USAF HISTORICAL STUDIES

THE GERMAN AIR FORCE IN WORLD WAR II

LIST OF PUBLICATIONS AVAILABLE IN THE SERIES

USAF HISTORICAL STUDIES: NO. 153

The German Air Force Versus Russia, 1941

By Generalleutnant Hermann Plocher

Edited by Mr. Harry R. Fletcher
USAF Historical Division

With an Introduction by Telford Taylor

USAF HISTORICAL DIVISION
AEROSPACE STUDIES INSTITUTE
AIR UNIVERSITY • JULY 1965

ARNO PRESS • NEW YORK

Reprinted with the cooperation of the Department
of Defense and the Historical Division, the Air
University of the United States Air Force.

Library of Congress Catalog Card No.: 68-22547

Manufactured in the U.S.A.
by Arno Press, Inc., New York, 1968

INTRODUCTION TO THE SERIES

The publication of this series of official historical studies is at once a most significant contribution to our knowledge of the Second World War and a landmark in the development of commercial publishing.

So much is published nowadays—far beyond the capacity of any individual even to screen—and so much is printed that ought never to see the light of day, that one tends to forget the considerable amount of writing well worth reading which rarely or never gets published at all. These volumes are an excellent example. Military monographs by foreign officers whose names are unknown to the public are not attractive items to most commercial publishing houses. But sometimes, as in the present case, they are unique sources of information which should be available in public if not in private libraries. Less often, and again as in the case of these volumes, they are surprisingly well written, and in many parts fascinating to the general reader as well as to the historian or military specialist.

The foreword of the Air Force Historical Division describes the inception and purposes of its German Air Force Historical Project and the circumstances under which these studies were written. Together with others to be published or made available for research in the future, the fruits of the Project are an analytic survey, at once comprehensive and intensive, of the Luftwaffe's structure and operations.

Not the least remarkable feature of the series is its authorship. With the single exception of Dr. Richard Suchenwirth—a one-time Austrian Army Officer and more recently a historian and educator in Munich—they are all former Luftwaffe generals, of low to middling seniority, who were intimately and responsibly involved with the events and problems of which they write. All seven were born within the decade 1891–1901, and thus in their forties or early fifties during most of the war years. Lieutenant-colonels or colonels when the war began, they filled a wide variety of staff and administrative assignments. Only two (Deichmann and Drum) attained three-star rank (*General der Flieger*), and only one (Deichmann) was ever given a major field command.

In military parlance, accordingly, they are all "staff" rather than "command" types, and for present purposes that is a good thing. Staff officers are responsible for the smooth functioning of the military machine; they must anticipate and provide for contingencies, and are expected to possess good powers of analysis and imagination. They spend much time drafting orders, which requires the ability to write with clarity and brevity. All these qualities are reflected in their product; our seven generals must have been good staff officers.

Banned by the Treaty of Versailles, the German air arm was condemned to a clandestine and embryonic life until 1933, and the Luftwaffe's existence was not publicly acknowledged until 1935. Hermann Goering and his colleagues in its command thus had only six years prior to the war in which to assemble and organize an officer corps. Its younger members—those who were lieutenants and captains when the war came—were recruited and trained during those years (1933–39), but the upper reaches of the corps had to be manned in other ways.

The need for experienced staff officers was especially acute, and this was met largely by transferring army (and a few navy) officers to the newly established air arm. Thus it is not surprising to find that all but one (Morzik) of our generals were professional soldiers who made their careers in the *Reichsheer* of the Weimar Republic, and received general staff training at the time Adolf Hitler was coming to power. So far as possible, the officers to be transferred were selected from those who had served in the air arm during the First World War, as had Deichmann and Drum.

Morzik alone represents the other principal type of senior Luftwaffe officer. He was not of the "officer class"; he had been a non-commissioned officer in the air arm during the First World War. Between the wars he led an adventurous and varied life as a commercial pilot, a successful competitor in aviation contests, a Junkers test pilot, and a flying instructor. Like his more famous superiors—Udet, Loerzer, von Greim, and Goering himself—Morzik was a free-lance knight of the air, and one of a considerable company commissioned from civil life in the 1933–35 period.

These generals are writing about events of which they were a part, in the course of a war in which Germany was catastrophically, and the Luftwaffe even ignominiously, defeated. What they have written is certainly not objective in the sense that it is detached; they see with the eyes and speak the language of the air arm, and readily find explanations for their own failures in the mistakes of the Army leadership—often with good reason, to be sure. But their work is objective in the sense that it is dispassionate. Their studies bespeak a deep curiosity about their conduct of the war and the causes of their defeat, and they have, on the whole, endeavored to put the record straight by the lines they are able to perceive.

There is, however, a great deal that they did not perceive. Few, if any, are those who can write at length about other men without revealing a great deal about themselves, and our authors are not in this respect exceptional. At least during this century, the German military profession has been rightly celebrated for its technical and tactical competence, but its record in the field of grand strategy has been abysmal. By and large these studies do not often venture into the rarefied atmosphere of the highest levels of command, and when they do, the results are unimpressive. Plocher's account of the reasons for the German attack against the Soviet Union,[1] for example, is superficial and diffuse. Of course he was not party or privy to the decision, but in telling us what he has heard there is little effort to winnow fact from fable, or to assess the considerations and alternatives.

In other respects, these volumes are not to be faulted so much for what is said as for what is left unspoken. Describing the Russian soldier, Uebe tells us that it is his "inherent character" to be "ruthless" and to place "a relatively lower value on human life" than "Western" peoples do.[2] For myself, I am inclined to discount popular stereotypes about national characteristics, and to judge rather upon a record of behavior. Beyond question the Russian soldier was often ruthless and worse, but what of the German soldier in Russia? Neither Uebe nor any of his colleagues carries the story in that direction. To be sure the Luftwaffe, by the nature of its operations, was not much involved in the exterminations, forced labor impressments, and other atrocities in which the Army was extensively implicated. But this hardly justifies Plocher's chest-thumping conclusion that: ". . . the incom-

---

[1] Plocher, *The German Air Force versus Russia, 1941*, pp. 1–3 (1965).
[2] Uebe, *Russian Reactions to German Airpower in World War II*, p. 1 (1964).

parable performances of the individual German soldier in combat in the East are above criticism. This applies to all ranks, from the lowest private to general officers, on the land, in the air, and on the seas."[3] Unhappily, the German military records tell quite a different story.

Fortunately such departures from the factual dimension are rare, and the authors have given us a unique and invaluable fund of information. Two of these studies concern the high command of the Luftwaffe, and two more cover particular Luftwaffe functions —air lift and ground support. The remaining six all concern the fighting on the eastern front between the German and Russian forces—a ferocious conflict on a scale greater than any other in human history.

Three of the eastern front studies, all by Plocher, constitute a chronological account of Luftwaffe operations on the eastern front in 1941, 1942, and 1943, one year to each volume. It is a mammoth undertaking of nearly 1,200 pages, well organized, and abundantly supported and illustrated with maps, charts, and photographs.

Plocher was chief of staff of an air corps on the southern part of the front, and remained in the east until the middle of 1943. Thus he witnessed at first hand the Luftwaffe's highly successful operations during the first few days of the campaign in July 1941, in the course of which the entire Russian air force was virtually annihilated, as well as the great encirclements at Minsk, Kiev, Bryansk, and elsewhere, which netted over two and a quarter million Russian prisoners and drove the Soviet forces back to the gates of Leningrad and Moscow and the banks of the Don. No doubt the Wehrmacht's failure to achieve decisive success was more the fault of the Army leadership than of the Luftwaffe, but the air generals made serious mistakes of their own, of which Plocher stresses two of major strategic proportions: (1) failure to carry out strategic bombing attacks on Russian armaments industries, and (2) dispersion of the slender air strength at the extreme northern end of the front, so that Murmansk and Archangel remained in Russian hands, as ports through which the western Allies could help the Russians to recover, following their nearly disastrous losses in the opening months of the campaign.

With the Russian air arm largely destroyed and strategic operations neglected, the Luftwaffe became, in practical terms, part of the German army—"flying artillery," supplemental transportation, additional ground forces. There were few Russian aircraft for the German *Flak* to shoot at, so the anti-aircraft units became front-line artillery.

Later on, as the Army got into even deeper trouble, the Luftwaffe was pulled in after it. Bombers were misused on ground-attack and airlift assignments; efforts to supply encircled German armies by air caused the Luftwaffe catastrophic losses. New Russian aircraft began to appear on the scene, and the balance gradually shifted so that by the end of 1943 the Germans no longer enjoyed air superiority, and the Luftwaffe became, as Plocher puts it, a "fire brigade," constantly on emergency call to plug up holes or salvage hard-pressed Army units.

How the Russians responded to the Luftwaffe's operations is the subject of Uebe's report. Except for the first few days, when the Soviet planes were destroyed in close array on their own airfields, like our own aircraft on Clark Field in the Philippines in December 1941, the Russians reacted to the overwhelming German superiority with great adaptability, and skill in the arts of camouflage and deception. Rails laid on ice did not sink with the thaw, for supports had been built under the ice; ships that appeared half-sunk and useless were under repair, with the bow flooded to elevate the stern. "As events show," writes

[3] Plocher, *The German Air Force versus Russia, 1943,* p. 266 (1967).

Uebe, "Russian reaction to German Air Force operations, however primitive and make-shift in character, and however crude they might have first appeared to be to their more enlightened Western opponents, proved throughout the course of the war to be highly efficient, effective, and ultimately an important factor in the defeat of Germany." A lesson for the American military command in Vietnam?

These same qualities were strikingly manifest in the Russian partisan operations behind the German lines, as described in a short but vivid study by General Karl Drum. The partisan units depended on air transportation for reinforcements, leadership, supplies, evacuation of wounded, and other necessary assistance, and all this was accomplished with obsolete aircraft and improvised equipment, utilizing air-drop or well-concealed air strips. Upon occasion, men were "delivered" to the partisans by parachuteless air-drop, wrapped in straw and dropped from low-flying planes into deep snow. The Germans, counting on a blitzkrieg victory, had made no preparations for anti-partisan warfare. No aircraft were earmarked to deal with the Russian air-supply, no single anti-partisan command was established to deal with the problem as a whole. Brutal occupation policies boomeranged by driving the population into the arms of the partisans. The German failure to take effective countermeasures is a striking demonstration that overwhelming superiority in heavy weapons and a sophisticated military tradition are no guarantee of success against surprise and deception.

Perhaps the most interesting and valuable of the eastern front volumes is Schwabedissen's extensive and perceptive study of the Russian air force as it appeared to the Germans. Through interchange of equipment and manufacturing and training facilities during the Weimar period, the antagonists were well known to each other. The Russian air performance in Spain and Finland had not been impressive, and in 1941, just prior to their attack, the Luftwaffe had a pretty accurate picture of the opposing force: it was far larger than the Luftwaffe, but much inferior in equipment, leadership, and training. The Germans expected to smash it to bits, and they succeeded.

What the Germans failed to reckon with was the Russians' recuperative powers. Most of their aircraft were destroyed on the ground rather than in the air, so that personnel losses were not high. The armament industries were rapidly moved eastward, and an early winter hampered Luftwaffe operations and gave the Russians a badly needed respite. By the winter of 1941–42 new Russian air units, better equipped, were beginning to appear at the front.

Still vastly superior in operational capacity, the Luftwaffe remained dominant in 1942, but in 1943 Russian numerical superiority, and techniques improved by experience, began to tell. During the last two years of the war, general air superiority passed to the Russian side of the front. But superior German technique enabled them to operate and achieve local successes right up to the end of the war; the Russians never achieved the total superiority enjoyed by the Allies on the western front.

German military air transport operations were opened by spectacular successes in the West. By parachute, glider, and landed aircraft, German airborne units descended on the major airfields of Norway and Denmark, on the airfields and tactically crucial bridges in Holland, and on the famous fort Eben Emael in Belgium. Morzik's fine account covers these operations in detail, as well as the later successful but costly assault on Crete, and the planned but never executed airborne operations in England, Gibraltar, Malta, and elsewhere.

The transport workhorse of the Luftwaffe was the three-engined Junkers 52, opposite number to our C-47s (otherwise known as DC-3s, Dakotas, "gooney birds," and now in Vietnam as "dragonships"), and well-known to all European travelers of ancient enough vintage to have flown Lufthansa during the thirties. A sturdy and versatile airplane, it was turned out by the thousands, but by the end of the war there were less than two hundred left. Most of the rest lay shattered and scrapped in Russia, near Demyansk and Stalingrad.

Morzik's account of the Demyansk and Stalingrad airlifts is gripping and enlightening. Retreating from the Moscow sector, the German Second Corps (roughly 100,000 men) was encircled at Demyansk in February 1942. Hitler forbade a breakout to the rear, and decided to supply the Corps by air. This was accomplished, but at a cost of 160 railway trains of gasoline, 265 Ju-52s, and consequent loss of trained crews and disruption of the pilot-training program. The psychological cost was even higher, for the apparent success of the operation made spuriously credible Goering's promise, ten months later, to supply Paulus' Sixth Army of over 300,000 men, encircled at Stalingrad. By then the Luftwaffe had only 750 Ju-52s left; half of them, and many bombers pressed into service as transports, were lost in the futile effort.

Airlift operations were the product of special circumstances, and strategic bombing the Luftwaffe neglected from birth to death. Day in and day out, its basic role was direct support of Army operations: attacking enemy troop columns, strong points, and tanks; impeding the flow of enemy reinforcements or cutting off their avenues of retreat; general intelligence reconnaissance. After 1941, Army support comprised over 75% of the Luftwaffe's operational activity—too large a proportion, as General Deichmann points out in his treatise "German Air Force Operations in Support of the Army." Deichmann traces the development of German air theory from its beginnings in the First World War, and explores the manner in which those theories shaped the Luftwaffe and governed its operational potential. The military air specialist will find this an exceptionally informative study.

In "The German Air Force General Staff," Nielsen takes us into the weird world of the Luftwaffe high command, well stocked with colorful characters, many of them adequately unattractive. Hitler was not much interested in air power and left Goering a free hand as long as things went well. After the period of spectacular initial successes, Goering suffered a sharp decline in influence, and the Fuehrer interjected himself into the Luftwaffe's management. He was not helpful; his decisions were the product of ignorance and favoritism and simply completed the process of demoralization.

Nielsen's study is focused on the general staff—i.e. the group of specially trained officers who held staff assignments—but its perspective is much broader, and includes the interplay of personality and rivalry at the top. Until his fall from grace, Goering's domination was complete, with one exception—Erhard Milch, his second-in-command, who had his own contacts and standing with Hitler and the Nazi Party. A former director of Lufthansa and a man of great energy and administrative ability, Milch was ambitious to the point that his attitude on proposed measures was governed less by the merits than by his estimate of their probable effect on his personal situation. Thus he initially opposed the creation of a general staff, and, when overruled, bent his energies to ensuring that the chief of the general staff would not impair his status as the No. 2 man. The consequence was a running battle between Milch and the succession of chiefs—seven during the Luftwaffe's less than twelve years of life—who served, basically, as Goering's advisors in the field of combat operations.

The results of his jerry-built command structure and riven leadership are graphically portrayed in Professor Suchenwirth's "Historical Turning Points in the German War Effort." Since the Luftwaffe ended the war in a state of total disintegration, the title postulates a study of crucial decisions which proved disastrous.

Perhaps the worst mistakes were made before the war began, and were the almost inevitable consequence of the personal shortcomings of the Luftwaffe leaders. Hans Jeschonnek—a career army officer barely old enough to have had a bit of flying experience at the very end of the First World War—was the Luftwaffe chief of staff from early 1939 to his suicide in 1943. Blindly devoted to Hitler and, until near the end, to Goering, he swallowed whole Hitler's assurances that the war would be a short blitzkrieg. Accordingly, he took no interest in training, neglected air transport, opposed the development of a long-range bomber, and focused all of his considerable ability on army support, and especially on the dive bomber. During the first year of the war these weaknesses did not show, but the Luftwaffe's failure over Britain and its inadequacy to the sustained demands of the eastern front were the direct result of such miscalculations, of which Jeschonnek was by no means the only author. Udet, Milch, Goering, and Hitler himself all contributed greatly to the Luftwaffe's misconstruction, misuse, and miserable fate.

In 1936, when Francisco Franco asked Hitler for help in moving his forces from Africa to Spain, Ju-52s were sent to do the job. Nine years later, as the Third Reich crumbled, Ju-52s—what was left of them—were still the standard Luftwaffe transport aircraft, and in this circumstance the Luftwaffe's intrinsic weakness is strikingly reflected. Messerschmitt 109s and 110s, Dornier 17s, Heinkel 111s, Ju-87 "Stukas," and Ju-88s were all on hand before the war began. With the sole exception of the Focke-Wulf 190—somewhat but not significantly superior to the Me 109—not a single new major aircraft type was added to the Luftwaffe until the last year of the war. Then came the first jet aircraft and the V-weapons, but it was too little and too late.

In retrospect, it is apparent that the Luftwaffe reached its peak of effectiveness before the war had even begun. Germany's bloodless conquest at Munich was achieved largely by the fear of Goering's bombers—a threat that was real enough, though exaggerated far beyond its true dimensions. Spectacular as they were, the Luftwaffe's triumphs in Poland, Norway, Holland, and even against the French (whose air force was woefully decrepit) were not scored against major opponents. As early as Dunkirk the veil was torn, and from then on the story is one of decline, gradual until the winter of 1941–42, rapid thereafter.

And so it came about that the story told, and well told, in these volumes can be fairly summarized in just seven words: how not to run an air force.

Telford Taylor

USAF HISTORICAL STUDIES: NO. 153

THE GERMAN AIR FORCE VERSUS RUSSIA, 1941

by

Generalleutnant Hermann Plocher

Edited by Mr. Harry R. Fletcher
USAF Historical Division

USAF HISTORICAL DIVISION
Aerospace Studies Institute
Air University
July 1965

Everyone who desires to become a strategist has before him a book entitled "Military History" . . .

I must admit that the reading is not what one might call stimulating in its entirety. One has to work his way through the mass of scarcely palatable ingredients. But behind it all one still arrives at the facts, often cheering facts, and upon the basis of this finds the knowledge of how everything has come about, how it had to come about, and how it will happen again.

Alfred Count von Schlieffen,*

From an address given at the Centennial of the German War Academy in Berlin on 15 October 1910.

---

*Alfred Count von Schlieffen (1833-1913) served as Chief of the Prussian General Staff from 1891 to 1906. His study Cannae: Principle of the Victory of Annihilation through Envelopment is world famous and has become a basic study for the field of Military Science.

FOREWORD

The German Air Force versus Russia, 1941, written by General-leutnant Hermann Plocher, and revised and edited by Mr. Harry Fletcher, is one of a series of historical studies written for the United States Air Force Historical Division by men who had been key officers in the German Air Force during World War II.

The overall purpose of the series is twofold: 1) To provide the United States Air Force with a comprehensive and, insofar as possible, authoritative history of a major air force which suffered defeat in World War II, a history prepared by many of the principal and responsible leaders of that air force; 2) to provide a firsthand account of that air force's unique combat in a major war, especially its fight against the forces of the Soviet Union. This series of studies therefore covers in large part virtually all phases of the Luftwaffe's operations and organization, from its camouflaged origin in the Reichswehr, during the period of secret German rearmament following World War I, through its participation in the Spanish Civil War and its massive operations and final defeat in World War II, with particular attention to the air war on the Eastern Front.

The German Air Force Historical Project (referred to hereinafter by its shorter and current title, "The GAF Monograph Project") has generated this and other especially prepared volumes which comprise, in one form or another, a total of more than 40 separate studies. The project, which was conceived and developed by the USAF Historical Division, was, upon recommendation of Headquarters Air University late in 1952, approved and funded by Headquarters USAF in early 1953. General supervision was assigned to the USAF Historical Division by Headquarters USAF, which continued principal funding of the project through 30 June 1958. Within the Historical Division, Dr. Albert F. Simpson and Mr. Joseph W. Angell, Jr., respectively Chief and Assistant Chief of the Division, exercised overall supervision of the project. The first steps towards its initiation were taken in the fall of 1952 following a staff visit by Mr. Angell to the Historical Division, Headquarters United States Army, Europe, at Karlsruhe, Germany, where the Army was conducting a somewhat similar historical project covering matters and operations almost wholly of interest to that service. Whereas the Army's project had produced or was producing a multiplicity of studies of varying length and significance (more than 2,000 have been prepared to date by the Army project), it was early decided that the Air

Force should request a radically smaller number (around 40) which should be very carefully planned initially and rather closely integrated. Thirteen narrative histories of GAF combat operations, by theater areas, and 27 monographic studies dealing with areas of particular interest to the United States Air Force were recommended to, and approved by, Headquarters USAF in the initial project proposal of late 1952. (A list of histories and studies appears at the end of this volume.)

By early 1953 the actual work of preparing the studies was begun. Col. Wendell A. Hammer, USAF, was assigned as Project Officer, with duty station at the USAREUR Historical Division in Karlsruhe. General der Flieger a. D. Paul Deichmann was appointed and served continuously as Control Officer for the research and writing phases of the project; he also had duty station at the USAREUR Historical Division. General-leutnant a. D. Hermann Plocher served as Assistant Control Officer until his recall to duty with the new German Air Force in the spring of 1957. These two widely experienced and high-ranking officers of the former Luftwaffe secured as principal authors, or "topic leaders," former officers of the Luftwaffe, each of whom, by virtue of his experience in World War II, was especially qualified to write on one of the topics approved for study. These "topic leaders" were, in turn, assisted by "home workers"--for the most part former general and field-grade officers with either specialized operational or technical experience. The contributions of each of these "home workers," then, form the basic material of most of these studies. In writing his narrative the "topic leader" has put these contributions into their proper perspective.

These studies find their principal authority in the personal knowledge and experience of their authors. In preparing the studies, however, the authors have not depended on their memories alone, for their personal knowledge has been augmented by a collection of Luftwaffe documents which has come to be known as the Karlsruhe Document Collection and which is now housed in the Archives Branch of the USAF Historical Division. This collection consists of directives, situation reports, war diaries, personal diaries, strength reports, minutes of meetings, aerial photographs, and various other materials derived, chiefly, from three sources: the Captured German Documents Section of The Adjutant General in Alexandria, Virginia; the Air Ministry in London; and private German collections made available to the project by its participating authors and contributors. In addition, the collection includes the contributions of the "home workers." The authors have also made use of such materials as the records of the Nuremberg Trials, the manuscripts prepared by the Foreign Military Studies Branch of the USAREUR Historical Division, the official military histories of the United States and the United Kingdom, and the wealth of literature concerning World War II, both in German and English, which has appeared in book form or in military journals since 1945.

With the completion of the research and writing phases in 1958, the operations at Karlsruhe were closed out. At that time the project was moved to the Air University, Maxwell Air Force Base, Alabama, where the process of editing and publishing the studies was begun by the USAF Historical Division.

Basic revising and editing of the monographs has been handled by Mr. Edwin P. Kennedy (1958-61), Dr. Littleton B. Atkinson (1961-62), Mr. Gerard E. Hasselwander (1962-63), and the present Editor, Mr. Harry R. Fletcher. Final review and editing has been the responsibility of Dr. Albert F. Simpson, Chief, USAF Historical Division, with the assistance of Dr. Maurer Maurer, Chief of the Division's Historical Studies Branch.

The complexity of the GAF Monograph Project and the variety of participation which it has required can easily be deduced from the acknowledgments which follow. On the German side: General Deichmann, who, as Chief Control Officer, became the moving force behind the entire project, and his assistant, General Plocher; General Josef Kammhuber, a contributor to, and strong supporter of, the project, who became the first chief of the new German Air Force; Generaloberst a. D. Franz Halder, Chief of the German Army General Staff from 1938 to 1942, whose sympathetic assistance to the project was of the greatest value; the late Generalfeldmarschall Albert Kesselring, who contributed to several of the studies and who also, because of his prestige and popularity in German military circles, was able to encourage many others to contribute to the project; and all of the German "topic leaders" and "home workers" who are too numerous to mention here, but whose names can be found in the prefaces and footnotes to the individual studies.

In Germany, Colonel Hammer served as Project Officer from early in 1953 until June 1957. Colonel Hammer's considerable diplomatic and administrative skills helped greatly towards assuring the project's success. Col. William S. Nye, USA, was Chief of the USAREUR Historical Division at the project's inception; his strong support provided an enviable example of interservice cooperation and set the pattern which his several successors followed. In England, Mr. L. A. Jackets, Head of Air Historical Branch, British Air Ministry, gave invaluable assistance with captured Luftwaffe documents.

The project is indebted to all of those members of the USAREUR Historical Division, the Office of the Chief of Military History, and the USAF Historical Division, whose assistance and advice helped the project to achieve its goals.

At the Air University, a number of people, both military and civilian, have given strong and expert support to the project. The several Commanders of Air University during the life of the project in Karlsruhe (1952-58) without exception were interested in the project and gave it their full backing. Other personnel at Headquarters Air University who contributed time and experience include: the several Directors of the Aerospace Studies Institute since 1952; Dr. James C. Shelburne, Educational Advisor to the Commander; Mr. J. S. Vann, Chief of Special Projects Branch, DCS/Operations; and Mr. Arthur P. Irwin, Chief, Budget Division, DCS/Comptroller.

The project is grateful to Lt. Col. Leonard C. Hoffman, former Assistant Air Attaché to Germany, who gave indispensable aid during the project's last year in Germany, and to Mr. Joseph P. Tustin, Chief Historian of Headquarters, United States Air Forces in Europe during the years when the project was at Karlsruhe, who rendered substantial assistance by solving a variety of logistical and administrative problems.

Mrs. Mary F. Hanlin deserves special thanks for her expert typing of the final draft.

AUTHOR'S FOREWORD

My intimate involvement with the Russian campaign dated from the earliest beginnings of the preparations for BARBAROSSA. I served for many months during the war against the Soviet Union as a General Staff officer of the Luftwaffe and as the commanding officer of an air division. A pre-World War II course of study at the Army War College (Kriegsakademie) in Berlin was invaluable in helping me to secure a clearer comprehension of problems related to army tactical and strategic operations.

This present work is based upon a detailed study of the available source materials of the time, including books and essays on military science published in Germany and abroad, as well as documents and war diaries which originated in the various German military headquarters. Prominent former commanding generals and senior officers of the Luftwaffe, officers of the General Staff, and experienced troop commanders of all ranks and branches of the Luftwaffe assisted me with invaluable advice, reports, and commentaries. It must be pointed out, however, that little documentation was to be had regarding the preparations for BARBAROSSA and the course of the campaign in 1941. Therefore, a clear presentation of the events of the time was possible only by making a lengthy and laborious comparison and evaluation of the available information with the oral and written contributions furnished by my collaborators.

Insofar as was possible, every effort has been made to achieve objectivity in the presentation of the historical events of the period which reflect directly upon the leadership of Germany, and upon the services rendered during the war by all German units in Russia.

The German conflict with the Soviet Union naturally produced a great mass of military experiences of a tactical, technical and strategic nature. These experiences and the conclusions drawn from them are not merely the products of my own personal and critical evaluations, but directly reflect the recollections and opinions of many staff and front line commanders of the Wehrmacht, almost too numerous to mention, who served on the Eastern Front. Their collaboration with me in this present undertaking was the result of a soldierly sense of duty to the memory of their comrades who died in good faith for their fatherland, and in the hope that the useful application of these lessons and experiences will, in the future, keep warfare from German soil.

December 1953   Hermann Plocher,
                                                 Generalleutnant a. D.

PREFACE

The great Prussian General Carl von Clausewitz has said that the specific aims of warfare are to "destroy the enemy's forces," to "occupy his country," and, ultimately, "to force him to conclude a peace on your own terms." It was precisely Hitler's inability to secure the first two of these conditions that prevented him from achieving a victory over the Soviet Union and eventually led to Germany's defeat.

The war on the Eastern Front provided each of the great antagonists with an opportunity to discover the strengths and shortcomings of the other which had not theretofore been evident. The offensive against Russia was not based on a meticulous and detailed plan by the German General Staff, but centered around a number of general directives issued by Hitler, most of which rested upon the assumption that German military power was, and would continue in the future to be, irresistible.

Perhaps in the East, more than in any other German war theater, the position of the Reich was most largely determined by the fortunes of the Wehrmacht on the ground. It was, in short, an "Army show," in which both the Luftwaffe and the Navy held supporting and subordinate roles. Because of this fact, military literature here and abroad has tended to place special emphasis upon German Army operations and to neglect the importance of the Luftwaffe in determining the outcome of events. In awareness of this, the author has devoted only such space to ground force actions as is required to lay the framework for German air operations.

In this, the first of several of his studies dealing with the Campaign in the East, General Plocher makes a critical examination of deficiencies in planning, failures to provide for unexpected contingencies, and the German High Command's dangerous underestimation of Soviet capabilities, all of which led to unpleasant and stunning surprises. In tracing the events of 1941, the author describes the optimistic opening of the war, the great early victories, and the eventual failure to secure the strategic objectives of the campaign, leading to a radical change in plans and a sobering reappraisal of the Soviet enemy. General Plocher has made ample use of the principal documentary sources available at the time, and the testimony of numerous former Luftwaffe officers who had firsthand knowledge of the events. Although several years have elapsed since this study was written, it is worth noting that no significant new materials have since come to light to alter the general tenor and conclusions of his work.

The original of this manuscript has been abridged, and several of the longer quotations have been sharply reduced in an effort to improve the narrative for the reader. Extensive editing has been carried out by the USAF Historical Division, yet a determined effort has been made to preserve the character of General Plocher's work, the essence of his commentary, and the significance of the remarks and opinions presented by others.

In conformity to general practices arising from the difficulty of finding precise American equivalents for grades and positions of German general officers, all ranks above colonel have been left in the German form.

ABOUT THE AUTHOR

Generalleutnant Hermann Plocher was born 5 January 1901. His career in the German military service began in October of 1918 as an officer candidate in the 126th Infantry Regiment. He was commissioned 1 December 1922 in the 13th (Wuerttemberg) Infantry Regiment, a unit whose junior officers included such able men as Erwin Rommel and Hans Speidel. Three years later Plocher began training as a pilot, and in 1928 went with other German officers to the Soviet Union to take special courses in aerial combat and reconnaissance during the period when such activities were proscribed in the Reich. Following his promotion to Captain on 1 April 1934 he attended the Army War College (Kriegs-akademie) in Berlin, receiving special air force training, and a year later was assigned to the Organization Branch of the Luftwaffe General Staff.

In August of 1936 Plocher, then a Major, was sent to Spain as part of the German contingent to assist General Franco, and participated actively in the Spanish Civil War. In October of 1937 he was appointed Chief of Staff of "Legion Condor." By virtue of his record, Plocher earned on 1 March 1938 an extraordinary promotion to Lieutenant Colonel.

Prior to the outbreak of World War II he was assigned to the Luftwaffe General Staff as Chief of Plans and Mobilization. He then assumed the post of Chief of Staff of the V Air Corps (redesignated 1 April 1942 as Luftwaffe Command East) on 5 January 1940 and served with this organization during its campaigns in the West and in the Soviet Union. On 1 February 1943 he took command and directed the formation of the 19th Luftwaffe Field Division, and in April, following his promotion to Generalmajor, went with his unit to Normandy. General Plocher assumed command on 1 July 1943 of the 4th Air Division, and in October became Chief of Staff of the Third Air Fleet (Western Front). Following his promotion on 1 July 1944 to Generalleutnant, he became Commanding General of the 6th Airborne Division (Western Front). On 10 May 1945 he surrendered to Canadian forces in the Netherlands.

From 1953 until the spring of 1957, Generalleutnant Plocher gave generous and valuable assistance to the USAF Historical Division's German Monograph Project in Karlsruhe, Germany, adding his contributions to those of his colleagues to round out the story of German Air Force operations during the war. In March 1957 he returned to active duty in the new Luftwaffe where, as a general officer, he held key positions until his final retirement at the turn of the year 1961.

As a former commander of German air and ground forces and as a General Staff officer of considerable experience and ability, he is ideally suited to document the course of events on the Eastern Front, where he played such a significant role.

CONTENTS

Chapter 1

THE BACKGROUND OF THE WAR AGAINST RUSSIA

Reasons for Germany's Decision To Wage War

Hitler's decision to open a military campaign against the Soviet Union was his most dangerous gamble of World War II, and one which set the stage for Germany's greatest catastrophe. The question has often been asked how Germany, with its particular military, economic, and geographic resources, could have dared to attack an opponent which enjoyed so many natural advantages, for without question such an undertaking was bound to tax the Reich's reserves to the limit and to dangerously weaken its forces in other areas.

Germany was in dire need of raw materials, especially foodstuffs, for the prosecution of its war effort, and its expanding population required additional living space (Lebensraum) in which to achieve its economic and national aspirations. These needs could be satisfied in the Soviet Union, the conquest of which would also permit Germany to achieve a successful end to the war in the West.

In 1940 the Wehrmacht was clearly superior to the Soviet armed forces, but Russian rearmament would rapidly alter this relationship to Germany's disadvantage. Time was, then, a most important factor in deciding to go to war against the colossus in the East. The war against Britain was far from concluded, and the United States, then substantially supporting her, was demonstrating an increasingly hostile attitude toward the Axis powers. In such a situation a protracted war against Russia could have disastrous consequences.

Political Reasons for War

The steady expansion of Soviet power and the suspicious manifestations of Russian representatives during the many political, military, and economic conferences with Germany after 1939 served to strengthen Hitler's belief in the inevitability of war with the Soviet Union.

Among the more important political issues between the two governments were the Russian occupation of Rumanian Bessarabia and Bucovina, Russia's demand for German recognition of Bulgaria as a

1

part of the Soviet sphere of influence, Russian insistence upon a permanent agreement with respect to the final status of Poland, continued demands for German support of Soviet efforts to secure naval bases in the Dardanelles, and Russian insistence upon complete freedom of action in dealing with Finland. Since these demands were invariably made to coincide with periods of crisis for Germany, the conviction was naturally held in the Reich that the Russians would exploit every opportunity to act against Germany's plans and interests. On 12 November 1940, Soviet Foreign Minister V. M. Molotov inquired into the "meaning of Germany's declaration of guarantees to Rumania," much to the consternation of German political leaders, whose suspicions were later deepened and confirmed by the Soviet treaty of "friendship" with Yugoslavia.

Hitler was aware of Germany's exposed and vulnerable flank in the Balkans, and the memory of the once dangerous Salonika Front of 1918 doubtless exerted a powerful influence upon his thinking. The large number of conferences with Bulgaria, Rumania, Yugoslavia, and Hungary, in which the Germans sought to bring the Balkans under the influence of the Reich, were further indications of Germany's awareness of the potential dangers from the southeast. The obvious solution to the problem was to divert Soviet attention and interests toward Persia and India where it could strike a blow at Britain's most important sources of power, but Hitler, in his negotiations, neither supported nor pursued these ideas with the necessary firmness. Always continental in thought, he was habitually mistrustful and cautious, indeed, almost apprehensive of any global policy.

Ideological Reasons

The clear impossibility of reconciling the philosophy of German National Socialism with the political and ideological views of the Soviet Union continued to be a factor of importance.* In the persisting insurmountable antagonisms separating the two powers, the so-called Russo-German Friendship Treaty of 1939 changed nothing, for their differences were neither resolved thereby nor diminished. In Hitler's eyes, the Soviet Union had always been the ideological enemy which, because of its extortionist policies, would sooner or later attack Germany from the rear, and do so as soon as the world political situation seemed to require

---

*It is worth noting that President Franklin D. Roosevelt persisted in the belief that the two villains, Hitler and Stalin, would somehow resolve their differences, even after months of bloody warfare. This point of view was held by few Germans.

or Russian armaments permitted. Because Hitler thought that the Communist system in Russia had not been fully consolidated, he was convinced that the Soviet government, if attacked soon enough, would thus be unable to sustain itself against heavy external blows, and would quickly collapse.

Economic Reasons

In the conduct of its war against the West, Germany had a considerable dependence upon raw materials imported from Russia. The continuance of this supply was in part, and often almost exclusively, dependent upon the uncertain "good will" of the Soviet Union. A military occupation of European Russia would bring wheat from the Ukraine, coal and other ores from the Donets Basin, nickel from the Kola Peninsula, oil from the Caucasus, and wood from White Russia, all essential goods for war, without which a German victory would be doubtful. At the opening of the Winter Help Drive on 30 September 1942, Hitler declared, "The enormous area of Russia should be made available for the nourishment of the German people, for the assurance of their supply of raw materials, and, in a greater sense, for the maintenance of Europe."

Military Reasons for War

The Soviet attitude toward the Reich remained perpetually uncertain, and many Germans viewed the Soviet sphinx as a constant latent source of danger. Russia had been attentively and anxiously observing Germany's rise to power, and had already begun to take corresponding defensive measures, among which were the seizure of the Baltic States, Bessarabia and Bucovina, and parts of Finland. From 1939 to May of 1941 the number of Soviet divisions had increased from 65 to 158, and many of these were concentrated along the western frontiers. While such forces were ostensibly defensive in character, they nevertheless constituted a grave menace to Germany. The inference of this becomes more obvious in the light of a statement made by a Russian officer in 1945 to Field Marshal Albert Kesselring* that "Russia would have achieved a maximum level of armament and combat readiness by 1943."[1]

---

*For brief biographical sketches of important persons who appear in the study, see Appendix II.

Thoughts Become Reality

On 29 July 1940, General der Artillerie Alfred Jodl issued at Hitler's behest precise instructions for a concentration of power in the East, a "Buildup East" (Aufbau Ost), to the National Defense Branch of the High Command of the Armed Forces (OKW). Logistical, operational, and administrational measures required for a war against Russia were then prepared by Generalleutnant Walter Warlimont, Chief of the National Defense Branch of the Wehrmacht, and sent to Field Marshal Wilhelm Keitel, Chief of the High Command of the German Armed Forces.

On 31 July 1940 Hitler informed the Commander in Chief of the German Army, Field Marshal Walther von Brauchitsch, and the Chief of the Army General Staff, Generaloberst Franz Halder, of his plan to attack Russia. Halder thereupon ordered a study on the proposed campaign to be made by Generalleutnant Erich Marcks (which was later completed by Generalleutnant Friedrich Paulus).

The War Economy and Armament Office, headed by General der Infanterie Georg Thomas, had been informed on 14 August 1940 of the Fuehrer's intention to discontinue all supply shipments--these were being made under the terms of the Russo-German trade pact--to Russia after the spring of 1941.[2] Appropriate steps for an expansion of the war were then taken in November, when Goering announced Hitler's decision for a buildup of forces in the East.[3]

Although Grossadmiral Erich Raeder, the Commander in Chief of the Navy, was apparently not apprised of Hitler's plan until late 1940 or early 1941, the matter was clarified on 8 or 9 January 1941 when the Fuehrer told Raeder that "Germany would be able to continue the war against England under completely tolerable conditions once the danger in the East had been eliminated," and that "the collapse of the Soviet Union would constitute a great relief to Japan and would thus increase the dangers for the United States in entering a war against Germany."*[4]

---

*Admiral Raeder thought for a time that his efforts had been successful in dissuading Hitler from his plan by suggesting a penetration of Africa, Dakar, and the Mediterranean. Mein Leben (My Life), Vol. II, Tuebingen: Verlag Fritz Schlichenmayer, 1957, pp. 246-249.

As early as mid-November of 1940, when Generalmajor Otto Hoffman von Waldau informed the officers of the Operations Staff of the Luftwaffe of the details of the plan for a campaign against Russia, many of them had already surmised the existence of such a plan because of Marshal Goering's previous demand for a buildup of Luftwaffe ground forces in the East. However, photo-reconnaissance flights which were proposed as a consequence of this plan were banned by Hitler on the ground that they might incite the Russians to war prematurely. It can therefore be assumed that when Goering was informed of Hitler's decision for war on 4 January 1941, it had long been expected by senior Wehrmacht officers. [5]

Probable Duration of the Campaign

Hitler really believed that the war in the East could be concluded in three or four months, and busied himself, even prior to the attack on Russia, with plans for later operations in the Near East. Spoiled by successful "lightning wars" in 1939 and 1940, Hitler and the top commanders of the armed forces unfortunately made too favorable an estimation of the situation.

While the High Command did not expressly object to the Fuehrer's timetable, and, in early June 1941, even asked for the formulation of a clear plan "for subsequent operations to be conducted after the smashing of the Russian armed forces,"[6] a later remark by General Halder indicates that he was "firmly convinced when Hitler began the Russian campaign in 1941 that it was with the preconceived notion, which was neither shared nor supported by the Army General Staff, that Russia could be forced to make peace in 1941."[7]

Field Marshal Erhard Milch, State Secretary of Aviation, likewise remained unconvinced that the Soviet Union could be defeated in a "Blitz" campaign.[8] On 5 December 1942 he declared:

> . . . At that time [January 1941], of course, everyone knew that the action in the East was coming. That was long before June. I had been then asked whether or not we should prepare for winter. This was months in advance. I thereupon gave the order to prepare everything for winter; the war will last several years in the East. At that time the official opinion was otherwise. I know the East, its scope, and I had been there often. I have seen much of the world and know exactly what we are risking there.[9]

The official German government viewpoint was best expressed by Foreign Minister Joachim von Ribbentrop in his boast to the Italians that if Germany and Russia came to blows the Soviet Union of Stalin would "disappear from the map within eight weeks."[10] Hitler, too, spoke of a "short campaign in the East" during a conference with von Brauchitsch on 5 December 1940 at the Reichs Chancellory,* but Reichsmarschall Hermann Goering (Commander in Chief of the Luftwaffe) had serious doubts about it. In a speech before a gathering of Gauleiters (Nazi District Party Leaders) at Munich, 8 November 1943, Goering commented bitterly on the supposed "brevity" of the campaign:

> . . . And then came the Russian campaign! . . . at that time I had also hoped that we would not need to discontinue the campaign against England. In the beginning it was said: these wings should go to the East for the first four days only, in order to increase the impact [of the German Wehrmacht]. What once went to the East never returned; it remained in the East.[11]

Considerations Against an Eastern Campaign

Colonel Josef "Beppo" Schmid (GSC)/ and many other Luftwaffe leaders voiced their immediate disapproval of a war against the Soviet Union. Until Hitler's decision was announced in January 1941, they had been firmly convinced that the Fuehrer would observe Germany's historic fears of a two-front war.[12] Von Waldau viewed this additional prospect of war as a dangerous and irresponsible dissipation of strength for the Luftwaffe, which then urgently required rest and rehabilitation following its commitment in Poland, Norway, the Lowlands, and France, and pointed out that victory in the Battle of Britain (then reaching its climax) would be forfeited by a voluntary abandonment of the attack through a transfer of flying units to the East.[13] Such an event would be seen by the enemy as an absolute miracle, since it would permit British war plants to carry on without danger from German air attacks. Also the support of Germany's Italian ally had to be considered, which meant that the Wehrmacht might have to fight on a Mediterranean front, with a further dissipation of Luftwaffe power.

---

*See Halder Diary, Vol. VI.
/Best known as a Luftwaffe intelligence officer. See Appendix II.

Field Marshal Milch considered the idea of a campaign against Russia to be a catastrophic mistake whereby the war would be lost altogether. He therefore urged Goering to try to prevent it at all costs and thus exert a historic influence upon the outcome of the war.[14] The Reichsmarschall indeed attempted to dissuade Hitler from his plan by insisting that army material requirements would quickly take precedence over those of the Luftwaffe, thereby weakening German air power, and suggested "an attack through Spain upon Gibraltar," to which Hitler is said to have commented, "Goering, why don't you stop trying to persuade me to drop my plans for Russia? I've made up my mind!"[15]

The naval high command (OKM) strongly opposed a war against Russia. Raeder repeatedly drew Hitler's attention to the fact that England was the "principal enemy," whose Achilles' heel, her shipping, was being crippled and destroyed by the Axis, but that the campaign could be carried through to a successful conclusion only if U-boat construction could be stepped up. Therefore, naval leaders soundly rejected an immediate expansion of the war by an attack on the Soviet Union.

Hitler and the Wehrmacht leaders shared mutually pessimistic views of Russia's military and political intentions and believed that the Soviet Union would eventually cause trouble. Yet, despite these apprehensions, the military commanders believed that an immediate extension of the war, especially to the East, would overstrain the performance capability of German military power and its war economy. It was therefore the decision of Hitler, "as both statesman and general," that plunged the Wehrmacht, and thus the Luftwaffe, into its greatest and most formidable undertaking.

Directives and Orders for Operation BARBAROSSA

Fuehrer Directive No. 21 (OKW Directive No. 21), outlining the projected campaign against the Soviet Union, was the result of numerous studies,* map exercises, and Fuehrer Conferences. (FRITZ, the original code name for the operation, was personally rejected by Hitler

---

*The roles of Marcks and Paulus in planning BARBAROSSA are discussed in Tippelskirch, p. 199, and Walter Goerlitz, Der Zweite Weltkrieg (The Second World War), Vol. I, Stuttgart: Steingrueben Verlag, 1951, p. 215. See also Appendix I.

and replaced by the name BARBAROSSA, probably to stress the idea of a crusade against Bolshevism.)*

The first paragraph of Directive 21 stated that "Soviet Russia is to be crushed in a quick campaign before the end of the war with England." A short campaign against Russia was to be recognized as a necessity in the interest of the overall course of the war, based upon the optimistic belief that a "lightning campaign" was possible in the East as well as in the West.

Paragraph three outlined Luftwaffe strength as envisioned for the operation. Although the strongest possible forces were to be used for the campaign in the East, the directive required the retention of sufficient forces to defend German and allied territory, and to prosecute the war against England/ and its shipping. In this paragraph the threatening dissipation of Luftwaffe forces can already be discerned. Section III B, "Luftwaffe," of the directive lists the tasks of the German Air Force: (1) to eliminate Soviet air forces, (2) to support German ground operations, (3) to interrupt Soviet communications, and (4) to provide paratroopers and airborne personnel if the occasion should require. //

Operations against the Soviet arms industry, especially in the Urals, were postponed until after the end of mobile ground operations, probably because any earlier attempt to carry out such missions would seriously overtax the Luftwaffe. Therefore, German air strikes were to be mainly tactical in nature, often in close support of ground forces, with the objectives of eliminating Russian air forces and disrupting Soviet communications. Because of this, Luftwaffe directives were

---

*See Halder's commentaries on 3-7, 12, and 24 December 1940, Halder Diary, Vol. V, Karlsruhe Document Collection. The name BARBAROSSA was taken from the name of Emperor Frederick Barbarossa (1152-1190) or "Red Beard" (a figure well known to every German school boy), who intended to restore the Roman Empire in the West, and had great success until his untimely death enroute to the Third Crusade. At that time he had already participated in one Crusade and was acclaimed as the recognized military leader of Christendom against the Infidel.

/Germans almost habitually use the term "England" in referring to Great Britain. Because of aircraft range limitations their air war against Britain was virtually against England alone, but in their references to English shipping and the war effort, Great Britain is clearly meant.

//Paratroopers in the German Wehrmacht were under the command of the Luftwaffe.

subject to the orders and directives of the German Army High Command as shown by the Army deployment directive for BARBAROSSA, signed by von Brauchitsch on 31 January 1941.[16]

Luftwaffe Directives

A copy of the Luftwaffe employment directive for BARBAROSSA has never been found, although it must have been closely identified with Directive No. 21 and the Army employment directive, and have contained the following:

(1) In conformity with the main points of effort of the Army, the Second Air Fleet, supporting Army Group Center, would be the strongest, and would include the II and VIII Air Corps and the I Antiaircraft Artillery Corps.

(2) In Army Group South the left wing (the stronger) was to be supported in the same way by the V Air Corps and the II Antiaircraft Artillery Corps under the command of the Fourth Air Fleet, while the numerically weaker IV Air Corps of the Fourth Air Fleet was to be committed to support the remainder of the front of Army Group South.

(3) In the northern battle area the First Air Fleet--with the I Air Corps and the forces of Luftwaffe Commander Baltic--would cooperate with Army Group North. In the High North, Luftwaffe operations were to be conducted with partial forces of the Fifth Air Fleet.

Significance of the Directives for the Luftwaffe

Although Luftwaffe Field Regulation 16, entitled "The Conduct of Aerial Warfare,"[*] entailed the idea of strategic air operations against Russia, such plans were to be postponed until the Army had reached the Volga-Arkhangelsk line. Since strategic operations were envisioned for a later date, however, plans had to be made accordingly. Strategic air warfare would oblige Luftwaffe commanders to break off their support operations early enough to make adequate preparations. If this was impossible, they would have to quickly form new, strategic air units in the rear areas. Sufficient radio, navigational, and other technical equipment, long-distance bombers (the "Ural bomber"),[†] long-range

---

[*]See Luftwaffe Service Manual No. 16 (L. Dv. 16), F/I/2a, Karlsruhe Document collection.
[†]See footnote, p. 43.

9

fighters for escort duty, and other logistical support would have to be granted for such a program without reservation.

Experiences in Poland and the West had taught Luftwaffe leaders to expect a decided personnel and material attrition during close support operations. The Luftwaffe therefore had to make continuous and vigorous efforts to replace its losses, to increase its close support units, and, insofar as was possible, to build up its reserves. To accomplish this, however, the German war industry would have to concede top materiel priorities to the air force, which was most unlikely in view of the heavy demands made upon the German Army.

A Luftwaffe View of Russian Military Geography

Area

At the end of 1940 the Soviet Union was the largest contiguous national land formation in the world, comprising the greater part of eastern Europe, northern Asia, and northwestern Central Asia, an area of 8,354,393.19 square miles (approximately one-seventh of the earth's surface).[17] It was bounded on the north by the Arctic Ocean; on the west by the Baltic Sea, Norway, Finland, Poland, Germany, Hungary, and Rumania; and on the south by the Black Sea, Turkey, Iran, Afghanistan, India, and China.[18]

In the strictest sense of the word, Russia is understood to be that part of the Soviet Union which is bounded on the east by the Ural Mountains and the Ural River and on the south by Turkey, Iran, and the Black and Caspian Sea coasts, the Manych Valley, and the Caspian Sea, on the north by the White and Barents Seas and by Norway, and in the west by Finland, Poland, Germany, Hungary, and Rumania. The administrative division of the Soviet Union is not identical with this definition of territorial limits, but this area today still constitutes the political, cultural, and economic center of the Soviet Union. In geography and culture it is a transitional area between Europe and Asia.

Surface Configuration

The characteristically broad expanses of the Russian landscape appear almost monotonous in comparison with the lands of central and western Europe. Except for the peripheral areas of the Kola Peninsula (4,068 feet), the Yayla Mountains in the Crimea (5,059 feet), the Caucasus Mountains (Mt. Elbrus 18,472 feet), and the Ural Mountains (5,512 feet), the land seldom rises much above 1,312 feet above sea level.

Flat and far-reaching heights, or hilly terrain, rise about 650 feet above the extensive lowlands. These hilly areas can be seen in northwestern Karelia and the Kola Peninsula, to the east and south in the so-called Russian Highlands, the Valdai Hills, and the Timanskiy Range.*

Rivers, Lakes, and Marshes

Russia has some of the largest rivers in the world, the Volga, Dnepr, Don, Kama, and Severnaya Dvina, all well over 1,000 miles in length. Although Russian rivers are largely unregulated, most of them are connected with each other through a system of canals. In contrast to the rivers of central and western Europe, Russian rivers are characterized by weak, uniform descents (except for the Dnepr with its rapids) and by asymmetrical valleys, as seen in the Volga and Dnepr. The relatively higher elevations of western banks of Russian rivers, in contrast to their low-lying eastern banks, tend to favor forces attacking from west to east.

Most of the Russian rivers flow from north to south or from south to north; only one large river flows from east to west. This river, the Pripyat, which begins around the Mazurian Lakes region of East Prussia and northern and central Poland and meanders eastward to the Dnepr, forms a tortuous, almost insurmountable obstacle, with its immense branching of tributaries and interspersed marshy areas. It thus acts as an effective geographical divide, separating the land into a northern and a southern theater for operations, which accounts for the great gap between the combat zones of Army Group Center and the Second Air Fleet and that of Army Group South and the Fourth Air Fleet.✝ Such meandering streams as the Pripyat were admirably suited for Soviet defensive purposes.

Marshy areas and deltas of rivers in Russia were difficult to traverse in the summer except by boats, and were almost intolerable for man or beast because of the enormous swarms of mosquitoes and other insects. In the winter they were likewise hard to cross, even when the surfaces were frozen over. Unfortunately for the Germans, northern and central Russia abounded in such regions.

---

*Valdai Hills are 1,056 feet above sea level, and the Timanskiy are 850 feet.

✝See Maps Nos. 1 and 3. See also Chart No. 2.

Russia was filled with large lakes, one of which, Lake Ladoga, was virtually an inland sea and by far the largest lake on the European continent.

Surface Vegetation and Its Use

The extreme North, the Murmansk coast, and the Arctic islands consist of tundra covered by lichens and moss and sometimes by dwarf-like shrubbery and bushes. South of this tundra belt lies the great forest zone, which is divided into two very different areas, the southern part which has significant cleared areas and the larger northern zone, in which tracts lying far from the rivers are still covered by vast, untouched forests in their primeval state.

In World War II these great forested areas of the East limited military operations severely and offered constant protection for Soviet defenders. They had to be laboriously combed through by the Infantry, since to by-pass them would be to risk leaving them as concentration centers for large military and partisan forces. Undeniably, such areas tied down strong forces which could well have been used elsewhere.

To the south, the area of the steppe forest--very small and largely deforested by man--gives way to the grassy steppes which sometimes assume a prairie-like appearance.

Mineral Deposits

The Soviet Union enjoys a virtual self-sufficiency in raw materials, with the exception of rubber (generally imported from the East Indies), and is especially rich in chemicals, iron, and non-ferrous metals. Nickel is found in the Kola Peninsula and in the central and southern Urals, iron and manganese in the Krivoy Rog and Nikopol areas, some low-grade iron and coal south of Moscow (around Tula), coal in the Donets Basin, oil in the northern Caucasus, and salt and coal in the Urals.[*]

Climate

A nation's climate determines its soil characteristics, ground vegetation, and the life of its people. In Russia, an armed force invading from the west encounters climatic conditions which are entirely different from those found in western or in central Europe.

---

[*]See Map No. 2.

By virtue of its tremendous north-south territorial expanse (some 2,485 miles), Russia has a share in four climatic zones:

(1) The arctic climate, found in the coastal area of the White Sea, featuring low temperatures, frozen ground, tundra, and low precipitation but relatively high atmospheric humidity.

(2) The Mediterranean climate, found only along the southern coast of the Crimean Peninsula and the northeastern shore of the Black Sea, with high temperatures, pronounced summer droughts, and winter rains.

(3) The North Temperate Zone comprising the mass of central and northern territory lying between these extremes.

(4) The subtropical dry climate, found in the southeast, in the Caspian lowlands, and in the western Caucasus, a barren and continental region.

Unlike most countries, temperatures in the Soviet Union in the winter diminish most markedly as one moves toward the East. In the summer, Russian temperatures increase noticeably in the direction of the Southeast.

Winter in the Soviet Union sets in solidly during November and December and, except in the South, is very cold (minus 31° to minus 49° Fahrenheit). The barometric axis of Europe is such that Russia experiences very long and deep snow cover and ice formations in the northern and central regions, combined with severe storms and with long-lasting ice cover on the rivers. Heaviest snows come in February and March.

Population

In October of 1940, Russia had a population of 193,200,000 persons, and a population density of 23 persons per square mile, most of which was located between the western boundary of Russia and the Volga River, especially in the Ukraine.

Since World War I this population had become increasingly urban in character, eight cities having populations of more than 400,000, while two of them, Leningrad and Moscow, had more than 3,000,000 inhabitants. An annual average population increase of about 3,000,000 persons gave the Soviet Union a strong human base from which to carry out military operations.

The Economy

Deeply mistrustful of the West, the Soviet Union set out after World War I to achieve economic and industrial independence. In order to do this and to conceal their progress from the outside they isolated themselves. Without question they made enormous progress between the wars in industrializing their nation, especially in steel and armament plants. Powerful hydroelectric stations also permitted them to decentralize their industries considerably. Although a strip of land 62 miles wide along the western frontier was almost devoid of large installations, masses of heavy industry were located in the eastern Ukraine, at Moscow, along the Volga, in the Ural and Altai Mountains, near Lake Baykal, and east of the lake. This corresponded very roughly with the locations of densest population.

Soviet Russia has vast agricultural resources. Although there are no cereal crops whatever in the Far North region, to the south of it lies the arctic barley zone, and still farther to the south the so-called oats zone, with oats, rye, flax, buckwheat, and hemp. In the steppes large amounts of wheat and sugar beets are grown. In the far South, along the Crimea and the northern Caucasus, is found the subtropical barley zone. But, best known of all is the rich, and most important crop producing area, the black soil belt (chernozem) of the Ukraine and the central Volga. The hurried collectivization and mechanization of agriculture in Russia after 1 October 1928 cost a large part of the livestock* and reduced the yields, but possibly increased the acreages under cultivation. Most Russian farmers were deeply dissatisfied with their national economy as it was in 1941.

Soviet Routes of Communication

Soviet communication networks were extremely thin compared with networks in western Europe. Only three percent of Russian roads had any type of stone surfacing and most of the roads were absolutely

---

*Not to mention the eradication between 1928 and 1931 of thousands of well-to-do farmers (Kulaks) who were in disagreement with the policy of surrendering the fruits of their labor to the government, and who had therefore refused to collectivize.

14

unimproved. Her railroad network was somewhat better, but throughout the entire Soviet Union only 52,000 miles of railroad tracks had been laid by 1941. Yet this was sufficient to make it Russia's most reliable means of transportation. Because of this fact, interdiction of Soviet rail lines was one of the prime objectives of the German Luftwaffe.

Upon the seas the Soviet merchant marine linked Russia with the outside world as well as with other parts of the Soviet Union. In 1938, the Russian merchant service carried 800,000 tons of shipping. Ninety percent of her entire foreign trade moved through Murmansk, Leningrad, the Black Sea ports, and Vladivostok. Although Russia had a rapidly developing air transportation system, it was inconsequential compared to the merchant marine.

The Soviet Form of Government

The Soviet federation included 16 soviet socialist republics: the Russian, Ukrainian, White Russian, Uzbek, Turkmen, Tadzhik, Kazakh, Kirgiz, Georgian, Azerbaijanian, Armenian, Moldavian, Estonian, Latvian, Lithuanian, and the Karelo-Finnish.* The greater part of the land and population of the Soviet Union are included within the Russian Republic.

The Ukraine probably represented the strongest mainspring for national independence movements, although it was, of course, economically, politically, and militarily closely bound to the rest of the Soviet Union. Autonomy of the republics was (and is) largely theoretical, since autonomy remained essentially limited to certain aspects of cultural life. The Soviet federation knew no national state. The support of the state was the proletariat, for whom the Soviet Union was supposed to be the great "fatherland of all working peoples."

---

*Only seven soviet socialist republics are listed by the author: the first six and the Transcaucasian Soviet F.S. Republic (by 1941 no longer a political entity). Of the above-listed republics, all but the Karelo-Finnish Republic are still republics of the U.S.S.R. (Karelo-Finnish Republic is now "autonomous.") The Moldavian S.S.R. was forcibly brought under Soviet control on 28 June 1940 when it was wrested from Rumania. Estonia, Latvia, and Lithuana were seized by Soviet troops 15-17 June 1940.

Conclusions for the Luftwaffe

The Luftwaffe's combat zone was to be roughly within the area bounded south to north by the mouth of the Danube River, Rostov-on-the-Don, Moscow, Tallinn (Reval), Memel (Klaipeda), and Leningrad, a territory of 579,150 square miles. It remained to be seen whether Luftwaffe logistics, aircraft, and planning would be equal to such a vast aerial undertaking.

The Wehrmacht, starting from a 995-mile-wide front, extending from the Danube estuary to Memel, had to advance against a front more than 1,240 miles wide, stretching from Rostov to Leningrad, and also had to open an additional front north of Leningrad, extending more than 620 miles from Lake Ladoga westward along the White Sea to the Barents Sea near Murmansk, and east of Petsamo (Pechenga)* to Norway. In terms of space alone the task was formidable.

The Collection of Intelligence Data

One of Germany's most difficult jobs was to secure intelligence information regarding the Soviet Union. Matters were complicated considerably by Russia's self-imposed isolation from the world. During the German-Polish and Russo-Polish war of 1939, little information was collected. Even the German air attachés on duty in Russia were unable to uncover anything of real value. Collecting intelligence material was made even more difficult after the signing of the Russo-German "Friendship Pact" of 23 August 1939, when the High Command of the Wehrmacht, as a matter of principle, forbade its agencies to assemble data on their "new ally." Soviet officers serving in Germany gave no assistance whatever, since they remained immutably silent.

Large numbers of reports came into German possession during the Russo-Finnish War of 1939-40. Viewed in retrospect, however, these reports served mainly to mislead German commanders, who overlooked the fact that the limited objectives of that war necessitated only the commitment of Soviet troops from the Military District of Leningrad.

After 1940 the German air attachés in Moscow, Tokyo, Ankara, Stockholm, Helsinki, and Washington were given the special assignments

---

*A valuable Finnish nickel mining center seized by the Soviet Union in 1939 and renamed Pechenga.

16

of ferreting out information regarding the Soviet Union, its military, political, and industrial progress and strength. Radio monitoring units were also established and enlarged in Bulgaria, Rumania, Hungary, the Protectorate (of Bohemia and Moravia), Poland, East Prussia, and Finland. Some of the most reliable information was compiled by these stations. In March of 1941 German agencies were burdened down with the additional task of collecting data for the campaign in the Balkans (Yugoslavia, Greece, and Crete). Photo-reconnaissance units working out of Werder* on the Havel River, and later out of Fritzlar† carried out successful photographic missions after October of 1940. Later a number of such organizations collected information on Russian industrial installations, troop and air stations, border fortifications, and supply depots, especially in European Russia, the Baltic States, and the Finnish-Karelian area. In the course of these operations only one plane was lost, a Ju-86, and this was due to bad weather. The crew was captured by the Russians near Vinnitsa and freed a few weeks later by advancing German troops.

In April of 1941 the Russians suddenly announced that a German group would be permitted to visit a number of aircraft and other defense plants in the Soviet Union. The visiting group of specialists, headed by Col. Heinrich Aschenbrenner, Air Attaché in Moscow, soon discovered that the myth of Soviet deficiencies in the area of workmanship was completely false. They also found out that Soviet industry had achieved a great degree of independence. Even in individual plants considerable self-sufficiency had been effected, and installations were widely dispersed.†† The German contingent was probably invited specifically to receive a warning from the Soviet Union, a message which, according to Colonel Aschenbrenner, was unmistakable in intent:

---

*Werder is located about seven miles southwest of Potsdam in Brandenburg.

†A small community in Upper Hesse, about fifteen miles southwest of Kassel, principally known in Germany as one of St. Boniface's most important missionary sites.

††Slow workers in Soviet factories were encouraged to increase their production by a clever system of piecework known as Stakhanov, derived from the name of a Russian miner who responded to Stalin's 1935 speech by exceeding his required tonnage quota of coal. This led to a "Stakhanov year" in 1936 and the founding of "Stakhanov clubs" by obedient workers who had exceeded their work quotas.

After the inspection of [Fighter] Aircraft Factory No. 1 at Moscow's Central Airport, an unequivocal warning was imparted to us by none other than the brother of the People's Commissar for Economics, Mikoyan, * who was busy as chief engineer in Factory No. 1, and after whom the famed Russian MIG fighters are named. There is not the slightest doubt that this occurred at the order of the highest [Soviet] authority. Mikoyan explained to me literally: "We have now shown you everything that we have and what we can do; and whoever attacks us, we destroy!" I passed this statement on, word for word, with corresponding commentaries to all duty stations concerned, without, however, so much as finding the slightest response.

Hitler reacted to the report of the armament commission with the following words: "Well, there you see how far these people are already. We must begin immediately." That our report would have a reaction of that kind, we had of course not expected, let alone wanted. [19]

German intelligence reports indicated that in general the Russian air forces, despite their numerical strength, were inferior to the Luftwaffe. The bulk of Soviet air units were in European Russia, except for heavy bomber units, and most of these were stationed at fields (many of them new) in the Baltic States and in what was formerly eastern Poland, with principal areas of deployment around Kovel, Lvov, Dubno, Sarny, Grodno, Bialystok, Kobrin, Slonim, Kaunas, Wilno, Daugavpils, and Siauliai. These airfields were designated in the following manner: (1) main airfields, which corresponded somewhat to German peacetime air bases, with permanently constructed facilities available, situated near large cities, with very large-- 1 1/4 miles square and larger--landing fields; (2) secondary air bases, conforming roughly to German home airfields, but without permanent installations or rail connections; and (3) advance airfields, situated close to the front, which were usable only as the weather permitted. Clusters of secondary and advance airfields were generally controlled by, and from time to time logistically supported by, a main airfield.

---

*Artem Ivanovich Mikoyan, aircraft designer and brother of Anastas Ivanovich Mikoyan, then People's Commissar for Economics, now Deputy Premier of the U.S.S.R.

The greater part of the Russian combat aircraft were obsolete before BARBAROSSA began, but a conversion of all combat units to modern planes was already in progress. This was especially advanced within the fighter units, which had been hitherto chiefly equipped with the I-15 (Chato), the I-16 (Rata), and the I-153 (Chaika) aircraft,* and which were now being supplied with the latest MIG and LAGG⧸ models. By the summer of 1941 about 200 to 300 I-18 fighters,⧸⧸ with alleged speeds of 372 miles per hour, were to be delivered to Soviet units. Russian fighters produced after the I-16 and I-153 were generally armed with four fixed machine guns, mounted in the fuselage, and two 20 mm. wing cannon (at that time they had no cannon which could be fired through the propeller spinner).

Bomber units in the Soviet Union were usually equipped with SB-3 and DB-3 aircraft.** Since the Russians intended as a primary objective to complete the conversion of all older organizations (especially those equipped with SB-2's) to these aircraft types, German commanders expected no substantial numerical increase in Russian bombers. In conformity to Russian standards, the conversion was quite slow.[20]

According to intelligence estimates the Soviet Union had 7 air divisions, with a total of 7,300 aircraft, in European Russia. These were found mainly in the Military Districts of Kiev, the West, and

---

*All radial-engine, single-seat fighters which flew in the Spanish Civil War. The I-15 biplane and the I-16 low-wing monoplane were 1932 Polikarpov designs, while the I-153 was a more powerful 1938 version of the I-15 having retractable landing gear. Their top speeds ranged from 224 m.p.h. in the I-15 to 300 m.p.h. in the I-16. Spanish Loyalist pilots named the I-15 Chato (the Flat-nosed One), the I-153 Chaika (the Gull), and the I-16 Mosca (the Fly). The latter plane was more widely known, however, by the name Rata (the Rat), which was given to it by Spanish Nationalist and German Legion Condor pilots. All of these planes were of mixed construction style and no match for the modern German fighters.

⧸The LAGG-3 fighter was a single-engine, single-place monoplane designed by S. A. Lavochkin, V. Gorbunov, and M. Gudkov.

⧸⧸Also known as the MIG-1 and I-61. Used in 1941, but soon replaced by MIG-3's.

**SB-3's were fast, twin-engine, three-place, midwing monoplane bombers (an improved version of the SB-2); the DB-3's were long-range, twin-engine, three-place monoplane bombers.

19

Leningrad, which had 1,300, 1,650, and 1,400 planes respectively.* German military leaders assumed that an additional 3 air divisions, of 2,000 planes, were stationed in Asia. Because of Germany's tie with Japan, however, they did not believe Russia would dare transfer units from that region to Europe.

Intelligence agencies could piece together only rough approximations of Soviet antiaircraft strength. They deduced that by June 1941 the Russians had 300 heavy antiaircraft batteries (1,200 guns), 300 light batteries (1,200 guns), about 150 antiaircraft machine gun units (900 machine guns), and about 100 searchlight units with corresponding listening equipment. Very heavy concentrations of antiaircraft artillery were located at Odessa, Moscow, and Leningrad.[21]

Even according to the most pessimistic reports, German leaders believed that the Luftwaffe would be absolutely supreme in quality and numbers over all battlefields in European Russia. Furthermore, the Soviet Union's abandonment of strategic air concepts in favor of close support operations, and the obsolescence of Russian bombers, indicated that Germany would be relatively safe from Soviet air attacks, while Russia would be vulnerable to the Luftwaffe.

The Soviet war economy, despite its favorable location, was not expected to be capable of fulfilling the requirements of the nation's armed forces in case of an all-out war.

German Preparations and Security

Under the provisions of Directive No. 21[†] preparations for Operation BARBAROSSA proceeded under maximum security. Planning

---

*2,000 of these planes were fighters, only about 300 of which were modern MIG types. It should be mentioned that the Russians had at least 10,000 training and practice aircraft which were put to good use as liaison and courier planes. See photographs Generalleutnant a. D. Walter Schwabedissen, The Russian Air Force in the Eyes of German Commanders, USAF Historical Studies No. 175, Maxwell AFB: Historical Division, ASI, June 1960.

†Section IV, which was used with Security Order (Fuehrer Order) No. 1, date unknown, prescribed in detail the conditions under which one might secure access to any secret information. See Field Marshal Keitel's Document Book No. 1 (extract), G/a, Karlsruhe Document Collection. See also Appendix I.

staffs were intentionally kept as small as possible, and only those officers who had been sworn to secrecy and had a "need to know" were brought into the discussions and groundwork. Operations against England were, at all costs, to retain the appearance of normalcy in order not to betray the air concentration in the East.

So rigid were the security regulations surrounding the operation that neighboring staff organizations often did not know what the other group was doing. In southern Poland, the Chief of Staff of the V Air Corps (leader of Planning Staff "P" preparing for BARBAROSSA) kept running into the Chief of Staff of the First Panzer Group, a personal acquaintance of long standing. They even lived in the same hotel. For reasons of security, however, both officers, when conversing, made use of various "white lies" to explain their presence in southern Poland. Fourteen days later before the opening of the campaign, they learned, much to their surprise, that they, as chiefs of staff, were under orders to collaborate particularly closely with each other.

Officers to be concerned with the planning of the campaign against the Soviet Union were informed that the decision for war had been made because of Russia's implacable political demands, all of which were unacceptable to Germany, and because of the dangerous buildup of Russian forces along the western frontiers of the Soviet Union.

In early January 1941, a conference was held by Generaloberst Halder and attended by a number of senior commanders and staff officers, including Generalleutnant Hans-Georg von Seidel, Quartermaster General of the Luftwaffe. Plans were then laid for the organization of Luftwaffe ground units and auxiliary units for the renovation of existing airfields, for the establishment of technical and special installations, for the construction of new fields, and for the stocking of supply bases and fields.

One of the principal tasks of operational planning staffs was the transfer of units from their bases in other theaters to the eastern staging area. Luftwaffe units in the West were then secretly directed to diminish the scale of their operations against Britain. This had to be done with extreme care to avoid betraying their intentions, especially in "spy-laden" Brussels and Paris, where every movement was likely to be reported to the enemy. Because of the reduced air activity over Britain and the necessity to build up reserves for the East, only the most promising and least hazardous objectives were assigned to the remaining western units. Special care was taken to avoid losing new aircrews by assigning them routine type missions until they had gained combat experience. Although by the end of May only a few German units were still flying against Britain, chiefly those not intended for early action against Russia, the transfer of German air units and the significance thereof went largely unnoticed by the British. As early summer approached, the battle over England was broken off.

Cooperation with the various German Army Groups was the immediate objective of planning staffs, so that the fighting power of the Soviet Union could be quickly destroyed and the country occupied by the Wehrmacht. Only about three months remained, however, until the attack deadline, a very brief period indeed. All Luftwaffe units involved were therefore not able to complete their plans in good time, and the Fourth Air Fleet, for example, was preoccupied with German operations in the Balkans and in Crete until 17 June, a scant four days before the beginning of BARBAROSSA.

German Airfield Construction

Airfields in eastern Germany, Poland, the Protectorate (of Bohemia and Moravia), and allied territories were improved and expanded, particularly those designated for early combat operations in BARBAROSSA. The Reichs Labor Service (Reichsarbeitsdienst or RAD) units were especially capable in accomplishing these tasks.

Airfields were particularly poor in southern Poland, and great efforts were required to bring them up to standard in time for the opening of the campaign. Foreign labor was used at many of these fields, but the Poles proved to be far less productive and technically capable than German workers,* and were always security hazards.

Lines of Communication

Adequate communication lines were virtually nonexistent in the parts of Poland seized by Germany in 1939, and even in that part of Poland which had been part of Germany prior to the Treaty of Versailles.

---

*Poles residing in areas which had belonged to Germany before 1919 often looked down upon those living in "old Poland," who had a much lower standard of living. Because of the general backwardness of Poland, Hitler, and indeed many other Germans, were fond of using the term "Polish" as a synonym for anything that was crude or primitive in character.

Since 1919 East Prussia had been connected with Germany only by the submarine cable which extended from Leba (Pomerania), and by two telephone lines along the railroad route.

Auxiliary and main trunk telephone lines were established by special advance teams from each air force and air fleet. Technical signal equipment for the various air corps was completely replenished through the generous assistance of General der Nachrichtentruppe Wolfgang Martini, Chief of the Luftwaffe Signal Communications.

Preparations by Headquarters of Air Administrative Commands

Air Administrative Commands (Luftgaukommandos) were thoroughly organized for the Russian war, and furnished administrative, logistical, and operational support for specific air corps selected for roles in the campaign. These Air Administrative Commands were often staffed by willing, but inadequately trained E-officers (Ergaenzungsoffiziere),* who had, as a rule, only a brief tactical and technical preparation for such positions. The more important of these posts were eventually filled by active regular Luftwaffe officers.

The mission of an Air Administrative Command was to improve the existing facilities in German and allied countries, to seize Polish airfields and supply installations, and to bring them up to standard and integrate them with the German Luftwaffe network. Progress was greatly facilitated by the action of Luftwaffe generals such as Field Marshal Kesselring, who intervened directly in the preparations when necessary in order to eliminate "red tape" and to hasten the completion of the work. In the course of the Russian campaign at least 105 airfields were built by the II Air Administrative Command alone.

---

*Former German Army officers with World War I service (usually lieutenants), who were given temporary commissions (generally as captains) in the new Wehrmacht to fill special new position vacancies. With no predecessors, they had to master all assignments on their own. Few qualified physically or otherwise for combat company or battery assignments. Their commissions had little to do with their former training, or whether they had ever, in fact, served in an air unit. They were paid in the grade of entry, and received no pensions. Moreover, they had a distinguishing mark on their uniforms to set them apart from other officers. Very willing to serve, their tasks were thankless at best, and many of these officers were unequal to them. See D/III, Karlsruhe Document Collection.

Air Administrative Commands for Special Duty

Luftwaffe Administrative Command staffs proved themselves in the West, against France, despite many initial defects. As "extended arms" of Luftwaffe Administrative Commands they were to maintain and supply Luftwaffe units, equip the Luftwaffe ground organization, provide for initial repair of captured airfields, and support air units in reconnoitering new airfields. Although these positions required the highest officer personnel qualifications, one often had the impression that regular stations, obliged to furnish officers for these special staffs, used this opportunity--in a complete lack of appreciation for the importance of the mission--to "get rid of" their undesirable officers. All of the map exercises and conferences could not compensate for basic human deficiencies and a lack of experience in supply operations.

Every Air Administrative Command Staff for Special Duty was ordered to cooperate with an air corps.* With their command posts situated closely to those of the air corps which they supported, an excellent working relationship usually resulted. Materially the problems for such special duty staffs were much greater. Motor vehicles, most of which were unsuited for Russian campaign requirements and were in poor mechanical condition, had to be hastily reconditioned. Great efforts were therefore made to utilize all available workshops prior to the attack to correct these problems.

Luftwaffe Personnel

The campaign in the Balkans and Greece had caused rather heavy personnel and materiel losses for Luftwaffe units, especially the VIII Air Corps. Among the bulk of the aircrew losses were many experienced combat veterans, men who could not easily be replaced. The replacement of aircrews for BARBAROSSA was numerically guaranteed, to be sure, but these positions could only be filled by new aircrews, lacking experience in both combat and formation flying. Their enthusiasm would naturally go a long way toward the creation of a solid striking force, but without adequate experience, considerable losses had to be expected.

Objectives in Russia

Operations in Russia were to take place within three large combat zones and an additional smaller zone. The northern and southern wings

---

*See Chart No. 2.

of the Wehrmacht were to capture the objectives of Leningrad in the North and the Ukraine in the South. Meanwhile the forces of Army Group Center were to hold the middle of the line intact. Moscow was at first only a remote objective, far less important than Leningrad, the birthplace of active Communism. If the Russians could be forced to withdraw to the East, relinquishing the industrial complexes along the Don and Volga Rivers, the German armed forces could press home their advantage.*

Germany's political leaders could not overlook the important economic goods offered in the southern war area and the psychological victory which would result from the destruction of Leningrad. The major question in the campaign, however, devolved upon the point of whether the German commanders, in their zeal to capture this region, would fully understand the separation of the significant from the even more significant.

_____

*See Maps Nos. 1, 2, and 3.

Figure 1
Generaloberst Hans-Juergen Stumpff
Commander-in-Chief Fifth Air Fleet

Figure 2
Generaloberst Alfred Keller
Commander-in-Chief First Air Fleet

26

Figure 3
Field Marshal Albert Kesselring
Commander-in-Chief Second Air Fleet

Figure 4
Generaloberst Alexander Loehr
Commander-in-Chief Fourth Air Fleet

27

Chapter 2

DEPLOYMENT OF GERMAN AND SOVIET AIR FORCES, JUNE 1941

Deployment of the Luftwaffe in the East

The mission of the Luftwaffe in the eastern theater was to destroy Soviet air forces on the ground and in the air and to give direct and indirect support to the German ground forces. Deployment of the Luftwaffe was closely adapted to the deployment of the German Army, in accordance with the Army's strategic objectives.

The field army of the Wehrmacht was divided into several major parts: Army Group South, Army Group Center, Army Group North, and Army Command Far North, to each of which an air fleet, or a portion thereof, was attached.[*]

Within the assembly area of Army Group South (Field Marshal Gerd von Rundstedt) was the Fourth Air Fleet under Generaloberst Alexander Loehr (with headquarters just north of Rzeszów). The right wing of the Fourth Air Fleet, consisting of the IV Air Corps (General der Flieger Kurt Pflugbeil), was deployed in eastern Rumania with its command post at Iaşi. The left wing, comprising the V Air Corps (General der Flieger Robert Ritter von Greim), lay in the area of Lublin-Zamość in southern Poland, with its command post at Lipsko, just south of Zamość. Also concentrated in southern Poland was the II Antiaircraft Artillery Corps of General der Flieger Otto Dessloch.

The Second Air Fleet (Field Marshal Kesselring), with its headquarters at the sport school at Warsaw/Bielany,[/] was situated within the deployment area of Army Group Center (Field Marshal Fedor von Bock). Its right wing, the II Air Corps, under the command of General der Flieger Bruno Loerzer, deployed in the Brest-Deblin area to the east of Warsaw, operated from a command post located at the casino of Otwock,

---

[*]See Map No. 3 and Chart No. 2.

[/]A small community on the west bank of the Vistula River, north-northwest and slightly over four miles from the center of Warsaw.

28

about 25 miles southeast of Warsaw. The left wing, the VIII Air Corps (General der Flieger Wolfram Freiherr von Richthofen) was placed in the region of the Suwalki Point, with its command post located on the north shore of Lake Wigry, east of Suwalki.* The final unit, but by no means the least important, of the Second Air Fleet was the I Antiaircraft Artillery Corps (Flakkorps) under the command of Generalmajor Walter von Axthelm. It was assembled in the area southeast of Warsaw, with its command post at Bohukaly, about 9 miles northeast of Brest-Litovsk.

Within the assembly area of Army Group North (Field Marshal Wilhelm Ritter von Leeb) was the First Air Fleet, commanded by General-oberst Alfred Keller, which operated out of its headquarters at Insterburg (now Chernyakhovsk), East Prussia. The First Air Fleet was comprised of the I Air Corps (General der Flieger Helmuth Foerster), stationed in eastern East Prussia, with headquarters at the grammar school at Gumbinnen (now Gusev), and the Luftwaffe Commander Baltic (Colonel Wolfgang von Wild), with headquarters at Metgethen, Samland district, East Prussia.†

In the Far North the post of Luftwaffe Commander Kirkenes was established to support operations in that area. Its headquarters was situated at the airfield at Kirkenes and was originally a detached unit (under the command of Colonel Andreas Nielsen, GSC), although it was later a part of the Fifth Air Fleet (Generaloberst Hans-Juergen Stumpff), which had its headquarters at Oslo.††

---

*Sometimes called the Suwalki Tip. This area was located just east of and immediately adjacent to the southeastern corner of the former German province of East Prussia. Most of this area is now encompassed by the boundaries of the Polish state.

†The German Province of East Prussia was captured by the Soviet forces in 1944 and 1945. Since then it has been divided between the Polish and Russian states in accordance with the de facto situation and the agreements of Yalta and Potsdam. The northern half has been incorporated into the Soviet Union as a part of the Russian Soviet Socialist Republic, while the southern half has been incorporated into Poland. Place names and economic relationships have therefore been altered completely by this change.

††See Figures 1-4.

Luftwaffe Assignments

The initial deployment area of the Luftwaffe in the East extended behind a German and allied army front approximately 995 miles wide, and faced an enemy front 1,490 miles in width, extending from Sevastopol to Lake Ladoga, Leningrad, and Kronshtadt by way of Rostov-on-the-Don and Moscow. The Karelian front formed an additional combat zone for the Luftwaffe to a depth of 215 miles (the entire Finno-German front extending about 620 miles).

Fourth Air Fleet*

The Fourth Air Fleet, in cooperation with Army Group South, was to proceed from Rumania and southern Poland toward the Crimea, the Sea of Azov, and the Don and Dnepr Rivers. Its IV Air Corps was to lend support not only to the German Eleventh Army advancing from Rumanian territory, but also to the Rumanian Third and Fourth Armies. This corps' front was about 370 miles wide; the distance from its bases at Focşani, Rumania, to the target area at Rostov was around 620 miles, and to objectives in the Crimea approximately 310 miles. The V Air Corps' mission was to support the Sixth and Seventeenth Armies, and especially the First Panzer Group of Army Group South in their advance from southern Poland against Kiev and Rostov. The initial front of the corps was about 215 miles in width; and the distance from its bases around Kraków in southwestern Poland to Rostov-on-the-Don some 930 miles.

The Luftwaffe ground organization in the deployment area of the Fourth Air Fleet was controlled by the XVII and VIII Air Administrative Command Headquarters at Vienna and Breslau (later at Kraków) respectively. These headquarters had to provide supplies for the units and, together with the 4th and 40th Air Administrative Command Staffs for Special Duty, were to build up and enlarge ground organizations in newly occupied territory during the course of the advance.

The tasks of the Luftwaffe Mission in Rumania were as follows: (1) organizing and directing active and passive defenses of the oil industry (drilling, pumping, refining, storage, and transportation), so vital to Germany's conduct of the war; (2) reorganizing and training the Rumanian

---

*See Map No. 1. See also Charts Nos. 2 and 3.

Air Force, both aircrews and antiaircraft artillerymen, in the latest German concepts in aerial warfare; (3) creating a Luftwaffe ground organization on Rumanian soil to receive German air units deploying for BARBAROSSA; (4) activating a Luftwaffe combat administrative command in Rumania for the impending operation and broadening the area of the command within the framework of the German advance to the East; and (5) promoting friendly relationships between German and Rumanian air forces in the hope of eventually establishing a firm alliance. *

Second Air Fleet/

The Second Air Fleet was to advance with Army Group Center out of northern Poland in the direction of Moscow. Since this area was the crucial point of the entire Eastern Front, the Second Air Fleet was especially well equipped with flying units. Its II Air Corps, on the right, was ordered to support the Fourth Army and, more particularly, the Second Panzer Group of Army Group Center. On the left wing the VIII Air Corps was to cooperate with the Ninth Army, but more specifically with the Third Panzer Group of Army Group Center. It should be noted that the initial front of these two air corps--between Brest-Litovsk and the area south of Suwalki--was only some 186 miles wide. The distance from Warsaw to Moscow, however, was about 680 miles.

Breakthroughs of border fortifications and further advances by the Second and Third Panzer Groups were to be supported by the I Antiaircraft Artillery Corps with its mobile and rapid-fire weapons.

Operating from its headquarters at Posen// the II Air Administration Command had the task of organizing, maintaining, and supplying a Luftwaffe ground organization in the newly occupied parts of the central sector. The 2nd and 20th Air Administrative Command Staffs for Special Duty were at the disposal of the command for the accomplishment of these assignments.

---

*See Appendix I.
/See Map No. 1. See also Charts Nos. 2 and 4.
//A German city and province until 1919. It then became a part of Poland. After the Polish campaign of 1939 it was reannexed to Germany. It is now a part of Poland and called Poznán.

First Air Fleet*

The First Air Fleet, in support of Army Group North, had to assist the army operations proceeding from East Prussia in the direction of the Dvina River and Leningrad. The I Air Corps, attached to the First Air Fleet, was to cooperate with the Sixteenth and Eighteenth Armies and, in particular, the Fourth Panzer Group of Army Group North. The initial army group front was about 125 miles wide; but the distance from Koenigsberg to Leningrad was about 528 miles. The coastal flank was to be guarded by the Luftwaffe Commander Baltic, which was assigned the task of attacking Soviet naval vessels and supporting ground force operations in connection with the assaults upon the Baltic islands of Saaremaa, Muhu, and Hiiumaa.

All ground organizations, including supply and maintenance units for the support of Luftwaffe units in Combat Zone North, were under the I Air Administrative Command at Koenigsberg. On hand for the reconstruction and development of new ground organizations in the captured territories were the 1st and 10th Air Administrative Command Staffs for Special Duty.

Fifth Air Fleet†

Units of the Fifth Air Fleet, operating under the command of the Luftwaffe Commander Kirkenes, based in northern Norway and Finland, were assigned the mission of supporting the advance of ground forces of Army Commander Norway against Murmansk and the Murmansk railroad, especially in the Kandalaksha sector. There was also a possible need for stronger forces to be used against the transport of Anglo-American goods across the Arctic Ocean. The terminals of these shipping movements were the harbors in Kolskiy Bay, particularly Murmansk, and the ports along the shores of the White Sea, especially Arkhangelsk, which became the most significant objectives for German air operations in the Finnish combat area. The overland breadth of the operational front was about 215 miles, while the distance from the home air base at Banak (at the southern tip of Porsanger Fjord) to Arkhangelsk was about 560 miles.††

Motorized elements of the entire Luftwaffe ground organization in the East, including antiaircraft artillery and signal services, were deployed by rail and motor convoys, a movement which was in great part completed

---

*See Charts Nos. 2 and 5.
†See Charts Nos. 2 and 6.
††See Map No. 1.

by 15 June 1941. Flying units were brought up to their prepared fields before 20 June in individual flights or in small, three-plane formations (Ketten), avoiding for security's sake all the larger urban areas. Units of the VIII Air Corps, which until a few days before "D-Day" were employed in the Balkans and Crete, were also successfully transferred to the new deployment areas in the East. On 21 June 1941 the Luftwaffe was in place for its most difficult operation.

Actual Luftwaffe Strength in the East, 20 June 1941

Immediately prior to the attack on Russia, the German Air Force had 2,000 combat planes in the East, consisting of 29 1/3 bomber groups (880 aircraft), 9 1/3 dive bomber groups (280 planes), 20 fighter groups (600 aircraft), 2 twin-engine fighter groups (60 planes), 2 ground attack groups (60 aircraft), and 12 long-range reconnaissance squadrons (120 aircraft). In addition, there were 230 noncombat planes in 5 air transport groups (150 planes) and 8 liaison squadrons (80 planes).

Fourth Air Fleet Strength

The Fourth Air Fleet, in support of Army Group South, had 600 combat aircraft in its organization. This included 12 bomber groups (360 planes), 7 fighter groups (210 planes), 3 long distance reconnaissance squadrons (30 aircraft), 2 air transport groups (60 planes) and 3 liaison squadrons (30 planes). There were also Army air units (Heeresflieger-Verbaenden) in the area of the Fourth Air Fleet, consisting of 5 long distance reconnaissance squadrons (50 aircraft), 14 close reconnaissance squadrons (140 aircraft), and 5 liaison squadrons (50 planes).

Antiaircraft artillery under the Fourth Air Fleet command was made up of 1 corps artillery staff, 3 regimental artillery staffs, and the units under these commands; 13 mixed antiaircraft battalions; and 4 light antiaircraft battalions.

Second Air Fleet Strength

Approximately 910 combat aircraft were available to the Second Air Fleet, assigned to support Army Group Center. This strength consisted of 8 bomber groups (240 planes), 8 1/3 dive bomber groups (250 planes), 9 fighter groups (270 aircraft), 2 twin-engine fighter groups (60 planes), 2 ground-attack groups (60 planes), and 3 long distance reconnaissance squadrons (30 aircraft). Also attached to them were 2 air transport groups (60 aircraft), and 3 liaison squadrons (30 aircraft). Army air units in this combat area were comprised of 4 long distance reconnaissance squadrons (40 aircraft), 11 close reconnaissance squadrons (110 planes), and 3 liaison squadrons (30 planes).

The Second Air Fleet had 1 antiaircraft artillery corps staff, 3 antiaircraft artillery regimental staffs, 16 mixed (light and heavy) battalions, and 7 light antiaircraft artillery battalions.

First Air Fleet Strength

This air fleet, supporting Army Group North, was the weakest of the three major air commands on the Eastern Front. About 430 aircraft were in this organization and ready for action on 22 June 1941. Its units included 9 bomber groups (270 planes), 3 2/3 fighter groups (110 planes), 5 long distance reconnaissance squadrons (50 aircraft), 1 air transport group (30 aircraft), and 2 liaison squadrons (20 aircraft). The army flying organizations in this area had 4 long distance reconnaissance squadrons (40 aircraft), 11 close reconnaissance squadrons (110 planes), and 3 liaison squadrons (30 aircraft).

Antiaircraft artillery strength in this zone consisted of 3 antiaircraft artillery regimental staffs, 8 mixed (light and heavy) battalions, and 3 light antiaircraft battalions.

Fifth Air Fleet Strength

On the extreme left of the German front was Army Command Far North (or High North), supported by the Fifth Air Fleet. This organization was clearly the weakest of all the front units. The Fifth Air Fleet possessed only 60 aircraft in all, divided as follows: 1/3 of a bomber group (10 aircraft), 1 dive bomber group (30 aircraft), 1/3 of a fighter group (10 aircraft), and 1 long distance reconnaissance squadron (10 planes). An army air organization situated in the area of Army Command Norway consisted of a close reconnaissance squadron of 10 planes.

A single mixed (light and heavy) antiaircraft artillery battalion was assigned to Army Command Norway.

Luftwaffe Strength and Space

On 22 June 1941 German combat aircraft, except for those belonging to replacement groups, were deployed as follows: 190 for home defense,

370 in the Mediterranean, 660 in the West, 120 in Norway (not counting units to be used there for BARBAROSSA), and 2,000 in the East, a total of 3,340 combat aircraft in the entire German Air Force.

It was a question whether the Luftwaffe in the East had sufficient range and power to strike targets in "Blitzkrieg" fashion beyond the Dnepr River. Judging by past standards, one could not expect more than 70 percent of the combat planes to be operational, and generally not more than 60 percent could be figured. The industrial centers in the lower Volga, in the Caucasus, and in the Urals and Siberia would therefore for all practical purposes remain out of the war zone.

Deployment of Soviet Air and Antiaircraft Artillery Forces

German intelligence agencies assumed the Soviet government to have about 7,000 combat aircraft in European Russia on 21 June 1941, and another 2,000 in Asiatic Russia.* According to an undetermined (possibly American) source, the Soviet air strength was deployed as follows:

Army Budënny - in the South

A total of 8 air divisions were assigned to this area, each division consisting of 3 to 5 air regiments of 80 aircraft each.

Army Timoshenko - in the North

This area had 2 air divisions, or about 480-800 aircraft in all.

Army Voroshilov - to the Rear of Timoshenko┼

Approximately 960-1,600 aircraft, organized in 4 air divisions were concentrated under this command.

---

*The German estimates based on 80 aircraft per air regiment and 3 to 5 air regiments per air division produce totals (in European Russia) varying from 5,420 to 9,200 planes. German leaders assumed 7,000 to be the probable total in this area.

┼Semën Mikhailovich Budënny, Semën Konstantinovich Timoshenko, and Kliment Efremovich Voroshilov, all Marshals of the Soviet Union.

The Moscow Area

Here, 7 air divisions were concentrated to defend the capital.

The Caucasus Region

Although not immediately needed for defense, 2 air divisions were located in this general area, rounding out the total number of 23 air divisions in European Russia. An additional 10 air divisions were supposed to be situated in the "Far East."[1]

Operation Barbarossa Is Delayed

Hitler had toyed with the idea of going to war against Russia in the autumn of 1940, but because of clearly insurmountable technical problems which would have precluded a deployment of the Luftwaffe in sufficient force, he quickly abandoned his notion. The plan was then rescheduled for May of 1941, but again events forced a postponement. One of these was an elementary natural occurrence, a late thaw in Russia; the other was a political incident with military consequences in Yugoslavia.

The Coup d'état in Yugoslavia

During the early morning hours of 27 March 1941 Prince Regent Paul of Yugoslavia was overthrown by Yugoslavian Air Force General Dušan Simovič,* and the young King Peter II, still a minor, was raised to the throne. Although ostensibly dedicated to a policy of neutrality, he immediately ordered a general mobilization along the borders of his new realm. This changed the entire political situation. Aware of the necessity of security in the South for his impending Russian campaign, Hitler reacted with lightning speed. About 1300 on 27 March, in the presence of von Ribbentrop, Keitel, Jodl and other leaders, the Fuehrer informed the top Wehrmacht commanders that Yugoslavia as a nation was to be destroyed and that it was politically important that this be swiftly accomplished.†

OKW Directive No. 25, comprising the oral directives of the conference, was signed by Hitler on the evening of 27 March and disseminated

---

*It is interesting to note that, as in 1914, a Serb set the stage for war in the Yugoslavian area.
†See Keitel's notes on this conference, G/VII/7, Karlsruhe Document Collection.

to responsible heads of the German Army, Navy, and Luftwaffe.* This proclaimed that the coup d'état in Belgrade had altered the international political situation, because of which Yugoslavia would have to be immediately dealt with as an enemy and destroyed as quickly as possible. Therefore, the Commander in Chief of the Luftwaffe, in the early hours of 28 March, ordered 7 bomber groups, 3 dive bomber groups, and a twin-engine fighter group to be assembled by 30 March in the Vienna area, under the command of the Fourth Air Fleet which was assigned to General-oberst Loehr. Its mission was to attack Belgrade and the ground organization of the Yugoslavian Air Force.

Hitler's decision also entailed a five-week postponement of BARBAROSSA.† General Halder remarked that the Yugoslavian intervention became a strategic problem since it delayed the attack upon Russia by about two months. [2]

The Late Thaw

But the beginning of BARBAROSSA was delayed not only by the Yugoslavian coup d'état, which obligated strong German air and ground forces to a new theater of war. Extraordinary weather conditions in the Soviet Union resulted in a very late thaw. Until the end of May the ground was boggy, with roads and unpaved airfields virtually unusable. These adverse conditions seriously retarded the rapid extension of German highway and road networks, the expansion of German airfields, and the construction of immense communication lines. Although these poor weather and terrain conditions permitted the German High Command and its troops to anticipate some of the natural forces against which they would be pitted in the vast Russian arena, the two-month delay of Operation BARBAROSSA was to have a tremendous--perhaps a decisive--impact upon the course of the entire campaign.

---

*See Directive No. 25, G/b, Karlsruhe Document Collection.
†Keitel's notes mention a four-week delay. G/VII/7, Karlsruhe Document Collection.

Chapter 3

THE BATTLE FOR AIR SUPERIORITY

The several army groups of the Wehrmacht on the eastern frontier opened their surprise attack upon the Soviet Union at 0330 hours on 22 June 1941. German armored forces were to shatter the Russian front north and south of the Pripyat marshes, after which isolated Soviet forces were to be individually attacked and destroyed, as close to the frontier as possible. A withdrawal of Soviet armies into the interior of the country was to be prevented at all costs.[1]

The Luftwaffe's primary mission was the destruction of Soviet air forces in western European Russia. All Russian operational airfields in close proximity to the border were to be attacked at once by all available air forces. Operations against Russian air and air force ground organizations were then to be continued until Soviet air power had been crushed. Army command staffs, recalling the Luftwaffe's successes in former campaigns, recognized the need to employ the bulk of available air combat units during the first days of the operation for the quick destruction of the Russian Air Force. If air superiority or, even better, air supremacy, could be achieved over Russia, the German Army could conduct its offensive without noticeable interference from Soviet aircraft, thereby reducing the ground force losses.

Information on the distribution of enemy air forces had been obtained prior to the campaign through high-altitude photographic reconnaissance performed by the reconnaissance group of the German Air Force High Command and by other intelligence methods, particularly the radio intercept services. This information had been made available as target data at all German tactical airfields in the East, each Luftwaffe command staff receiving data for the area in which its operations would most likely take place.

Following the basic patterns of the Polish and Western campaigns, squadrons of the German Air Force crossed the Russian border in the early dawn of 22 June 1941, concentrating their massed attacks upon Soviet air forces and air force ground installations.

The Luftwaffe's battle for air superiority in the East was begun against a numerically vastly stronger enemy. Nevertheless, the German

Air Force, favored by an abundance of good quality aircraft and favorable weather, launched continuous high-altitude and low-level attacks upon Soviet airfields, destroying hundreds of planes. It also shot down virtually all of the hostile aircraft which it encountered in the air. Bomber units flew as many as four to six missions daily, dive bombers, seven to eight, and fighters, five to eight, according to the distances from their respective bases to the front.

No explanation could be found for the failure of the Soviet command to take adequate air defense measures, which, in view of the political situation and the previous German use of air power, should have been warranted. Such obvious steps as the dispersal of fighter units situated on airfields close to the border, the transfer of bomber units to the interior, and the provision for antiaircraft defenses of air bases had been badly neglected.

The first attack caught complete air units upon the ground, unprotected.[2]* Within a few days the greater part of the Soviet air forces were destroyed. In the weeks that followed, the Russian Air Force appeared to be paralyzed; only small units, appearing at very infrequent intervals, participated in combat actions, and most of these were uncoordinated and unsystematic. The possibility of Soviet flying units halting or even delaying the swift advance of German Army groups, or of threatening the German homeland, was eliminated. Within a few days it became clear that the technical superiority of Luftwaffe aircraft, the relatively higher level of technical and tactical training of German airmen, and the high morale and aggressiveness of individual German aircrews were more decisive factors in combat than the actual numerical strength of these units might have suggested. By accomplishing its primary mission, the Luftwaffe contributed materially to the great victories of the German Army in the East during the opening weeks of the campaign.

Combat Situation East, 22-29 June 1941

On the first day of the attack Reichsmarschall Goering reported that only a few Russian aircraft had flown over East Prussia, some 20 enemy sorties penetrating to the Tilsit-Insterburg line. Of nine attacking enemy bombers, five were shot down by German fighters. Other sorties over the Reich were flown from the vicinity of Bialystok-Pultusk, Brest-Litovsk, and Kholm, but no bombs were reported to have been dropped.

---

*See Figures 5 and 6.

Figure 5
Soviet aircraft destroyed at Kaunas, Lithuania,
by the Luftwaffe, 22 June 1941

Figure 6
Soviet planes destroyed at Kaunas, Lithuania,
by the Luftwaffe, 22 June 1941

German air reconnaissance generally confirmed previous reports on the deployment of Russian air forces. No special camouflaging of planes or airfields was yet noticeable, and Russian aircraft were frequently parked "in rows on the fields or the edges thereof" in conformity to peacetime regulations. Apparently no surprise attacks had been expected. Thus individual combat reports carried the news that "extraordinarily large numbers of aircraft have been destroyed or damaged upon the ground." The attacks against the Russian bases had indeed proceeded as planned. Early on 22 June, German airmen, flying in the first attack wave and fully exploiting the factor of surprise, struck Soviet airfields near the border and other "specific individual targets," hitting 31 airfields, 3 suspected billets of high-level staffs, 2 barracks, 2 artillery positions, a bunker system, and an oil depot. In addition, Goering reported that a special operation had been carried out against the seaport of Sevastopol. The Luftwaffe's overall commitment in the first wave consisted of some 637 dive and conventional bombers and 231 fighters. Of these, only two were missing. Thus far the Russian fighter defense had proven to be unaggressive, turning away to flee when fired upon at long range, while no other well-directed air defense was in evidence. Towns, such as Brest-Litovsk, were fully lighted at night, indicating that the Russians had done little in the way of preparing for blackouts. [3]

During the first two days of the war, while the Luftwaffe continued its attacks upon Soviet air and air force ground installations, photo-reconnaissance uncovered a large number of hitherto unknown airfields, heavily occupied by enemy air units. Attacks upon these fields were so successful that on 29 June the High Command of the Armed Forces (OKW) was able to report the destruction of 4,017 Soviet aircraft, against a loss of only 150 planes for the Germans. Goering announced that in the first week of the campaign the Russians had lost 4,990 aircraft, while the Germans had lost only 179.[4] General Halder, Chief of the Army General Staff, commented on these victories on 22 and 24 June, noting that the "Russian aircraft shot down . . . [included] entire bomber squadrons flying without fighter escort."[5]

The 3rd Fighter Wing, commanded by Major Guenther Luetzow,* was cited by the High Command of the Luftwaffe on 9 July for a particularly

---

*Luetzow attained the rank of Colonel and has been credited with 103 aerial victories. Holder of the Knight's Cross with Oak Leaf, Swords, and Diamonds, he fell on 22 April 1945.

meritorious action. When an airfield, occupied by elements of his wing, was attacked by 27 Soviet bombers, the unit took to the air and shot down the entire attacking force in 15 minutes, without losing a single plane.[6]

Generalmajor von Waldau, Chief of the Luftwaffe Operations Staff, wrote in his diary on the evening of 22 June 1941: "the timing [of the air attack] was a complete success," opening the way for operations against the entire Soviet Air Force. Although he questioned the incoming reports of the day which claimed that more than 800 Russian aircraft had been destroyed by nightfall, he nevertheless believed that a decisive victory had been achieved. Clarification of the strategic situation was then of primary importance, but von Waldau believed in leaving the details in the hands of the air fleet commanders.[7] On 3 July he was able to make a better appraisal of the situation. He observed that Soviet military forces were quantitatively greater and better than preattack data had indicated. Surprised that the Russians had had some 8,000 planes ready for action in the western area, he was equally astounded to discover that 1,800 of those planes had been destroyed by the Luftwaffe on the first day of the war, with relatively negligible German losses.[8]*

Combat Situation East, June - October 1941

Field Marshal Kesselring (commanding the Second Air Fleet) wrote after the war "thanks to the tactical air planning and to the tireless, willing effort of the units, it was possible on the strength of excellent photo-reconnaissance to achieve 'air superiority' within two days." According to Kesselring, Goering had not at first believed the reports of the opening week which came in from the Eastern Front, claiming that some 2,500 Russian planes had been destroyed upon the ground and in the air. Goering had the figures checked, only to discover that the actual count ran 200 to 300 planes higher than Kesselring had claimed. Operations of the German Army would not have progressed as smoothly and as rapidly without the Luftwaffe "prelude." Kesselring described the destruction of squadrons of "clumsy" Russian medium bombers on 23 June 1941. Arriving at regular intervals, in tactically weak formations, they were easily downed by the German fighters. Furthermore, the Luftwaffe had thereby succeeded in destroying the basis for the Russian bomber fleet buildup so that during

---

*See von Waldau's diary, Karlsruhe Document Collection.

later campaigns Russian bombers scarcely put in an appearance, an achievement of the German Air Force in the East which was never really appreciated. [9]

Winston Churchill later noted the similarity of the Russian Air Force's misfortune on the first day of the campaign (albeit on a far greater scale) to the earlier fate of the Polish Air Force. [10] General Kurt von Tippleskirch,* in his postwar history, attested to the great effectiveness of the Luftwaffe in support of ground operations and its strong influence upon enemy morale. Noting the passiveness of the Russian air forces, he added that the German Air Force had not succeeded in annihilating the enemy air forces as it had in previous campaigns, apparently because of the vast extent of territory involved and the demands made upon its forces for the support of the ground fighting. [11]

Tippleskirch recognized the "advantages" of the Luftwaffe in direct and indirect support of the Army, but he completely misunderstood the effect of the struggle for air superiority upon ground operations. The Soviet air forces had to remain inactive during the first months of the campaign in the East because they had been nearly destroyed and could not attack German ground forces on a large scale. It is true that the complete destruction or the continuing neutralization of remaining Soviet air forces had not succeeded. The reason was that the bulk of the Luftwaffe now had to begin to carry out its second mission--its future main task--the direct and indirect support of the army.

It would have been correct for the Luftwaffe to have continued the fight against Soviet air forces with all available power, for they should not have been allowed to recover after the initial knockout blow. But this would have meant not only commitments against the enemy air forces in the air and on their bases but also against Russian production, the factories of the air armament industry. The latter was impossible, however, because of the inferior range of German twin-engine bombers and the lack of a long-range four-engine bomber capable of making regular assaults upon aircraft plants,⧸ especially against industrial installations in the Moscow

---

*General der Infanterie Kurt von Tippelskirch, who headed the Fourth, Fourteenth, Twenty-First Army Commands, and finally Army Group Vistula.

⧸General Walter Wever, Chief of the Luftwaffe General Staff, 1935-36 (killed in an air crash in 1936), advocated a four-engine bomber force in the 1930's. He called the bomber needed for such operations the "Ural bomber." For an interesting discussion of this problem see Richard Suchenwirth, Historical Turning Points in the German Air Force War Effort, USAF Historical Studies No. 189, Maxwell AFB: USAF Hist. Div., RSI, June 1959, pp. 40-44.

and Voronezh areas, which, at the time, had not yet been evacuated to the East. Only during September and October 1941, after capture of the territory around Kiev and Smolensk provided a jump-off area, were a few attacks made upon the aircraft industry at Voronezh by the Second and Fourth Air Fleets. But these were simply independent operations, initiated by the air fleets concerned. A large, planned operation, such as those envisioned under the German principles for "The Conduct of Aerial Warfare," ordered and controlled by the Commander in Chief of the Luftwaffe, never took place. Even after winning the take-off bases, so badly needed because of the limited operational range of German bombers, no strong, destructive, daylight attacks could be flown because: (1) sufficient forces were not then available for such operations; (2) long-range escort fighters, essential for daylight attacks, were also unavailable; and (3) the Soviet aircraft industry had by then already been transferred to the East, especially those plants producing specialized items such as optical instruments.

The failure to strike the Soviet aircraft production centers permitted the undisturbed Russian plants to steadily replace the enormous losses of the first weeks of war. In addition, hostile air activity gradually increased in certain areas, and by late summer became troublesome to German ground operations and helped to cause appreciable Wehrmacht losses. It was impossible for the Luftwaffe to perform simultaneously its two assigned missions, the achievement of air superiority and support of the ground forces, since the German air units in the East were numerically weak and the operational territory was so vast. In attempts to perform both missions at the same time, the effectiveness of one effort or the other was found to diminish. Yet at the beginning of the Russian campaign the Luftwaffe successfully accomplished its primary mission of annihilating the Soviet air forces at hand and securing air superiority (almost air supremacy). This was due to the superior equipment, training, and aggressiveness of the German Air Force, and the willingness of its personnel to make great sacrifices.[12]

The second mission (supporting the ground forces), which required all the air power available, began about 25 June. Sorties against Soviet air forces and their ground installations were then flown only occasionally and incidentally, and only when the steadily increasing Russian air activity became too bothersome for the German ground forces or caused them unbearable losses. Because of this primary mission of supporting the Army, operations of the German Air Force became increasingly involved with ground operations and finally completely dependent upon them. Consequently, it is necessary to study the Wehrmacht ground operations, with which the

Luftwaffe was so intimately involved, and without a knowledge of which the air operations cannot be understood.*

_____
*See Map No. 3.

Chapter 4

FOURTH AIR FLEET OPERATIONS LEADING TO THE
ENCIRCLEMENT BATTLE OF KIEV

Advance of Army Group South to the Dnepr River

Army Group South (comprising 26 regular and 4 light infantry divisions, 4 motorized divisions, and 5 armored divisions), commanded by Field Marshal Gerd von Rundstedt, began its advance on 22 June with orders to destroy Soviet forces west of the Dnepr River in Galicia and the western Ukraine, and to establish bridgeheads east of the Dnepr in front of and south of Kiev.[1]* Its left flank (Sixth and Seventeenth Armies and First Panzer Group) was to drive forward to Kiev, seize the Dnepr bridges, and open the way for continued operations east of the river. Its right flank (Eleventh Army and Rumanian and Hungarian units) was to remain in position during the initial advance period. This force, commanded by Generaloberst Eugen Ritter von Schobert, was ordered to contain as large a Soviet force as possible and to defend the vitally important Rumanian oil deposits. Aggressive action for the right wing was planned for a later stage.

Opposing these forces were two strong Russian groups under Marshal Sëmen Mikhailovich Budënny. Of these forces, 11 infantry divisions, 1 cavalry division, 2 armored divisions, and 7 motorized-mechanized brigades were deployed in Bessarabia, with the rear elements east of the Dniester and the bulk stretched in a thin line along the Prut River. Another Russian group of 27 infantry divisions, 17 cavalry divisions, 3 armored divisions, and 4 motorized-mechanized brigades was deployed on the frontier between Chernovtsy and the Pripyat River. In the rear were 1 armored division, 12 infantry divisions, 3 cavalry divisions, and 3 motorized-mechanized brigades situated as far back as the Sluch River and the headwaters of the Bug.[2]

The Russians were tactically surprised by the German attack, which quickly captured the Bug River bridges intact and penetrated Soviet border defenses at all key points. The Sixth Army (left wing of Army Group South) under Field Marshal Walter von Reichenau advanced across

---

*See Map No. 4.

46

the Styr River, where it and the First Panzer Group[*] of Generaloberst Ewald von Kleist were halted by fierce Russian armored counterattacks, first from the south and then from the north.[3] After bitter tank battles around Lutsk and Dubno (northeast of Lvov) the Russians were pushed back. The Seventeenth Army (center of Army Group South) under General Karl-Heinrich von Stuelpnagel soon encountered very strong enemy forces in well-developed positions northwest and west of Lvov (Lemberg) which it was at first unable to dislodge.

On 2 July 1941 the Eleventh Army (right wing of Army Group South) attacked toward Mogilev on the Dniester, the Rumanian Third Army advanced toward Chernovtsy, and Hungarian units seized Kolomyya, making contact with the southernmost units of the Seventeenth Army which had reached the Zbruch River after heavy fighting. Since strong Russian forces, particularly armored forces, had been concentrated south of the Pripyat marshes, it is probable that the Soviet command had expected the main German attack to come from the Gouvernement Général (Poland), probably on the assumption that the German command would concentrate against the Ukraine.[4] Army Group South with its First Panzer Group had not yet secured full operational freedom, but was compelled to use all of its armies to force back the enemy. Heedless of losses, the Soviet command had resisted tenaciously and had repeatedly extricated its forces from threatened envelopment.

The Sixth Army and the First Panzer Group arrived at the Sluch River about 4 July, with the Seventeenth Army on their right and rear along the Zbruch River, and Hungarian forces farther to the south. The Eleventh Army and the Rumanian Third and Fourth Armies were in the Bucovina and north Bessarabia areas. On 5 July Army Group South resumed its offensive. The left wing (Sixth Army and First Panzer Group) breached the Stalin Line at Novograd-Volynskiy, and the Seventeenth Army (center) did so at Bar. The first large-scale encirclement battle in the South now began to take form around Uman.[†] Protected to the east by a part of the Sixth Army, the First Panzer Group (now pushing ahead north of Uman) wheeled to the southeast through Boguslav and pushed to the south as far as Pervomaysk, preventing the withdrawal of sizable Soviet forces to the east and southeast. Contact was soon made with elements of the right wing of Army Group South, which pushed rapidly ahead to Pervomaysk, closing the ring around Uman. When the encirclement battle ended on 8 August, the High Command of the German Armed Forces

---

[*]See Figure 7.
[†]See Maps Nos. 4 and 9.

47

Figure 7
German armored column advancing into
Russia, Summer 1941

Figure 8
Fourth Air Fleet staff in Russia, Summer 1941
L. to R.: Col. Hermann Plocher, Maj. Alarich Hofmann, Maj.
Karl-Heinrich Schulz, Col. Richard Schimpf, Generalmajor
Guenther Korten, General der Flieger Ritter von Greim, General-
major Walter Sueren, Generaloberst Alexander Loehr, General
der Flieger Kurt Pflugbeil.

48

reported the capture of 103,000 prisoners, including the commanding generals of the Soviet Sixth and Twelfth Armies, 317 tanks, and 858 guns.

While protecting its northern wing against attacks by the Soviet Fifth Army from the area of Korosten, the German Sixth Army continued its advance to the east, threatening to envelop Kiev, the ancient capital of the Ukraine, on the west bank of the Dnepr. Meanwhile (about 25 August), the First Panzer Group brought practically all the territory west of the Dnepr River bend as far as Kherson under German control and established two bridgeheads across the Dnepr at Dnepropetrovsk and Kremenchug.

Farther south the Russians had evacuated Bessarabia in time, but part of the forces were pocketed in the Kirovograd area and destroyed; the rest withdrew across the Dnepr. Odessa was invested by the Fourth Rumanian Army, but was not taken until 16 October because the Rumanian forces were too weak to attack.

Meanwhile, a crisis had developed south of Kiev. On 7 August, while the battle at Uman was still in progress, a newly arrived Soviet force of 2 cavalry divisions, 1 armored division, and from 3 to 4 infantry divisions attacked across the Dnepr at Kanev. In swinging southeast, the First Panzer Group had left a gap between it and the Sixth Army. Into this gap poured the Russians, who then drove forward as far as Boguslav, seriously threatening the communications of both German forces. Weak German rear elements barely halted the enemy's advance, and only after several critical days could units be moved in from the north and south to counterattack and drive the Russians back across the Dnepr.

Operations of the Fourth Air Fleet

The mission of the Fourth Air Fleet (Generaloberst Alexander Loehr)* in support of Army Group South's operations was as follows:†

(1) Attack the Soviet air forces, achieve air superiority, and thereby prevent any counter-air action against the German Army units.

(2) Render direct and indirect support to the army group, concentrating on the left flank as the Sixth Army and First Panzer Group advanced

---

*See Figures 4, 8, and 9.
†See Maps Nos. 6, 7, and 8.

to the Dnepr at Kiev to prevent the withdrawal of strong Russian forces across the river.

(3) Attack and eliminate the Soviet Black Sea Fleet and its bases.

(4) Interdict Russian merchant shipping on the Black Sea and the Sea of Azov.

The IV Air Corps (General der Flieger Kurt Pflugbeil), a part of the Fourth Air Fleet, was linked with the operations of the Rumanian Air Force and cooperated in protecting the vital oil fields from Russian air attack, supported the operations of the Eleventh Army and the Rumanian Third and Fourth Armies, and attacked the Soviet naval bases around the Black Sea.

The V Air Corps under General der Flieger Robert Ritter von Greim was assigned the task of operating from the Zamośc-Lublin area against Russian air forces, particularly fighters, and of securing air superiority within the first few days of the campaign. After the third or fourth day, the First Panzer Group and the Sixth Army of Army Group South were to be supported in their rapid drive on Kiev, with the air corps assuming responsibility for their rear flanks. Air support was also to be given to the Seventeenth Army in case a critical situation should arise during its push toward Kiev from the south.

The II Antiaircraft Artillery Corps (Flakkorps) under General der Flieger Otto Dessloch was to provide antiaircraft protection, particularly for the First Panzer Group whose ground operations it was to support whenever necessary.

The staff of the Luftwaffe Mission in Rumania under General-leutnant Wilhelm Speidel was responsible for the air defense of the oil-producing area around Ploeşti, the oil storage and shipping installations at Constanţa, the bridge over the Danube at Cernavodă (the most important point of the oil pipeline), the oil shipping port of Giurgiu on the Danube, and the airfields of the Luftwaffe Mission. The strength of the Russian air forces in the southern area was estimated at eight air divisions.

Operations of the IV and V Air Corps

During the early hours of 22 June 1941 units of the IV and V Air Corps attacked the Soviet operational airfields which had been reported in their areas. Intelligence data obtained prior to the campaign revealed particularly heavy concentrations of Soviet air power in the V Air Corps area, especially around Brody-Lutsk-Dubno, Lvov, Stanislav-Tarnopol, Terebovlya, and in the area of Belaya Tserkov-Kiev-Ovruch-Zhitomir-Berdichev. The V Air Corps could thus assume that its first opposition would come from some 448 single-engine Russian fighter and ground-attack aircraft and 282 twin-engine bombers, with most of the fighters being based on airfields close to the frontier.[5] For supplies the Soviet air forces in the area depended upon equipment depots at Lvov and Kiev-Postvolynski. In the IV Air Corps zone the main concentrations of Soviet air power had been identified around Beltsy (Balti in Bessarabia) and Odessa.

The Russians were completely surprised by the Luftwaffe's attack. By employing all units to the utmost--Luftwaffe bomber units flying from three to four missions daily and fighter units carrying out six to seven missions a day--the Russians were dealt a decisive blow. On 9 August the general commanding the Soviet Sixth Army told his German captors: "The Russian air losses were terrible in the first days and the Russian Air Force has never recovered from this blow."[6] From 22 to 25 June 1941, units of the V Air Corps alone attacked 77 Russian airfields in 1,600 sorties, destroying 774 Soviet planes on the ground and 136 in the air.[7]*

In these operations, the small SD-2 bomb,✝ an item not always in adequate supply, was used extensively by the 51st Bomber Wing. It proved to be an efficient fragmentation bomb, particularly against live targets, troop concentrations, and moving vehicles, and also had excellent effects upon aircraft on the ground. The next larger bomb, the SD-10, was withdrawn from use for a long period because of several accidents resulting from collisions of the released bombs, which then detonated prematurely immediately under the aircraft. Consequently, 110- and even 550-pound bombs had to be used against these targets, although the desired broad fragmentation effect could not be attained with these bombs, even with the use of normal quick or super-sensitized detonators.

---

*See Figure 10.

✝The SD-2 bomb was a small, antipersonnel bomb, loaded with approximately 4 1/2 pounds of high explosive, and fragmenting roughly into 250 pieces. See "Abwurfmunition und Fliegende Koerper" ("Bombs Dropped from Airplanes and Flying Bodies"), C/VI/w, Karlsruhe Document Collection.

Figure 9
Combat situation conference in Russia, 1941, Fourth Air Fleet
L. to R.: Col. Werner Moelders, Commanding 51st Fighter Wing,
Generalmajor Guenther Korten, Generaloberst Alexander Loehr.

Figure 10
Soviet airfield at Mlinov, 8 miles northwest
of Dubno, Poland, June 1941

On the first day, V Air Corps units also attacked the main telegraph office and army telephone exchange in Lvov, a divisional telephone exchange reported in Lutsk, and the air equipment depot at Kiev-Postvolynski. Favorable weather conditions as far east as the Dnepr River brought generally clear skies and good visibility for these actions.

On 23 June units of the IV Air Corps attacked Nikolayev, northeast of Odessa. Reconnaissance discovered a total of 62 airfields, of which 51 were occupied by 1,270 aircraft, concentrated mainly in and around Kiev, Stanislav, and Odessa.

For a few days both air corps of the Fourth Air Fleet continued to pit most of their strength against the Russian air forces. Their attacks were so devastating that after the third day of warfare air operations could be shifted mainly to direct and indirect support of the ground forces. The Commander in Chief of the Luftwaffe made the following report on 6 July concerning the successes on the left flank, the area of main effort: "In the battle against the Soviet Union, the V Air Corps in the period 22 June - 3 July destroyed more than 1,000 aircraft on the ground."[8] Generaloberst Halder, Chief of the Army General Staff, remarked on 30 June in his war diary that "the Luftwaffe is reinforcing its forces in front of Army Group South and in Rumania." He noted further that very great air victories had been achieved against the Soviet air forces and the withdrawing enemy columns in front of Army Group South, and that "on this day [30 June 1941] over 200 enemy planes were shot down. The enemy is reportedly already using antiquated four-engine models."[9]

The situation report of the High Command of the Luftwaffe (including the first consolidated report of the success of the Fourth Air Fleet) claimed that "in Combat Zone South units of an air fleet command" shot down 41 aircraft and destroyed 45 more on the ground on 30 June, and the air fleet, while supporting the ground forces from 22 to 30 June, destroyed 201 tanks, 27 bunkers, and 2 armored fortifications.[10]

The V Air Corps Support of the Advance to the Stalin Line

After 23 June, the left (northern) wing of Army Group South received the definite support of German air units. Enemy forces concentrating about Lvov were thrown back to the east, to their weakest position, between Kristinopol and Sokal. The Styr River was reached by the First Panzer Group. On 26 June the Russians mounted an exceedingly strong tank attack, including 52-ton tanks, from the Kholoyuv-Brody line against the First Panzer Group's open flank. Units of the V Air Corps went into action in continuous, low-level attacks against this threat and against large motorized forces reported to be concentrating in the Toporov-Brody area. According to reports of the First Panzer Group, this action, carried out in a crucial moment, stopped an attack which was then under way by an entire Russian motorized corps and created conditions which permitted the First Panzer Group to continue its advance.

The Sixth Army had driven strong enemy elements into the densely wooded Lutsk-Rovno area where they constituted a serious threat to the army's northern flank, especially since these enemy forces were controlled by the Soviet Fifth Army. On 1 July, after a number of minor skirmishes, strong Russian forces struck across the highway known as the Panzer Road North (Vladimir-Volynskiy-Lutsk road) at Klevan and Olyka and drove deeply into the flank and rear of the First Panzer Group. The situation was critical. Concentrated attacks by the V Air Corps, however, inflicted such severe casualties upon the Russian forces in the Dubno-Rovno-Lutsk area as to break the effective power of the enemy. The V Air Corps destroyed 40 tanks and 180 other vehicles, and damaged and clearly put out of commission innumerable motor vehicles, including tanks.* General-major von Waldau commented in his diary on 15 July that, while motoring from Dubno with Col. Hermann Plocher (then Chief of Staff, V Air Corps), he had seen "hundreds of Russian tanks, many of which [were] super-heavy, lying south of Dubno," and that "the equipment of the Red Army amazes us again and again."[11]

Early in the course of the campaign the German High Command realized that the Russians, with surprisingly methodical planning, intended to break contact and offer renewed resistance further to the rear in the Stalin Line or behind the Dnepr River. To prevent, or at least delay, such a movement, V Air Corps units increased their attacks upon all identified and reported withdrawal movements on roads and railways. These attacks were directed against traffic and troop transit centers, such as Lvov, Brody, Zolochev, Zhitomir, Berdichev, Staro-Konstantinov, Belaya Tserkov, and Kazatin; they also struck some high-level headquarters and thus seriously interfered with Soviet operations. Particularly effective action was achieved against Russian retrograde movements on 30 June when Lvov was captured. Roads east and southeast of the city were jammed with traffic, often moving in columns of two or three abreast on a single road.

---

*See Figures 11 and 12.

54

Figure 11
Soviet tanks destroyed by the Luftwaffe
near Dubno, Poland, 1941

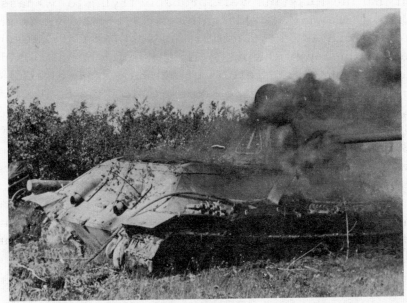

Figure 12
Soviet tank burning after German air attack,
Dubno, Poland, 1941

Interdiction of railroad traffic was highly important and essential in preventing the regrouping and transfer of Russian troops and materials.* At the same time, rolling stock was to be delayed for later capture by German troops to facilitate the movement of supplies over Russian rail lines. Initially, railroad interdiction operations were conducted only west of the Dnepr, concentrating in the Shepetovka-Kazatin-Kiev-Korosten area. Day and night these attacks were carried out by entire Luftwaffe units or, during inclement weather, by flights of a single aircraft. By 9 July rail traffic west of the Dnepr was substantially blocked. According to the captured Commanding General of the Soviet Sixth Army, this reduction of rail traffic made it almost impossible after the fifth day for the Russians to supply their troops. In southern Galicia, in the Gusyatin area, the leading and rear elements of a string of railroad trains were destroyed on 5 July, enabling the SS "Viking" Division (5th SS Panzer Division, largely recruited in the Scandinavian area) to capture on the following day 30 undamaged, loaded trains.[12]

In regard to the success of railroad interdiction operations, Halder observed on 11 July that "the Luftwaffe now appears to have succeeded in cutting the Russian railroads even in the far rear area" and that the number of sections with marooned trains were increasing. He also considered the heavy rail traffic below Kiev to be due to congestion from a large-scale Soviet evacuation of economic resources rather than movements of troops. Halder thought that the Russians were probably trying to by-pass the obstructions by withdrawing via Odessa or to the north, but he noted that serious obstacles (such as 34 isolated trains south of Cherkassy) were already present on the lower Dnepr.[13] On the following day Halder recorded: "Air reconnaissance shows the results of our harassing attacks on the enemy rail system in the rear"; there were large traffic jams on the railroads south of Kiev, in the region south of the Orsha-Smolensk line, between Vitebsk and Smolensk, and heavy antiaircraft defenses were located around Vitebsk and Berdichev.[14]† On 13 July the German Wehrmacht reported that the Luftwaffe had already "prevented any possibility of a large-scale counterattack by destroying the enemy railroad system."[15]

Besides the heavy casualties inflicted by the continuous attacks upon highways and railroads, the resultant delay of all movements hindered the Russians from carrying out a more timely withdrawal to the east.

---

*See Map No. 6.
†A report of General der Flakartillerie Rudolf Bogatsch.

At the Goryn River the First Panzer Group was delayed an unexpectedly long time because its units had become badly mixed, supply difficulties had arisen, its flank was threatened from the north, and its widely extended forces had to be closed up from the rear. Nevertheless, the Commanding General of the V Air Corps attempted by discussion with the army commander of the forward moving ground forces to accelerate the advance so that the ensuing favorable situation could be exploited to secure operational freedom. This effort was unsuccessful, as was his request to the Commander in Chief of the Luftwaffe for dive bomber units to facilitate more effective air support for the First Panzer Group.

Breaching the Stalin Line

Little time was lost at Polonnoye-Novyy Miropol in breaking through the Stalin Line toward Berdichev on 6 July, but exceptionally strong bunker positions delayed until 9 July the breakthrough at Novograd-Volynskiy, where, after sustained attacks against the emplacements, artillery positions, and approaching Russian reinforcements, the line was breached and the advance begun upon Zhitomir. Heavy Soviet counterattacks, particularly against the 9th Panzer Division in Berdichev, were shattered by sustained bomber attacks.

On 15 July Generalmajor von Waldau noted that the Sixth Army, and the First Panzer Group which preceded it, had experienced "the severest fighting" after crossing the border, where they had been ceaselessly attacked by Russian armored and infantry forces. The need for constant defensive action against steady Soviet penetrations into rear area communications prevented any territory from being taken until the situation was secured in two major tank battles at Rovno-Dubno and later at Zhitomir-Berdichev. Von Waldau asserted that the Luftwaffe should claim much of the credit for the success of these battles because its close fighter cover of German tank spearheads prevented effective Soviet counter-air measures and eliminated all threats to the flanks.[16]

Following the breach of the Stalin Line, Russian retrograde movements increased, and the V Air Corps* continued to concentrate upon moving columns and railroads. The Dnepr bridges at Cherkassy, Kanex, Kiev, and Gornostaypol were attacked for the first time. Despite 42 hits upon 6 bridges, complete destruction of the structures was not achieved, partially

_____

*See Figure 13.

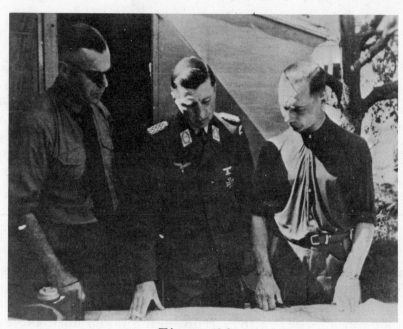

Figure 13
Combat situation conference in Russia, 1941, V Air Corps
L. to R.: Col. Hermann Plocher, Chief of Staff, Generalmajor Otto
Hoffmann von Waldau, Chief of Luftwaffe Operations Staff, Maj.
Fritz Kless, Operations Officer, V Air Corps.

because the heaviest bombs could not be loaded aboard the bombers owing to the poor condition of the runways.

On 12 July the Luftwaffe began interdiction operations east of the Dnepr River to prevent the advance of Russian reinforcements. On 14 July the rail junction at Bakhmach was attacked with good results. During these railroad interdiction operations some 1,000 railroad cars, many of them in the stations and loaded with ammunition, were destroyed. [17]

On the following day Halder mentioned General Bogatsch's report that the Luftwaffe had noticeably interrupted rail traffic in the Leningrad area, between Smolensk and Moscow, around Bryansk, especially in the southern area, and had damaged the bridges at Kiev, while the bridge at Cherkassy had sustained very serious hits. [18]

Besides rail interdiction operations, strong attacks were carried out against vehicular traffic moving in as many as four columns abreast and against troop traffic centers in the Proskurov-Staro-Konstantinov area. Exceptionally heavy losses were inflicted upon the Russians by the SD-2 bombs.

By 16 July armored units reached the Irpen River in front of the city of Kiev and established a small bridgehead south of the Zhitomir-Kiev road. Because of an order from the Fuehrer requiring the rear elements of the First Panzer Group to provide cover against enemy operations from Kiev and to abstain from immediate attacks upon the city, [19] no effort was made to seize the Kiev bridges over the Dnepr by storm. Reverses to the weak lead elements and the threat of Russian attacks on the flanks of the widely extended units did not allow further risks. The concern of the highest command echelons with these problems is evident from an entry in Halder's diary which indicates that Hitler did not want the armored units of Army Group South to be vainly sacrificed. [20] His concern was unfounded, however, since the Sixth Army infantry was still in the area of Novograd-Volynskiy and making progress (albeit slowly because of Soviet pressures from the Pripyat swamp area) in the direction of Korosten.

At this time Army Group South decided to postpone its plans to establish a bridgehead east of Kiev, and to drive instead toward the south in order to halt the withdrawal of Russian forces still situated west of the Dnepr River. To accomplish this, the III Corps of the First Panzer Group was to cover the left (northern) flank of Army Group South, while the Sixth Army advanced toward the southeast, its left wing along the Dnepr. Simultaneously, the remainder of the First Panzer Group was to drive southward toward Uman to envelop Soviet units in front of the German Seventeenth

Army, and to assist the Sixth and Seventeenth Armies in destroying the remaining Soviet Army units west of the Dnepr.

These latter operations were supported by units of the V Air Corps, Fourth Air Fleet. As anticipated, the movement of bombs, fuel, and other supplies destined for German air units became increasingly difficult. In the area from which they were now operating (after advancing their bases from Lublin and Zamosc) there were very few passable roads. At first all supplies were moved exclusively by air, using Junkers Ju-52 transports. The advance movement of V Air Corps bases and supply services depended upon: (1) the speed of construction of the permanent main signal communication line and lateral lines, (2) the speedy reconnoitering and preparation of new airfields, or the adaptation of existing Soviet air bases (Soviet airfields along the fringes of the Pripyat marsh area frequently had very wet surfaces), and (3) the load capacity of the roads over which the forward movements would take place.* Excessive traffic frequently jammed these roads, often delaying for days the various supply columns and ground force troops. The Chief of Staff of the V Air Corps and his supply officer repeatedly flew over the supply routes searching for fuel supply columns. They landed alongside moving columns of armored and motorized troops and, by asserting the authority of their offices, intervened to insure that the vital fuel columns were given the proper priority accorded by their written traffic authority.

Owing to the continuous action, the operability of German flying units depreciated steadily and considerably. Only a few serviceable aircraft were available for reconnaissance. Frequently, integration of Army-Luftwaffe operations resulted in army group reconnaissance coinciding with that of the Luftwaffe, and the thought of combining army and Luftwaffe long-range reconnaissance recurred many times. But no definite decision on the matter was made and no express orders were issued.† These deliberations are shown in the war diary of General Halder, in which he relates that, while talking with Field Marshal von Bock (Army Group Center) on 10 July about air reconnaissance, it was noted that the long-range squadrons assigned to Bock's forces (except for those with the tank forces) "still have 3 machines ready to fly in one squadron and none in the others. Only two serviceable planes are available for night reconnaissance. Therefore, the Luftwaffe offers to combine the army and Luftwaffe reconnaissance. I [Halder] urgently advised against it and referred to the conflict between

---

*A responsibility of the 4th Air Administrative Command for Special Duty.

†See Generalleutnant (Ret.) Hermann Plocher, "Air Reconnaissance and Antiaircraft Defense," Karlsruhe Document Collection.

the Commanders in Chief of the Army and the Air Force on this question prior to the start of the offensive."[21]

Russian Air Operations until Mid-July 1941

Those elements of the Soviet air forces escaping destruction in the first days of the campaign attacked chiefly the German armored spearheads and supply columns, trying thereby to delay the German advance. Their high-altitude and low-level attacks were directed primarily against bridges and bridge sites near such places as Lutsk, Dubno, Rovno, Ostrog, Polonnoya, Ovyy Miropol, Novograd-Volynskiy, and Zhitomir. With dash and obstinacy the Russians repeatedly attacked points known to be heavily defended by German forces, where Luftwaffe fighter and antiaircraft artillery concentrations inflicted heavy losses upon them.[22]

IV Air Corps Operations on the Right Flank of Combat Zone South

On 22 June 1941 and during the next few days there was little ground combat activity in the Rumanian area. The only exception occurred on 22 June when a German infantry division launched a surprise attack across the Prut River at Skulyany (Sculeni) north of Iași (Jassy) and established a bridgehead.

As in the main concentration area of the Fourth Air Fleet on the left (northern) flank of Combat Zone South, counter-air operations were also carried out at dawn on 22 June by IV Air Corps units, mounting successful and sustained attacks from their Rumanian bases against Soviet airfields, especially those around Beltsy (Balti) and other places which had been reconnoitered. Within the next few days, all enemy airfields which air reconnaissance reported to be manned were brought under Luftwaffe attack. In the Crimea and the Odessa-Nikolayev area especially strong concentrations of Soviet air forces were detected and reported.[23]

Russian fighter units were mainly concentrated in the Iași-Beltsy-Kishinev area and were repeatedly engaged in battle by German fighters, which inflicted heavy losses upon them. On 25 June alone, 44 Soviet fighters were shot down against a loss of two German planes. Continual reconnaissance was maintained over the Black Sea ports, and the Soviet Black Sea Fleet was located and kept under constant surveillance. Most of these naval forces, particularly the larger ships, remained at Sevastopol. Large numbers of freighters were usually at the port of Odessa. In a special operation, IV Air Corps bombers repeatedly mined the ports of Nikolayev, Odessa, and Sevastopol.

When, on 2 July, the Eleventh Army concentrated its forces and, moving from the bridgehead at Iaşi, launched an attack across the Prut, the IV Air Corps shifted its main effort from counter-air to direct and indirect support of the army. Henceforth, the air corps operated continuously in support of the ground forces in their advance through Beltsy to Mogilev on the Dniester and later toward Kishinev, assisting the Rumanians on their way to Odessa. Simultaneous with the German Eleventh Army movements, the Rumanian and Hungarian forces also opened an assault, each supported by its own air units.

In addition to the direct support of the ground forces, IV Air Corps units attacked all rail and highway traffic in the Odessa area, the lower reaches of the Dnepr, and the Zaporozhye-Dnepropetrovsk-Mogilev-Podolskiy area in order to prevent the arrival of fresh Soviet forces and materiel, and later to hinder the eastward withdrawal of the enemy over the Dnepr and Dniester. Primary targets were the rail, vehicular, and ponton bridges across the two rivers, such as the Dniester bridges at Bendery, Rybnitsa, and Soroki, and the Dnepr bridges at Zaporozhye and Dnepropetrovsk. About mid-July German and Rumanian troops crossed the Dniester and advanced to the east and northeast under the continuous support of IV Air Corps units.

Battle of Encirclement at Uman

Covered on the north by the Sixth Army, the First Panzer Group pivoted late in July from the Belaya-Tserkov area toward the southeast, in the direction of Pervomaysk, while the Rumanian Third Army and the northern wing of the German Eleventh Army advanced eastward through Balta. The Seventeenth Army continued its frontal assault to the east, while the Sixth Army was given the assignment of defending the northern flank of Army Group South to the west and northwest of Kiev.

Again committed to the area of main effort, the V Air Corps was to assist the First Panzer Group in a quick drive southeast and, if necessary, support the advancing Seventeenth Army. At the same time, Russian rail and vehicular communications in the rear areas and east of the Dnepr River were to be attacked and counter-air operations continued. This was indeed a big order for the limited forces available. Pressures of time required ever more urgently the full employment of all Luftwaffe forces for the exclusive task of supporting the army in all sectors of its operational area. As a result, the conduct of aerial operations grew progressively into complete conformity with ground force actions. The Luftwaffe, because of its speed and versatility, became more and more the sole means for relieving critical ground situations.

The Russian retrograde movements continued, indicating that the Soviet high command intended to withdraw all available forces across the Dnepr River in order to establish a new line of defense. The bulk of V Air Corps units, therefore, continuously attacked Russian columns west of the river and repeatedly interrupted rail traffic, particularly in the Kremenchug-Cherkassy, Kanev-Mironovka, and Smela-Znamenka areas. East of the Dnepr all railroads in the Konotop-Glukhov-Gorodishche-Priluki-Bakhmach area were also attacked to prevent the arrival of Russian reinforcements and materiel.[24]

Continuous rainfall and heavy thunderstorms turned roads and paths into quagmires, so that German ground movements were considerably slowed and in some cases made impossible. Thus only by the regular sorties against Soviet railroads and highways by V Air Corps units were the German forces able to inflict heavy losses upon the enemy. Ruthless attacks by bombers and fighters, usually at low altitudes and often carried out under exceedingly difficult conditions, in rain and with low cloud ceilings, slowed the Russian withdrawal, but could not prevent the escape of some Soviet elements to the east.*

By 22 July the ring around the Russian forces at Uman was contracted. Again and again German bombers and dive bombers successfully attacked to prevent enemy breakouts and to repel relief attacks launched from outside the encirclement. In systematic attacks dive bomber units broke the resistance of the encircled forces, particularly in the Uman-Golovanevsk-Novo-Arkhangelsk region.†

In spite of extremely difficult supply problems, Luftwaffe fighter units could be transferred to airfields within favorable striking distance of their targets. Very quickly these units achieved air supremacy over the pocket area and shot down at least 157 Russian aircraft. During the battle of encirclement itself, approximately 420 motor vehicles and 58 tanks were destroyed and 22 batteries put out of action. The large quantities of other weapons, vehicles, and materiel of all types destroyed in the battle could not be estimated. These successes demonstrated the decisive part played by the fighter, bomber, and dive bomber units of the V Air Corps in annihilating the entrapped Russian forces at Uman, the first large-scale battle of encirclement fought in the southern area of the Russian front.

----

*See Figure 14.
†See Maps Nos. 4 and 7.

Figure 14
Effects of German SD-10 fragmentation bombs
on retreating Soviet forces near Kiev, 1941

Figure 15
Dam at Zaporozhye, Russia, taken by German
armor with air support (V Air Corps), 19
August 1941, shown after its demolition

64

Meanwhile, the Sixth Army had continued its attack and forced the Russians back along a line from Kiev to Korosten. Very slowly the army gained ground to the east. But serious doubts arose concerning the security of its northern flank. The obscure, trackless, marshy, and wooded terrain undoubtedly presented the Soviet Fifth Army with favorable opportunities for surprise attacks against the deep flank of the German Sixth Army. Furthermore, the partisan threat was daily becoming worse, and could not be overlooked. Yet the numerous requests, applications, and demands of the Sixth Army for air support had to be rejected, even in urgent situations. The scant air power available had to be used in the decisive Uman area. It was, therefore, only natural that much friction and discord developed between Sixth Army and V Air Corps.

Finding themselves in serious combat situations, German Army units urgently called for dive bomber and bomber support, and from all quarters came the complaint that the fighters were not around and were not protecting the ground forces from the incessant nuisance raids of Soviet ground attack and bomber aircraft. This constant appeal to the Luftwaffe for air support and the necessity to refuse it (hitherto always readily provided) in favor of the concept of concentrating forces for a major effort severely strained the mutual confidence of command and troops between the ground forces and the Luftwaffe. Complaints became the order of the day. Even Army Group South and the Fourth Air Fleet often had to decide which ground units were to be supported and by what air units.

However, it was impossible for the few fighter forces available in this gigantic operations zone, extending from Korosten through Kiev and from Kremenchug to Zaporozhye, to protect all ground forces. It could not be satisfactorily explained to unprotected and unsupported ground units that the only fighter wing in the entire area, the 3rd Fighter Wing, based at Byelaya Tserkov, could not simultaneously protect the Sixth Army in the Korosten-Kiev area, the Seventeenth Army at Uman, and the First Panzer Group at Zaporozhye. Units felt that they were being neglected, and refused to consider the importance of the principle of power concentration, except when they themselves were in the area of main effort. Every unit wanted fighters overhead and bombs dropped ahead of its front.

Appropriate training in this respect for commanding officers of all ranks and for the troops as well was absolutely necessary, but such indoctrination should already have been given during peacetime and not have to be tried for the first time during a critical war situation.

The V Air Corps supported the XXIX Corps (Sixth Army of Army Group South) in its drive toward Kiev from the south (approximately 4-7 August 1941) by neutralizing Soviet field fortifications, individual enemy bunkers, and artillery positions south and southwest of that city and by hampering Soviet reinforcements moving westward across the Dnepr. During this period the Russians were extremely active in the air and their efforts to concentrate air power in the area were clearly noticeable. The large Luftwaffe air base at Belaya Tserkov, the German front line infantry, and all bridges within Combat Zone South were ceaselessly attacked by Soviet warplanes. In spite of numerical inferiority, the Luftwaffe 3rd Fighter Wing intervened again and again, and successfully provided cover for German ground troops in the area.*

The V Air Corps Halts the Soviet Advance at Boguslav and Kanev

After the encirclement battle at Uman it was a question of destroying the Russian forces still west of the lower Dnepr and of establishing a bridge-head across the river from which operations could continue. For this purpose the First Panzer Group was to drive on to Dnepropetrovsk and Niko-layev and seize any intact bridge over the Dnepr. The Eleventh and Seventeenth Armies (the right wing and center, respectively, of Army Group South) were to follow to the east and southeast and mop up the area west of the Dnepr. The Sixth Army's mission of providing cover for the north flank of Army Group South in the Kiev-Malin-Korosten area remained unchanged. In this operation the V Air Corps was to provide support for the First Panzer Group and continue counter-air and rail interdiction operations.

In the midst of preparations for this operation, when some movements were already under way, the Russians launched a tank and cavalry attack across the Dnepr south of Kiev at Kanev on 7 August, at first in approximately divisional strength, surprising and breaking through the extremely weak outposts and supply installations in that sector. That the Russians planned to drive through Boguslav to Belaya Tserkov in order to break the German envelopment of Kiev was revealed when a simultaneous Soviet attack was made from the north at Malin. Sixth Army elements, consolidated as Army Group von Schwedler,✝ were dispatched against this serious threat. The 11th Panzer Division of the First Panzer Group, already driving southeast, was turned around and again sent northward.

---

*Major Guenther Luetzow, Close Air Commander North, controlled the III Group, 77th Dive Bomber Wing and Groups I and III, 3rd Fighter Wing.
✝Named for General Viktor von Schwedler, Commander of the Army Group.

But the divisions which were to seal off the penetration were still far from the scene, and Russian pressure became stronger. An army bakery company and a veterinary company held out at Boguslav under the greatest difficulty and with outstanding courage. From Belaya Tserkov heterogeneous units, improvised for the emergency, were brought without heavy weapons to Boguslav and sent into action. From the airfield at Belaya Tserkov, itself already under heavy Soviet air attacks, light and heavy antiaircraft artillery units were thrown platoon by platoon and gun by gun into action in the area of penetration. Between Boguslav and Korsun-Shevchenkovskiy there was not a single German soldier. A serious crisis threatened. In this situation the V Air Corps, on its own initiative, attacked with every unit available and annihilated the Soviet tank and cavalry forces which had broken through. After Army Group von Schwedler arrived on the scene the V Air Corps was assigned the task of supporting von Schwedler's counterattack.

The action of the flying units was truly dramatic. They knew scarcely any details about the real situation, since there was no time for reconnaissance work before going into action and a normal transmission of orders was not possible. Organizations and their aircrews could only be told that strong Soviet tank and cavalry forces had penetrated into the Kanev-Korsun-Shevchenkovskiy-Yanovka-Boguslav area with the probable intention of breaking through toward Belaya Tserkov. All Luftwaffe units were committed. Each sought its own targets, tanks being given priority. On 7 August, bombers, dive bombers, and fighters took off individually and in three-plane flights (Ketten), and were able to carry out determined, low-level bombing, dive bombing, and strafing attacks despite severe weather conditions of rain, winds, and low ceilings (165-260 feet). Landing only to refuel and reload with bombs and ammunition, these planes continuously attacked every enemy observed in the breakthrough area, achieving excellent results. At the same time, the aircraft reconnoitered so that an overall picture of the situation could gradually be formed. During the first three days alone the Luftwaffe destroyed a total of 148 motor vehicles and 94 tanks, and with improving weather its attacks tended to have a lasting effect, especially around Yanovka.

The enemy ceaselessly continued to try to bring in new forces from the Kanev-Zolotonosha sector in order to press his attack. Therefore German dive bombers continued to attack the bridges at Kanev; one bridge was destroyed and a ponton bridge south of the city eliminated for a long period by numerous direct hits.

After four hard and exhausting days of fighting, the composition of the attacking Russian force became clearer. It was the Soviet Twenty-Sixth Army, comprising three fresh infantry divisions, two depleted infantry divisions, two cavalry divisions, and one or two armored divisions.

Under pressure by the reinforced Army Group von Schwedler, now on the scene and counterattacking, and by the steady attacks of the Luftwaffe dive bombers, the Soviets were forced backward south of Kiev in the vicinity of Kanev. Still they attempted to force a breakthrough to the west by a ruthless commitment of their forces, but were decisively frustrated in this effort by German air attacks, which inflicted extremely severe losses upon Russian units. Luftwaffe fighters were particularly successful against occasional very strong enemy air attacks, shooting down 139 Soviet planes, while bombers of the V Air Corps successfully attacked hostile operational airfields on the east bank of the Dnepr.

On 13 August the Russian command began to withdraw its remaining troops at Kanev across the Dnepr, thus abandoning its offensive plan. In unbroken waves, German dive bombers now struck at the Soviet troops massed at the Kanev bridges, where on 15 August the Russians suffered particularly heavy personnel and materiel losses. By then the bulk of the enemy which had penetrated into the Boguslav-Kanev sector had been destroyed and the remainder thrown back across the Dnepr. Small elements were able to make their way to Cherkassy.

According to the report of Army Group von Schwedler, only the sorties of the V Air Corps stopped the already accomplished Soviet break-through for the two long, tense days until army reinforcements arrived. Thus the air corps had averted a serious crisis which otherwise would have had far-reaching consequences for the entire operation in the Ukraine. The commitment of the Luftwaffe in the Kanev area was thereby over and its interrupted task* could be resumed. The continuation of the operation of Army Group South was now possible without too detrimental a loss of time as a result of the unstinting, unflagging, and brave efforts of all units of the V Air Corps.

---

*The V Air Corps was to support the First Panzer Group advance to the Dnepr to cut off Soviet forces still west of the river and also to continue counter-air and rail interdiction operations.

Air Operations During the Mop-Up West of the Lower Dnepr

Beginning on 17 August bomber units were used in day and night sorties against the traffic center of Dnepropetrovsk, the main targets being the railroad station, thoroughfares, and bridges. These attacks were designed to delay an orderly retreat of strong enemy forces and to prevent the establishing of defenses by the Russians on the eastern banks of the Dnepr. *

The Fourth Air Fleet had specified that Dnepropetrovsk was to be the sector of main effort for Luftwaffe fighter forces. Although the constant action of the past several weeks had considerably reduced the fighting strength (to a total of 44 fighters in all of the V Air Corps units), nevertheless these achieved considerable success, for the Commander in Chief of the Luftwaffe reported that on 17 August fighter units (the I and II Groups, 3rd Fighter Wing and the III Group, 52nd Fighter Wing) of the V Air Corps downed 33 Soviet aircraft and destroyed three others on the ground. Of those shot down, 29 were bombers, mostly DB-3's and SB-3's. And to make the German air victories more impressive, on 30 August Major Luetzow's 3rd Fighter Wing shot down its 1,000th Russian plane. ⫟

Inadequate supplies of fuel and ammunition and excessive distances to targets complicated V Air Corps operations during this period. The distance problem later compelled the air corps to base some units on the Krivoy Rog airfield, where supply conditions were especially bad. Fuel and ammunition could be brought in only by air. The terrain and distances which the services of supply had to surmount steadily grew to gigantic proportions. In most cases, supply columns found that the extremely bad roads made it impossible for them to keep pace with the advance of tactical units. Movements were completely impossible in the sticky mud which resulted from a few hours of rain upon the famous black soil of the Ukraine. ⫟⫟ And the railheads were still too far west, for, despite feverish efforts to restore destroyed sections of track, much delay occurred after each advance before railheads could be moved forward to the proximity of front line troops.

---

*See Map No. 8.

⫟Lt. Col. Count Schoenborn, Close Air Support Commander South, controlled the I Group, 77th Dive Bomber Wing, Group II of the 3rd Fighter Wing, and Group III of the 52nd Fighter Wing.

⫟⫟An old Ukrainian proverb goes: "In summer one bucket of water makes one spoonful of mud; in autumn one spoonful of water makes a bucket of mud."

Despite the fact that German flying officers detailed for duty at Lipetzk in the Soviet Union from 1926 to 1931 had continually reported that German motor vehicles were fully unsuited for the sand and mud conditions of Russia, the German Armed Forces entered the Russian campaign with completely inadequate vehicular equipment. Most German cars and trucks were suited only conditionally for the road and terrain conditions encountered in the East, and during the mud seasons most of them were entirely useless. The German troops attempted to help themselves out of this predicament. With the aid of voluntary Russian laborers* and working in improvised shops, they repaired captured Russian vehicles (especially the very good 1 1/2-ton cross-country model), with which they organized their own supply columns. These measures, however, were no more than an expedient.

Disregard of the early reports and the failure to draw proper conclusions from them in equipping the Wehrmacht must be considered as serious mistakes of the German command, mistakes which in 1941 and later were to work strongly to the disadvantage of the mobility of both the Luftwaffe and German Army units in Russia.

On 19 August the 9th Panzer Division captured the dam at Zaporozhye and established a bridgehead on the east bank of the Dnepr, but shortly thereafter the division was forced to give up the bridgehead./ On 26 August the 60th Motorized Division succeeded in seizing the ponton bridge at Dnepropetrovsk and also in establishing a bridgehead on the far shore.

To achieve closer cooperation with, and more effective close-air support of, the First Panzer Group through the creation of more rapid command channels, the organization of Close Air Support Commander South// was established under the V Air Corps, with instructions to operate directly with the First Panzer Group against Soviet preparations for a counterattack in front of the bridgehead held by the 60th Motorized Division. Meanwhile, bombers attacked all highways and railroads leading westward to the bridgehead, and took a heavy toll of the Russian forces already approaching, thus weakening Soviet striking power before the counterattack could begin.

---

*So-called Hiwis (Hilfswilliger or Hilfsfreiwilliger), volunteer auxiliaries, generally foreigners, brought in for driving, construction, and other similar tasks.

/See Figure 15.

//Nahkampffuehrer Sued or Nafü Süd. See footnote p. 69.

Because of the round-the-clock German air attacks a real easing of the situation was achieved. The enemy pressure decreased noticeably so that after 28 August a substantial expansion and reinforcement of the Dnepropetrovsk bridgehead became possible.

Meanwhile, the Seventeenth Army had concentrated its forces until by 31 August it was ready to cross the Dnepr at Deriyevka, east of Kremenchug. A diversionary attack, which was already begun at Cherkassy to deceive the Russians, led them to concentrate their forces near Cherkassy and to use their air forces for a considerable time in a determined effort against this attack.

The office of Close Air Support Commander North* was established by the Sixth Army (north flank of Army Group South). His task was to delay the withdrawal of the Soviet Fifth Army over the Dnepr from the area north of Kiev by attacking troop traffic centers and columns on the roads leading eastward. These west-to-east movements of the Soviet forces were first positively confirmed on 19 August by night air reconnaissance. Generaloberst Halder observed in his diary that "this possibility" had been expected "for days."[25] In addition to units of the Close Air Support Commander North, the bomber units of the V Air Corps were also committed against these roads. The attacks were always successful, although the enemy attempted to minimize his heavy losses by marching at night or in small bands on secondary roads and in extended order.

In a surprise attack the German 111th Infantry Division seized the timber bridge over the Dnepr east of Gornostaypol, sent armored units across, and established a bridgehead in the direction of Oster; its advance was first halted at the Desna River. The loss of this very important bridge induced the Soviet command to make a strong commitment of its air forces. The bridge site was continually attacked by Russian bombers and fighters, mostly at low altitudes (as low as 30 feet), using bombs, machine guns, and "Molotov cocktails." The fighters assigned by the V Air Corps to protect the bridge and river crossing--despite a very low level of operational readiness (averaging only eight planes per group)--were able to protect the bridge, and by 24 August had shot down 33 aircraft. On that date a local fog at the Belaya Tserkov airfield prevented fighter aircraft from taking off for their advance fields at Gornostaypol. But favorable weather within the operational area of the Soviet air units and at the Gornostaypol bridge enabled Soviet Rata (I-16) fighter aircraft to attack the bridge at altitudes of about 30 feet and to drop gasoline containers to

_____

*Nahkampffuehrer Nord or Nafü Nord. See footnote, p. 66.

71

ignite it. Apparently the antiaircraft fire of the Army units at the bridge was too weak to provide adequate protection. Aware that only a few fighter aircraft were available, and with knowledge of the poor weather conditions, the responsible German ground forces command should have immediately provided stronger antiaircraft defenses for this important bridge. Because of the low-level approach of the attacking planes, a more successful defense should have been possible by massed heavy antiaircraft artillery fire, especially in view of the low cloud cover. The loss of the bridge adversely affected further river crossing operations and considerably delayed the attack by the Sixth Army.

On 1 September the Seventeenth Army, effectively supported by the Close Air Support Commander South, established a bridgehead across the Dnepr at Kremenchug. Fighter units successfully defended the river crossing and downed 12 Soviet aircraft on the first day. These units also attacked Soviet ships, including monitors, antiaircraft batteries, and barges, armed motor boats on the Dnepr, and batteries on the east bank of the river. The Seventeenth Army acknowledged the excellent protection of the river-crossing points by the German fighter forces and gave them the greater part of the credit for the successful defense of the positions.

Soviet air units assaulting the Kremenchug bridgehead were attacked with highly favorable results at their airfields and bases around Kharkov, Poltava, and Kiev by bomber units of the V Air Corps. For the next few days German air units operated continuously against enemy troop movements and concentrations which had been detected opposite the bridgehead, and contributed substantially to the expansion and defense of the bridgehead, which was to serve as the southern point of departure for the next major operation: the encirclement of the armies under Budënny at and east of Kiev.

During this period, on the southern flank of Army Group South, the IV Air Corps supported the advance of the Eleventh Army across the Dniester and later across the lower reaches of the Dnepr at Borislav. The Fourth Rumanian Army invested Odessa, and many of the IV Air Corps' attacks were directed against the evacuation of Russian troops and materiel from Nikolayev and Odessa. The operations of 18 August were particularly successful when more than 30,000 tons of shipping (warships and merchantmen) were sunk or damaged at Odessa.[26] The harbor installations at Sevastopol were likewise attacked repeatedly with bombs and mines. The harbor of Novorossiysk was mined.

In early September the IV Air Corps concentrated its efforts upon supporting the Eleventh Army (on the extreme south flank of the German

Eastern Front) in its crossing of the Dnepr, an especially difficult operation in the open terrain with only a single ponton bridge available for such a wide stream. Strong enemy air attacks against the crossing sites caused but little delay. The starting point for an attack on the Crimea had been won through the energetic support of the IV Air Corps.

The Situation in the South at the Beginning of September

Supported by the Fourth Air Fleet, Army Group South had seized the territory west of the Dnepr from numerically superior Soviet air and ground forces and had established bridgeheads at Borislav, Dbnepropetrovsk, and Kremenchug, which became the starting points for the next operations. By versatile leadership and the closest collaboration with the various Army command headquarters, the Fourth Air Fleet and its component units, the IV and V Air Corps, had vigorously and successfully supported the ground troops. In many critical situations the swift and flexible Luftwaffe had been the sole and final assistance in averting serious threats to ground operations, indeed, even in turning such threats into victories. Often the principle of concentrating power at key points had to be accomplished with the utmost determination against the strongest enemy resistance. In opposition to individual--and, understandably human--wishes and demands, the Luftwaffe leadership, conscious of its responsibility, would permit no splintering or dissipation of its numerically weak, constantly shrinking, combat strength.

When, for example, General der schnellen Truppen* Breith, upon return from a visit to Army Group South, reported that the liaison between the armored troops and the Luftwaffe (Generaloberst Greim and his V Air Corps) was not always in accord,[27] he seems to have made a biased report. The present author is very well acquainted with the situation at that time. It was not that the liaison between the armored forces and the Luftwaffe was not in harmony; it was because the total Luftwaffe strength deployed in the area of Army Group South was simply too weak to handle all of the demands made on it, and, in addition, the combat readiness of the Luftwaffe had seriously declined because of its steady combat activity.

Successful use of air power at points of main strategic significance was the decisive factor in the summer campaigns of 1941. Von Waldau noted on 14 August that the Fourth Air Fleet had skillfully conducted its operations and that its practice of assigning missions daily had proven to be correct, although the number of demands made it "far from easy" to select the most essential tasks.[28]

---

*General of the Mobile Troops (lit. "fast troops") Hermann Breith.

73

Employment of Antiaircraft Artillery in Combat Zone South

The II Antiaircraft Artillery Corps under General der Flieger Dessloch was deployed in the operational area of the Fourth Air Fleet. The corps was to provide: (1) antiaircraft protection for the mobile units of the ground forces, primarily of the First Panzer Group; (2) support for the Army units, above all, the armored corps and divisions, which were fighting to break strong enemy opposition by attacking pockets of resistance, fortifications of all kinds, and tanks; and (3) protection of airfields, particularly those used by bombers and dive bombers.

The antiaircraft artillery units which were assigned to the Luftwaffe commanders with the army groups or armies (Koluft)* had first of all to provide antiaircraft protection for the army units. Only in an emergency were they to be employed in ground combat.

From the beginning of the campaign all units of the II Antiaircraft Artillery Corps were deployed with the advancing armored and motorized infantry columns so that they could protect the armored spearheads, which the enemy again and again attempted to stop with his bombers and ground-attack aircraft. Moreover, the antiaircraft artillery units--employed in ground fighting--provided valuable arms support for the ground forces by reducing bunkers and pockets of resistance, particularly in the breakthrough of the Soviet border positions, the Stalin Line, and the fortifications at Kiev. They contributed materially, often decisively, to the steady advance of German motorized and armored units.

With the crippling of the Soviet air forces the need for defense against hostile air attacks declined and the use of antiaircraft artillery in ground fighting increased considerably. This artillery, which was used more and more as an armor-piercing weapon, achieved particular success in the tank battles in the Dubno-Rovno-Lutsk area, in the severe tank fighting at Zhitomir and Berdichev, and in the encirclement battle of Uman. Hundreds of destroyed tanks pointed the way to the antiaircraft artillery batteries. The original main task of antiaircraft artillery units, that of air defense, was steadily displaced by that of ground combat, which

_____

*Koluft or Kommandeur der Luftwaffe (Commander of the Air Force) was a German Air Force commander who was assigned to the headquarters of an army group or army as an adviser of the headquarters operations staff on all matters pertaining to the employment of assigned air units, and was also the superior officer of personnel in those Luftwaffe units.

eventually became its primary mission. This was an immediate result of a shortage of effective armor-piercing arms in the Army and the overall mission of the Luftwaffe to support the ground forces.

The great success of the antiaircraft artillery in Combat Zone South is shown by some of the reports which were made from a large number of "exceptional performances" mentioned in situation reports of the High Command of the Luftwaffe. These reports reveal clearly that the principal use of the antiaircraft artillery units had shifted from air defense to almost exclusive ground fighting in support of the Army:

(1) According to the report of 17 July, between 22 June and 15 July the II Antiaircraft Artillery Corps brought down 92 planes and destroyed 250 tanks and 51 bunkers. These successes were achieved as follows: the "General Goering" regiment destroyed 67 aircraft, 193 tanks, and 22 bunkers; the 6th Antiaircraft Artillery Regiment destroyed 17 planes, 4 tanks, and 23 bunkers; and the I Battalion, 7th Antiaircraft Artillery Regiment accounted for 8 aircraft, 53 tanks, and 6 bunkers.

(2) The 23 August report enumerated the total successes of the II AA Corps during the battle for Uman as follows: 53 aircraft shot down; 49 tanks, 93 trucks, 59 machine-gun nests, and 7 observation posts destroyed, as well as 1 infantry battalion, 1 infantry company, and 3 artillery batteries; 1 heavy battery, 1 gun, and 140 motorized vehicles captured; and 1,155 prisoners taken in 35 successful engagements.[29]

Lastly, the antiaircraft artillery contributed materially to the victories of Army Group South and the Fourth Air Fleet in the Bessarabian and western Ukrainian zones of operations.

Combat Assignment of the Luftwaffe Mission in Rumania

Since October 1940, Generalleutnant Wilhelm Speidel had commanded the Luftwaffe Mission in Rumania, first as Chief and later as Commander in Chief. On 24 June 1941 Generalmajor Bruno Maass replaced Speidel's first chief of staff, Col. Gerhardt Bassenge, GSC, who joined the Operations Staff of the Rumanian Air Force as the Luftwaffe adviser.

When the Russian campaign began, the original functions of the Luftwaffe Mission in Rumania ceased and its combat assignment under BARBAROSSA became its urgent new task. Placed under the command of the Fourth Air Fleet shortly before the campaign opened, its mission was to serve as an advance or field Luftwaffe administrative command, responsible for developing a ground organization (which already had been started during the preparations for Operation BARBAROSSA) and an aircraft warning system, and for defending the vitally important Rumanian oil-producing areas. To carry out this work the mission staff was expanded and reinforced with qualified personnel.

For the development and expansion of the ground organization to serve units of the IV Air Corps, the Fourth Air Fleet assigned the 40th Luftwaffe Administrative Command Staff for Special Duty (Generalmajor Hermann Ritter von Mann),* which later in the course of the advance was employed in the southern Ukraine and the Crimea.

The following air defense areas were established to protect the oil-producing and processing installations in Rumania under the direction and responsibility of the Luftwaffe Mission in Rumania: the Ploesti area with oil wells and refineries, Constanta with oil storage and shipping installations, the Danube River bridge at Cernavodă (the most vulnerable point of the oil pipeline), the oil shipping port of Giurgiu on the Danube, and the airfields of the mission itself.

German forces available to the mission were one antiaircraft artillery divisional headquarters staff; several antiaircraft artillery regiments; several, frequently changing, additional antiaircraft artillery battalions; air signal units (especially aircraft warning services); an air defense brigade with special units for extinguishing oil fire; Luftwaffe construction units; and the command staff of the 52nd Fighter Wing. The III Group of the 52nd Fighter Wing was equipped with Messerschmidt Me-109's and was later replaced by I Group of the 2nd Training Wing, also an Me-109 unit. The total strength of Luftwaffe forces deployed in Rumania comprised about 50,000 men.

Rumanian fighter units were not assigned to the Luftwaffe Mission in Rumania, but German air defense areas included in many instances Rumanian antiaircraft artillery units, and tactical arrangements were made for cooperation between German and Rumanian fighter units. Rumanian antiaircraft artillery was included within the German aircraft warning network, which the signal officer of the Luftwaffe mission, Colonel Prinz,/

---

*Hermann Ritter von Mann Edler von Tiechler, Generalleutnant 1 November 1940.

/Probably Otto Prinz, who was later Inspector of Armed Forces Signal Communications Headquarters, High Command of the Armed Forces (Inspizient der Wehrmacht Nachrichten Kommandanturen, OKW). Generalmajor 1 September 1943.

had developed and considerably extended in Rumania and Bulgaria since the spring of 1941. But the civilian air defense was an exclusive responsibility of the Rumanian authorities. From his headquarters at Ferme Lupescu, immediately north of Bucharest, the mission commander (General Speidel) directed the operations of the units assigned to him. In the course of these actions an advance command post was organized at the forward airfield at Tiraspol from which Speidel directed the employment of his forces, while the chief of staff carried out the routine affairs at the Ferme Lupescu headquarters. [30]

The scope, nature, and effect of Soviet air attacks against Rumanian territory are indicated in the following selected reports of the High Command of the Luftwaffe:

(1) The report of 26 June stated that more than 50 Soviet sorties were flown over Rumania "in the report period," with Constanţa as the principal target, and that after several attacks on preceding days, the city was attacked four times on 25 June and at dawn of the following day, causing slight damage. One Russian formation of 20 to 30 aircraft making a dawn flight against Ploeşti flew erroneously toward Constanţa, where it was dispersed by German fighters, losing 17 of its planes. Soviet aircraft, operating from 23,000 feet, dropped 17 demolition bombs upon Bucharest, damaging a few houses and injuring some of the populace. [31]

(2) The 14 July report noted that the Astra, Romana, and Orion oil refineries on the southern outskirts of Ploeşti were attacked upon the afternoon of 13 July by six Soviet aircraft flying at 6,500 feet. The attack destroyed 5 large and 6 small lubricating oil storage tanks and 12 loaded railroad tank cars, and so seriously damaged 1 oil distillation plant that it would remain inoperable for a short time. Fighters shot down four of the attacking aircraft. Near Tulcea, three Soviet aircraft were sighted during the afternoon, and at night enemy aircraft penetrated to Galaţi, Iaşi, Tulcea, and south of Constanţa, but no bombings were reported. [32]

(3) On 10 August, Soviet aircraft, operating between 9,800 and 13,000 feet in clear skies, thrice attacked Cernavodă, dropping some 17 bombs upon the city. The Danube bridge was the apparent target since two bombs struck the bridge structure, lightly damaging the stringers and a pier of the bridge and igniting an oil pipeline. Traffic was interrupted principally by the fire damage. A factory producing screws also received slight damage. At 0557 of the same morning, in slightly cloudy weather, seven Soviet SB-2 bombers attacked the harbor at Constanţa from an altitude of 1,600 feet, but the 25 bombs released were dropped prematurely

into the sea because of heavy antiaircraft artillery fire. They were not intercepted by German fighters. A formation of 10 Soviet DB-3 long-range bombers was sighted some 25 miles east of Constanța, but it jettisoned its bombs and withdrew at 0612 because of coming under attack by German fighters. During these attacks Russian pilots evinced a skillful use of weather and lighting conditions for defense, and showed an adroit ability to change altitudes to advantage.[33]

(4) A summary of events, printed in the report of 26 October, showed that from 22 June to 21 October 1941 units of the Luftwaffe Mission in Rumania had shot down 143 enemy aircraft (73 by fighters, 69 by antiarcraft artillery fire, and 1 by other units). Mission fighters also destroyed 4 tanks.[34]

Flights over Rumania by individual, and sometimes by several, Soviet reconnaissance aircraft and bombers were also carried out on days not covered by the foregoing reports. The penetrating enemy aircraft usually turned away immediately upon encountering antiaircraft artillery fire and avoided combat with German and Rumanian fighters whenever possible. The Russians' training in night flying was obviously very poor. Furthermore, the Rumanians complicated Soviet night air operations by using cleverly devised dummy installations with decoy fires and other deceptive features. A small lake north of Bucharest which was suitable as a navigational point had been drained to deprive Soviet airmen of such a favorable opportunity for orientation. When the German operations against the Crimea began in the autumn of 1941, the hitherto almost daily Russian air attacks diminished considerably. The number and effect of the few Soviet air penetrations were no longer worthy of mention because the Russians at this time concentrated all their air power in the bitter struggle for the Crimea.

Von Waldau recorded in his diary on 15 July that "in the Rumanian zone all efforts of air attacks against the fuel depots of Constanța and Ploești failed. The bulk of the penetrating Russians were shot down."[35]* Thus, from the first day of operations all enemy air objectives in Rumania, despite almost daily air attacks, were protected successfully without suffering great damage, and as a consequence, the entire oil production and the defenses thereof could proceed essentially as planned without limitations. The decisive result of this achievement was the safeguarding of regular fuel deliveries to Germany for its conduct of the war. German losses in these operations were slight.[36]

---

*Von Waldau is probably glossing over the rather minor losses, such as those indicated in the report for 14 July 1941. Some material damage was indeed caused in the raids of 13 July.

Chapter 5

SECOND AIR FLEET OPERATIONS LEADING
TO THE BATTLE OF KIEV

Army Group Center Operations

The first great objective assigned to Army Group Center (Field
Marshal von Bock) under the provisions of the High Command of the
Armed Forces (OKW) Directive No. 21 of 18 December 1940 (Operation
BARBAROSSA),* was the following:

> In the operational area divided by the Pripyat marshes
> into a northern and a southern half, the main concentration
> of effort is to be formed north of this [marsh] area. Here
> two army groups are to be committed.

> To the southern of these two army groups--center of
> the entire front--falls the task of routing the enemy forces
> in White Russia by especially strong armored and motor-
> ized units breaking out of the area around and north of
> Warsaw.[1]

On 22 June, Army Group Center consisted of 31 infantry, 7
motorized infantry, 1 cavalry, and 9 armored divisions.[2] Army Group
Center planned to exploit the favorable curve of the boundary projecting
toward Warsaw by employing a large-scale pincer movement to envelop
and destroy the Soviet forces concentrated in the Bialystok-Minsk area.
For this purpose, the Second Panzer Group (Generaloberst Heinz
Guderian) was to advance from the Brest-Litovsk area in a flanking
movement from the south, while the Third Panzer Group (Generaloberst
Hoth) was to advance from the Suwalki Tip in a flanking movement from
the north. The Fourth Army (Field Marshal Guenther von Kluge) was
to follow up the Second Panzer Group, and the Ninth Army (Generaloberst
Adolf Strauss) was to follow the Third Panzer Group.

Army Group Center was opposed by Soviet forces which were
almost equal to it in strength. These forces, under Marshal Semën

---

*See Appendix I and Map No. 3.

Konstantinovich Timoshenko, were composed of 36 infantry, 8 cavalry, and 2 armored divisions and 9 motorized mechanized brigades. The larger part of these forces was concentrated in the border area of Bialystok, while approximately one third lay as far back as the Minsk area.[3]

The armies and panzer groups of Army Group Center began their advance into Russia at 0330 on 22 June, their movements proceeding as planned. In the double battle of Bialystok and Minsk, the first battle of encirclement in the eastern theater, strong Soviet forces were destroyed, although some elements succeeded in escaping to the east from both pockets. The High Command of the Armed Forces reported on 11 July that 328,898 prisoners--including several senior general officers--had been taken and that 3,322 tanks, 1,809 guns, and large quantities of other war material had been captured.[4] With this success Army Group Center had burst open the gate to the center of the front.

Armored units then continued eastward and broke through the Stalin Line, which was anchored on the Dnepr and Dvina Rivers and supported by the strongly fortified settlements of Rogachev, Mogilev, Orsha, Vitebsk, and Polotsk. By-passing Mogilev on both sides, the Second Panzer Group forced its way on 11 July across the Dnepr and on 16 July took Smolensk in an attack from the south. The Third Panzer Group advanced through Vitebsk to Yartsevo, and with its right wing closed the ring to the north and northeast around the Soviet forces near Smolensk, except for a narrow gap only a few miles wide to the east.

This led to the second great battle of encirclement (named for its focal point, Smolensk) which continued for nearly four weeks.* The battle was fought in an area bounded on the west by the Dnepr and extended in a great ring around Smolensk, commencing at Bykhov and passing along the upper Sozh River north of Roslavl and through Yelnya and Belyy to Velikiye Luki. In the individual battles around Mogilev, Orsha, Polotsk, and Smolensk the Soviet forces were wiped out. On 5 August the last resistance collapsed in the steadily contracting pocket. Again the Russian prisoners numbered in the hundreds of thousands, while thousands of tanks and guns were also added to the booty.

While the fighting in the Smolensk area was still in progress, Guderian's Second Panzer Group fought at Roslavl against strong enemy

---

*See Maps Nos. 5 and 9.

forces attempting to break open the Smolensk pocket from the south and southeast. Finally, between 9 and 24 August the enemy was compressed in the Gomel-Klintsy area by elements of the Second Panzer Group and the Second Army[5] and for the most part destroyed. Soviet forces near Mozyr were thrown back to the east, and after heavy fighting in the Velikiye Luki area the northern wing of Army Group Center made contact at Kholm with the southern wing of Army Group North. Meanwhile, the infantry corps had closed up on the central front of Army Group Center and in the vicinity of Yelnya the army group had to go over to the defensive. Until the end of August very strong Soviet forces attacked this protruding bulge in the front with the intent of retaking the Smolensk area. In general, these powerful, threatening Russian counterattacks could be repulsed by hard fighting,[6] but early in September strong enemy pressure forced the withdrawal of the Yelnya salient.

A land bridge between Army Groups Center and South was effected as a result of the successful encirclement battle of Gomel during the latter half of August.* Until then, the Pripyat marshes, which separated the groups, had been a constantly threatening area, a gap serving as a favorable assembly area for dispersed enemy forces and partisan bands.

Thus the German Army created the conditions which were necessary for the later and great encirclement movement far to the east of Kiev which closed in a gigantic ring around the armies of Marshal Budenny.

Operations of the Second Air Fleet

Mission of the Second Air Fleet

When Germay launched its attack against Soviet Russia, Field Marshal Kesselring's Second Air Fleet (II Air Corps [General der Flieger Loerzer] on its right and the VIII Air Corps [General der Flieger von Richthofen] on its left) was required to coordinate its operations closely with those of Army Group Center.⸸ Commensurate with the principle of concentrating forces at key points, the Second Air Fleet was the strongest air fleet in the eastern theater. Its mission was to eliminate Soviet air

---

*See Maps Nos. 8 and 9.
⸸See Figures 16 and 17.

Figure 16
Arrival of Field Marshal Kesselring to inspect
Second Air Fleet units in Russia, 1941

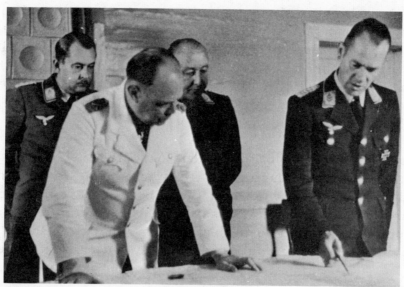

Figure 17
Combat situation conference in Russia, 1941, Second Air Fleet
L. to R.: Col. Ewers, Adjutant, Field Marshal Kesselring, Col.
Hans Seidemann, Chief of Staff, and Lt. Col. Klaus Uebe.

Figure 18
Fortress of Brest-Litovsk after destruction
by the Luftwaffe, 1941

power, thereby achieving air superiority or supremacy, and to support the ground operations of Army Group Center, particularly those of the Second and Third Panzer Groups.[7] Opposing the Second Air Fleet were two Soviet air divisions in the border area, backed by seven others farther to the rear, some identified and some presumed. Especially strong concentrations of air units were reported in the Kobrin-Slonim-Grodno-Bialystok area.

Despite the strength of the Second Air Fleet it could not fully carry out both of its tasks during the first days of the campaign. Thus, the first and most important task for the bulk of the air fleet units was to secure air superiority and, if possible, air supremacy. Kesselring later commented that it had been clear to him "that even these tasks could not be completely accomplished at once, but only one after the other."[8]

Initial Air Operations

For tactical ground reasons the High Command of the Armed Forces (OKW) had, contrary to the wishes of the Luftwaffe which could not make a night formation flight, ordered the attack to begin at 0330. For that reason there existed a danger that the Soviet air forces, warned by the early ground attack, would take off in the early dawn of 22 June 1941 in order either to throw themselves against the German units on the ground and in the air or at least to evade German air attacks by moving to alternate fields in the rear.

To cope with either or both of these possibilities, appropriate instructions were issued. Lt. Col. Paul Deichmann, Chief of Staff of the II Air Corps,* later related that the Luftwaffe yielded to the Army's objections and accepted the "unfavorable" attack time, which was bound to give the Soviet air units a 40-minute advance notice. In order to prevent Soviet exploitation of this warning, however, the II and VIII Air Corps (Second Air Fleet) adopted a somewhat dangerous plan of operations. Three Luftwaffe planes, manned by crews with night flying experience, attacked each Russian airfield upon which fighter aircraft were based.

_____

*Also Chief of Staff of the German Supreme Commander South (Kesselring) 1942-43, and, after World War II, Project Control Officer of the USAF Historical Division German Monograph Project in Karlsruhe, Germany. See biographical section.

Flying at maximum altitudes over "unsettled marsh and forest areas," these aircraft crossed the border and arrived undetected over the enemy fields to bomb them at the very moment the German Army opened its initial assault. These air attacks were intended to cause such confusion at the enemy fighter bases that the take-off of aircraft would be delayed. The attacks were a complete success. "Only at one field," Deichmann observed, "was a fighter unit met which was just taking off. The bombs fell in the midst of the . . . unit so that the aircraft lay destroyed in take-off formation at the end of the field." During the first few days of the campaign the II Air Corps thus met the Soviet fighter defenses and systematically destroyed "all aircraft" on fields within a 185 mile radius.[9]*

The precisely prepared operational plans for the first day of the air attack, including target assignments and arrangements for continuous attacks against every enemy aircraft located, made it possible to achieve within the first three days in the combat zone of Army Group Center air superiority which, although limited in time and space, was soon extended to outright air supremacy. The apparently incredible reports that approximately 2,500 enemy aircraft had been destroyed were doubted by most people, including Goering, but a careful check, made after the German ground forces had occupied the terrain, proved conclusively that the actual figures were even higher than had been reported.[10] Thus the first task of the Luftwaffe, the neutralization, paralysis, and destruction of Soviet air forces, had been achieved by the unprecedented tactical victories of German air units.

Beginning on the third day of operations in Combat Zone Center, the direct and indirect support of the ground forces became the primary task of the Second Air Fleet, taking precedence over all other operational demands, even those of a strategic nature.

------

*This evidence is supported by General v. Richthofen who wrote in his diary on 22 June: ". . . the single-engine fighter and dive-bomber pilots could not yet fly in formation. . . . Thus certain aircrews experienced in night flying . . . attacked the Soviet bases with bombs at the moment when German ground forces opened their attack. The confusion produced was so great, . . ." that no enemy air units had taken off before the German bombers arrived. See von Richthofen diary, Karlsruhe Document Collection.

Influence of II and VIII Air Corps on the Battles of Encirclement at Bialystok and Minsk

On 22 June the enemy had been completely overwhelmed in Combat Zone Center: his border positions were broken through at all points and every bridge over the Bug River was taken intact. On the right wing of Army Group Center an attack was launched by the Fourth Army and the Second Panzer Group. The principal river crossing over the Bug took place within the effective range of the guns of the fortress and citadel of Brest-Litovsk. Although the fortifications were obsolete, the thick walls of the fortress still offered sufficient protection for a number of batteries which could exert a considerable effect upon German troops crossing the river. Furthermore, since the armored units had orders to push forward to the east after crossing without taking time to reduce the fortifications on both banks, the Russian batteries posed a serious threat. For that reason, at daybreak on 22 June, the II Air Corps (Second Air Fleet)--ordered to work closely with the Fourth Army and, more especially, the Second Panzer Group--was to eliminate or at least neutralize the enemy batteries in the area of the fortress of Brest, especially those in the citadel.

Still another danger existed for the armored elements advancing on the north flank. Here, north of Brest-Litovsk, in the otherwise nearly level terrain, a conspicuous commanding range of hills extended to the east and west, paralleling the line of advance of the armored units. These hills were reported to be strongly fortified and emplaced with numerous gun batteries, thus forming a potential flanking danger to the advance of the Second Panzer Group. Rocket batteries (Nebelbatterien) had been provided to combat these artillery positions, but these batteries could only reach the western side of the hills.[11]

In order not to endanger the first points of the armored spearheads to the east, the appropriate ground forces command requested the II Air Corps to eliminate or continually keep out of action the Russian batteries in the Brest fortress area and in the hills to the north. Based upon experiences in the campaign in France, especially in the crossing of the Meuse River near Sedan on 13 May 1940 and later, Guderian (Second Panzer Group) did not attach much importance to single concentrated attacks against known battery positions, but requested instead that a number of dive bombers, even if only a few, be kept constantly in the air over the two danger zones to immediately attack any battery that opened fire.

Although this tactic contradicted standing operating procedures for dive bomber units (normally they would be employed in close, concentrated attacks of annihilation), the II Air Corps decided for once to commit its dive bombers as the panzer group requested. The bombers were to pin down and keep silent all enemy batteries, since this was more important than the destruction of only a part of the enemy gun positions. Furthermore, the dive-bomber flights were ordered to attack every enemy target located, particularly the artillery, before returning to base after being relieved by another flight. In this exceptional operation complete success was achieved, for the enemy batteries remained silent during the entire period.

The German armored group advanced swiftly, with the infantry divisions of the Fourth and Ninth Armies following closely behind. Bitter fighting continued only around Brest-Litovsk, where the important citadel still held out for several days and blocked the railroad and highways over the Bug and Mukhavets Rivers with small arms fire.[12]* General Deichmann later commented that a few days after the successful crossing of the Bug at Brest, a regimental commander of the 45th Infantry Division arrived at the air corps command post at Biala Podlaska and requested help in capturing an encircled Red Army commissar school at Brest, which defended itself stubbornly and hampered the forwarding of supplies to the Second Panzer Group. Both regimental and divisional resources and attacks by corps dive bombers (then able to carry only 1,100-pound bombs) had proven inadequate for destroying the school's fortifications and thereby breaking the garrison's resistance. As a solution the air corps then used heavy bombers, one of which was manned by a specially selected crew and carried a bomb weighing nearly two tons which had been brought up from the rear. This bomb tore open the fortification and capitulation soon followed.[13]⁄

---

*See Figure 18.

⁄The High Command of the Luftwaffe reported the success of this special attack on 30 June 1941. Five bombers scored six direct hits with 1,100-pound demolition bombs (SD-500) on the right (north) side of the citadel on the morning of 28 June, but the garrison's resistance remained unbroken. Late in the afternoon seven bombers dived upon the fort, one of them dropping an SC-1800 bomb weighing almost two tons and the others dropping twelve 1,100-pound bombs (SC-500), all of which struck the target and forced the garrison to capitulate. See Oberbefehlshaber der Luftwaffe, Abt. Ic, Geheim Kdos, Lagebericht Nr. 660, 30.6.1941 (C.i.C. of the Luftwaffe, Intelligence Branch, Top Secret, Situation Report No. 660 of 30 June 1941), p. 18. Karlsruhe Document Collection.

The Second Panzer Group, followed by the Fourth and Ninth Armies, reached Slonim and the Third Panzer Group reached Wilno on 24 June, the same day on which Napoleon I had taken Wilno and Kaunas in 1812. In continuous sorties the II Air Corps supported the advance of the Second Panzer Group, while the VIII Air Corps smashed all resistance to the more northerly Third Panzer Group.

On 25 June, despite constant resistance by Russian tank units, German armored forces took Slonim and Baranovichi and sealed off from the south the Soviet forces in the Bialystok-Wilno-Minsk-Baranovichi area. In the meantime, other German ground forces closed ranks toward the northeast and captured Bransk, Bocki, and Hajnovka. In repeated counterattacks, using motorized forces, the Russians sought to break through the envelopment, especially in the region of Grodno, near Kuznica, east of Osowiec, and at Slonim. German motorized troops, advancing by way of Kobrin to Kartuz-Bereza, continued on to Byten, some 19 miles south of Slonim.[14]

The High Command of the Luftwaffe reported on 28 June that most of its bombers and dive bombers were committed against the Soviet forces caught in the Bialystok-Zelva-Grodno area and that these enemy forces, some apparently disbanding, were seeking refuge in the forests to the east or south, but were being hampered in their withdrawal by roads blocked with destroyed vehicles and vast forest fires in the areas around Suprasl (northeast of Bialystok) and Bolshaya Berestovitsa (east of Krynki).[15]

In order to evade the destructive attacks of the Luftwaffe, the enemy withdrew mainly at night. By day he divided his retreating forces into very small units, which fell back, exploiting the generally very difficult terrain and often proceeding cross-country far from roads and pathways. The Luftwaffe's bombing attacks frequently came too late, since the enemy, warned by the appearance of the reconnaissance plane, went into the forests before the bombers arrived.

This form of retreat compelled the High Command of the Luftwaffe to adopt a new operational procedure, the so-called armed reconnaissance. Flying on a broad front in flights of three planes or in formations of five to six, the bombers did their own scouting and immediately attacked every enemy target seen.

The impetuous advance of the German armored groups created deep, open, and either unprotected or weakly protected flanks which formed a lasting danger to the Wehrmacht. Again and again strong enemy forces attacked the flanks; again and again critical situations resulted which could be cleared up only by the swift and versatile Luftwaffe. Thus on 24 and 25 June strong bomber and dive-bomber units of the VIII Air Corps continuously attacked and smashed Soviet armored units in the Kuźnica-Odelsk-Grodno-Dabrowa area, destroying numerous tanks and motorized vehicles. Von Richthofen wrote in his diary that when strong Soviet tank and cavalry forces from Bialystok and Lunna attacked the VIII and XX Army Corps (Ninth Army) near Grodno and Kuźnica on the afternoon of 24 June, the "commitment of the entire air corps followed." By evening the Soviet attack was halted, with 105 tanks destroyed. "All crews had abandoned their tanks in terror during the attack, [and] horses without riders, broken loose from the wagons, galloped about the land." Von Richthofen also noted that the morale of the German XX Corps, west of Grodno at Nowy Dwór, was excellent and confident, and that the support by the air corps was "greatly appreciated."[16]

A serious crisis also arose at Lida. The enemy had successfully counterattacked and formed strong bridgeheads over the Neman River at Mosty, Orlya, Bolitsa, and Ruda, from which he began an attack toward Lida, with his main effort at Ruda. Only weak security forces opposed him. The Soviet attack quickly gained ground and thereby became a serious threat to the flying units of the VIII Air Corps, which had been moved up to the area around Lida. If the Third Panzer Group had been forced by the counterattack to divert elements for the protection of its extended flank, this would have been a great defensive victory for the Soviet forces. Therefore, the main point of attack by the VIII Air Corps was immediately transferred against this dangerous Russian operation.

The air units based at Lida, including a ground-attack group, fought primarily to protect their own bases. Dive bombers attacked all enemy forces which moved north over the Neman. Because of the difficult terrain, the forward boundary for bombing attacks by the twin-engine fighters and bombers was the Neman. Large enemy elements, especially artillery, were destroyed before they could join in the fighting. The flying units in front, based around Lida, were able to continue to attack successfully despite deterioration of the weather. Sufficient time was thereby gained by the action of the VIII Air Corps to permit the V Army Corps to be brought up to help beat off the menacing Soviet attack. The early advance of the ground-attack units of the air corps had worked with success, increased the number of possible sorties, and thus raised the effectiveness of this arm to the highest degree. The decisive aid of the Luftwaffe helped to achieve a defensive victory, and the Third Panzer Group retained freedom of action in its further advance.

The long-range reconnaissance squadrons of the Second Air Fleet and its II and VIII Air Corps, together with the reconnaissance units attached to the army group and the armies, carried out continuous air reconnaissance embracing the entire operational zone of Army Group Center and the Second Air Fleet in which the most important target areas were covered by overlapping aerial photographs. An air photo of Orsha taken during the first days of the campaign showed, among other things, a large number of vehiclelike objects drawn up in many rows close to a large hangarlike building. On the strength of this air photo, the II Air Corps received a personal order from Goering that combat vehicles stored at Orsha were to be immediately attacked with all forces. According to a High Command of the Luftwaffe (OKL) report of 25 June, a supply depot, observed north of Orsha on the preceding day by long-range air reconnaissance, was occupied by some 2,000 tanks and combat vehicles.[17] This was also mentioned by General Halder in his diary entry for 26 June 1941.[18]

Although II Air Corps' headquarters believed that the vehicles to be attacked were not combat vehicles but possibly agricultural machinery or something of a similar nature, the explicit orders of Goering, nevertheless, had to be carried out. Accordingly, the supposed tank depot (possibly repair shop)--the aggregation of vehicles and the large hangar next to it-- was attacked on 27 June by all available forces. On the following day the Luftwaffe High Command reported a successful attack by 20 bombers upon the motor vehicle park at Orsha, hitting "four hangars and striking among the parked vehicles at the freight station," as well as the bombardment of "a large building" northwest of these targets.[19] When Orsha was later captured, it was discovered that the "tank depot" reported by air reconnaissance and attacked by the bomber unit was merely a collecting point for horse-drawn vehicles. Most of the equipment stocked in the large building (saddles and items for cavalry and horse-drawn vehicles) had been destroyed. This operation has been mentioned, first, to show that even the highest leadership of the Luftwaffe, the Commander in Chief himself, directly intervened in the operations orders of the higher and intermediate Luftwaffe operations staffs. Secondly, it illustrates how an insufficient evaluation of a reconnaissance report as an alarm message was transformed into an incorrect employment of fighting forces.

The ring about the enemy forces at Bialystok was closed and the first "pocket" in the East was formed by the rapid advance of the Fourth and Ninth Armies. Despite the strongest commitment of the Luftwaffe, it and the armies initially succeeded only in delaying the exit of the Soviet forces to the east. But when the ring closed, the II and VIII Air Corps of the Second Air Fleet were employed repeatedly against violent and desperate Russian attempts to break out to the east and the southeast.

On 1 July the Russian forces in the pocket were destroyed or captured. The armored groups, whose wings had again pushed to the front, supported by relays of flights of all of the flying units of the Second Air Fleet, encircled anew in the Minsk-Novogrudok area the enemy forces which had escaped from the Bialystok pocket and the new Soviet forces which were found west of Minsk.

In the fighting against the retreating enemy infantry and motorized columns, it had soon become evident that the commitment against so-called highway traffic centers was not as effective as it had been in the more highly developed West. Although during the campaign in the West the entrances and exits of a community were frequently closed and the through traffic blocked by dive-bombing attacks, this procedure was not to be followed in the East because Soviet settlements--villages and even the smaller cities--were laid out in an unplanned and dispersed fashion and generally consisted of single wooden or earthen houses. Massive stone buildings were to be found only in the centers of the medium- and large-sized cities.* The Soviets could simply march or drive around these debris obstacles without traffic jams occurring at a highway junction. Favorable and more effective, however, were the attacks launched against crossing sites over smaller rivers or even over brooks, especially when these streams rose during periods of high water in the spring or autumn or even after heavy thunderstorms.

On 27 June the two armored groups closed the second great pocket just west of Minsk. Four Soviet armies were encircled and nearly destroyed. In an order of the day, Field Marshal von Bock of Army Group Center emphasized that the success of this battle of annihilation was possible only through the support of the Second Air Fleet (which had fought in close cooperation with the army group).

While the continuous support of the Third Panzer Group by von Richthofen's close support corps (VIII Air Corps) in the fighting on the northern wing of Army Group Center encountered no difficulties because of the corps' special composition, organization, and equipment, which enabled it to perform its mission well, conditions on the southern wing of the Second Air Fleet (II Air Corps) were considerably less favorable.[20] Here, in the first few days in the combat zone of the II Air Corps the armored spearheads pressed rapidly ahead to the east, driving along two roads. At first substantial enemy forces to the sides of these roads

---

*See Figure 19.

Figure 19
Russian village showing the common
dispersed character of houses

remained completely unmolested. Then, in incessant and often extremely bitter fighting, the infantry divisions of the Fourth Army gradually mopped up the Soviet elements in the by-passed territory.

The close-ground-attack units of the II Air Corps were employed immediately in front of Guderian's armored spearheads in order to break at once any resistance that developed.[21] The limited range of these units made it necessary to move their bases quickly to points close behind the armored group, for only thus was it possible to achieve a close cooperation between the armored forces and their supporting units. The fighters also had to be brought forward early to provide at the same time protection for the support units, since an eventual revival of enemy air activity had to be reckoned with, despite the devastating losses suffered by Soviet flying forces in the early days of the campaign.

It now turned out that it was impossible for the II Air Corps to direct the bomber units and the long-range reconnaissance aircraft (which for logistical reasons were based farther to the rear), carry out the supply of all units, maintain contact with the Fourth Army and the Second Panzer Group, and at the same time insure constant close cooperation between the close-support air units (often based over 60 miles farther to the front) and the individual armored corps.

After a few days of action, therefore, it proved necessary to provisionally establish a so-called close-support air commander (Nahkampffuehrer), Col. Martin Fiebig, who henceforth directed the light units (with the help of a small operations staff acting under orders of the II Air Corps) and cooperated closely with Guderian's armored group and its air corps.

In indirect support of the ground forces, the Luftwaffe made successful attacks from 26 June upon the railroads lying in the zone of operations, those leading to this zone, particular railway junctions, and especially the rail routes of Minsk-Borisov-Orsha and Minsk-Molodechno and the rail junctions of Orsha, Zhlobin and Osipovichi. Close by, occupied Soviet airfields were successfully attacked again and again, in particular the airfields in the Minsk-Bryansk-Smolensk-Polotsk area, during the early morning and late evening hours of 29 June, and a major effort against the airfields around Gomel was made on 2 July.

In the combat area of the encirclement battles it was often extremely difficult to distinguish between friend and foe. Often the enemy could be recognized only because he left his vehicle upon the approach of German aircraft and tried to reach the nearest woods.

Because of the difficult terrain, the constantly changing ground situation, and the frequently poor contact between ground forces and air units, the German ground forces were easily in danger of being bombed by mistake. Despite the precautionary measures ordered, such errors were not completely avoided. Guderian wrote that on 1 August, while he was on the line of advance of the 23rd Infantry Division, he had been involved in an attack by German bombers which inflicted "serious losses" upon nearby personnel.[22]

The attack zones which had been initially established by the higher operations staffs of the Luftwaffe and Army (no bombs were to be dropped on the German side of these lines) proved to be ineffective in the rapid, widely dispersed movements of the armored forces. The bomb lines were too rigid and became obsolete too quickly to be useful. Fortunately the forward German ground units had been repeatedly ordered to identify themselves upon the approach of German aircraft by displaying swastika flags, ground signal panels, smoke signals, and Very pistols, a procedure which was always possible during periods of German air superiority.[23] This practice became difficult only when enemy air activity revived and when the Soviets also made use of German recognition signals.* Therefore many attacks upon Soviet troop concentrations and columns did not take place because the approaching German flyers were unable to make positive identification of the troop units. Moreover, severe losses often occurred when Luftwaffe aircraft dived low enough to determine the target's identity. Frequent changes in flare signals were therefore an absolute necessity.

The establishment of the enemy's identity was facilitated considerably by the increased use of Luftwaffe signal service liaison troops, as well as by fighter-control and dive-bomber-control units which operated with the most advanced ground troops. By their assistance the objectives and required time of attack could be radioed to the flying units. Thus combat Luftwaffe planes were brought in proximity to the targets, or directed to new objectives when the ground situation had suddenly changed.

---

*Soviet troops were avid users of German identification signals. German prisoners were often interrogated to determine precisely what signs were in current use, and these procedures were then put into practice among Soviet forces. Sometimes Russian troops were dressed in German uniforms. See Generalleutnant Klaus Uebe, Russian Reactions to the German Air Force, USAF Historical Studies No. 176.

But it was demonstrated again and again that the ground forces needed to be thoroughly trained in the strict use of the recognition signs. The anxiety, frequently well founded, that the signals might also become known to the enemy, who would exploit them for his own attacks, often led to a disregard of their use.

The crossing sites of the retreating enemy over the Neman, Berezina, and Shara Rivers and the congestion of Soviet troops and vehicles of all kinds at these points were attacked with favorable results again and again by strong Luftwaffe forces. Before any operation against railroad and highway bridges was carried out an agreement with the controlling army staff in this sector of the front was urgently needed in order to clarify which bridges should not be destroyed because of their value for the smooth advancement of German armored and other ground units. In such cases, the attack must be limited to missions against the enemy forces jamming the bridges. An outstanding success was the destruction of the large railroad bridge at Bobruysk, which was doubtless of special importance to the Russians for the supply of new forces and materiel of all kinds.[24]

If the Russian was already a master of rapid, though mainly primitive, repair of destroyed railroad bridges and sections of track, his performance in repairing the Bobruysk bridge was particularly impressive. In 24 to 36 hours over 1,000 skilled workmen, laboring under the direction of the People's Commissar for Communications, restored the bridge so that it could be crossed. Western railroad specialists, for safety considerations, would certainly have refused to permit trains to proceed over such bridges, but the Russian, in his stubbornness and with his disdain for human life, traveled over them without hesitation.

While the Second and Third Panzer Groups, supported by the close support forces of the Luftwaffe, advanced on both flanks of Army Group Center, German bombers attacked on a greater scale and with good effects the roads and railways and the railway junctions in the Mozyr-Roslavl-Smolensk-Vitebsk-Polotsk-Daugavpils area.

Halder remarked in his diary that the Luftwaffe now appeared to have interdicted the Russian railroads, even those far in the Soviet rear: "The number of track sections occupied with standing trains is increasing satisfactorily. " He noted that this continuing work had resulted in a great number of freight cars being shunted onto sidings to the east of Gomel (Unecha) as well as on lines situated to the west and southwest of this center. Many of these were "loaded with wagons and tanks. " Halder believed that this situation indicated either an attempt to provide dispersed mobile units with new materiel or an attempt to move the mobile units.[25]

On 30 June the High Command of the Luftwaffe reported on the German Air Force participation in the encirclement battle at Minsk, noting that strong units of bombers and dive bombers attacked the fleeing enemy, concentrating on the areas north of Ruzhany (southeast of Volkovysk), at Derechin (east-northeast of Volkovysk), and Novogrudok. Their objectives were "columns and river crossings," with rail interdiction operations in the Russian rear, the main efforts being launched against the junctions of Smolensk and Polotsk.[26]

At this point, the Soviets attacked with strong air forces in an attempt to stop Guderian's armored forces from crossing the Berezina at Bobruysk and later the Dnepr. On 30 June large daylight air battles were waged over the Bobruysk area, where Soviet air forces sought to check the German crossing. In the aerial combat over this sector the Russians lost 110 aircraft.[27] Guderian, observing these air battles, attested to the excellence of the cooperation of Col. Werner Moelders* and his airmen, but complained that the liaison with the II Close Air Support fliers under General Fiebig did not work quickly enough. Guderian also noted that air reconnaissance had detected fresh Soviet forces assembling in the Smolensk-Orhsa-Mogilev area.[28]

In regard to the armored group commander's criticism of Fiebig, it should be noted that smooth and close cooperation between the armored units and Fiebig's command could not have been properly performed in the brief period of the command's existence (since the end of June 1941). In the field of signal communications, especially, there must still have been malfunctions and breakdowns, since the command and troops had insufficient experience in this special duty of giving direct support to the ground forces. Moreover, suitable radio equipment was still lacking. Fiebig's performance was further upheld in a later comment by Kesselring, who declared that "experiences must naturally be acquired first," but that Fiebig had "developed into a close-support air commander comparable to von Richthofen."[29] It should also be observed that by this time the ground

----

*An extremely able officer who entered the service in the mid-1930's. He was the top fighter ace among German airmen in the Spanish Civil War (1936-1939), and in June of 1941 was the top fighter ace in the German Air Force and commander of the 51st Fighter Wing, attached to the II Air Corps.

96

troops had become outrageously spoiled by the continuous employment of Luftwaffe units in direct support on the battlefield. Von Richthofen noted in his diary on 5 July that the Army refused to realize that the Luftwaffe could not be dribbled out to all places, but must be concentrated at major points.* Every sortie required time. Planes had to be refueled, loaded with bombs, and then flown to the new objective. Everyone in the Army wanted to take over the Luftwaffe, but the Army was completely unaware of the potentialities of air power.[30]

Second Air Fleet Support of the Army During the Encirclement Battle at Smolensk

After the encirclement battle at Minsk, the Second and Third Panzer Groups pushed toward a new Soviet enemy which apparently intended to defend the Dnepr-Dvina (rivers) line. The next task of Army Group Center was to strike this foe, destroying as much as possible in a new battle of encirclement in the Smolensk area. To carry out this task, Army Group Center depended above all upon getting Guderian's Second Panzer Group across the Dnepr under any circumstances. The II and VIII Corps were to support the Dnepr crossing near Mogilev on 12 July by a sudden concentrated daybreak attack. The VIII Corps, with its operations staff and a part of its units, was situated in the area of Lepel, with other components around Molodechno.

It was determined in a detailed conference, held at Second Panzer Group headquarters at Borisov, that all forces of the Second Air Fleet were to be concentrated under the direct command of the II Air Corps. Units of the II Close Support Air Commander (Fiebig) were to engage front line objectives, while VIII Air Corps units were to operate in the northern part of the attack sector (because of ranges involved) and would overlap, in part, the target area of General Fiebig's forces. An exception was the bomber units of the II Air Corps, who were also committed to direct support of the ground forces, but in the rear of the attack zone. After the first, sudden, concentrated attack, the VIII Air Corps would again support the Third Panzer Group. Since Guderian's Second Panzer Group succeeded on 11 July in forcing the Dnepr crossing by surprise,

---

*The RAF, operating in the Western Desert in 1942, and the AAF operating in Tunisia in late 1942 and early 1943, had the same complaint. The RAF by the end of 1942 and the AAF by April 1943 had corrected this unwise and dangerous Army practice.

these assault plans were never carried out. This abandoned short-term operational plan clearly shows, however, how quickly, in even the larger scope of the air fleet, strong forces could be assembled to produce a sudden concentration of heavy, annihilating firepower at a given point.

After crossing the Dnepr on both sides of Mogilev on 11 July, the Second Panzer Group pushed forward with its right wing and its center as far as the Sozh River and on 16 July reached Smolensk from the south. With this crossing over the Dnepr, the enemy air activity, like that at an earlier period at the Berezina, was considerably stronger than usual, just as it was on the other fronts. Guderian later commented that strong enemy artillery fire and numerous bombing attacks launched on 11 July against the bridge site of the 10th Panzer Division had made crossing operations more difficult than for the XXXXVII Panzer Corps.* A bridge near the SS-Division "Das Reich" (2nd SS Panzer Division) had also been damaged by these air attacks.[31] But Guderian also verified the successes of German fighters in destroying their aerial opponents again and again, or in securing in specific areas temporary air superiority or even air supremacy. Moelders' fighters, operating from advance fields located just behind the front lines, achieved air supremacy over the assembly area for the Dnepr crossings. "Wherever he [Moelders] showed himself," wrote Guderian, "the air was soon clear."[32]

In the meantime, the Third Panzer Group had pushed forward by way of Vitebsk to Yartsevo and had wheeled its right wing around toward Smolensk. After weeks of heavy fighting the infantry divisions of the Fourth and Ninth Armies, which had moved slowly up from behind, almost completely closed the circle around the enemy forces west of Smolensk. As usual, the close support forces of the Second Air Fleet supported successfully the envelopment movements of the armored groups and the advance of the unmotorized armies. In this operation the ground-attack wing, the 210th Bomber Wing (equipped with Me-110 twin-engine fighters) attached to the II Air Corps, destroyed 915 Soviet aircraft in 1,574 sorties flown between 22 June and 26 July 1941. Ninety-two of these planes were put out of action in aerial combat. On the ground, 165 tanks, 2,136 motor vehicles, 194 cannon, 52 trains, and 60 locomotives were either put out of action or destroyed.[33]

Some interesting comments were made on 11 July by von Richthofen (commanding the VIII Air Corps) concerning leaflet drops

---

*The roads or routes of approach of the 10th Panzer Division were poor and the bridge position barely adequate.

during this period of close support activity. The Russians in front of the
Third Panzer Group began to desert in small parties and, at the request
of the German ground forces, leaflets were dropped stating that deserters
would not be shot (as had been rumored by Soviet leaders). Deserters who
came over on the strength of these leaflets maintained that probably even
more of their comrades would desert, but that too few of the leaflets
bearing promises of safety were to be found. Since the Russians believed
that a leaflet of this kind would be valid for only one person, many were
afraid to desert without having such a "special life insurance certificate."
After that, improved leaflets were dropped which were valid for more
than one person. The expected deserters, however, failed to appear.
Thereupon, the VIII Air Corps itself prepared new leaflets which were
dropped during its dive-bombing attacks. In contrast to the long-winded
earlier leaflets, the air corps leaflet was of classic brevity: "No one
is shot! But, if you do not desert immediately, we will come again!"
The result was a clear increase in the number of deserters.[34]

Unfortunately, the Smolensk pocket had not been closed tightly.
Through a small gap east of Smolensk only a few miles wide, substantial
Soviet forces escaped destruction or capture. Kesselring commented in
1955 that, after personally inspecting the gap, he had requested Hoth of
the Third Panzer Group and von Bock to launch an attack from the north
and close the opening, and that he had guaranteed air support, but
"unfortunately nothing happened. My proposals by way of the Commander
in Chief of the Luftwaffe were also fruitless."[35]

Although during daylight hours the continuous attacks on the
escape gap by close-support air units succeeded at least in limiting or
delaying the movement of Soviet fighting forces, the enemy used the
breach very successfully at dusk and during the night. Kesselring estimated that over 100,000 Soviet troops escaped from the Smolensk pocket.[36]
As in earlier battles of encirclement, this battle had shown that the
Luftwaffe alone was incapable of closing openings in an encirclement ring.
During the day the Luftwaffe could strike the enemy with destructive force
in waves of air attacks, but at night neither an exact target designation
nor a fix on the target was possible in the completely obscure terrain,
with its numerous small woods and shrubbery which offered no check-
points. Employment of paratroopers or airborne troops which would
have been especially suitable for closing gaps could not take place
because these special units had suffered very heavy losses in the capture
of Crete and were not available for a special mission of this kind.

A situation--at times critical--also existed north of Yartsevo,
when an enemy fighting force attacked across the Vop River from the area

north of and around Dorogobuzh. This attack, supported by strong artillery and tanks, was initially successful against the weak German security forces. The Russians even succeeded in occupying the highlands west of the Vop and in advancing somewhat farther along the Tsarevich River. In the meantime, the VIII Air Corps had brought forward a part of its close-support forces to a position just back of the front in the Dukhovshchina area. Since 23 July the air corps command post also lay just to the east of Dukhovshchina. As soon as the Russian assault was recognized, the close-support units were immediately committed and inflicted severe losses upon the enemy in ceaseless attacks. Even the 99th Antiaircraft Artillery Regiment, attached to the VIII Air Corps for airfield defense, was employed to parry the menacing enemy thrust. The destructive effect of the 88 mm. antiaircraft artillery gun in direct fire, with its high firepower, as well as the effects of 20 mm. and 37 mm. antiaircraft artillery weapons, inflicted devastating losses on the Russians.

But, despite the high losses, the enemy again pushed forward over the difficult terrain. The situation became critical not only for the ground forces, but also for the airfields and thus for the operation of the flying units. The command post of the VIII Air Corps organized itself for defense; the units assumed the defense of their operational fields. The ground situation changed so often that Luftwaffe units generally did not know when they took off whether they would be able to land at their old fields after the sortie. Once more, the flying units fought for the protection of their own bases. Over and over again every unit attacked the enemy found directly in front of it, flying the utmost number of sorties. German units had received certain standing orders, since every formal issuance of orders would only have delayed operations. As in previous operations, the high-speed fueling apparatus with its flexible hoses again proved itself particularly valuable, for it made possible the simultaneous fueling of as many as nine planes, which could be parked at distances sufficient to safeguard them against possible bomb hits.

Fluctuating weather conditions also influenced the employment of the flying units. Because of the numerous sorties, a shortage of supplies occurred very soon which was for a time so severe that it appeared questionable whether another strong enemy attack could be warded off. Air transport units were therefore employed to bring up supplies to the front lines, and it was at this time that these units sustained their first losses.

Fortunately, this attack across the Vop River remained an isolated action of the enemy forces which were desperately defending themselves in the Smolensk pocket. Additional German ground forces were brought up, which succeeded in checking the enemy after hard fighting. During these operations, the order had been received from the Commander in Chief of the Luftwaffe to transfer the VIII Air Corps to Combat Zone North. This air corps, therefore, intended to assemble its forces in the Vitebsk area and to rehabilitate them for the ensuing commitment, leaving only weak close-support forces under Lieutenant Colonel Hagen behind. But, in the critical situation which had arisen, units of the VIII Air Corps were the only forces immediately available for defense against the enemy attack. In this emergency, therefore, its units were again committed to combat action upon the order of the Second Air Fleet. The VIII Air Corps inflicted heavy personnel losses upon the enemy, stopped his advance, and thereby won the necessary time to parry the Soviet attack with newly arrived ground forces. A Soviet attempt to tear open the northern section of the Smolensk pocket was thereby prevented. The enemy, despite considerable casualties, was able to hold a small bridgehead west of the Vop River for the next few days, but this resistance was cleared up during the further contraction of the pocket.

At the end of the fighting, the VIII Air Corps was transferred to the combat zone of the First Air Fleet. On 3 August Field Marshal Kesselring issued an order of the day to the corps, stating that the VIII Air Corps was leaving his command for "temporarily different employment." His order mentioned that a short period of preparation for the Russian war and six weeks of war "lie behind us"; it praised the VIII Air Corps for its role in the rapid successes of the Ninth Army and the Third Panzer Group, and especially praised von Richthofen, the commander of these "superbly trained and aggressive [air] units." Kesselring concluded his order of the day by extending his "heartiest wishes" to the VIII Air Corps in its coming operations and the hope that "without great losses the VIII Air Corps shall again attach equally great laurels to its victorious banner!"[37]

During the last days of July and the beginning of August, while the close-support forces of the Second Air Fleet made its annihilating sorties, particularly against the enemy forces in the Smolensk pocket, the twin-engine fighter and bomber units attacked the roads and railways leading from the east to the Bryansk-Vyazma-Velikiye Luki line, and on 14 July for the first time hit the railroad and superhighway between Moscow and Smolensk.* These attacks were intended to suppress at the very outset all enemy operations undertaken for the liberation of the Smolensk area. Thus, the railroad station installations at Orel were very successfully attacked during the night of 30-31 July by units of the II Air Corps, which dropped some 30 tons of demolition bombs and 3,600 incendiary bombs.

---

*See Figure 20.

Figure 20
Interdiction of railroads leading to the
Smolensk area by the Luftwaffe, 1941

Southeast of Smolensk, the Soviets also attempted to tear open the pocket by strong counterattacks. Here the GAF's II Air Corps was employed with success by the Second Air Fleet. The High Command of the Luftwaffe reported on 31 July that bomber and dive-bomber units supported the ground forces by attacking Soviet columns and artillery emplacements in the area between the Smolensk-Roslavl rail line and the highway to Vyazma, and by smashing a Soviet attempt to push forward with tanks around Shatalovo, some 37 miles southeast of Smolensk. These attacks destroyed 67 trucks, 17 tanks, 2 antiaircraft artillery batteries, 6 artillery pieces, 2 trench mortar batteries, 6 teams of horses, 1 fuel depot, and 1 ammunition dump. Knocked out of action were 3 antiaircraft guns and 1 antiaircraft artillery battery, while 6 trucks, 5 tanks, 1 locomotive, and 15 railroad cars were damaged. Railroad stations at Korobets and Stodolishche, parts of a cantonment, and a village near Staraya Sheveleva were set on fire. The Luftwaffe High Command reported that direct hits and very near misses on four to five heavy tanks caused only one tank to smoke. Enemy casualties from these attacks could not be accurately estimated.[38] At this time, the enemy flying forces were also being continuously attacked in the air and at their bases. From the beginning of the campaign until 31 July 1941, the 26th Twin-Engine Fighter Wing "Horst Wessel"* alone destroyed 620 Soviet aircraft in aerial combat and in low-level attacks.[39]

On 5 August the encirclement battle of Smolensk was essentially over, with only small, trapped enemy units still offering desperate resistance. Units of the Second Air Fleet had a decisive share in this successful and great battle in Combat Zone Center. During the last days of the battle around Smolensk, the bulk of the dive-bomber and bomber units of the II Air Corps were employed against railroads and highways, especially in the Roslavl-Sukhinichi-Bryansk-Unecha area, since for days air reconnaissance had reported new Soviet forces moving up against the projecting salient of Yelnya; however, bad weather frequently impaired the employment of the flying units in this area. During the fighting in the Smolensk area enemy air activity had increased, especially against the southern wing and the center of Army Group Center. Especially troublesome were the continuous attacks upon the German front lines by Soviet ground-attack planes. Although these attacks were generally of relatively slight effect, they nevertheless influenced the morale of the ground forces, particularly when the latter were engaged in heavy defensive fighting in sectors such as, for example, the Yelnya salient.

----

*Named after an early Nazi Storm Troop (SA) leader, Horst Wessel, who was murdered in Berlin.

The struggle against these ground-attack aircraft was very difficult because they approached from afar and at low level, flying singly, in two-plane formations, and in weak squadron strength; dropped their bombs on the front lines; and immediately turned back toward their own territory. Scrambling German fighters usually arrived too late to block the attack, and their pursuit of the Soviet ground-attack aircraft, which were retiring at low altitudes, was too costly for the unarmored German fighters because of the strong Soviet ground fire. An air-defense patrol would have been the most favorable antiaircraft measure, particularly because the Russians, in their familiar stubbornness, repeatedly attacked at the same point, in the same sector, and at the same times. Such a defensive operational procedure was not possible, however, because of the inadequate numerical strength of the available fighter units. Moreover, such a procedure did not correspond in other respects to the German operational principles for fighter pilots.

Favorable results were only possible with the so-called visual take-off (Sichtstart), that is, when German fighters could see the enemy aircraft as they were about to take off from advance fields close behind the front and could, as it were, "pin" these aircraft as they took off. However, such airfields were seldom available because of the terrain. The best protection, therefore, was a strong defense by the ground troops themselves with automatic weapons (the same system of defense employed by the Soviets). This was true for the entire Eastern Front and for the entire period of the campaign.

The II Air Corps received a special secondary assignment when it was ordered to support the 1st Cavalry Division* on the southern wing of Army Group Center. This division had advanced along the northern edge of the Pripyat marsh area and had suffered serious losses in the dense vegetation of the difficult, swampy terrain. A large number of river monitors caused the cavalry division particular trouble, and armed Russian motor boats also repeatedly joined in the fighting. These vessels were very difficult to locate and combat, because the banks of the many tributaries were overhung with trees and bushes. For weeks, elements of the II Air Corps were employed against these monitors; and although a large number of them were destroyed, others were able to operate in the marshlands for a long time, much to the disadvantage of the ground forces, which had to fight their way laboriously through this region while suffering grievous losses. Later on, the endlessly overextended

---

*Commanded by Generalleutnant Kurt Feldt, an officer with cavalry service dating back to the turn of the century.

southern flank of these German units was constantly harassed by attacks from this region.

With the swift advance of the German armored units, the major concern of the Luftwaffe High Command was the timely forward movement of bases for flying units, particularly of the close-support units. At the same time, the signal communications essential for command purposes had to be established up to the front. Only those airfields could usually be occupied and used which lay close to the routes of the armored units and the main line of march. The most pressing supply requirements—especially spare parts—were flown forward by air transport. The Luftwaffe supply columns moved forward only with difficulty over the few available roads which were even halfway passable for heavy vehicles. Bad weather frequently delayed the advance of supply items important for military operations.

The few airfields were generally overcrowded and therefore decidedly vulnerable to air attack. A concentrated enemy air attack could have caused extraordinary damage. Fortunately, the Soviet command missed such opportunities.

Strong defense of these airfields by antiaircraft artillery was necessary. The ground elements of the air units, together with the anti-aircraft artillery, also assumed the defense against attacks by enemy infantry and armored forces which had been bypassed or dispersed by German armored forces, as well as by partisans, which were becoming increasingly stronger. It now proved worthwhile for every man of the ground organization, including technical personnel, to be trained in ground fighting and armed accordingly. Airfield personnel learned very quickly to organize for all-round defense immediately upon occupying an airfield. From stocks of captured materiel, the ground organization units obtained heavy weapons, ammunition, and even tanks, which they put in running order and used to protect their fields. Such self-initiative was shown, for example, by Col. Gottlob Mueller in the ground defense of his airfield at Bobruysk, using captured Soviet tanks which had been put in effective working condition.

Kesselring later wrote regarding the advance, organization, and defense of the air bases that the advance of the Luftwaffe's ground organization along the roads was much more difficult than that of the Army because there were not enough motorized vehicles and no tracked vehicles. With few permanent bases available, advance airfields which were no longer directly protected by Army troops had to be reconnoitered and prepared. The resultant security measures further burdened the ground personnel, already too few in number, at these fields. The Luftwaffe administrative commands and their staffs for special duty deserved the highest praise for making possible the continuous employment of the flying units, "particularly the close support corps [VIII Air Corps] and the II Close Support Air Commander [Fiebig]."[40]

The importance of a permanent personal liaison and operational arrangement between the operations staffs of the Luftwaffe and the Army had proven itself in all the battles. Since one could scarcely get through the heavily used, frequently blocked advance routes by motor vehicles or motorcycles, aircraft--generally the Fieseler Fi-156 "Storch"-- remained the only means of communications.[41]*

After repeated costly experiences with the confused, frequently changing ground situation, it had become necessary for liaison planes to fly at low altitudes along the German-held roads, in order to avoid being shot down by dispersed enemy ground forces or to avoid having to make an emergency landing on a cross-country flight, far from the roads. A frightful example of what could happen occurred in the first days of the campaign when Luftwaffe Colonel von Gerlach was shot down while on a cross-country liaison flight from one advance route to another; German troops later discovered his brutally mutilated body.

Support of the Right Wing of Army Group Center by the II Air Corps in the Gomel-Bryansk-Roslavl Area

Before the battle for Smolensk was over, a few armored and infantry corps were concentrated under Guderian to destroy a strong enemy group which was attacking from the Roslavl area toward the northwest. Supported by II Air Corps units, Guderian's troops successfully encircled this enemy group and destroyed it near Roslavl during the first three days of August before it could approach the Smolensk pocket. Guderian's XXIV Panzer Corps, under General der Panzertruppe Freiherr Geyr von Schweppenburg, then pushed forward from Roslavl in the general direction of Klintsy, in order to cooperate with the Second Army in the envelopment (from the line west of Mozyr-Rogachev-Krichev) of two Soviet armies which stood north and west of Gomel, forming a deep dangerous wedge between the rearward bending flanks of Army Groups South and Center. German ground troops, assisted continuously by the close support of the II Air Corps, destroyed this mass of enemy

---

*Col. Rudolf Meister (GSC), Chief of Staff to von Richthofen, once had an accident with his liaison plane. His 50-mile return by ground transportation took 11 hours.

strength in the encirclement battle of Gomel-Klintsy, with only small remnants getting away to the southeast. During this period, between 9 and 24 August, bomber units of the II Air Corps successfully attacked troop movements and concentrations, notably in the Chernigov-Konotop-Gomel area. Moreover, continuous attacks followed on all railroads which approached the southern wing of Army Group Center from the east and southeast, in order to prevent both a retreat of enemy forces to the east and the arrival of new Soviet forces and supplies from the east. Since 22 August, a weaker enemy force on the northern wing of the army group (in the Velikiye Luki area) had been successfully destroyed with VIII Air Corps support. At the same time, Second Air Fleet bombers-- primarily under the command of the II Air Corps--repeatedly attacked the occupied Soviet air bases which had been reported by air reconnaissance and radio intercept services. Because of these attacks the Soviet air attacks decreased noticeably, thereby substantially relieving the ground forces. On 9 September the High Command of the Luftwaffe, summarizing this action against enemy forces, reported that the II Air Corps had destroyed 2,660 planes (1,380 shot down and 1,280 eradicated on the ground) between 22 June and 30 August.[42]

During this fighting on both wings of Army Group Center, the elements of the group which had pushed farthest to the east in the center met very strong opposition and went over to the defensive in the so-called Yelnya salient. The Soviets attacked continuously with strong artillery support.* In this tense situation, however, the weak German forces again and again successfully warded off these heavy counterattacks, and, despite great losses, held their positions. It was understandable that the Army urgently requested Luftwaffe support for the heavily engaged ground troops in their defense of the salient.[43]

The forces of the Second Air Fleet, however, were too weak to meet all the desires and requirements of the ground forces in Combat Zone Center. The few flying units, which had been in continuous action since 22 June and were therefore seriously reduced in combat readiness, were insufficient to carry out several tasks at the same time. Therefore, the Second Air Fleet decided, with Goering's consent and in accordance with the principle of concentrating forces at key points, to commit all forces of the II Air Corps for the support of the right (southern) wing of Army Group Center in the Mozyr-Konotop-Roslavl-Rogachev area. This decision was possibly made because it seemed to be of decisive importance

----
*Editor's Note: These attacks were alleged to have been ordered by Stalin.

to assist the Second Army under Generaloberst Maximilian Freiherr von Weichs, which was far to the rear and faced with an ever menacing danger from Russian units to the south, to move forward as quickly as possible by eradicating these hostile forces.

Furthermore, by gaining the area south and southwest of Bryansk as a base of departure--about on a line from Pochep to Unecha--a vast envelopment movement could be created from the north against the armies of Marshal Budënny, which stood east of Kiev.

In his diary entry for 27 August General von Waldau, Chief of the Operations Staff of the Luftwaffe General Staff, commented on the satisfactory beginning of the operations by the Second Army and Guderian's Second Panzer Group, which culminated in the capture of the crossings over the Desna River. Von Waldau believed that if the rail line between Kiev and Konotop could be reached within two to three days, "a thrust could be made deep into the rear of the Russian forces" and developments would progress favorably at the Dnepr front, while the north front of Yelnya remained on the defensive.[44]

The closing up of the Second Army in the vicinity of the Yelnya salient would in itself relieve the German forces there. The Army High Command (OKH) was divided on whether to hold or to yield up the salient. However, it disagreed with the Luftwaffe command by insisting that the air arm, as a first priority, support the salient. These opposing views are evident in Halder's diary entry of 3 August 1941, in which the Chief of the Army General Staff commented that the Yelnya salient provided "dominating positions" whose abandonment would affect the area to the north. "The holding of the 'bridgehead' is costing us much blood." Halder felt personally that the salient should be held and that the Russian artillery should be met by German counterfire and a widening of the bridgehead.[45] On the following day, Col. Adolf Heusinger (GSC), upon returning from the Fuehrer Conference (held at headquarters, Army Group Center), reported that the successful operation against Roslavl was expected to relieve the Yelnya situation and that the abandonment of Yelnya was "out of the question."[46]

Field Marshal von Bock telephoned the Commander in Chief of the Army, Field Marshal von Brauchitsch, on 14 August, complaining of Goering's order to shift air support from Yelnya to Rogachev despite army group objections, and commenting that Guderian wanted to give up the Yelnya salient but that the army group command did not. On the following day the Russian attacks continued and the question of whether to hold Yelnya was still undecided by Army Group Center. On 21 August

Halder protested the action of Goering to Field Marshal Keitel at the High Command of the Armed Forces (OKW). By 1 September strong Soviet attacks in the Yelnya salient and to the south of it began to take on the appearance of a "regularly planned large-scale operation." On the following day, abandonment of the salient was finally decided upon by Halder, von Bock, and von Brauchitsch during a conference at the headquarters of Army Group Center. Three days later (5 September 1941) the Yelnya salient was evacuated.[47]

In 1955, Kesselring, replying to questions about the Luftwaffe's support of the Yelnya salient, stated:

> Nothing is known about the conversation of von Bock; I do not, however, consider this impossible, since at the time the Second Air Fleet, with only a part of its forces, had to support the Second Army (von Weichs) and later the Second Panzer Group (Guderian) on the right wing of von Bock's army group against enemy forces advancing in the direction of Gomel-Roslavl.

> The fact is that Guderian wanted to abandon the Yelnya salient. When I heard of that, I flew forward to the command post of the Second Panzer Group (Guderian) to discuss everything further with Guderian regarding support. However, I met only the Operations officer, to whom I explained my view that I would immediately give the armored group all possible Luftwaffe support, if the Yelnya salient could thereby be held.

> Finally I flew to my command post and immediately ordered the concentration of all flying forces in front of the Yelnya salient. The order remained in effect a few days. Inordinately soon thereafter, however, the abandonment of the Yelnya salient was ordered.[48]

A number of documents of Luftwaffe High Command (OKL) provenance describe the commitment of air units in the Yelnya area. The situation report of 31 August 1941, concerning the sector east of a line from Roslavl to Yelnya to northeast of Smolensk, bears a commentary on a resumed Soviet offensive which made use of rehabilitated units. Although these troops, supported by armored vehicles, succeeded in breaking the German main line of resistance, the offensive was halted by action of the Luftwaffe.[49]

109

Beginning early on 30 August the Russians launched renewed attacks against the German front lines south and northeast of the Yelnya River bend which were preceded by hours of artillery barrages. Tanks were used to spearhead the infantry attack. At this time three Luftwaffe bombers attacked tank concentrations and massed troops 16 to 27 miles to the southwest of Shatalovo, registering a number of hits on moving armored vehicles. Troop concentrations at the Desna bridges south of Shatalovo were struck by German bombers, several bombs landing amid massed Russian infantry units.[50]

On 4 September strong Soviet forces, supported by tanks and artillery, pressed forward an attack against the sector from Roslavl to Smolensk. According to the High Command of the Luftwaffe, the statements of Russian prisoners revealed that "several [Luftwaffe] armored battalions" had recently arrived from Asia and were "assigned to the infantry divisions to bolster their fighting power." At the same time, however, German forces made slight gains east of Velikiye Luki. In support of them were 89 dive bombers, 20 light bombers, and 1 bomber, which were used against truck and tank columns, bridges, infantry, and artillery positions in the Desna River region from Sosnitsa northward to the sector south of Yelnya.[51] The German position remained, nevertheless, precarious. On 7 September the Luftwaffe reported the abandonment of the Yelnya salient "for reasons of economy of forces." Wehrmacht units thereupon withdrew behind the Desna, with the enemy following slowly behind.[52]

The bulk of the flying units of the II Air Corps, however, remained in action in front of the Second Army and the Second Panzer Group, facing enemy forces south and southwest of Bryansk. The successful advance of the Second Army, constantly supported by forces of the air corps, proved in the final result that the Luftwaffe was correct in placing its main effort and commitment in the area west (and later east) of Gomel, to the southwest of Bryansk, and in front of the Second Army and Guderian's armored group, then advancing from Roslavl toward the south and southeast. This air effort was maintained despite the counterclaims of army command posts in the area.

A concentrated commitment of the II Air Corps in the Yelnya salient would at best have been able to achieve only a tactical defensive victory on a relatively small sector of the front. At worst, the salient could be temporarily withdrawn for a few miles without adverse operational consequences. In contrast, the concentrated employment of Luftwaffe forces in front of the Second Army and the Second Panzer Group in and east of the Gomel area enabled the right wing of Army Group Center, which was behind the others, to advance and thereby eliminated the deep Soviet wedge between Army Groups South and Center. This air action was therefore of decisive importance. After the war, General der Infanterie Kurt von Tippelskirch wrote that the Soviet forces involved consisted of 17 infantry, 1 armored, and 5 cavalry divisions, and yielded, "78,000 prisoners, 144 tanks, and 700 guns," with the remaining forces falling back to the southeast. "This victory," asserted von Tippelskirch, "was already the prelude to the great battle of annihilation around Kiev, which began on the last days of August."[53]

The II Air Corps' ceaseless direct and indirect support of the Second Army and the Second Panzer Group was a decisive contribution toward winning this northern jump-off point for the encirclement of Kiev, the greatest battle of its kind in the eastern campaign.

Antiaircraft Artillery to the Front!

Assembled in Combat Zone Center under the command of the Second Air Fleet was Generalmajor Walter von Axthelm's I Antiaircraft Artillery Corps, consisting of two motorized regiments (the 101st and 104th), each of which had three heavy battalions and one light battalion. Working in close cooperation with the Second Panzer Group, the corps was to support the breakthrough of the Soviet border fortifications, protect the armored group from air attacks during the advance, and help in breaking up all enemy resistance.

Additional heavy and light antiaircraft artillery battalions of the Luftwaffe were attached directly to the ground forces under the control of commanders of the Luftwaffe (Koluft) who were assigned to the armies, army groups, and armored groups.

When the army batteries opened fire at 0315 on 22 June, shortly before the beginning of the general attack, the batteries of the I Antiaircraft Artillery Corps also commenced firing. In direct fire the antiaircraft artillery destroyed bunkers and special pinpoint targets in the Soviet field positions and border fortifications, such as known observation posts, towers, and entrenched tanks. The flat trajectory and the high rate of fire of their guns enabled the Luftwaffe antiaircraft artillery to achieve particular success against these kinds of point targets.*

---

*See Figures 21 and 22.

Figure 21
Heavy (8. 8 cm.) antiaircraft gun supporting
ground forces against Soviet armored
attacks, Eastern Front, 1941

Figure 22

Night firing by 8.8 cm. antiaircraft gun in support of
German ground forces on the Eastern Front, 1941

Figure 23

An 88 mm. gun being pulled from the mud
by a German tank, Russia, 1941

At the opening of the general attack, the heavy and light batteries of the I Antiaircraft Artillery Corps crossed the Bug River with the first armored units. Included within the points of the armored spearheads, the batteries henceforth had as their first and most important mission the defense of the forward-rolling armored units from any air attack which would delay their advance. Although the condition of the advance routes was terrible, the antiaircraft artillery batteries had to keep pace with the armored units.[*] Wherever the leading tank was to be found, there also stood the first antiaircraft gun.

The successful destruction and crippling of the enemy flying forces by the Luftwaffe's air units in the first days of the campaign also had its effects in Combat Zone Center, with the result that enemy air attacks occurred only sporadically and in low numerical strength. Seen as a whole, the effect of these Soviet air attacks was extremely slight. Thus in the central combat zone the secondary mission of the I Antiaircraft Artillery Corps became more and more its primary task: combating Russian tanks and furnishing artillery support for the Army in action against enemy pockets of resistance. As was the case on other fronts, here, too, whenever strong enemy resistance was to be broken or hostile tanks came forward to counterattack, the call invariably resounded at all points: "Antiaircraft artillery to the front!"

Batteries of the I Antiaircraft Artillery Corps consistently provided the expected effective support. For example, a report of the High Command of the Luftwaffe on 3 July 1941 announced that from 22 to 28 June the heavy antiaircraft artillery units of the corps had brought down 21 Soviet planes, while firing an average of 28 rounds per aircraft. Fourteen planes were shot down by German light batteries, which expended 1,170 shots in the process. Two additional planes were destroyed by German quadruple 20 mm. machine guns, which fired about 200 rounds against each aircraft. The corps also destroyed 45 personnel carriers, 34 tanks, and numerous pockets of resistance manned by personnel with machine guns and antitank weapons.[54]

Other similar successes were mentioned in reports of the High Command of the Luftwaffe, which indicated the nature of the actions and the results achieved. Included in such reports were units of the I

_____

*See Figure 23.

Antiaircraft Artillery Corps, as well as antiaircraft artillery battalions assigned to the Army and under the control of commanders of the Luftwaffe (Koluft).[55]*

A particularly important victory was the repulse of persistent Soviet attempts in early July to eliminate the Borisov bridgehead or to destroy the bridge by aerial attack. The antiaircraft artillery units kept this highway bridge across the Berezina River open and intact, rendering a valuable contribution to the continued operations of the Second Panzer Group.†

Especially effective was the action of the antiaircraft artillery in the area around Bobruysk. While the battle for the town was still in progress, the Soviets continued to hold an airfield south of the town from which close support and fighter aircraft continued to operate. In a bold surprise attack antiaircraft artillery personnel seized this airfield, capturing 59 aircraft intact and a large number of damaged and destroyed aircraft, large quantities of fuel, and more than 10,000 bombs of all sizes. Desperate Soviet efforts to retake the field in counterattack failed in the face of blazing defensive fire by the antiaircraft guns.

A few days later Guderian's armored units prepared to cross the Berezina at Bobruysk. Heavy units of the antiaircraft artillery and the flying units of the 51st Fighter Wing were then alerted to protect the crossing site and river-crossing movements. From intercepted Soviet radio messages it was known that the Soviet forces had been strictly ordered to halt the German advance across the Berezina at Bobruysk at all costs, and that all bomber units based on airfields between Bobruysk and Moscow were to be concentrated in attack against the German crossing site. In fact, it was at Bobruysk that the Soviets renewed their massive bombing attacks. The bridge was bombed continuously by aircraft flying at an altitude of approximately 6,500 feet. But the assembled batteries of the 10th Antiaircraft Artillery Regiment concentrated upon the crossing site, overwhelmed the approaching bombers with sustained fire, scattered the formations, and shot down a number of planes. Groups of the 51st Fighter Wing under Colonel Moelders dived after the scattered bombers and completely destroyed them. By exemplary cooperation, the German antiaircraft

----

*See p. 111.

†See the interesting eye-witness accounts of these actions during early July 1941 in the diary of Col. Hans-Wilhelm Doering-Manteuffel, Commander of the 101st Antiaircraft Artillery Regiment, G/VI/3a, Karlsruhe Document Collection.

artillery and fighter units repulsed with heavy losses the Soviet air attacks at the crossing sites. The German armor, motorized infantry and artillery, and their supply columns continued to roll eastward over the Berezina without interruption.

The antiaircraft artillery was also effectively employed in air defense and ground combat in the later battles around Roslavl, near Gomel, and especially on the Desna near Trubchevsk (50 miles southwest of Bryansk). In the severe fighting in the Yelnya salient, the batteries of the I Antiaircraft Artillery Corps were the strong backbone of the defense of all the ground forces there for more than four long weeks.

During its combat employment between 22 June and 30 August 1941 the I Antiaircraft Artillery Corps shot down 259 airplanes, while antiaircraft artillery units under the control of Koluft Army Group Center brought down 500 aircraft and destroyed 360 armored vehicles between 22 August and 9 September.[56]

Chapter 6

KIEV

Prelude

While the entire German Eastern Front continued its fluid advance against a stubborn and tenacious enemy, a serious command crisis arose between Hitler and the Army High Command over the question of the further prosecution of the Russian campaign once the three army groups had achieved their initial objectives. As Supreme Commander of the Armed Forces, Hitler had taken a much larger part in both the strategic and tactical operations of the eastern campaign than he had in all of the preceding campaigns and operations.[1]

The greatest disagreement concerned the primary objective. Halder, von Brauchitsch, the commanding generals in Army Group Center, and the Luftwaffe's Field Marshal Kesselring adhered firmly to the goal of destroying the Soviet military power, which they believed could best be accomplished by a continued rapid drive toward, and seizure of, Moscow. Moscow was important not only because, as the seat of government, it was the symbol of the Soviet regime but also because it was an important industrial and armament center and the hub of the entire railroad system in European Russia. Its loss would mean not only a loss of prestige for the Soviet government in world opinion--one may remember the effect which the loss of Paris had in 1940 upon the French armed forces and populace--but it would also mean the loss of an important nerve center of the Soviet Union.

Kesselring, who had been the Luftwaffe commander in Combat Zone Center, declared after the war that leaders in that sector pondered over the matter of a continuation of the drive on Moscow, while the troop units, "unfortunately, stood inactive at their positions for too long a time."[2] According to Kesselring, allowing for the inevitability of bad weather and its effects in Russia, Moscow could still have been taken had Hitler not wasted costly weeks in lengthy "deliberations and secondary operations." If the drive had been continued early in September, Kesselring believed that the Soviet capital could have been captured before the arrival of both winter and the enemy's Siberian divisions. In all probability it would then have been possible to push forward a screening bridgehead to the east, which would have complicated Russian flanking maneuvers and the supply of other fronts. The capture of Moscow would have cut off European

117

Russia from its Asiatic resources, and the seizure of the economically vital city of Leningrad, the Donets Basin, and the Maykop oil region "would have been no insoluble task in 1942."3*

Hitler reasoned differently, for he wanted to operate on the flanks and seek a decision there. Furthermore, he placed the economic goals of seizing the war economy of the Leningrad area, the Ukrainian granary, the Donets Basin, and the Caucasian oil fields, and the capture of the Crimean air bases which threatened the Rumanian oil fields ahead of purely military objectives. Within Hitler's own staff, as well as in the Army High Command, this trend of thought met with opposition and serious doubts. Until late in August, the decision upon which the campaign's success might depend was sought in conferences; through new directives (often impossible to carry out); through continual admendments to the directives; and by "reciprocal memorandums."4

On 21 August, after much annoying vacillation, Hitler finally settled the dispute by issuing a directive to the Commander in Chief of the Army--Goering received a copy--which advised von Brauchitsch that the most important goal before the arrival of winter was not the capture of Moscow, which was what the Army believed to be the best strategy, but the seizure of the Crimea and the Donets Basin, "the strangulation of the Russian oil supply from the Caucasus region," the encirclement of Leningrad, and a link-up with the Finnish forces. To achieve these goals Hitler ordered adjoining units of Army Groups South and Center to attack the opposing Soviet Fifth Army, not only in order to push it from its positions behind the Dnepr River, but to destroy its forces before they could be withdrawn behind a line in the Desna-Konotop-Sula sector. Only thus could Army Group South be relatively free of danger so that it could seize a foothold east of the Dnepr and resume its advance in the direction of Rostov-on-the-Don and Kharkov. A rapid crossing of the Dnepr in the direction of the Crimea was to be made by German mobile units before Soviet reinforcements could arrive. The capture of the Crimea would provide security for the Rumanian oil fields and allow Wehrmacht forces to advance rapidly into the Caucasus, from which place the Reich could bring pressure to bear upon Iran.

North of the Pripyat marshes the Second Army (right wing) of Army Group Center was to eliminate Russian salients which bulged into its front, while the left wing of Army Group Center (Ninth Army) was to establish contact with the Twenty-Seventh Army (right wing) of Army Group

_____

*See Maps Nos. 1 and 3.

North in the high ground west of Toropets. Meanwhile the Eighteenth Army (northern wing) of Army Group North was to encircle and drive beyond Leningrad, linking up with the Finnish Army.

Only after the Soviet Fifth Army had been destroyed, Leningrad encircled, and contact made with the Finnish forces, could German military units be made available for an attack upon Moscow and against the forces of Marshal Timoshenko as had been planned in Directive No. 34 of 12 August.[5]*

A study signed by Hitler on 22 August 1941, concerning how the coming operations in the East were to be carried out, shows not only the reasoning by which Hitler rejected the Army's proposals and issued his directive of 21 August, but cites the efforts of the highest leadership of the Luftwaffe to build up concentrations of main effort. This document is not mentioned to emphasize any differences in operational concepts between the Army and the Luftwaffe, but, rather, to show that the Luftwaffe's efforts to adhere to the principle of power concentration were recognized at the highest levels of command. In the study, Hitler pointed out that the campaign was intended to eliminate Russia as a continental ally of Great Britain and as the last hope of Britain for a favorable outcome of the war. Only by annihilating Russia's armed forces and by capturing or devastating the essential economic foundation required to reorganize those forces could this objective be achieved. Hitler considered "the destruction or seizure of vital sources of raw materials" to be "more decisive than the occupation or devastation of industrial areas." Manufacturing facilities--particularly when machinery had been evacuated-- could soon be reestablished and also imported from overseas, but the replacement of coal, oil, and iron through imports was hopeless.

Thus, Soviet forces were to be destroyed, and any Soviet program of rearmament prevented "by the capture or elimination of the regions of raw materials" and the means of production. Russian naval and air forces in the Baltic region were also to be destroyed. All Russian airfields in the Black Sea area--particularly around Odessa and on the Crimean Peninsula--were to be quickly seized to prevent any fatal air attack on the vital Rumanian oil producing region and also to encourage Iran to hope for German support in the event of Anglo-Russian threats to that country. Moscow, said Hitler's study, was of far less importance than were these objectives.

---

*See Maps Nos. 1 and 3.

In order to achieve these goals, individual army groups and army commanders were to be permitted freedom of action in their operations as long as they did not compromise or endanger the overall concept of the campaign. This concept was not to be based upon "the frequently divergent views, intentions, or expectations of the individual army groups or armies," but rather, all unit commanders at the front were to "scrupulously" follow the instructions.

In this tremendous theater of war, decisive results could be achieved only by a concentration of forces in whatever sector was deemed to be of sufficient importance to the overall plan. In accordance with this idea, air and ground forces had been concentrated in Army Group Center from the beginning of the campaign--not on the assumption that final victory lay only in that area, but with the intention of breaking through the Soviet resistance at that point and, after reaching the initial Dnepr River objective tentatively chosen by Hitler, to stop and shift the two armored groups (one to the north, one to the south) for the support of operations in other parts of the front.

The hope, which was justified by later events, that the drive in the center would lead to the encirclement and annihilation of large hostile forces, led to the continuation on 3 July of the offensive of Army Group Center. But even the initial objectives had been placed so far forward that the infantry lost valuable weeks trying to reach the advanced armored units instead of using that time to destroy the power of the Soviet ground forces, with the result that the Russians were able to extricate elements of their organizations which, after rehabilitation, again stood in opposition to Army Group Center.

At the outset of the campaign it was possible for the Wehrmacht systematically to develop a power concentration to include all arms. However, in view of the great extent of the Eastern Front, it soon became clear that similar massive concentrations of power could only be developed with those arms which by their very nature were "sufficiently mobile" and maneuverable and were alone suited for such purposes. This meant that in future operations, whether on a large scale or on the basis of a single division, the decisive points upon which strong concentrations of forces must be employed had to be clearly recognized. Furthermore, the wide extent of the front would in almost every instance prevent a timely movement of infantry troops to a given area; only the motorized Army units and the Luftwaffe could concentrate and reinforce their troops in a short time over long distances. Because of this, neither the motorized ground forces nor the Luftwaffe were to be integrated into any army group, army, or air fleet, but were instead to be placed under the exclusive operational control of the supreme command.

Hitler admonished the Army to instill within its ranks an understanding of this irrevocable principle of command, just as Goering had done in the Luftwaffe. He observed that if the Army's viewpoint had prevailed over the Luftwaffe, the air forces would have been dispersed even to the army corps level and would no longer be capable of performing the tasks demanded by a continental conflict. Hitler declared that any departure from the overall concept would inevitably result in an impossible situation, forcing the Army High Command to "adjust its plans to the tactical conceptions and requirements of the individual army groups and armies." Hitler also believed that while a proper disposition of forces required lengthier preparations, it was actually a guarantee of success because time would be thereby saved which might otherwise be lost through dispersals and dispositions of units.

Hitler blamed the stalemated situation in the north on Army Group North's partial disregard of an order (which was never identified by the Fuehrer). But he saw that with the available forces, the army group could not throw its right wing around Leningrad quickly enough to encircle or destroy the city and its defenders. Units originally designated for later assignment to Army Group North (numerically the weakest of the army groups) were now ordered up, and Hitler expressed the hope that the three divisions dispatched would enable Army Group North to secure its south (right) flank. He also hinted that the quicker the reinforced army group, in cooperation with Luftwaffe units assembled by Goering, succeeded in its mission, the sooner its forces--particularly the motorized units-- could be used with those of Army Group Center to advance upon Moscow.

"Equally important, indeed more decisive," said Hitler, "was the rare opportunity presented by a Soviet force occupying a triangular-shaped, 185-mile-deep salient between Army Groups Center and South." According to Hitler, this Soviet force, surrounded by two army groups, could be destroyed if the viewpoint of the high command prevailed over that of the army groups involved. Objections by Army leaders that too much time would be lost thereby and that Wehrmacht units committed to this action would then no longer have the technical capacity to advance upon Moscow appeared to Hitler to be inconclusive when compared with the inviting opportunity at hand. The Army suggestion that the destruction of Soviet forces east of the Dnepr between Army Groups Center and South would require the assistance of Army Group South was shrugged off by Hitler with the comment that, even if the task might be easier with additional help, "it could not be overlooked or left unresolved [by the Wehrmacht] under any conditions.

Hitler did not know whether the center of the attack force, the Sixth Army of Army Group South (then stalled by the Soviet Fifth Army to its east), could force a crossing of the Dnepr River in the vicinity of Kiev or whether this problem could be solved by an attack from the south toward Mirgorod and Poltava by the Seventeenth Army (right wing) of Army Group South, thus checking Russian forces before they had made good their withdrawal to the east. To the left of the Sixth Army the Second Army of Army Group Center continued to move to the southeast toward Gomel, strengthening the southern flank of Army Group Center and tightening the ring around the Soviet forces east and west of Kiev. On the far left wing of the operation the Second Panzer Group began its drive to the south from an area around Klintsy. All armored elements of Army Group Center which were not indispensable as reserves were ordered to be sent to Army Group South for use in a drive into the Donets Basin. Such transfers of units took valuable time, however, and permitted the Russians to proceed with their withdrawal.

The tardy buildup of the right wing of the German force for the encirclement of the Kiev area prevented Army Group South's Sixth Army (the center of the attack force) from engaging the main body of the Soviet Fifth Army around Kiev. Hitler believed these delays were necessary in order to complete the destruction of the mass of enemy troops situated east and west of Kiev before they withdrew to the base line of the salient. Hitler also held that criticisms of this operation and the resulting postponement of the assault upon Moscow were invalid because the elimination of Soviet forces on the right flank of Army Group Center would enhance, rather than impair, a further advance to the east. If Soviet forces were not destroyed they would continue to threaten the southern (right) flank of Army Group Center, and serve to reinforce new Russian positions in the rear.*

In Hitler's opinion no one would have questioned the wisdom of an operation for encirclement of Russian troops east of the Dnepr if the salient near Kiev had developed at the start of the campaign, and in any case the circumstances--chiefly the opportunity to destroy a large Soviet force--did not warrant any different action. Once operations around Kiev

---

*See Maps Nos. 4, 6, 7, and 8.

had been brought to a conclusion, Hitler's promised thrust (which was not to fail in any circumstances) toward Moscow was to begin. For this offensive he considered the formation of powerful motorized armies to be indispensable, especially for operations on the flanks. These forces-- which were to be kept intact rather than dispersed--were to pause when necessary to destroy entrapped Soviet forces. Hoping that Army Group South could cross the Dnepr near Zaporozhye or Dnepropetrovsk and seize the Soviet air bases in the Crimea which threatened the Rumanian oil fields, Hitler delayed approval of the army group's proposed dispositions, which he thought prematurely determined the final direction of advance of the group's motorized units. In the event that a crossing could be achieved in a short time between Kiev and Kremenchug, motorized units of Army Group South were to rush ahead to dislodge the new Russian position or to assist in the destruction of Soviet forces still within the salient. Should this opportunity fail to materialize for Army Group South, the supreme command was to direct the completion of this task by motorized units of Army Group Center.

Hitler made the Army High Command solely responsible for implementing these assignments, just as the Commander in Chief of the Luftwaffe was to be responsible for the logical and strategically concentrated employment of the Luftwaffe.[6]

No further objection was advanced by any of the leading commands of the Wehrmacht or by the High Command of the Armed Forces itself against the new Fuehrer directive, which became binding and subsequently decisive in effect.

Coordinated Operations of Army Groups South and Center

Army Group South, in cooperation with the southern wing of Army Group Center, was to envelop and annihilate the Soviet forces remaining along the middle Dnepr and the lower Dnepr Rivers so that operations against Kharkov and the Donets Basin could continue at an early date. Operations were to proceed as follows:

(1) The First Panzer Group was to drive north from the Kremenchug bridgehead, wheel toward the Sula River section, and block the Soviet forces withdrawing from the west between Romny and Lubny. Later, the III Panzer Corps was to attack eastward from the Dnepropetrovsk bridgehead.

(2) The Seventeenth Army in the area of Kremenchug and northwest of Cherkassy, with a bridgehead east of Kremenchug, was to use

its XI Corps to block the Sula River section downstream from Lubny, Most of the army's forces, however, were to drive on Poltava to secure the line along the Vorskla River and to facilitate the later armored attack from the Dnepropetrovsk bridgehead toward the Donets Basin.

(3) The Sixth Army, deployed from north of the Seventeenth Army to north of Kiev, was to advance from its bridgehead across the Desna River near Oster and Morovsk to the Yagotin-Priluki line. The XXIX Corps was to take Kiev from the west. Army Group South was to advance in a general offensive when the envelopment from the north began to develop.

Army Group Center was to push elements of the Second Army toward Olishevka to facilitate the advance of the Sixth Army from the Morovsk bridgehead. The Second Army, which was deployed in an arc beginning west of Chernigov and running northeast to Novozybkov, with its strength concentrated on its eastern flank, was to advance through Nezhin to Lokhvitsa to intercept the Soviet forces withdrawing before the Sixth Army. The Second Panzer Group, located southwest and south of Pochep, with its main front facing south and with components constantly covering the eastern flank, was to proceed across the Bakhmach-Konotop line against Romny to close the Romen River section between Bakhmach and Romny and join forces with the First Panzer Group advancing from the south.

On 25 August 1941 the forces of Army Group Center opened their offensive to the south. German armored units drove through the boundary between the army groups of Timoshenko and Budënny and penetrated deep into the rear of Budënny's group, which had sought to protect the northern Ukraine by defending the areas north and south of Kiev and east of the Dnepr. Budënny had already lost his opportunity to achieve a planned and orderly withdrawal of his unit to the east. The Soviets, quickly recognizing the far-reaching significance of the German operations, attempted to frustrate the Wehrmacht's intentions by making a spirited defense of the Desna lowlands. After weeks of bitter fighting, the Second Army of Army Group Center advanced as far as Nezhin. On 14 September the Second Panzer Group reached Romny, 124 miles east of Kiev. Its eastern flank (which had steadily lengthened to some 136 miles) was constantly attacked by Soviet forces, especially around Trubchevsk, Yampol, and the area south of Putivl.

On 10 September Army Group South's First Panzer Group and Seventeenth Army moved out of the Kremenchug bridgehead toward the northeast, north, and northwest. Six days later at Lokhvitsa the First

Panzer Group joined components of the Second Panzer Group advancing from the north. The ring was closed around five Soviet armies. Now began the actual encirclement battle of Kiev, the greatest battle of annihilation in the entire Russian campaign.

The Seventeenth Army advanced its right wing to Poltava to cover the east flank of the First Panzer Group, while other strong elements of the Seventeenth Army wheeled to the northwest. At the same time, the Sixth Army of Army Group South attacked across the Dnepr River on both sides of Kiev, isolating that Soviet strong point, and on 19 September the city and fortress were taken. The autumn mud season seriously hampered the movements of the armies, especially the smooth advance of the armored groups. Nevertheless, the ring around Budënny's armies grew steadily tighter and stronger. German infantry forces finally compressed the enemy into the Kiev-Cherkassy-Lokhvitsa area, while the armored units beat off Soviet counterattacks from the east which sought to relieve the pocket. These armored forces also drove repeatedly into the pocket, dividing it into still smaller pockets.

Although in some areas strong Soviet forces were destroyed to the last man in bitter hand-to-hand fighting, the number of prisoners taken in the encirclement seemed incredibly large. Yet, all reports of prisoners taken and material captured were later confirmed. When this encirclement battle ended around 26 September, the Germans had captured 665,000 prisoners, 3,718 guns, 884 tanks, and immense quantities of other materiel.*

Did the results of this tremendous battle confirm the views of Hitler or those of his generals as to how the war on the Eastern Front should be fought? After the war, General der Infanterie von Tippelskirch declared that "the magnitude of the local success spoke for Hitler. Yet, only the outcome of the entire campaign could show whether the extent of the tactical victory . . . stood in correct proportion to the resultant loss of time for the continuance of the operations. If the objective of the campaign was not achieved, therefore, the Russians had indeed lost a battle, but won the campaign."[7] Generaloberst Guderian, Commander of the Second Panzer Group during the Kiev battle, later acknowledged that the battle had been "a great tactical success," but he doubted that the tactical victory "would also produce great strategic results." It was vital for German forces to achieve decisive results before the onset

---

*See Maps Nos. 6, 7, and 8. See also Figure 24.

Figure 24
The endless mass of Soviet prisoners,
encirclement battle of Kiev, 1941

Figure 25
Air interdiction of the Kiev pocket, 1941

126

of the autumn mud period or of winter, and although the planned operation for a tighter siege of Leningrad already had had to be abandoned, the Army High Command believed that the Soviets could not establish effective defensive positions in the South and that Army Group South could win the Donets Basin and reach the Don before the arrival of winter. The main effort, however, was to be directed at Moscow with the reinforced Army Group Center. Some army commanders, like Guderian, questioned whether there was still time for that.[8]

The Luftwaffe Shatters Budĕnny's Armies

In the gigantic encirclement battle at Kiev units of two air fleets were for the first time required to support the coordinated operations of the several armies and panzer units of two army groups, South and Center. Over a million Soviet soldiers with a vast quantity of materiel were enclosed within a pocket of some 15,440 square miles.

The Luftwaffe supported ground operations by air reconnaissance, establishment of air superiority over the battlefield, isolation of the pocket against external Soviet counteraction, and by direct attacks against the entrapped enemy ground forces. Air reconnaissance units supplied the Army and Luftwaffe commands with essential data for the evaluation of strategic and tactical situations, thus permitting a timely commitment of forces in an auspicious strategic or tactical direction. Enemy positions inside and outside the pocket from which relief attacks might be launched were kept under constant surveillance by German airmen.

The fighter units, achieving air superiority over the battlefield, prevented any serious Soviet air interference with German ground forces and protected close support units of the Luftwaffe as they carried out successful, devastating, and virtually undisturbed attacks against Russian troops and materiel in the pocket.

Luftwaffe bomber units isolated the battlefield against Soviet ground intervention by continuous (and effective) attacks against the roads and railways leading into the pocket from the southeast, east, and northeast. By making constant sorties against rail junctions and highway traffic centers, by repeated interdiction of track sections and the destruction of numerous trains, and by the destruction of bridges, these bombers also complicated or prevented both the advance of Soviet reserves attempting to break the encirclement and the escape of sizable forces from the pocket. The German isolation of the Kiev pocket was exemplary, with the bombers of the V Air Corps (Fourth Air Fleet) operating from the

Kirovograd area in the south and those of the II Air Corps (Second Air Fleet) operating from north of Gomel and Orsha in the north.[9]*

The Right Wing of the Pincer Movement

The First Panzer Group, advancing rapidly from the south under the constant support of the Close Support Air Commander and fighter units of the V Air Corps (Fourth Air Fleet) reached Lokhvitsa to join elements of the 3rd Panzer Division of Guderian's Second Panzer Group of Army Group Center. In an earlier desperate move the Soviets, using the only rail line still in their hands, the line from Romodan to Poltava, attempted to transport as much supplies, equipment, and personnel as possible to the east, saving whatever could still be saved. Trains-- heavy rail movements--were observed moving within sight of each other. In extremely heavy attacks on this rail line and against Soviet troops marching on both sides of the roads, the long-range bombers of the V Air Corps inflicted severe losses, in particular upon elements which had already escaped east of the Khorol-Lokhvitsa line.[10] At the same time, units of the Close Support Air Commander of the V Air Corps attacked enemy columns and field positions in the Lubny-Lokhvitsa- Priluki-Yagotin and the Akhtryrka-Gadyach-Mirgorod areas.

A series of local Soviet attempts to effect a breakthrough in the Lubny area were smashed with the support of V Air Corps units. A critical situation which developed in the Lubny-Lokhvitsa area, because of the inadequate strength of the advance German ground forces (First Panzer Group of Army Group South) was equalized only by the Luftwaffe. Further, units of the Seventeenth Army (right wing) of Army Group South had to prevent the formation of a new Soviet force in the Mirgorod- Gadyach-Akhtyrka-Poltava area (made up of elements which had escaped the pocket and reinforcements from the east), since such a force, under energetic leadership, could undoubtedly be capable of delivering promising relief attacks from the Mirgorod-Gadyach area toward the Sula River sector. At the same time, the Seventeenth Army, attacking toward Poltava, also would be supported by these air attacks. Long-range bomber forces of the V Air Corps, therefore, repeatedly struck at the numerous withdrawing Soviet columns in this area, preventing them from reorganizing their units and reestablishing their defenses and forcing them to retreat in disorder to the Kharkov-Akhtyrka area, leaving some elements around Poltava. German fighter pilots were

---

*See Maps Nos. 6 and 7. See also Figures 25 and 26.

Figure 26
Damage to Russian materiel
in the Kiev pocket, 1941

very successful in establishing air superiority over the Soviet air arm in the battle area, and by 14 September had shot down 44 enemy aircraft. In addition, V Air Corps units in this period destroyed 560 trucks and 3 tanks, damaged 267 trucks, destroyed or badly damaged 17 trains, and repeatedly interrupted traffic on 5 railroad lines. Further continuous bombing of the Soviet air bases at Kharkov and Poltava destroyed large numbers of aircraft.

After the completion of the envelopment, the enemy divisions within the pocket were attacked daily by waves of aircraft. The Soviet command was no longer in a position to employ its troops in organized operations and to force a way through the iron ring. With the increasing contraction of the pocket, dive bombers were able to attack dense concentrations of enemy troops and vehicles, inflicting exceedingly heavy casualties.

At this point a fuel shortage, which had threatened for days in the area of the Fourth Air Fleet, exerted such an extremely adverse effect upon operations that on 16 and 17 September only a few bombers could be sent into action. Repeated requests to the air fleet by the V Air Corps, asking for timely and sufficient fuel supplies, were futile, even after the air fleet had begun to exert its influence in the matter, since the tremendous distances and inadequate available transport space did not allow a smoothly functioning supply system. Nor was an adequate reserve of supplies to be expected at the airfields in the near future.

On 18 September the German Sixth Army began its offensive to the east. Its XXIX Army Corps was to capture the Kiev citadel after breaching the fortified defense system. As always, air attacks were to soften up the fortress for the ground attack. General der Artillerie Fritz Brand (OKH) declared that Kiev was to be reduced to "rubble and ashes" and the Luftwaffe was to do "half of the work."[11] For this attack, therefore, the V Air Corps transferred the III Group of the 77th Dive Bomber Wing and the III Group of the 52nd Fighter Wing to Belaya Tserkov. Bunkers and artillery positions in the fortress approaches and fortifications on Lysa Hill were successfully attacked, enabling the ground forces to advance quickly and to capture the fortress around noon on 19 September.[12]

The dive bombers, now sent in to break the last bitter resistance and to annihilate the pocketed enemy forces, struck very dense masses of troops, vehicles, and equipment of all kinds around Borispol, Voronkov, and Staroye. On 29 September alone, at least 920 vehicles were definitely destroyed and extraordinarily heavy and unprecedented losses of men and materiel were inflicted upon the enemy. A later inspection of the battle-field impressively confirmed the chaotic and destructive impact of the air attacks. Prisoners agreed that Soviet combat morale had long been declining because of the Luftwaffe. The commander in chief of the Sixth Army, while visiting the completely demolished Borispol, saw the annihilating effects of the dive bomber attacks on closely massed Russian forces--in some instances, eight columns of vehicles had been moving abreast--and recognized the merits of the Luftwaffe in quickly breaking Soviet resistance in sectors of main effort and, especially, in facilitating the swift continuation of operations.

In summation, the following comments can be made with respect to the fighting along the southern half of the Kiev pocket:

(1) Even before the actual battle of annihilation began at Kiev, ceaseless day and night attacks by V Air Corps units against the rail lines to the east decisively delayed the timely withdrawal of strong Soviet forces from the Kiev area and weakened the enemy through continuous disruption and destruction of his supplies.

(2) The V Air Corps enabled the Seventeenth Army to establish the bridgehead at Kremenchug which was decisive for the envelopment movement and contributed positively to the rapid advance of the First Panzer Group northward until it made contact with the Second Panzer Group.

(3) Before the ring was closed between Lubny and Lokhvitsa, the Luftwaffe prevented the withdrawal of substantial Russian forces toward Kharkov.

(4) A developing Russian threat to the flanks and rear in the Mirgorod-Gadyach area was nipped in the bud.

(5) The contraction of the pocket, as well as the swift capture of the Kiev fortress, was in large measure due to the work of the close support units of the V Air Corps.

(6) The annihilation of the entrapped Soviet masses within the area southeast of Kiev represented the high point which was achieved up to that time in the destructive effectiveness of the bomber and dive bomber.

During the battle around Kiev (12 to 21 September) the V Air Corps flew 1,422 sorties and dropped 1,251,440 pounds of bombs, 96 containers, each holding a number of incendiary bombs (Brandbomben-Schuett-Kasten 36), and 1 1/2 racks of propaganda leaflets, with the following results: (1) 65 aircraft of the Soviet Union were shot down with 42 more being destroyed on the ground; (2) 23 tanks, 2,171 motor vehicles, 6 antiaircraft artillery batteries, 52 railroad trains, 28 locomotives, and 1 bridge were destroyed; (3) 355 motor vehicles and 36 trains were damaged; (4) 41 horse-drawn vehicles were damaged or destroyed; and (5) 18 sections of railroad track were broken up. At the same time, German Air Force personnel losses were limited to 4 officers killed and 3 missing, and 5 noncommissioned officers and airmen killed, with 15 missing and 5 wounded. Aircraft losses were also low, with 17 planes destroyed, 9 receiving over 30 percent damage, and 5 with less than 30 percent damage.[13]*

The Left Wing of the Pincer Movement

In the northern area of the Kiev pocket the II Air Corps of the Second Air Fleet supported the advance of the Second Army and, more especially, of the Second Panzer Group (later Second Panzer Army) of Army Group Center. After heavy fighting, the ground forces, aided by strong air support, crossed the Desna River--its wide, marshy banks formed a difficult natural obstacle--and broke through the enemy field positions on the far shore. While the II Air Corps employed its bomber units en masse against railroads, units of the II Close Support Air Commander rendered invaluable assistance to the Second Panzer Group in its drives on Konotop and, later, on Romny.[14]

Dive bomber and ground attack units, cooperating directly with Guderian's armored corps and divisions, repeatedly broke local Soviet resistance which attempted desperately to hold the German spearheads and the enveloping flanks. These air units also effectively supported the ground defenses against massed Soviet attempts to break out through the weaker positions on the northern and eastern fronts of the pocket. In addition, through waves of attacks, which inflicted exceedingly high losses on the Russian forces within the steadily contracting pocket, these units contributed much to break the will and destroy the fighting power of the entrapped armies. The strong and diversified character of these sorties is shown by the following reports and observations:

---

*See Maps Nos. 6 and 7.

132

After the war, General Guderian commented on the effectiveness of the Luftwaffe, remarking that while visiting an artillery forward observation post on the north bank of the Rog [Rozhok] River on 26 August to observe the impact of the dive bombers on Soviet positions defending the river, he noted that although the bombs were well aimed little damage was done. "Nevertheless, the morale effect, which held the Russians down in their foxholes, permitted the river to be crossed almost without losses."[15]

On 10 September, General Halder wrote with regard to Army Group Center that the Second Panzer Group had taken Romny and was advancing towards its First Panzer Group counterpart (v. Kleist). Halder thought it curious that the Second Panzer Group had not been attacked on its eastern flank, and thought that perhaps "the numerous destructions of railroads by our Luftwaffe are a part of it."[16]

The High Command of the Luftwaffe report for 2 October mentioned the outstanding performances of the 3rd and 53rd Bomber Wings of the II Air Corps and listed the severe destruction which they had wreaked upon Russian targets between 22 June and 9 September. The 3rd Bomber Wing, for example, accounted for 21 planes in the air and 450 more on the ground. It also destroyed 30 tanks, 488 motor and other vehicles, 349 railroad trains, 7 armored trains, and 14 bridges, while it interrupted rail traffic 332 times. In addition, 290 sorties were flown against troop concentrations, columns, barracks, 21 supply depots, and 27 artillery and field positions, while 1,334,000 propaganda leaflets were dropped over enemy lines.[17]

The highly effective results achieved by the 210th Ground Attack Wing (II Air Corps) between 22 June and 27 September were also noted by the OKL. During this time the wing shot down 96 Soviet aircraft and destroyed 741 more on the ground; it also destroyed 148 tanks, 166 artillery pieces, 3,280 motor and other vehicles, 49 railroad trains, 1 armored train, 68 locomotives, and 4 bridges. The wing was also able to silence 47 artillery batteries, to cut repeatedly seven railroad lines, and to successfully carry out numerous attacks upon troop units, positions, depots, and cantonments.[18]*

Also mentioned by the High Command of the Luftwaffe was the performance of the 51st Fighter Wing (II Air Corps), which on 8 September

---

*Attacks made with Me-110 two-engine fighters, equipped with SD-2 fragmentation bombs (each bomb weighing 4 1/2 pounds). See Figure 26.

1941 achieved its 2,001st air victory. The figure includes victories on both the Western and Eastern fronts. By 10 September, on the Russian front alone, the wing had shot down 1,357 planes and had destroyed 298 more on the ground. In 354 strafing attacks by the unit on Soviet airfields, columns, battery positions, troop concentrations, railroad installations, and other targets, the wing successfully helped to overthrow enemy resistance, "destroying 142 tanks and armored cars, 16 guns, 34 locomotives, 432 trucks, 75 vehicles of various types, and 1 armored train."[19]

Luftwaffe antiaircraft artillery--incorporated with the advance assault troops--defended the ground forces, especially the armored spearheads, against attacks by Soviet ground attack aircraft along the entire front of the encirclement. In ground fighting the antiaircraft artillery fought against pockets of resistance and provided valuable defensive firepower against enemy armor attempting to break out or to counterattack. Many local crises were mastered by committing anti-aircraft artillery batteries to ground combat.[20]

An outstanding example of the effective employment of antiaircraft artillery against ground targets is that of the 104th Antiaircraft Artillery Regiment, commanded by Col. Hermann Lichtenberger. On 18 September 1941, Soviet forces, supported by numerous tanks, attempted to break through the thin ring encircling the Kiev pocket just east of Romny. Only two weak battalions of the German 10th Infantry Division (Motorized) were then available to repel the attack, and Generaloberst Guderian (who, on 16 September, had shifted the command post of his Second Panzer Group from Konotop to Romny) requested help from Generalmajor von Axthelm, commanding the I Antiaircraft Artillery Corps. The latter, whose command staff had arrived at Romny on the morning of the 17th, summoned by radio the batteries of the 104th Antiaircraft Artillery Regiment, then situated five miles northwest of Romny. These units, led by Lichtenberger, arrived through the mud and immediately went into action against the decisive Soviet tank assault, made by T-34 tanks, then already within a half mile of the city. As the batteries arrived on the scene, they began by rapid firing to simulate a superiority in firepower. On the front line, unsupported by infantry, the batteries provided their own infantry cover from supply train personnel, while their guns neutralized several Soviet batteries and set numerous tanks on fire. The 104th Antiaircraft Artillery Regiment thereby succeeded in crippling and delaying the strong Russian attacks until elements of the SS-Panzer Division "Das Reich" and the 4th Panzer Division could arrive. On 19 September and during the following days the Russian forces were thrown back with heavy tank losses. The regiment received the thanks of Guderian and the plaudits of the High

134

Command. Colonel Lichtenberger and Captain Fahlbusch, one of his battery commanders, were awarded the Knight's Cross of the Iron Cross.[21]

The heavy commitment of antiaircraft artillery batteries and flying units of the Second and Fourth Air Fleets in support of army operations helped materially to accelerate the Wehrmacht advance in the East. This support was given despite adverse conditions, and was of crucial importance because every day gained for operations was essential if the objectives of the campaign were to be achieved before the onset of winter.

Chapter 7

FIRST AIR FLEET OPERATIONS IN ARMY GROUP NORTH AREA

Operations of Army Group North

At the beginning of the Russian Campaign, Army Group North, commanded by Field Marshal Wilhelm Ritter von Leeb, was committed to action with the Sixteenth Army on the right (south) and the Eighteenth Army on the left (north). Behind the adjacent wings of the two armies stood the Fourth Panzer Group, ready to make a breakthrough. Army Group North, numerically the weakest of the three great army groups on the Eastern Front, controlled 20 infantry, 3 motorized infantry, and 3 armored divisions. Its mission consisted of three principal tasks: to destroy Soviet forces deployed in the Baltic region; to seize the Baltic ports; and to capture Leningrad and Kronshtadt, thereby depriving the Soviet Navy of its bases.[1]

Because of the location of the Russo-German border in the northern area and the consequent lack of large areas for troop concentrations, there would be from the first no opportunity to carry out (as did Army Group Center) a large-scale envelopment of Russian forces. Therefore, after breaking through the border positions Army Group North would rely upon advancing a strong right wing, preceded by hard-hitting mobile units, to reach as quickly as possible the Opochka-Pskov area, where it was to check the withdrawal of Soviet units from the Baltic region and thus open the way for the continued rapid advance on Leningrad. OKW Directive No. 21 of 18 December 1940 provided that Army Group Center was to support these operations by wheeling mobile units from the Smolensk area toward the northeast.[2*]

The Soviet forces in front of Army Group North were deeply echeloned. Under Marshal Kliment Efremovich Voroshilov, seven infantry divisions were deployed in the relatively weak border fortifications. To the rear 22 infantry and 2 cavalry divisions and 6 motorized-mechanized brigades were concentrated in separate groups in the Wilno-Kaunas area, around Siauliai, and in and south of the Pskov area.[3]

---

*See Maps Nos. 3, 4, 8, and 9.

The weak border defenses were quickly breached on 22 June. Advancing on a broad front, units of Generaloberst Erich Hoeppner's Fourth Panzer Group reached the Dvina River at Daugavpils on 26 June and established a bridgehead.* One corps of the unit was temporarily held up near Kedainyai, north of Kaunas, by heavy Soviet tank attacks. Following behind in forced marches were the Sixteenth Army under Generaloberst Ernst Busch and the Eighteenth Army under Generaloberst Georg von Kuechler, the latter unit occupying Riga, Latvia, on 29 June.[4]

The northern wing of the Fourth Panzer Group, leading the field, captured Pskov on 9 July, and on the following day its southern wing reached Opochka. The Eighteenth Army mopped up the southern Baltic region against slight enemy resistance, occupying Liepāja (Libau), Latvia, on 28 June and Ventspils on 1 July. By 10 July one army corps had reached the Tartu-Pärnu line.

Up to this time, Army Group North had not been able to envelop and destroy the strong enemy forces at hand. The Soviet front had given way in all sectors as the German forces sought to come to grips with Russian armies. According to an entry in his diary on 23 June, Halder thought that the Soviets had long prepared to withdraw, probably behind the Dvina River. Russian resistance did not begin to stiffen until the Wehrmacht crossed over the old pre-1939 Soviet border south of Lake Peipus.[5]

Since 11 July 1941 Finnish troops had been attacking on the isthmus toward Leningrad, and on 13 July Army Group North also resumed its drive toward that city. Although the Finns' attack tied down considerable Soviet forces, enabling the northern wing of Army Group North to make good progress, a dangerously deep and open flank developed on the southern wing of the army group, which was advancing in a general northeasterly direction. The army group's right wing was behind the general advance, and a steadily widening gap developed between Army Groups Center and North, constituting a grave source of danger to both army groups. Soviet movements in this area had to be watched continuously. Halder noted on 4 July that a Soviet movement was proceeding from Moscow into the area west of Velikiye Luki and therefore "between the inner wings of Hoth and Hoeppner," while a second Soviet advance was moving northward around Lake Ilmen into the Pskov area.[6]

---

*See Figures 27 and 28.

Figure 27
The Dvina bridge and Daugavpils,
Latvia, in June 1941

Figure 28
Air view of the fortress of Daugavpils,
Latvia, June 1941

138

But Army Group Center constantly required all of its forces to clear up the critical situations developing on its extended flanks and so could not support Army Group North by wheeling mobile units north or northeast, as had been stipulated in the basic operational directive.[7] In the meantime, the High Command of the Armed Forces had ordered that Army Group North would have to perform its assigned tasks with its own forces alone.[8]

The Eighteenth Army cleared Latvia and Estonia, but the bulk of the enemy force was able to fall back across the Narva River before the Fourth Panzer Group (which, on 17 August, had taken the city of Narva from the south) could close the narrow stretch of land between Lake Peipus and the Gulf of Finland.

The Sixteenth Army had to cover the Eighteenth Army's drive on Leningrad against attacks from the east or southeast. On 10 August the Sixteenth Army occupied Kholm and, after very heavy fighting, established a defensive front at Staraya Russa on the Lovat River. A surprise attack by strong Soviet forces across the Lovat led to a very serious crisis, particularly in view of the fact that large Russian units had turned abruptly to the north. In cooperation with Fourth Panzer Group tank units (which were rushed south from Luga) and an armored corps from the left flank of Army Group Center, the units already in the area were able to restore the situation and destroy the Soviet group in bitter combat along the western slopes of the Valdai Hills. During this fighting the Sixteenth Army advanced its southern (right) wing to a line extending from Ostashkov to the eastern shore of Lake Ilmen. Driving ahead to Petrokrepost (Schluesselburg) the Eighteenth Army sealed off all eastern and southeastern approaches to Leningrad. It was hoped that with Finnish support the city could be encircled and captured.

By the end of August, Army Group North had inflicted heavy losses upon the enemy, but it had not achieved a genuine strategic victory. In the early days of September the Eighteenth Army had forged ahead as far as the Neva River east of Leningrad and thus occupied the entire southern coast of the Gulf of Finland, except for a Soviet bridgehead around Lomonosov (Oranienbaum) and pressed forward to encircle heavily fortified Leningrad. The attack on the eastern and southeastern outer perimeter defenses, which began on 5 September, brought favorable results, and on 8 September Petrokrepost was taken by assault.[9]

A joint Army-Navy-Luftwaffe operation launched on 14 September against the Baltic islands of Muhu, Saaremaa, and Hiiumaa was successfully concluded on 21 October. A more detailed treatment of this operation appears later in this chapter.

In mid-September the Fourth Panzer Group and the armored corps of the Third Panzer Group (brought up from the south a few weeks before to support the Sixteenth Army) were disengaged from Army Group North and transferred to Army Group Center for the planned operation against Moscow, an action which seriously weakened Army Group North. Halder recorded on 5 September that during a Fuehrer conference held that day it had been announced that the Leningrad objective had been achieved, that henceforth the city would be a secondary theater of operations, and that all armored and Luftwaffe units were to be transferred elsewhere. Moreover, it had been decided that, in an impossibly few days, an attack--in which the role of the Sixteenth Army was obscure--was to be launched against Marshal Timoshenko's forces. That evening a discussion between Col. Adolf Heusinger, Generalleutnant Friedrich Paulus, and Halder brought forth the conclusion that the attack could not be undertaken before the end of September.[10]

Despite being severely weakened, Army Group North continued its attack early in October and, after breaking through the Volkhov front with elements of the Sixteenth Army, pushed forward in stubborn, bitter combat as far as Tikhvin. However, the southern wing bogged down in front of the Valdai Hills in the face of strong Russian resistance.

Under the pressure of a very heavy Soviet counteroffensive the spearhead of the Sixteenth Army, which had been pushed forward as far as Tikhvin, had to be withdrawn in December of 1941 to a defensive position on the west bank of the Volkhov. The Eighteenth Army established contact on the Volkhov, and Petrokrepost remained in German hands. On Christmas Day 1941 an apparent halt to the fighting came over the entire front of Army Group North.[11]

Operations of the First Air Fleet

Mission

Under the command of Generaloberst Alfred Keller,* the First Air Fleet (with its headquarters at Norkitten, some 12 miles west of Insterburg)✝ in coordination with Army Group North, was to: (1) destroy

---

*See Figure 29.
✝East Prussia, annexed by the Soviet Union and renamed Chernyakhovsk.

Figure 29
Generaloberst Keller, ready to fly to one of his
First Air Fleet units, Russia, 1941

the enemy flying forces in its combat zone and thereby gain air superiority; (2) create conditions which would permit the units of Army Group North, particularly the Fourth Panzer Group, to advance quickly upon Leningrad; and (3) attack the Soviet Navy in its Baltic bases, in Kronshtadt and Leningrad. Under the air fleet's control were the I Air Corps under General der Flieger Helmuth Foerster and Luftwaffe Commander Baltic, Col. Wolfgang von Wild. With these forces the First Air Fleet intended to: (1) attack all occupied Soviet airfields within the range of its own bombers, operating against Russian aircraft in the air and on the ground, to prevent any counter-air activity against German Army operations; (2) provide fighter protection for the advancing ground forces, especially armored units, against possible enemy air attack; (3) interdict Soviet highway and railroad traffic; (4) attack the Soviet Baltic Fleet at sea and in its bases with bombs and mines, tie up merchant shipping in the Baltic, and stop traffic through the White Sea-Baltic Canal (Stalin Canal), the last task to be accomplished mainly by destroying the lock installations at Povenets, the highest locks (about 328 feet above sea level) of the canal, thus preventing the transfer of some 45 submarines, about 15 destroyers, and various mine-laying vessels from the Gulf of Finland to the Arctic Ocean; (5) directly and indirectly support the ground forces with bombers; and (6) attack the Soviet air armament industry, concentrating on Leningrad.

Special antiaircraft artillery forces in the form of an antiaircraft artillery corps or a division were not available to the First Air Fleet in 1941 as they were to the air fleets in Combat Zones Center and South. Instead, the Luftwaffe antiaircraft artillery battalions and regiments were assigned to the Luftwaffe commanders (Koluft) attached to the headquarters of Army Group North, the Sixteenth and Eighteenth Armies, and particularly the Fourth Panzer Group. Their primary task was to provide antiaircraft protection for the armored spearheads and the main advance routes, especially at river crossing sites. Only in cases of emergency were these units to be employed in ground combat.

First Air Fleet Operations in the Baltic Area, 22 June to early August 1941

All bomber units of the First Air Fleet took off in clear weather about 0230 on 22 June from their East Prussian bases and crossed the border between 0300 and 0330 to attack the identified Soviet operational airfields. Air and ground reconnaissance had presented a clear picture of the condition of the Soviet flying forces, their strength, their composition, and the garrisoning of their air bases. This data was continually checked and amplified with great success by the long-range reconnaissance squadrons.[12]

In Combat Zone North the opening attacks of the First Air Fleet units took the Russians completely by surprise. A great part of the Soviet flying units were destroyed by these attacks and by those which took place during the following few days. Assessments made after the capture of the area yielded the same picture of tremendous destruction as had been found in Combat Zones South and Center. Many hundreds of wrecked aircraft were found, mostly I-16 Rata fighters but also numerous so-called Martin bombers (SB-3's), burned out and torn to shreds on the airfields which had been plowed up thoroughly by German bombs of all sizes. The field installations, mostly of wood construction, were burned out or otherwise destroyed. As a result, the Luftwaffe construction troops and the German Labor Service (Reichsarbeitsdienst) battalions later had to work long and hard to restore these airfields and to remove the gigantic quantities of debris.

Through these annihilating blows, the First Air Fleet achieved air superiority within the first few days in its zone of operations and induced the Russians to transfer their remaining air units behind the Dvina River. Then, the emphasis in air fleet operations shifted to the support of Army Group North's advance toward the Dvina, with the main effort over the sectors of the armored spearhead of the Fourth Panzer Group. By 1 July the Wehrmacht reached the Dvina on a broad front, and the cities of Riga, Jēkabpils, and Daugavpils were captured, with bridgeheads being successfully established at these places.* The I Air Corps performed a particularly valuable service to the ground forces by shattering a Soviet counterattack, heavily supported by tanks, in the area south and southwest of Siauliai. In close cooperation with the Army, the air arm destroyed more than 250 tanks.[13]

From the beginning of the Russian campaign, single planes and formations of planes of the enemy flew over East Prussian territory. These were so effectively met by German antiaircraft artillery and fighters that after some three to four days no substantial penetration by Soviet aircraft occurred. Reports of the High Command of the Luftwaffe describing these air penetrations show, for example, that on 22 June some 70 to 80 Russian aircraft, deployed in a number of raids, flew over German territory and occupied Poland, damaging some property and killing and injuring a few civilians. On the following day, 10 Soviet

---

*See Figures 27 and 28.

bombers slightly damaged the gas works and the wharf area at Koenigsberg. On 25 June some 28 Russian planes made bombing attacks over Germany, occupied Poland, and Norway; eight planes hit Memel (Klaipěda), killing 23 persons, leaving 250 homeless, damaging houses and a chemical factory, partially interrupting electric power and the water supply, and mining the harbor. However, seven Soviet planes which attacked Tilsit were shot down before they reached their targets.[14]

The superiority of German fighters over Soviet bombers was especially impressive when an entire formation of 20 enemy bombers, returning from a largely ineffective attack on Gumbinnen, was intercepted and shot down between Gumbinnen and Goldap by a fighter group based at Trakehnen.* A few hours later the first Soviet prisoners were interrogated by the air fleet intelligence officer and their statements were immediately evaluated for the next German sorties. A Soviet bomber formation of 43 planes was completely destroyed in the same way a short time later by fighters of the I Air Corps, and during the daylight hours of 4 July fighter and twin-engine fighter units shot down another 20 out of 25 bombers which were attacking the advance units of an armored group.[15]

Units of the Luftwaffe Commander Baltic carried out continuous attacks against enemy shipping and mined the waters of the Baltic Sea around Kronshtadt. On 29 June a 2,200-pound Luftwaffe high-explosive bomb struck a lock gate of the White Sea-Baltic Canal, which interrupted all traffic over that route.

On 2 July Army Group North attacked from its bridgeheads east of the Dvina and breached the old Russian border fortifications. A week later, the advance reached a line extending generally from Opochka through Ostrov, Pskov, and Tartu to Pärnu, and the flying units of the I Air Corps were moved forward to bases in the Daugavpils-Riga area. On the first day of this offensive the First Air Fleet supported the attack against the Soviet fortifications in this sector, but on the second day shifted its operations mainly to the interdiction of Soviet retrograde movements by rail and road. This action against the Russian defenses east of Pskov greatly aided the German advance.

_____

*The northern half of East Prussia, seized by the Russians in World War II, has been incorporated into the Soviet Union. Thus Tilsit is now Sovetsk, Gumbinnen is Gusev, and Trakehnen is probably Anderskemen. Goldap was given by the Allies to Poland. De jure recognition has never been given to these acquisitions, which are tied in with the problem of the final settlement of Germany's boundaries and the "Cold War."

At the bridgehead across the Velikaya River at Ostrov another very heavy attack by Soviet bomber units was repulsed on 6 July with 65 of the 73 bombers being shot down. After this costly defeat the Soviets desisted from further attacks in large formations.

On 14 July the High Command of the Luftwaffe reported that between 22 June and 13 July the I Air Corps had shot down 487 Soviet planes and destroyed 1,211 aircraft on the ground, a victory which prevented an effective intervention by Soviet flying forces. The 1st Bomber Wing,* moreover, had carried out "particularly effective attacks" while directly and indirectly supporting Army operations. Similar support was rendered to the German Navy by the 806th Coastal Group under Lieutenant Colonel Emig.[16]/

By 30 July the right wing (the Sixteenth Army) of Army Group North reached Lake Ilmen. In the center, the Fourth Panzer Group, driving on Luga, had encountered south of that city a strongly organized fortification system in which the enemy tenaciously resisted. For weeks the Sixteenth Army had a major problem, for until mid-August all supplies had to be brought forward by transport planes, since the only road extending from Pskov to Gdov was repeatedly closed by scattered, but still fighting, Soviet forces in the almost impenetrable forests. The High Command of the Luftwaffe reported on 29 June that since 23 June bombers had daily supplied the advancing armored units, Army reconnaissance aircraft, and airfields with ammunition, fuel, and aircraft weapons.[17] The OKL report of 6 July noted that on the previous day the Army and the Luftwaffe had been supplied by air "with fuel, aircraft ammunition, replacement parts for fighters, rations, communication equipment, [and] medical supplies, as well as . . . news."[18]

Meanwhile, Army Group North's left wing (Eighteenth Army) had pushed forward from Riga to the Gulf of Finland and to Pärnu on the east side of the Gulf of Riga. The First Air Fleet supported this advance, concentrating its units with the Fourth Panzer Group. With the exception of targets immediately ahead of the forward armored units, strong Luftwaffe bomber forces attacked the highway and railroad traffic northeast and east of Pskov, while other bomber units were employed against rail traffic in Estonian territory and on the Leningrad-Moscow railroad.[19]

---

*Attached to the I Air Corps.

/The 806th Coastal Group was attached to the Luftwaffe Commander Baltic. The group's commander, Colonel Emig, was killed in action during this operation.

145

The important railroad junction at Bologoye, always heavily occupied by 20 to 30 locomotives and 1,600 to 1,800 freight cars, was successfully attacked in several operations, especially those of 25 and 27 July. Counter-air operations were also carried out against Soviet airfields around Leningrad and in the Lake Ilmen region.

Small Russian forces scattered behind the front in very thinly settled and generally marshy areas had to be constantly eradicated by difficult guerrilla warfare. The monotony of the landscape and the extremely poor and inaccurate maps placed extraordinarily high demands upon the orientation abilities of the I Air Corps crews committed to operations in these areas.

In the meantime, units of the Luftwaffe Commander Baltic continued their operations against the Soviet Navy and merchant shipping and laid mines in the Gulf of Finland. For example, on 11 August it was reported that bombers operating against Soviet warships and merchant-men had severely damaged two destroyers, sunk a 2,000-ton merchant vessel, and damaged a 3,000-ton merchantman so badly that it was a total loss.[20]*

A Reinforced First Air Fleet Supports Army Group North Operations Against Leningrad†

In OKW Directive No. 34 of 30 July 1941 Adolf Hitler ordered a continuance of the attack on Leningrad. The order concentrated on the attacking forces between Narva and Lake Ilmen in order to "surround Leningrad and establish contact with the Finnish Army." The Luftwaffe was to shift its main attack operations to the northeastern front by the transfer of the VIII Air Corps to the First Air Fleet. This change was to be made in time for the beginning of Army Group North's main attack, early on 6 August.[21]

Pursuant to these instructions, the VIII Air Corps was withdrawn from Combat Zone Center during late July and early August and trans-ferred to the Dno area to reinforce the First Air Fleet. Here, in concentrated action, the corps was to support the breaching of the

---

*The 4th Bomber Wing, which had just been transferred (mid-August 1941) from the western theater of operations to the First Air Fleet, did not assist the campaign against Allied shipping, but took part in the opening air attacks upon Moscow.

†See Maps Nos. 11 and 12.

fortifications at Luga and the advance of the Eighteenth Army on Novgorod. Halder's diary indicates that this use of the VIII Air Corps must have been discussed and decided at the highest command level (between Hitler and Goering) without asking for the opinion of the Commander in Chief of the Army, Field Marshal von Brauchitsch.[22]* Hitler's interference in the transfer of the VIII Air Corps and his interference in the control of operations (the dislocation of the Luftwaffe's main point of effort from Combat Zone Center to Combat Zone North) and in tactical control (the precise disposition of the air corps in Combat Zone North) are clearly evident. On 30 July General Jodl informed Halder that Hitler had now decided that Army Group North must take Leningrad and that the attacks against the Moscow-Leningrad railroad were to be abandoned. Furthermore, the Luftwaffe was to build up its strength in Combat Zone North in order to assist the ground forces in mopping up Estonia, and no air units were to be withdrawn until the success of the army group's efforts was assured.[23] The Fuehrer had given precise instructions for the employment of the First Air Fleet and the VIII Air Corps, first in attacking Novgorod, and later in supporting an attack by forces under General der Panzertruppen Hans Reinhardt.[24]

The Fourth Panzer Group, with the effective support of the VIII Air Corps, broke through the Soviet system of fortifications on 11 August. Ten days later, Army Group North had reached the northern tip of Lake Ilmen and the Gulf of Finland, and its position extended roughly along a line passing through the captured cities of Novgorod, Kingisepp, and Narva.

Typical of the diversified and effective employment of the First Air Fleet during this period were the operations of 10 August. On that day strong dive bomber and bomber units attacked a variety of targets in the Lake Ilmen-Mshaga River-Luga-Kingisepp area, destroying 10 tanks, more than 200 vehicles, 15 artillery batteries, and individual emplacements, silencing several antiaircraft artillery batteries, setting five transport trains on fire, and destroying several ammunition and fuel dumps. Besides this damage, the command posts of several important Soviet commands were bombed. These attacks, including those on Saaremaa Island, resulted in 54 Soviet planes being shot down.[25]

---

*Halder commented, "The commitment of the VIII Air Corps [was ordered] for the support of the Lake Ilmen group without in any respect informing the Army High Command."

147

By 26 August units of Army Group North in Estonia had advanced to Tallinn (Reval), which they captured two days later with support from the concentrated forces of the I Air Corps and the Luftwaffe Commander Baltic. Particularly successful here were air attacks on 28 and 29 August against Soviet merchant vessels which were embarking from Tallinn loaded with troops and evacuated materiel.*

On 30 August the High Command of the Luftwaffe reported that most of its bomber units were being used against Russian vessels fleeing from Tallinn, enemy warships and merchantmen in the Gulf of Finland as far as the Bay of Kronshtadt, and individual ships on the Neva River and in the Ladoga Canal.[26]/ Stronger bomber forces continued to attack the retrograde ship movements during the next few days.

A strong Soviet counterattack against the advancing left wing of Army Group North (running along a line from Staraya Russa to Kholm to Lake Ilmen to the east) required a further concentrated effort by the Luftwaffe. Units of the First Air Fleet made a decisive contribution to the successful conclusion of the defensive battle south of Staraya Russa, which continued until 24 August.

Besides this direct support of the ground forces, the I Air Corps in the month of August carried out numerous attacks against the railroads leading from Leningrad to the west, south, and southwest, as well as the rail lines south and east of Lake Ilmen.

The Soviet air forces limited their operational activity almost wholly to the immediate vicinity of the front lines. The few flights which they made into the German rear service area and over Germany itself were carried out by very few aircraft and had no appreciable effect, except as nuisance raids. An example of this could be seen in the High Command of the Luftwaffe report of 9 August that "on the night of 8-9 August two to three Soviet Russian aircraft" utilized the "almost closed cloud cover" to approach Berlin via Stolpmuende. One plane dropped its bombs without effect and turned away when it encountered gunfire in the antiaircraft artillery zone in the northern part of the capital, while the other aircraft dropped their bombs in open country. The intruders were

---

*See Figures 30 and 31.
/Ladoga Canal consists of two parallel canals, running east from Petrokrepost (Schluesselburg) along the southern coast of Lake Ladoga. The canal closest to the lake is the Novo-Ladozhskiy (New Ladoga) Canal, while that to the immediate south is called the Staro-Ladozhskiy (Old Ladoga) Canal.

Figure 30
Harbor of Tallinn (Reval) after its occupation
by German forces, end of August 1941

Figure 31
Soviet transport attacked by the Luftwaffe,
Gulf of Finland, Summer 1941

also fired upon by antiaircraft artillery at Stettin and Kuestrin,* but bad weather prevented German night fighters from intercepting them.[27]

To suppress, or at least to limit, the slowly reviving Soviet air activity, bomber and fighter units of the First Air Fleet continuously attacked the Soviet flying units at their bases. From the beginning of the campaign until 23 August the I Air Corps alone destroyed 2,514 enemy planes. Of these, 920 were shot down in the air and 1,594 were destroyed on the ground. An additional 433 planes were probably destroyed.[28] On 23 August the High Command of the Luftwaffe (OKL) made special mention of the 26th Twin-Engine Fighter Wing of the I Air Corps. The wing had carried out two attacks on 19 August on a Soviet air base at Nizino, 17 miles southwest of Leningrad; the first attack silenced the antiaircraft artillery and the second set 30 fighters on fire, destroyed 15 more, and shot down 3 in aerial combat. The wing thereby increased its total of enemy planes destroyed to 854, of which 191 had been shot down.[29]

North of Lake Ilmen the Sixteenth Army had advanced through Chudovo and on 8 September captured Petrokrepost, while the Fourth Panzer Group had advanced through Gatchina into the area just south of Leningrad. On 23 September the Eighteenth Army reached the coast of the Gulf of Finland at Petrodvorets, placing the entire southern coast of the Gulf in German hands. Leningrad was completely surrounded except for a pocket around Lomonosov.†

On 26 September the planned siege of Leningrad began. To support this operation the bulk of the forces of the First Air Fleet had been committed mainly to the area south and southwest of Leningrad, where they were to carry forward the attack of the Fourth Panzer Group and the Eighteenth Army. Targets of military importance in Leningrad, as well as Soviet naval vessels in Kronshtadt, were also repeatedly attacked with good results. Toward the end of September, continuous operations by concentrated forces halted strong Soviet attacks south of Lake Ladoga and thereby prevented an opening of the ring around Leningrad. In addition to supporting the ground forces in repulsing Soviet breakout attempts at Leningrad, and in defending against attacks on the screening front south of Lake Ladoga, the First Air Fleet had to take continuous action against the supply and evacuation traffic to and from Leningrad by way of Lake Ladoga.[30]

---

*Both cities are situated on the Oder River.
†See pp. 140 and 142.

Bomber and Dive Bomber Operations Against the Soviet Baltic Fleet

In the second half of September, the warships at Kronshtadt were attacked repeatedly with good results. The attacks were directed in particular against the two battleships Oktiabrskaya Revolutia (October Revolution) and Marat, which had been under constant surveillance by German air reconnaissance. According to situation reports of the High Command of the Air Force, bombers and dive bombers on 22, 23, and 24 September attacked the two battleships, a cruiser of the Kirov class, a second cruiser, several destroyers, a few miscellaneous naval vessels and some merchant ships--sighted mainly at or near Kronshtadt (they hit the cruiser Kirov again on 29 September)--causing heavy cumulative damage, including fire, to the battleships (although apparently there was no fire on the Marat) and the cruisers, with many of the destroyers and merchant vessels sunk, damaged, or set afire. Aerial photographs taken on 23 September show that the heavily damaged bows of both battleships were at times under water.[31]*

These attacks on the Soviet warships, exemplifying a successful use of aircraft against naval targets, were carried out in the face of very heavy ship and land-based antiaircraft artillery fire. Flying into such defenses, Lt. Hans-Ulrich Rudel of the 2nd Dive Bomber Wing, who became the most highly decorated officer in the Luftwaffe, made a direct hit with a 2,200-pound bomb on the Marat on the morning of 22 September.[32]/

---

*On 23 and 24 September 1941 the 2nd Dive Bomber Wing attacked units of the Soviet Baltic Fleet. After heavy bomb hits, although some guns were still serviceable, the battleship Marat was beached. The Oktiabrskaya Revolutia was hit outside the harbor; the cruiser Maksim Gorki was heavily damaged at Leningrad when a group commander of the 2nd Dive Bomber Wing, his plane fatally damaged, dived next to the cruiser. See Gerhard Huemmelchen and Juergen Rohwer, "Vor Zwanzig Jahren," Marine-Rundschau ("Twenty Years Ago," Navy Review), LVIII, Okt. 61, p. 299.

/See Figure 32. See also "Rudel" in the biographical section in the back of this study.

Figure 32
Soviet battleship Marat sunk by direct hit from the Ju-87
of Hans-Ulrich Rudel, 22 September 1941

Figure 33
A Siebel Ferry, a German attempt to stop Russian supply
movements across Lake Ladoga, Russia, 1941

Upon completion of the encirclement of Leningrad,* the VIII Air Corps--despite all protests of Army Group North--was transferred back to the Second Air Fleet in Combat Zone Center to support the advance of the ground forces on Moscow. Halder's notes of 12 August indicate that he had been told by the army group's liaison officer that retention of the air corps was necessary until the Moscow-Leningrad railroad was reached on about 25 August. A month later Field Marshal von Leeb (Army Group North), "stormily" insisted that he retain control of the air corps, but the forthcoming operation in Combat Zone Center had priority.[33]

On 14 August the combined operation of the Luftwaffe, Army, and Navy began against the Baltic islands of Muhu, Saaremaa, and Hiimaa. For this operation, the First Air Fleet had reinforced the units of the Luftwaffe Commander Baltic with a bomber group, a twin-engine fighter group, and a replacement fighter group and had concentrated them into a combat organization under the command of Generalmajor Heinz Helmuth von Wuehlisch. Then, during the course of the capture of Saaremaa, the combat unit was disbanded.†

First Air Fleet Operations at the Volkhov River and Tikhvin

During the second half of October, the main point of effort of the First Air Corps was concentrated upon the support of the motorized XXXIX Army Corps penetration of the Soviet defenses on the Volkhov River and the subsequent German advance on Tikhvin. For the support of the Tikhvin advance, the First Air Fleet established a "Luftwaffe Commander Tikhvin," which was to cooperate closely with the army corps. The Commander of the 77th Bomber Wing, Col. Hans Raithel, who was also named Luftwaffe Commander Tikhvin, established his command post at the headquarters of the XXXIX Army Corps, then at Trubnikov Bor. His units were comprised of the 4th Squadron of the 122nd Long Range Reconnaissance Group, one group of the 54th Fighter Wing, the 77th Bomber Wing, one heavy antiaircraft artillery battalion, and air signal units. Preparation for the advance were largely improvised by the Army and the Luftwaffe.

---

*Editor's Note: The reference to the "surrounding" of Leningrad is somewhat misleading. Leningrad was effectively encircled only on the land routes, leaving Lake Ladoga open as a possible source of supply. The Ladoga route enabled the city to resist capture throughout the war.

†A detailed description of the Luftwaffe's role in this operation is presented in the next section of this chapter.

Maj. Rudolf Loytved-Hardegg, Intelligence Officer of the First Air Fleet (temporarily assigned as General Staff officer to the Luftwaffe Commander Tikhvin), later described the operation against Tikhvin:

The building of the bridgehead at Gruzino succeeded without substantial local support by the Luftwaffe. The enemy held out in the vicinity of the bridge site in a monastery, whose walls withstood even the heaviest bombs. Only on the second or third day was this troublesome defensive post smoked out by engineers with flame throwers. Sorties of the bombers took place mainly in the depth of the attack sector against enemy concentrations [and] highway and railroad objectives (Novgorod-Borovichi-Tikhvin-Chudovo area.)

The enemy air force replied with small, but often very troublesome attacks upon the advancing divisions, the bridge sites, headquarters, and rear supply services. They were usually carried out in low-level flight by three to five twin-engine aircraft.

The adverse weather and rough terrain favored surprise attacks and complicated our own defenses on the ground and in the air. A timely arrival of our own fighters was difficult to accomplish, and generally they were able to down only one of the Soviet planes. The enemy exploited well the moments when our fighters were away.

The experiment of transferring one of our fighter groups to Chudovo or to another field close to the front was unsuccessful, and there remained only the advance landing field at Siverskiy which was too far back for even Me-109 speeds. As a rule . . . scramble take-offs from there were therefore too late.

On the second or third day after the attack a thaw set in . . . . The armor came to a standstill; the crews had to dismount. The armored spearhead advancing on the Gruzino-Tikhvin road had not reached the important road bottleneck (a swampy area crossed by a corduroy road which was easy to block) lying near Serebryanka. Here arose the first opportunity for the Luftwaffe Commander [Tikhvin] for direct intervention in the ground fighting. The combat team of Captain Poetter (77th Bomber Wing), experienced in close combat at Saaremaa, received the mission to keep the bottleneck open, destroy the enemy found there, and to combat the reinforcement of the position by new forces until the dismounted tank crews and infantry were near.

This was an extremely difficult task (especially for Ju-88's), since enemy movements were difficult to detect in the wooded, bushy country, and area attacks upon woods suspected of harboring enemy concentrations were out of the question with the [inadequate] air strength available.

The mission was successfully completed, despite the fact that Captain Poetter himself was shot down in one of the first low-level attacks. He and two of his crew, wounded, were able to rejoin our troops the next day. The assumption that the much liked officer was still alive had urged on the tank crews to speed [their] advance and his own combat team to make unflagging sorties.

* * * * * * *

The correct judgment of the Luftwaffe's action was extraordinarily difficult here. It was clearly evident that the available number of flying units was insufficient . . . for the detachment of a strong close support unit. Moreover, dive bombers and ground attack aircraft, which were essential to such a unit, were also lacking.

As so often happens, the disproportion between the number [of aircraft] in units and those found in operations staffs also worked to disadvantage. Even in the given situation, the staff of the Luftwaffe Commander Tikhvin increased this disproportion. The necessity for a tactical air command near the front in the Tikhvin sector could have been realized equally well by an advance command post of the I Air Corps or by an air liaison party well equipped with signal communication equipment.[34]

This last view must be acknowledged to be absolutely correct. With the shortage of personnel and materiel, as well as of time for preparations, the smoothly functioning command machinery of the I

Air Corps at an advance command post would have been sufficient, especially since the operation involved was limited in time and space.

Besides the direct support of the troops advancing against the tenaciously resisting Soviets, the Luftwaffe units attacked all railroad lines leading toward the flanks of the XXXIX Army Corps to prevent the approach of fresh enemy forces. Another interesting operation of the First Air Fleet which deserves mention was the attempt to ignite the large oil storage lakes at Shcherbakov by high-explosive and incendiary bombs, an effort which was completely unsuccessful.[35]

Important military targets in Leningrad were also continuously attacked with good results, although the city was very heavily defended by numerous antiaircraft artillery batteries of all calibers and many balloon obstacles.[36]

Tikhvin was captured on 9 November and held for an entire month by heavy defensive fighting against strong counterattacks from numerically superior Soviet forces. Besides supporting this defensive action, I Air Corps units carried out interdiction attacks against rail traffic east of the Volkhov River and Lake Ilmen.[37]

Beginning late in the autumn and early winter of 1941, the results of air reconnaissance operations became steadily more fragmentary. This was due less to the increasing Soviet fighter and antiaircraft artillery defenses than to unfavorable flying weather;[38] even during sunshine there were blinding effects and haze. Also, in comparison to the gigantic area to be reconnoitered, the reconnaissance squadrons were much too weak, a disproportion which became still more obvious in trying to detect the columns of vehicular traffic after the marshes, rivers, and lakes froze over. The Russian dependence in summer upon a few highways ceased in winter for all tracked and even conventional vehicles. Because of this greater freedom of action, the reconnaissance of Soviet routes now became the reconnaissance of areas, which required considerably more time and resources. With the strong commitment of units to other sectors of the front, there was also a decrease in reconnaissance in the forward areas by bomber crews and by fighters, which had hitherto formed a valuable supplement to the normal air reconnaissance effort.

With regard to Soviet rail movements, which were carried out principally at night in the front areas, the German command was essentially dependent upon inferences drawn during the day from traffic observed at the various railroad stations. The station at Bologoye, the most important junction in the northern combat zone, showed the greatest variation in activity and was, therefore, attacked on numerous occasions, while the stations at Tikhvin and Parakhino-Poddubye were attacked less often.

Immediately after Lake Ladoga had frozen over, a heavy, steadily increasing Russian supply traffic developed, which moved across the ice, to and from Leningrad. Since it was impossible for the ground forces to cut this supply artery, the First Air Fleet was ordered to interrupt the traffic over the so-called ice road on the lake. Between 25 November and 3 December, elements of the First Air Corps attacked the ice road, especially at its southern extremity. Although considerable casualties and great materiel losses were inflicted upon the enemy, the attacks did not permanently interrupt this important line of supply.[39] It was found that traffic over large frozen lakes could not be stopped by shattering the ice surface with bombs. Holes which were blasted here and there by large caliber bombs very soon froze over again. Moreover, the tremendous ice area enabled the Soviets to detour quickly around any obstacles in their supply route.

It may be noted here that before Lake Ladoga froze over, an attempt had already been made to prevent supplies from crossing the lake. For this purpose, so-called Siebel Ferries (named for their designer Reserve Colonel Fritz Siebel) armed with antiaircraft guns were employed from the Finnish occupied shore.* These ferries involved a great expenditure, but their employment on Lake Ladoga was always fundamentally unsuccessful. Motor torpedo boats or heavy motor boats would certainly have been better and have achieved better results.

The continuing bad weather and the extreme cold throughout December greatly impaired the combat activity and operational preparedness of the flying units of the First Air Fleet. The elemental force of winter, with its directly paralyzing effect upon man and machine, was the most powerful ally of the Russians. Its effects could not then, and cannot in the future, be completely assessed but they were enormous.

On 27 October the forces of the Luftwaffe Commander Baltic had been disbanded. Only the 806th Coastal Group (bombers) remained in Combat Zone North assigned to the I Air Corps, while the remaining units were transferred to other fighting fronts.

_____

*See Figure 33.

157

In the face of superior enemy pressure the Germans evacuated Tikhvin on 12 December, and all the forces of the Sixteenth Army which had pushed east of the Volkhov River had to be withdrawn to a defensive position on the west bank of the river. During these movements, which were continued until 23 December under especially difficult combat and weather conditions, the mass of the I Air Corps was employed to ease the pressure on the ground forces. Concurrently, the supply traffic across Lake Ladoga and the rail traffic in the combat area of the First Air Fleet were continuously attacked. Because of the importance of railroad interdiction, fighters were also frequently employed in "sweeps" against locomotives, trains, and railroad installations.

The operations of the First Air Fleet during 1941 also included the commitment of Luftwaffe units as infantry. During very critical situations the First Air Fleet was compelled to use all of its available resources to help close grievous gaps in the ranks of the Army. While recently rehabilitated units of the 7th Air Division--then the only paratroop division available--were thrown prematurely into the battle for Leningrad, regular infantry units (such as the 14th Luftwaffe Regiment and the organization of Generalmajor Eugen Meindl) were formed from volunteers from Luftwaffe ground organizations, the antiaircraft artillery, and the signal service of the First Air Fleet. All were immediately employed at the centers of the fighting. These units fought successfully shoulder to shoulder with their hard-struggling comrades of the Army. Their relatively briefer training in ground combat naturally made their losses disproportionately high, but their bearing and fighting spirit contributed vitally to the stiffening of the defensive front.* They became the core of the Luftwaffe Field Divisions which were organized in 1942.

Luftwaffe Participation in Operations BEOWULF I & II

Planning

The capture of Tallinn (Reval) on 28 August and the winning of the western coast of Estonia by German ground forces prepared the ground work for the seizure of the Baltic islands of Muhu, Saaremaa, and Hiiumaa

_____

*Editor's Note: Some German Army commanders, such as Generaloberst Hans Friessner, thought that the employment of inadequately trained Luftwaffe personnel for infantry tasks was a misuse of manpower. See Generaloberst (Ret) Hans Friessner, Verratene Schlachten (Betrayed Battles), Hamburg: Holsten Verlag, 1956, p. 228.

by an attack from the mainland. Responsibility for the execution of this undertaking (Operation BEOWULF) was entrusted to the commanding general of the XXXXII Army Corps, comprising the 217th and 61st Infantry Divisions, to which elements of the Navy and Luftwaffe were assigned. Thus BEOWULF was a joint operation of all the armed forces under one commander.

To seize the islands, two plans, initially involving only the islands of Muhu and Saaremaa, were considered. At the end of June 1941 Army Group North decided in favor of Plan BEOWULF II, which provided for troops operating from the west coast of Estonia, with assembly area at Virtsu, to cross the large strait between the mainland and Muhu and take the islands by an attack from the east.

The reasons for the decision by Army Group North in favor of BEOWULF II over BEOWULF I (which provided for troops operating from northern Kurland, with assembly areas at Roja and Ventspils, to land on Saaremaa in Fettel Bay* and at Salme and take the islands from the south and southwest) were:

(1) There was no need for a rapid seizure of the islands, since the Soviet forces there could not seriously interfere with operations on the mainland or with supplies by sea. It was also believed that the Soviet airfields on the islands could be eliminated by counter-air action.

(2) The passage across the relatively narrow large strait promised to be shorter and therefore safer than a crossing from Kurland. Furthermore, the danger of flanking operations by Soviet naval units was considerably less in the large strait.

(3) The landing on the east side of the islands was expected to be easier, since most of the fortifications were situated on the southwestern and western sides and were especially designed for defense against attacks by sea, such as the amphibious operation of the German Army and Navy against Saaremaa during World War I.†

The Terrain and the Enemy

On the whole the terrain on the Baltic islands is level. A few dunes, most of them covered with coniferous trees, range in height from 160

---

*Editor's Note: Fettel Bay is the name given in the German manuscript, but the Estonian-English version could not be determined.
†See Map No. 10.

159

feet to 223 feet.   In 1941 only a small part of the islands was cultivated; the remainder was wasteland, heather, and swampy terrain with pasture land and scrub forests.   Stone walls served as boundaries for farm lands, and there were numerous dolmens on Muhu Island, but owing to danger from rock slides, neither the walls nor the dolmens provided good cover. Muhu was connected with Saaremaa by an embankment about 2 1/2 miles long.   The fog which prevails in the Baltic except during the summer months could severely hamper the progress of the operations.

The total strength of the Soviet forces stationed on the Baltic islands was estimated at 20,000.   It was assumed that some 10,000 would be in the strongly organized western part of Saaremaa, with the remainder distributed between Muhu, Hiiumaa, and the eastern part of Saaremaa. At points commanding the sea, some 15 coastal batteries, considered to be of heavy and extra-heavy caliber with armored shields or good concrete embrasures were emplaced.   It was later confirmed that the estimate of Soviet troop strength and distribution was correct, but that the effectiveness of the batteries had been overestimated, since the guns were only of medium and heavy caliber and only two batteries had armored shields.   And while some of the remaining batteries had concrete embrasures, others were emplaced in field artillery positions.   A strong fortification system with concrete bunkers was found only on the Sõrve Peninsula, the southernmost part of Saaremaa.

In contrast to the mainland Soviet forces, the garrison on the islands was well fed and equipped.   The core of the defense was provided by naval infantry (marine) and coastal artillery units, whose personnel were confirmed communists and fanatical fighters.   Bases for light naval forces were situated in Triigi Bay, Kihelkonna Bay, and at Kuressaare (on the northern, western, and southern coasts of Saaremaa respectively).

The only large airfield for landplanes on the Baltic islands was the field at Mönnuste on Saaremaa, but this was inadequate for modern planes such as the Ju-88.   A larger naval air station was located at Papisaare* on the western coast of Saaremaa.   In addition, a large number of smaller landing fields were available for landplanes and seaplanes, fields which the enemy used skillfully with his few (20-30) obsolescent aircraft.

---

*Papisaare is the German name for this base.   The Estonian name for this has not been found, and may have undergone other changes after its incorporation into the U.S.S.R. in 1945.

German Forces

Army. Directing the entire operation was the commanding general of the XXXXII Army Corps, who controlled the 61st and 217th Infantry Divisions. The 217th was entrusted with all covering missions, such as the occupation of the coastal area, artillery flank protection at the crossing points, and early seizure of Kessu Island which threatened the right flank of the crossing. This enabled the 61st Infantry Division to employ all its units as assault troops. Prior to the attack, the 61st assembled three infantry regiments along the Lihula-Virtsu road, with a reinforced reconnaissance battalion in the Saastana area, all ready for embarkation. It was intended, after feints had been made by German naval units against the northern, western, and southern coasts of Saaremaa, to land with the bulk of the division at three places: Lalli (Võlla),* Kantsi,ᵻ and Tusti on the east coast of Muhu. The reinforced reconnaissance battalion was to land at Nõmmküla on the north coast of Muhu on order to attack from two bridgeheads toward the Muhu-Saaremaa causeway.

A company especially organized for combat patrols and equipped with boats and cargo sailing ships was to eliminate the coastal batteries or capture the causeway. The date of the operation depended upon the slow process of moving forward the vessels required for the crossing, but the crossing was tentatively scheduled for the period 11 to 15 September.

Navy. For the crossing operation the German Navy provided Siebel ferries, naval landing barges, fishing boats, and conventional barges, all assembled at Virtsu and in the bays to the south. Craft for the security of the operation and for the feint attacks consisted of mine sweepers, motor mine sweepers, artillery barges, armed fishing trawlers, coastal sailing ships, and barges of the so-called experimental unit. These forces were placed under the control of the Commander of Mine Sweepers North (Fuehrer der Minensuchboote Nord), Kapitaen zur See Kurt Boehmer, and were assembled at Pärnu and Riga, mainly at the latter.

Other naval forces for the diversionary operations were concentrated at Liepāja (Libau), Ventspils, and Turku (in Finland) under the command of the Chief of the 2nd Torpedo Boat Flotilla, Korvettenkapitaen Heinrich Erdmann, or the Commander of Torpedo Boats,

---

*Võlla is the Estonian name for this site, Lalli the German name.
ᵻKantsi is not on the coast, but in the interior of Muhu, and is the approximate location of this action.

Kapitaen zur See Hans Buetow. The German Navy planned to carry out three feints:

(1) Operation South Wind (SUEDWIND) was to simulate a landing in the area of Kuressaare and Fettel Bay. At dusk on the day preceding the attack (D minus 1) the units, proceeding at slow speeds, were to be so located that enemy reconnaissance or agents would be certain to observe them. At dawn on D-day, they were to change to a reverse course.

(2) Operation West Wind (WESTWIND) was to simulate a landing on the west coast of Saaremaa. A naval force consisting of the 2nd Torpedo Boat Flotilla, the 2nd and 3rd Motor Torpedo Boat Flotillas, three submarine chasers, and three steamers were to be standing some 30 miles offshore on the late afternoon of D minus 1. After dark it was to change course to an opposite heading. On the night preceding D-day the motor torpedo boats were to stand by in waiting positions outside of Soela Strait and Taga Bay and off Cap Ristna, where they were to be relieved at dawn by the 2nd Torpedo Boat Flotilla.

(3) Operation North Wind (NORDWIND) was to simulate an attack from the rocky Finnish coast. Two Finnish armored ships, a minelayer, and two steamers were to carry out a brief approach on the Baltic islands until dark on D minus 1.*

Air Force. For the execution of Operation BEOWULF II, the First Air Fleet organized within its chain of command/ the staff of the Luftwaffe Commander "B" (Generalmajor von Wuehlisch). Assigned to von Wuehlisch were:

(1) Luftwaffe Commander Baltic (Colonel von Wild) with the 806th Coastal Group (Ju-88's), three squadrons of the 125th Reconnaissance Group,// the I Group of the 77th Bomber Wing (Ju-88's), the II Group of

----
*See Map No. 10.

/This staff was authorized and formed for a specified period only, as required for command purposes and coordination of the planned operation.

//On 26 July 1941, the 125th Reconnaissance Group had the following aircraft: Heinkel He-60, single-engine, two-place, biplane, utility, with floats; Heinkel He-114, single-engine, two-place, biplane with short bottom wings, close-reconnaissance seaplane; Arado Ar-95, single-engine, three-place, biplane, with floats; and the Arado Ar-196, single-engine, two-place, low-wing monoplane, coastal reconnaissance and ship-based seaplane. See also Appendix 29, Book 2, original German draft of this study, Karlsruhe Document Collection.

the 26th Twin-Engine Fighter Wing (Me-110's), the Operational Squadron of the Replacement Training Group of the 54th Fighter Wing (Me-109's), and, after 21 September, the 506th Coastal Group (Ju-88's).

(2) The 10th Antiaircraft Artillery Regimental Staff with three heavy and three light antiaircraft artillery batteries.

(3) The 10th Luftwaffe Signal Regiment with one telegraph construction battalion, one field trunk cable construction company, one teletype and telephone platoon, and one radio platoon. Further, there was a special Luftwaffe signal battalion with two signal companies in the airport area and one aircraft reporting director with an aircraft reporting platoon and a Freya radar installation.

The communication facilities and supply requirements of the ground organization for Luftwaffe Commander "B" were prepared and ready for operations after 9 September. The units under von Wuehlisch's command were deployed as follows: the staff of Luftwaffe Commander Baltic had its headquarters at Pärnu, the 806th Coastal Group and (after 21 September) the 506th Coastal Group were at Riga, while the 125th Reconnaissance Group had located its headquarters and 1st Squadron at Pärnu, its 2nd Squadron at Haapsalu, and its 3rd Squadron at Helsinki. Besides these units, the I Group of the 77th Bomber Wing was based at Kuusiku, and the II Group of the 26th Twin-Engine Fighter Wing was at Pärnu, while the Operational Squadron of the Replacement Training Group of the 54th Fighter Wing was deployed first at Pärnu and after 21 September at Mönnuste on Saaremaa Island where it was supplied by Gigant cargo gliders.*

The antiaircraft artillery was deployed in defense of the ground organization and the harbor of Pärnu, concentrating around Pärnu. A

---

*The Messerschmidt Me-321 "Gigant" cargo glider, capable of lifting a payload of about 22 tons. It was normally towed by three Me-110C's, by a single five-engine, twin-fuselage Heinkel He-111 Z, or by a Junkers Ju-290 A-1. The last named aircraft was the most ideal for the task, but was everywhere in short supply, so that the He-111 Z was usually employed. The Gigants mentioned above were probably towed by three Me-110 C's, since these were the towing aircraft then assigned to the 1st Gigant Squadron (5 Gigants and 15 Me-110 C's). See Appendix 34, Book 2, original German draft of this study, Karlsruhe Document Collection.

specially organized light antiaircraft artillery battery, mounted on 12 Siebel ferries, was assigned to the ground forces to directly protect the crossing operation. On the afternoon of 13 September the flying units reported that they were at the prescribed airfields ready for action.

The Course of Operations

The original plan to bring most of the attacking ground forces by convoy from Pärnu to Muhu, after a first wave--crossing in assault boats from Virtsu--had seized a beachhead on Muhu, had to be abandoned. Because it was not certain that mines, which had been laid by the Luftwaffe at an earlier period, could be swept clear in time for the operation, the crossing from Virtsu to Muhu was to be accomplished by the use of assault boats and Siebel ferries.

On 8 and 9 September the 217th Infantry Division launched a surprise attack on the weakly garrisoned islands of Hobu and Vormsi, east of Hiiumaa Island. These islands were taken--as was the island of Kessu, east of Muhu, on 10 September by elements of the 61st Infantry Division-- without significant resistance.* Vormsi Island fell on 10 September. Thus, the danger of a flank attack from the north by Soviet naval forces during the crossings to Muhu and Saaremaa was eliminated. Low ceilings, rain showers, and bad visibility limited Luftwaffe activity during these assault operations to fighter protection by the Replacement Training Group of the 54th Fighter Wing.[40]

The unfavorable weather also postponed until 14 September the attack on the 2 1/2-mile causeway joining Muhu and Saaremaa. On 12 and 13 September the 806th Coastal Group; the I Group, 77th Bomber Wing; the II Group, 26th Twin-Engine Fighter Wing; the Operational Squadron, Replacement Training Group, 54th Fighter Wing; and the three squadrons of the 125th Reconnaissance Group arrived at the assigned airfields, previously mentioned, where communications and provisions were in readiness. In like manner, the three heavy and two light batteries of the 10th Antiaircraft Artillery Regiment were moved to protect the airfield and crowded harbor of Pärnu, with elements of the remaining light battery being set up at the airfields at Kuusiku and Haapsalu.

---

*According to the author, the 217th Infantry Division was originally directed to seize the island of Kessu, but this was later changed so that it was taken by the 61st Infantry Division.

The German Navy carried out its three diversionary operations on 13 September to conceal the intended direction of the attack and to induce the Russians to disperse their forces. Three separate convoys approached the southern, western, and northern coasts of Saaremaa Island* and misled the Soviets into expecting attacks from those points. Air reconnaissance later confirmed that the Soviet command had actually dissipated its forces by deploying them along the coast. After nightfall the German transport steamers turned back on their courses, while the escort units remained on patrol in the offshore waters of the islands. Luftwaffe Commander Baltic units provided the air cover for these diversionary actions, but no Soviet air or naval units were encountered.

The details of the amphibious operation were settled on the afternoon of 13 September at a briefing held at the headquarters of the 61st Infantry Division, in the presence of the commanding general of the XXXXII Army Corps and the Navy and Luftwaffe commanders for the joint operation. Still to be answered were questions as to whether a landing on Muhu would come as a surprise to the Russians after the seizure of Vormsi, Kessu, and Hobu; whether the Soviets had shifted reinforcements, especially artillery, from the western part of the islands to the east side of Muhu; or whether the Navy's feints had really achieved their deceptive, force-shackling effect. Since the XXXXII Army Corps had originally intended to make a surprise landing on Muhu at dawn from assault boats (without artillery and air attack preparation), a predawn landing was requested by the 61st Infantry Division and subsequently given the force of an order by higher headquarters.

Luftwaffe Commander "B" was requested to bomb seven lanes through the mine fields, which were assumed to be along the shore in the landing sector, and to provide continuous air support for the attacking ground troops. The counterproposal to postpone the crossing until dawn and neutralize the enemy by simultaneously concentrated artillery fire

---

*The feint operation NORDWIND was really conducted by Finnish rather than German naval forces, and was carried out off the northern tip of Hiiumaa Island rather than Saaremaa. The Finnish coastal armored ship Ilmarinen struck a mine and sank while withdrawing from the operation on 13 September. See Olof Ekman, "Untergang des finnischen Panzerschiffes Ilmarinen," Marine-Rundschau, Vol. LIX, Okt. 1962 ("Sinking of the Finnish Armored Ship Ilmarinen," Naval Review), pp. 301-305. See also Friedrich Ruge, Der See-Krieg 1939-1945 (The Sea War 1939-1945), Stuttgart: K. F. Koehler Verlag, 1954, pp. 156-158.

and commitment of the Luftwaffe could not be considered because the Army had already issued its orders. The assault troop company was ordered to seize and destroy the coastal battery at Kübassaare on Saaremaa Island--the elimination of which was considered absolutely necessary by the Navy--in a surprise airborne and amphibious attack. The briefing ended with the order to begin Operation BEOWULF II early on the following day, 14 September. The landing at Muhu was to take place at 0450 after the preparatory artillery fire and the clearing of the seven lanes through the mine fields by the bombers.

The next morning, the first wave of the 151st Infantry Regiment of the 61st Infantry Division left the mainland in 180 assault boats bound for Muhu. About 15 minutes before they landed, "the neutralization of the enemy began with sudden, concentrated fire of the coast artillery [from the mainland] and aerial bombing and strafing."[41] The first wave landed between 0500 and 0530. It had been delayed 20 to 30 minutes by haze, light rain showers, and heavy swells. Some of the troops did not land at the intended points, having drifted off course because of the strong current in the strait. Because of this, the clearing of the seven lanes through the mine fields by Luftwaffe bombers was cancelled on the initiative of the commander of the bomber formation. The Soviets resisted tenaciously in prepared positions, in part heavily supported by artillery. Principal resistance was met in the Tusti-Kuivastu sector. The enfilading Russian artillery and antiaircraft artillery fire inflicted heavy losses on the approaching assault boats of the first wave and then upon the troops as they attacked across the open beaches. From his Fieseler Fi-156 "Stork," the Luftwaffe Commander "B" observed that German artillery fire from the mainland had little effect because poor weather conditions prevented adequate observation. In this critical situation bombers and twin-engine fighters (Me-110's) replaced the artillery. A narrow bridgehead was established during the morning, after the Luftwaffe had eliminated several Soviet batteries and directly supported the ground attack. In the afternoon enemy resistance decreased noticeably at some points. Nevertheless, only five infantry battalions and one artillery battalion had landed on the east coast of Muhu by 1800, the breakdown of numerous vessels and the heavy swell having considerably slowed the speed of the crossing. The concluding report of the XXXXII Army Corps on Operation BEOWULF II expressly confirmed that the success achieved on the first day was due in decisive measure to the unflagging assistance of the Luftwaffe, which had been committed at the right time and place.

Toward 1500, the 161st Reconnaissance Battalion reported that it had gained a surprise footing on the northern coast of Muhu, had broken the weaker Soviet resistance, and was marching south. All vehicles of the battalion were brought over there by evening. Before dusk two bridge-heads were won: the first, from Pallasma through Tupenurme to Raugi, and the second, from Tusti to the western edge of the forest between Tusti and Kuivastu.

The planned surprise seizure of the coastal battery at Kübassaare by an assault troop company failed. In the early dawn, one-third of the company, aboard freight gliders, landed immediately north of the battery. However, the amphibious force with two-thirds of the company was delayed by heavy seas and false orientation. At daylight the boats were driven off by gunfire, and the airborne force was encircled just north of the coastal fort.

The naval feints had proceeded according to plan. Units in Operations WESTWIND and SUEDWIND were fired upon by coastal batteries, and a Finnish armored warship, Ilmarinen, participating in Operation NORDWIND, struck a mine and sank on the 13th. Weak Soviet naval forces--motor torpedo boats--were repulsed by aerial attacks.*

On 15 September the movements across the strait to Muhu were still being hampered by hostile artillery fire and heavy swells. Around 1000 hours, the converging attack from the bridgehead--extending from north to east--began toward the causeway connecting Muhu and Saaremaa. Most of the assault troop elements, encircled near Kübassaare, left the penin-sula in pneumatic boats dropped by air and were later picked up by naval vessels. By evening of the following day (16 September), all of Muhu, except for a narrow sector along the west coast, had been brought under German control without more serious difficulties.

Meanwhile, air reconnaissance had established that the feint opera-tions of the Navy had caused the Soviet command on Saaremaa to deploy its force along the entire coastline of the island. In particular, no sub-stantial forces stood on the northeast coast opposite Muhu Island. There-fore, Luftwaffe Commander "B" proposed that, under Luftwaffe protection, the ground forces should push forward immediately on the next day over the causeway leading to Saaremaa. To delay the advance by waiting for reinforcements and by making further preparations would give the Soviets

_____
*Editor's Note: It should be noted that the author indicated earlier that "no Soviet air or naval units were encountered" by units of Luftwaffe Commander "B" during the diversionary naval operations. It may be assumed that whatever forces were present had a negligible effect on the German operation.

time to reinforce the eastern shore of Saaremaa. Moreover, since the units attached to Luftwaffe Commander "B" were available for only a few days for the operation against Saaremaa, the commander himself decided to create spontaneously within his own organization the conditions which would facilitate a crossing to Saaremaa as early as 16 September.

On the evening of 15 September, Luftwaffe Commander "B" advised the 61st Infantry Division and the infantry regiments still engaged on Muhu that the swift crossing to Saaremaa would be of special importance at that moment, since the Luftwaffe forces were available only temporarily, and an immediate attempt to cross would thus be supported by all the available air power. This assurance had substantial influence on the independent decision of Captain Pankow to move across the causeway to Saaremaa with his advance infantry forces.

Thus, on the morning of 16 September, bomber and twin-engine fighter units, attacking in waves, covered the infantry during the difficult crossing over the 2 1/2-mile-long stone embankment, which had been only partially demolished by the Russians. These air attacks neutralized the Soviet defenses so effectively that by evening three battalions had established a bridgehead about 7 1/2 miles wide and from 2 to 3 3/4 miles deep on Saaremaa without severe losses. On the following day this bridge-head was extended across the entire breadth of the island to a depth of 6 miles. The crossing to Saaremaa had definitely succeeded.

In addition, units of the Luftwaffe Commander "B" succeeded on 16 September in destroying or disabling in Triigi Bay a fleet of 20 ships, apparently assembled there for an evacuation. On the following day these flying units again protected the crossing movements from Soviet motor torpedo boats which had suddenly appeared on the scene.

With the establishing of a sufficiently sizable bridgehead, the most difficult part of the operation against Saaremaa had been mastered. On the afternoon of 17 September the Luftwaffe Commander "B"--prior to the disbanding of his command--transferred his command authority to the Luftwaffe Commander Baltic. The I Group of the 77th Bomber Wing (Ju-88's) and the II Group of the 26th Twin-Engine Fighter Wing (Me-110's) reverted to the command of the First Air Corps and were transferred to the Leningrad front. To replace them, the 506th Coastal Group, with 14 Junkers (Ju-88) bombers was sent on 21 September to the Luftwaffe Commander Baltic at Riga.

The coastal fort at Kübassaare was captured on 18 September after bitter resistance, and some 400 Soviet marines were taken prisoner. From then until 23 September the 61st Infantry Division proceeded without serious difficulty to occupy the island as far as the isthmus which leads to the Sõrve Peninsula. In these operations, units of the Luftwaffe Commander Baltic provided vigorous support through bombing and strafing attacks on batteries of artillery, pockets of resistance, and marching columns.[42]

During this period the ground forces were twice supplied by air from two Me-321 Gigant freight gliders which transported 24 tons of ammunition, rations, and fuel from the Estonian mainland to Saaremaa.

On 23 September the attack opened against the Sõrve Peninsula, where unexpected heavy fighting developed, fighting which lasted four days longer than the entire preceding occupation of Muhu and the greater part of Saaremaa. The small peninsula had been organized as a bunker position throughout its entire length and had been heavily mined. Therefore, more than 2,000 land mines had to be removed in a single day, and 41 bunkers had to be taken in battle. Supported by strong artillery, the Russian defenders resisted desperately in the belief that the Soviet Navy would soon hasten to their relief and that the Germans would shoot all prisoners. Here the moral of the Soviet troops, mostly marines, was far above the average for the typical Russian soldier.

The battle for the Sõrve Peninsula, which depended upon the closest cooperation with the infantry in order to launch attacks upon pinpoint targets, such as bunkers, machine-gun nests, and gun emplacements, required a reliable and flexibly adaptable means of transmitting information between aircraft and ground forces. Communication by the use of ground signal panels and other visual means was developed to a very high standard. On this occasion, as in former battles, the employment of Luftwaffe signal liaison teams with the foremost infantry elements proved to be extremely useful. These teams kept the command headquarters constantly and accurately informed by radio on the current situation and on the location of the changing front lines.

In part, the combat area on the peninsula was narrow, only 1 1/4 miles wide. This permitted only three aircraft, at the very most, to operate simultaneously, because attacks on pinpoint targets were carried out at low levels and the restricted area did not allow sufficient freedom of movement. On the ground the infantry advanced foot by foot, averaging a gain of little more than half a mile in a day.

The Soviets offered only slight resistance in the air. Approximately 15 Soviet fighters were based on Sorve and were indeed cleverly employed in low-level attacks against the German ground forces, but

169

they disappeared immediately upon the appearance of German fighters. At best they accepted combat with the slow-flying seaplanes of the 125th Reconnaissance Group.

On the other hand, the enemy's antiaircraft defense was remarkable. A strong medium antiaircraft artillery and machine-gun defense was distributed over the entire peninsula, and three heavy batteries were emplaced at its southern tip. All five of the German planes lost in the Sörve operation were brought down by this Russian ground defense.

The first signs of the collapse of resistance on Sörve were the transfer of the 11 Soviet fighters still on the peninsula to the mainland on 3 and 4 October, and an attempt by several commissars to escape during the night of 3-4 October in a motor torpedo boat. The boat was set afire by a bomber's guns and sank with all aboard.

A week after the fighting on Sörve had ended, the 61st Infantry Division began the attack on Hiiumaa, the last of the Baltic islands. Here, too, diversionary naval operations deceived the enemy with respect to the direction of the attack, which was launched from Saaremaa against the southern tip of Hiiumaa. Despite bad weather, the first German aircraft took off before daylight on 12 October, covering the noise of the approaching assault boats and landing craft with the sound of their engines so that at daybreak German infantry surprised the enemy completely and were able to land on the southern end of the island. By evening two bridgeheads were won, from which further advances followed on the next day. The occupation of Hiiumaa was accomplished in about nine days--in some instances against stubborn, individual defenders--and on 21 October the last vestiges of Soviet resistance were crushed. Just as in the capture of Saaremaa, the units of the Luftwaffe Commander Baltic supported the regiments of the 61st Infantry Division on Hiiumaa in an extremely effective manner by continuous air reconnaissance and constant intervention in the ground fighting. They experienced only weak fighter opposition, but in places encountered strong antiaircraft artillery defenses.

On 21 October the High Command of the Armed Forces (OKW) made the special announcement that, with the seizure of Hiiumaa, all of the Baltic islands had been brought under German control, a victory which was due to the exemplary cooperation of the Army, Navy, and Luftwaffe.

Sorties and Losses of the Luftwaffe

In the operations against Saaremaa Island a total of 1,313 sorties was flown: 488 by bombers, 318 by fighters, 118 by twin-engine fighters,

30 by reconnaissance aircraft, 318 by seaplanes, 39 by Mausi aircraft,* and 2 by air-sea rescue planes. In the operations against Hiiumaa a total of 211 sorties was flown. Eighty-six of these were carried out by bombers, 56 by fighters, 7 by reconnaissance aircraft, 53 by seaplanes, and 9 by Mausi aircraft. Total German aircraft losses were eight Ju-88's, two Me-110's, two Me-109's, and one air-sea rescue plane.

Results Achieved by the Luftwaffe

In the Saaremaa Island operation, air attacks on ground targets destroyed 26 batteries, 25 individual guns, 26 motor vehicles, 16 field emplacements, 7 bunkers, 2 observation posts, 1 ammunition dump, 7 permanent barracks, 6 cantonments, and 2 columns of horse-drawn vehicles. In addition, 20 batteries were bombed. Besides this, attacks upon ships destroyed 4 motor torpedo boats, capsized 1 minesweeper, set fire to 2 motor torpedo boats and 10 merchant vessels totaling some 5,500 tons, blew up 2 minelayers, sank 3 merchant ships totaling 2,200 tons, and badly damaged 4 smaller vessels. In the Hiiumaa Island operation many artillery and antiaircraft artillery emplacements, field positions, bunkers, and trucks were heavily bombed.

In all of Operation BEOWULF II the Luftwaffe destroyed 15 enemy planes: one I-16 fighter, nine I-153 fighters, and five MBR-2 flying boats.†

Soviet Morale and the Military Situation

During the Baltic island operations the Germans intercepted two revealing letters which uniquely illustrate the condition of Soviet morale and the military situation on the island of Saaremaa. Writing on Saaremaa to his Divisional Commissar (and Chairman of Political Guidance of the Soviet Baltic Fleet), the Regimental Commissar (and Chairman of the Political Branch of the Baltic Coastal Defense Area of the Soviet Baltic Fleet) described in his first letter the numerical superiority of German

---

*The term "Mausi" refers to aircraft especially fitted to detect and destroy magnetic mines at sea. Generally the Ju-52 transport (the tri-motor work horse of the Luftwaffe) and the Dornier Do-23, twin-engine, medium bomber, fitted with a large, electrically charged ring beneath the wing, detected the mines in low-altitude flights.

†A short-range reconnaissance flying boat, single-engine, four-place, monoplane.

ground and air forces; the damage inflicted upon the German amphibious forces as they approached Muhu and Saaremaa, as well as the downing of Luftwaffe planes; and the tremendous Soviet losses of personnel and materiel. These Russian losses, the commissar attributed to: (1) the overwhelming superiority of the Luftwaffe and its continuous attack on Soviet land and sea targets from 30 August to 10 September and after 13 September; (2) the betrayal of Russian movements by Estonian nationals; (3) the lack of sufficient Russian troops to man all the defenses and the lack of serviceable automatic weapons and reserves for stopping break-throughs by the Luftwaffe supported ground forces; (4) cowardice and panic among some Russian officers and men, together with the failure to attempt to restore telephone communications, which had been disrupted by the Luftwaffe; (5) the breakdown of political machinery, since all of the commissars had engaged directly in the fighting, with consequent severe losses; and (6) the failure of the higher political and military leadership on the mainland to fill the repeated requests for air support, automatic weapons, and troop replacements; instead, aviation gasoline and bombs had been tardily delivered after the aircraft for which they were intended had been destroyed to prevent capture, while stocks of unneeded wine were received instead of aircraft parts. The commissar closed his letter with the request for immediate air support, artillery shells, evacuation of the seriously wounded, and tobacco, mail, and news-papers for maintaining morale. In his second--and shorter--letter, written on 29 September, he reiterated the tremendous losses suffered from the German air attacks and begged for air support.[43]

The content of the commissar's letters clearly confirms the unusually great and decisive effect of the Luftwaffe's operations in the capture of the Baltic islands.

Lessons Learned

An operation involving the military, naval, and air services should be conducted by one overall commander in chief. A responsible staff should be assigned to him by each participating service. "The task most tedious in preparation and most difficult to accomplish is the procurement and assembly of equipment for the crossing [of the strait between the Estonian mainland and Muhu], as well as the crossing itself." Since their slow speed precluded rapid concentration, the vessels had to be obtained well in advance, and such an assemblage, which undeniably betrays intentions, was hard to camouflage, particularly from aerial reconnaissance. But diversionary operations pointing "to other places" were successfully carried out.

172

It was decided that the first wave should cross in a surprise assault in the dark, without artillery and air attack preparations, rather than after such preliminaries. Although it had been originally intended that predawn air support of the crossing was to comb lanes through possible mine fields on the beach, this could not be done. Night orientation prevented "sufficiently accurate bombing" and endangered the landing troops, since the lanes were to have been bombed just before the landing of the troops, in order to achieve the greatest possible surprise. The Luftwaffe, however, provided the second assault wave-- crossing in the daylight--with fighter protection and close air support. "To avoid losses in attacks upon ground targets a reliable identification of one's own front lines, especially the first wave, is necessary."

The lessons learned in the BEOWULF II operation recommended a number of techniques. The first assault wave should cross silently just before dawn; only after these troops had landed should artillery on the mainland begin firing upon targets close to the beach area; then, at daybreak, Luftwaffe units should furnish close air support to the first wave and "constant" fighter cover over the landing and crossing points. "It is of decisive importance to undertake flanking landings at as many different places as possible," as the 161st Reconnaissance Battalion demonstrated by landing easily, taking the enemy by surprise, and launching an attack upon the extended Soviet flank. Because the telephone cable between the mainland and the islands was taken intact, communications were no problem, but stand-by radio equipment and courier aircraft had been prudently provided. The Luftwaffe signal communication liaison party and the combined use of radio and radar equipment to direct the fighters were particularly valuable. As soon as a bridgehead was well established, prompt selection of land for airfields was important. A fighter squadron and a flight of close-reconnaissance aircraft were easily transferred to Saaremaa, because Gigant cargo gliders could supply them without delay.

As on the other fronts, propaganda leaflets dropped by air were effective; especially important (according to the testimony of a Soviet deserter-prisoner) was the situation sketch map printed on the back of the leaflet. With respect to the Russian treatment of German personnel captured during the operation, there were, for example, 12 German prisoners captured after the unsuccessful air landing operation near Kübassaare on the Sõrve Peninsula who were "robbed and then shot, being bound from behind." There was also the shooting--with "hands tied and eyes bound"--of fighter pilot Lieutenant Henkemeier, who had been "at first apparently well treated in the hospital at Küressaare" after being shot down and wounded, but who was liquidated when the Russians evacuated the city.[44]

Luftwaffe Commander Baltic*

The command of Luftwaffe Commander Baltic (Colonel von Wild), already mentioned in regard to First Air Fleet operations, had been activated at Swinemuende on 1 April 1941. It was organized to provide continuous armed reconnaissance in the eastern part of the Baltic Sea and Gulf of Finland to prevent "surprise attacks by enemy surface and submarine forces"; mine the harbors of Kronshtadt and Leningrad, the Neva River between Leningrad and Petrokrepost, and the White Sea-Baltic Canal; attack the canal lock installations in the Lake Onega area; provide submarine defense and escort convoys, as well as carry out antisubmarine warfare in the Baltic Sea east of 13° East longitude; and attack enemy merchant shipping whenever necessary.[45]

In order to perform these many-sided tasks, the Lufwaffe Commander Baltic was assigned the 125th Reconnaissance Group, equipped with Ar-95's, He-60's, and He-115's;✝ the 806th Coastal Group, with Ju-88's; the 9th Air-Sea Rescue Squadron; an air-sea rescue control center; the air traffic control ship Karl Meyer, which was used as a navigational aid and for rescue work; and two crash boats. Temporarily assigned later were the Operational Squadron, Replacement Training Group, 54th Fighter Wing; the 506th Coastal Group; the 1st Squadron, 196th Ship-Based Reconnaissance Group; and the 1st Squadron, 406th Coastal Group. The assigned tasks were to be carried out in close cooperation with the naval authorities committed in the Baltic. Reconnaissance was to be provided exclusively for naval purposes, particularly for the Commander in Chief of Cruisers, Vizeadmiral Herbert Schmundt, Commander of Mine Sweepers North, and Commander of Torpedo Boats. The latter had his command post at Helsinki. Reconnaissance activities were directed primarily toward determining the location of and keeping

---

*See Charts Nos. 2 and 6.

✝The Heinkel He-115 was a twin-engine, three-place, midwing, reconnaissance and torpedo bombing, utility floatplane. All organizational charts in the Karlsruhe Document Collection show that the 125th Reconnaissance Group had no He-115's. The other aircraft were all floatplanes.

surveillance over surface units of the Soviet Baltic Fleet, in order to give the German Navy sufficient warning in the event of Russian naval attacks.

Reconnaissance over the Gulf of Finland during the laying of German mine and net barriers between Tallinn and Helsinki was of primary importance. In addition, reconnaissance of Soviet submarines was particularly important and covered all of the eastern Baltic (insofar as this was possible with the weak reconnaissance forces available) in contrast to the reconnaissance of Soviet surface vessels, which could remain limited to definite areas. Mining operations against the naval base at Kronshtadt, the Neva River, and especially the White Sea-Baltic Canal, as well as the escort of convoys to Riga and Tallinn, were special tasks for the Luftwaffe Commander Baltic. A small number of mine-clearing aircraft, the so-called Mausi, were also employed successfully in sweeping operations, while the fighter squadron protected both the convoys and the reconnaissance aircraft as best they could with the number of airplanes available. Then, as heretofore mentioned, reinforced units of the Luftwaffe Commander Baltic furnished support to the joint BEOWULF II operation.[46]

German naval operations in the Baltic were also supported indirectly by Luftwaffe cooperation in the war against merchant shipping and in the successful bombing of Soviet naval vessels in port and at sea. If these operations were not coordinated in detail with the Navy, they nevertheless corresponded basically to the orders given to the Luftwaffe Commander Baltic, who also carried out attacks on the lock installations of the White Sea-Baltic Canal at Povenets. The attack of 15 July was especially successful, one lock gate being destroyed by a direct hit from a 2,200-pound bomb, completely stopping all traffic. After the first attacks, the Soviets put the installation back in order and began to transfer submarines and minesweepers to the Arctic Ocean. The exact time when repairs had been completed went unnoticed by the German air reconnaissance because of bad weather, but the German Navy requested, as it had before, a blockade of the Russian submarines and light naval craft in the Gulf of Finland until frost set in or until the canal might be closed by German ground forces, so the 806th Coastal Group carried out a further attack on the Povenets lock installations with 2,200-pound bombs which had new type detonators permitting low-level bombing. The attack was carried out with excellent results under the command of Major Buehring. Again a lock gate was destroyed and the lock basin severely damaged, but the attacking flight of Ju-88's was lost through premature detonations of the bombs. The use of this type of detonator was immediately stopped by the Chief of Luftwaffe Supply and Procurement.[47] However, the German

175

Navy continued to attach significance to the maintenance of the blockade of the canal by the Luftwaffe.

From 22 June until 31 August 1941 units under the leadership of the Luftwaffe Commander Baltic flew 1,775 sorties, as follows: the 125th Reconnaissance Group, 737 sorties; the 806th Coastal Group, 610; the Operational Squadron, Replacement Training Group, 54th Fighter Wing, 339; elements of the 1st Squadron, 406th Coastal Group, 15; the 1st Squadron, 196th Ship-Based Reconnaissance Group, 66; and the II Group, 1st Bomber Wing, 8 sorties. The last three units were attached to the Luftwaffe Commander Baltic only at times. Organizations of the Luftwaffe Commander Baltic succeeded in sinking 66,000 tons (BRT) of merchant shipping, including five destroyers, one torpedo boat, one patrol or picket boat, two motor torpedo boats, and one small boat.* An additional number of vessels comprising 17,000 tons of merchant shipping were so badly damaged that sinking was probable. The same was also believed to apply to one tanker, one submarine, one torpedo boat, and one escort vessel of 1,200 tons. A third category--ships which were definitely damaged or considered to be damaged by near misses--included: 1 heavy cruiser, 1 flotilla (destroyer) leader; 1 auxiliary cruiser of 6,000-7,000 tons, 17 destroyers, 5 motor torpedo boats, 2 minesweepers, 2 picket boats, 1 cutter, and 132,000 tons of merchant shipping. Luftwaffe Commander Baltic destroyed 46 enemy planes in the air and an additional 12 on the ground against losses of 11 Ju-88's, 3 Ar-95's, 1 Ar-196, and 5 Me-109's, a total of 20 aircraft.[48]

On 27 October the Luftwaffe Commander Baltic was disbanded, the 806th Coastal Group was assigned to the I Air Corps, and the 125th Reconnaissance Group was transferred, because of ice conditions, to Pillau for rehabilitation. The staff, together with a Luftwaffe signal company, remained for a short time at Tallinn, and was transferred at the beginning of November to Berlin. From there it moved early in 1942 to Saki in the Crimea as the staff of Luftwaffe Commander South.

The supply of the Luftwaffe Commander Baltic, which was on the whole accomplished by the I Luftwaffe Administrative Command Headquarters at Koenigsberg, came off smoothly except for a temporary shortage of fuel in July which, however, was quickly overcome by the intervention of the Quartermaster General of the Luftwaffe.✝ The

---

*Confirmed sinkings.
✝Generalleutnant Hans Georg von Seidel. (General der Flieger, 1 January 1942.)

Luftwaffe signal communications--wire and radio--were always available in the required capacity and in order. Liaison with the naval authorities was generally smooth and marked with a mutual understanding of individual weaknesses and shortcomings.

On the whole, the Luftwaffe Commander Baltic carried out successfully the assigned tasks within the limits of the forces available. Despite the very high fighting spirit of the crews and the best intentions of the command, these tasks could not be fully accomplished because the Commander Baltic had too few units and did not always have the type of planes best suited to the operations. This viewpoint was generally confirmed by the German Navy which, in its publication No. 601/12, noted that the Luftwaffe Commander Baltic units had supported naval operations in the Gulf of Finland. Units of the First Air Fleet were also detached to the Baltic area from time to time. But naval operations in the Baltic had been repeatedly complicated because the Luftwaffe's main point of effort in the East was in the area of the Second Air Fleet in Combat Zone Center. "Only with weak forces" were Russian coastal waters occasionally reconnoitered, German merchantmen protected, and Soviet naval targets attacked. "Further complicating [matters] was the local separation of the Navy headquarters from those of the Luftwaffe. Despite all difficulties, however, the good will of all command posts concerned must be emphasized, [for] they tried to carry out their extensive assignments with very meagre forces and were eventually successful. . . ."[49]

Chapter 8

AIR OPERATIONS IN THE FAR NORTH IN 1941
(FINNISH-KARELIAN AREA)*

Mission and Strategic Concentration

Command and Missions of the Three Wehrmacht Branches

Pursuant to Directive No. 21 (18 December 1940), the Commander of Gruppe XXI (later German Wehrmacht Command Norway), Generaloberst Nikolaus von Falkenhorst, who was also Chief of the Joint Command Norway, was ordered to make necessary preparations for and to direct operations in the Finnish area. In his capacity he controlled all branches of the Wehrmacht in the Norwegian-Finnish theater. His primary task was the defense of Norway, which made his mission in Finland from the very outset a secondary assignment, causing matters in the Finnish area to suffer. Von Falkenhorst was responsible for moving units into the Petsamo region in cooperation with Finnish forces to protect vital nickel mines, whose yield was urgently needed by the German war industry.

Murmansk was to be seized if sufficient forces were available for the purpose, so that Soviet ground, air, and naval activity in the region might be immediately restricted. To support this action, which aimed initially to sever all Soviet communications with Murmansk, German and Finnish units planned to launch an attack from the Rovaniemi area with the intention of reaching the Bay of Kandalaksha, from which point they could exploit the resulting advantages. The Murmansk offensive was given the code name Operation RENNTIER (Reindeer), and the drive on Kandalaksha was dubbed Operation SILBERFUCHS (Silver Fox).

Adequate naval support from the Kriegsmarine (German War Navy) was expected in these efforts, especially for the Chief of the Joint Command Norway and for General der Gebirgsjaeger Eduard Dietl's German forces on the Arctic coast.

---

*This chapter was written with the assistance of Generalleutnant (Ret.) Andreas Nielsen, Chief of Staff of the German Fifth Air Fleet, and, in 1941, also Chief of Air Command Kirkenes (Norway). See Appendix II.

In the course of German-Finnish discussions regarding future operations, it had been suggested that the well-known Finnish Field Marshal Karl Gustav Mannerheim should act as supreme commander of all German and Finnish troops operating in Finland. Although this proposal was warmly accepted by the High Command of the Wehrmacht, it was rejected by Mannerheim on the ground that he would thereby lose a large measure of his political and military independence, since the joint command would have placed him directly under the High Command of the Wehrmacht. Thus Mannerheim commanded Finnish troops in southern Finland, while Generaloberst von Falkenhorst, as Chief of the Joint Command of Norway, was responsible for operations in central and northern Finland. It was agreed, however, that the Finnish III Corps might be placed under German command in central Finland for the operation against Kandalaksha.

The Navy and Luftwaffe were permitted great independence of action, but only within the scope of their operational directives, and were to cooperate closely with von Falkenhorst's command in all joint operations. The permanent interdiction of the Murmansk railroad line, so essential to Soviet operations in the Finnish area, became the main task of the Luftwaffe, since naval forces were too insignificant to be able to render material assistance.

Strategic Concentration

Army. Before the outbreak of the war against Russia, the Chief of the Joint Command Norway, established a Command Headquarters Finland in Rovaniemi. Three combat organizations were set up to carry out the required missions in Finland. These consisted of the XIX Mountain Corps (General der Gebirgsjaeger Dietl) assigned to Operation RENNTIER, and the XXXVI Corps (General der Kavallerie Hans Feige) and the Finnish III Corps (General Siilasvuo), both of which were directed to undertake Operation SILBERFUCHS.

The XIX Mountain Corps, including the 2nd and 3rd Mountain Divisions,* was concentrated in and west of Kirkenes, so that forward elements could cross the Finnish border into Soviet territory immediately

---

*In the battle for Narvik (Norway) the 3rd Mountain Division, with only 4,000 troops, held off an allied force of 20,000 men. See Walter Hubatsch, Die deutsche Besetzung von Daenemark und Norwegen (The German Occupation of Denmark and Norway), Goettingen: Musterschmidt Wissenschaftlicher Verlag, 1952, p. 252.

upon the opening of Operation BARBAROSSA.

The XXXVI Corps was unable to concentrate its forces before the beginning of the war against Russia because of the possible political consequences of moving into Finland early. Some parts of this force had come from Norway, while other elements had to cross the Baltic Sea from Germany. The approach of this corps was covered by the Finnish III Corps, which was situated in an area about 60 miles south of Salla, around Kuusamo-Suomussalmi. The Finnish unit was to commence its attack upon Loukhi at the same time the Germans opened their attack upon Salla.

All three of these assault forces (each consisting of two divisions and additional corps troops) had only weak supporting artillery and no armored forces at all. The two German corps operated about 210 miles from each other, separated by impassable terrain, so that neither could come to the support of the other. The only lateral communication route was from Rovaniemi to Petsamo, the Arctic route, 120 miles to the rear of the most advanced assembly areas.

Navy. The Naval Commander Arctic Coast (with headquarters at Tromsø) was given the responsibility for naval missions in collaboration with army forces in the Finnish area. This force also furnished a number of naval coast artillery batteries for use from Petsamo to Kirkenes. Although a naval staff was organized in Kirkenes for use in the event of the capture of Murmansk, no naval craft, with the exception of those used for convoy duty, were available for the northern operations from the Naval High Command Norway (Marineoberkommando Norwegen), headed by Generaladmiral Rolf Carls.

Luftwaffe. The Air Command Northern Norway (Col. (GSC) Andreas Nielsen) was established in Bardufoss at the close of 1940 and given the job of preparing airfields and other ground stations in that area, including supplying Finnish airfields which might be used by the Luftwaffe. This organization was placed under the command of the Air Administrative Command Headquarters Norway.*

Since a suitable commander and staff personnel for combat operations in the area were lacking, a tactical staff was organized as Air Command Kirkenes under the direction of the Chief of Staff, Fifth Air Fleet, at Oslo. Units could not be moved to their new locations in advance,

_____

*See Chart No. 6.

nor troops oriented ahead of time, because of the danger of betraying the intended campaign to the enemy. The close relationships existing between German soldiers and some of the Norwegian populace, especially the Norwegian women, obliged Luftwaffe commanders to take special security measures.

Only the airfield at Banak, at the southern end of Porsanger Fjord, and the field at Kirkenes, in northern Norway, could be used for the concentration of air forces, because they were the only fields situated close enough for the range of German planes. These bases were immediately prepared and stockpiled with supplies necessary for combat operations. Kirkenes posed a special problem since it had to be supplied by sea. Because of this fact, as well as the key importance of the position, it was furnished with a long-distance radio station, but the danger of interception prevented it from being used except on very infrequent occasions. Natural geographical obstacles in Norway obliged German forces to make immense efforts to establish connections with the Fifth Air Fleet headquarters in Oslo.[1]*

The Opposing Soviet Forces

Command

Since German intelligence agents had been unable to secure precise information concerning Soviet headquarters before the outbreak of war,/ the Luftwaffe was unable to destroy those centers at the outset of the conflict. Most of these command posts were discovered only after the interrogation of captured Russian troops.

It was surprising that Russian commanders in the north seemed to expect no attack, especially when the German concentration movements on a broad front had been going on for some time. Nevertheless, Soviet leaders reacted with remarkable quickness and vigor to the German offensives, and were finally able to bring all progress in the Finnish area to a halt. In this achievement almost none of the credit was due to naval or air units, which lent very little support.

---

*See Map No. 11 and Charts Nos. 2 and 6.

/The intelligence agents also knew very little about Soviet leadership.

The Soviet Command had the advantage of being able to concentrate its forces near the border in peacetime operations, without creating an air of suspicion. These forces were well supplied by an integrated logistical network and by the Murmansk railroad, a lateral communication route behind the front which gave the Russians special advantages.[2]

The Soviet Army

Estimates of Soviet Army strength prior to the war were made principally from the meager gleanings of German intelligence agents and from reports from the Finnish forces. At least three Soviet corps were anticipated in the area, including considerable armored forces, a fact which was later confirmed at the battle of Salla. The Russians had a great deal more artillery than the Germans in the Finnish area, and much of it was of heavy caliber.

The greatest advantage of the Soviet Army, however, lay in the fact that its troops were generally recruited in regions where extremes of temperature were common, and had conducted maneuvers in the very sectors where operations were about to begin. Being thoroughly familiar with the terrain and its problems, the Russians had a singular advantage over the Germans who knew nothing of the area and who were guided chiefly by inadequate maps and charts.

The Soviet Navy

Germans were completely in the dark with respect to the present or potential strength of the Soviet Navy. At the opening of the campaign German air reconnaissance detected several submarines and six heavy and light cruisers in the naval port of Polyarny at Murmansk, but, because of excellent camouflage of dock installations and frequent changes of mooring, it was impossible to determine the precise strength of the Soviet Fleet in Arkhangelsk or other ports on the White Sea.

The absence of German naval units along the Arctic coast left Soviet forces free to interfere with German troop concentrations and supply movements, yet no such action developed. Soviet naval units concentrated upon defending their own coastal convoys and generally feared to engage even the weakest German Navy forces. The Soviet Navy, in short, lacked initiative and aggressiveness.

Soviet Air Force

Soviet flying forces in the northern area consisted of army and naval air units. German commanders were never able to ascertain whether these organizations functioned under a unified command. Most of the important Russian air bases in this region were around Murmansk, including the large airfield at Varlamovo, the fields at Murmashi (I and II), and a seaplane base at Kola Bay. Two airfields, Niva and Shongui, were also found near Kandalaksha, but these were of relatively minor importance. The facilities at these Soviet air bases were almost uniformly inferior, few of the fields having adequate navigational or communications equipment.

About 200 Russian aircraft were based upon these airfields at the beginning of the war. Eighty percent of these planes were single-engine types, many of which were obsolete. The bulk of the Soviet fighters were Rata I-16* aircraft, which were highly maneuverable, but scarcely a match for the German Me-109. Whatever the deficiencies of the I-16, they were somewhat offset by their advantageous numerical ratio in this area. Approximately 100 Soviet fighters opposed every 16 German fighters.

The Russian bomber force consisted mainly of SB-2's and IL-2's,/ although the antiquated SB-2's were being gradually replaced in the summer of 1941 by IL-2's and bombers of British manufacture.

Soviet aircrew training was grossly inferior to German training, and Russian morale suffered accordingly. Most Soviet air operations were carried out in accordance with normal peacetime routines, but heavy initial losses forced them to adopt ingenious methods of camouflage and deception to protect their planes in the air and on the ground.//

---

*See footnote, p. 19.

/The SB-2 is a twin-engine, midwing bomber and long-range reconnaissance plane. The IL-2 was the well-known "Stormovik" fighter-bomber, widely used by Soviet forces for close support work. It was a low-wing, cantilever type monoplane, heavily armored, and fitted with 2 cannons, 2 machine guns, and bomb racks. It was a V-type, single-engine plane. See Leonard Bridgman (ed.), Jane's All the World's Aircraft 1941, p. 126c.

//See Generalleutnant a. D. Klaus Uebe, Russian Reactions to German Airpower in World War II, USAF Historical Studies No. 176, Maxwell AFB: USAF Hist. Div., ASI, July 1964, Chapters 4 and 5. Cited hereafter as USAF Study 176.

Soviet airmen flew very few missions each day, and only an occasional flight penetrated into the German rear areas. Since only the leaders of Russian units were entrusted with the knowledge of the attack objectives, German pilots disrupted their missions by shooting down the lead aircraft. The remainder of the Russian formation then dispersed in haste and fled to base by the shortest route.*

Russian fighter pilots were singularly lacking in aggressiveness during most of the war. In order to draw them into battle German fighters often found it advisable to carry along a few bombs to bomb a village or town, so that Soviet fighters would be forced to come to its defense. German fighter pilots, compelled to remain above 18,000 feet over some of the major port targets because of accurate fire by Soviet naval batteries, often viewed the spectacle of Russian interceptors flying several thousand feet below them, simulating fierce combat maneuvers, firing into the empty air space ahead. As soon as the German planes left the area these planes returned to base.✝ This curious action was later explained by Russian prisoners, who testified that the Commissar had ordered all Soviet fighters to take off when an enemy bombing took place, and to engage the enemy in combat until he had left the target area. Because of their short flight durations, German fighters had to return to their bases within 15 minutes, in any case, allowing Soviet fighter units to report that they had "driven off the attackers." From the ground the sight must have looked impressive and credible.

German Army Operations

XIX Mountain Corps

While the main body of the German Army crossed into Soviet territory at dawn on 22 June 1941, units of the Joint Command Norway began the concentration of its forces in central and northern Finland. No hostile action was taken against them by Soviet forces.

On the extreme left wing of the far northern sector, the XIX Mountain Corps hastened to complete its concentration by 28 June.[3] On the following day, by the light of the "midnight sun," German mountain

---

*Ibid., pp. 91 and 92.
✝Ibid., p. 66.

forces of the XIX Mountain Corps began their drive on Murmansk across the still snow-covered tundra.[4]* Surprise was out of the question since the war against Russia had been in progress on other fronts for a full week, but well-coordinated blows by tenacious mountaineers (supported by Luftwaffe dive bombers) succeeded in breaking down most of the Soviet field fortifications.

The advance continued despite stiffening enemy resistance on the second day, but slowed perceptibly when the dive bomber group of the Air Command Kirkenes was transferred away for the support of the XXXVI Corps in its attack on Salla. Because of this the Litsa River was not crossed until 8 July. Strong Russian counteroffensives began on the following day, and mounted in intensity on 10 July.[5] The need for air support in this area was complicated by the fact that heavy sea traffic had been observed at this time moving from Murmansk through Motovski Bay to the Rybachiy Peninsula, and Luftwaffe assistance was needed there to support the weak corps forces in the Rybachiy Peninsula. The threat of this Soviet sea movement against the rear of the corps' northern flank slowed down the further advance so that little progress was made in July. Increasing Soviet counterattacks were repelled by the Wehrmacht although enemy flanking maneuvers from the south and constant threats of seaborne attacks from the north repeatedly placed the corps in critical situations.

German forces (XIX Mountain Corps and the XXXVI Corps) on the Finnish Front were ordered on 19 July to continue their offensive in accordance with Fuehrer Directive No. 33, even though delays would have to be expected in view of the impossibility of granting air support at the time. As soon as the fighting around Smolensk (to the south) had come to an end, the Luftwaffe intended to transfer a number of dive bomber units to Finland to support arctic units of the German Navy in easing the situation of the XIX Mountain Corps.[6]/ At the end of July, however, the Russians succeeded in landing a force from Motovski Bay in the rear of the Mountain Corps, which was thus forced to halt its offensive (on its main front) and resort to positional warfare.

As a result of this development, a new Fuehrer Directive (No. 34 of 30 July 1941) called for the discontinuance of the drive on Kandalaksha in order for the XXXVI Corps to transfer forces for the relief of the

---

*The attack had to commence in broad daylight because in these high latitudes the midnight sun was above the horizon throughout the day and night.

/ This battle ended on 6 August, but the expected transfer of dive bombers never took place.

northern flank of the XIX Mountain Corps. While the XXXVI Corps came to the rescue of the Mountain Corps, the Finnish III Corps, which had been more successful in its operations in that theater, was to be assigned the task of interdicting the vital Murmansk rail line.

The most tragic aspect of operations in this area was the apparent total ignorance on the part of the German High Command of existing conditions and the possible range of action in the Far North. It was utterly impossible to withdraw forces from the XXXVI Corps in the strength prescribed by the High Command of the Wehrmacht without exposing the uncovered flanks of that unit to dangerous Soviet counterattacks. This would inevitably have meant surrendering the initiative to the enemy. In any case, an acute shortage of transportation would have prevented the timely transfer of reinforcements over the only available route of communication (a distance of 480 miles). Forces moving to the front over this route would have arrived far too late to relieve the mountain troops.

The XIX Mountain Corps was therefore obliged to do as best it could, with assistance from the Luftwaffe when available. Having shifted to positional warfare on its main front, the corps launched an attack against the landed Soviet forces and annihilated them in a thorough operation. Soviet assault in the area of the Mountain Corps' main front (intended to eliminate the German bridgehead across the Litsa River) were meanwhile repulsed by army units in that sector, supported substantially by German air power.

At this time heavy Soviet artillery batteries, placed along the west coast of the Rybachiy Peninsula, had created a serious situation for the seaborne supply traffic of the Finland Army, especially since these guns commanded the entrance to the port of Petsamo. Attempts to neutralize these batteries, concealed as they were in rock bunkers, required the greater part of the then available air power, depriving ground forces elsewhere of more substantial support. This gradually forced German units, especially the mountain corps, to go more and more to the defensive.

In September, after regrouping, the XIX Mountain Corps attempted to recover the initiative, but only slow progress could be made against the now considerably reinforced Soviet forces. Shortly thereafter, the Russians commenced counterattacking, and all that could be achieved by the Germans was a rather negligible expansion of the existing bridge-head across the Litsa.*

The Battle at Salla and Operations by the XXXVI Corps and the Finnish III Corps

The XXXVI Corps did not complete its concentration movements until 30 June 1941, and opened its initial assault without artillery preparation or aerial bombardment on 1 July, three days after the XIX Mountain Corps had gone into action. Its attack was launched against the fortification system at Salla, a strong series of emplacements, some of which were constructed of reinforced concrete. The offensive bogged down in its initial stages. One unit of the corps (SS Division NORD),† which was used in a frontal assault in the center, panicked on the first day and broke, with the result that the entire division had to be withdrawn from combat. Several days were required to re-form the unit and return it to action. Fortunately for the German forces, Soviet commanders in the area failed to follow up their momentary opportunity.

Despite subsequent heavy air support by the Luftwaffe, German ground forces were unable to capture the fortifications at Salla until 9 July. Once these positions had been taken, however, the most serious obstacle to the conquest of Kandalaksha was removed. During the month of July, Finnish III Corps forces pushed vigorously ahead against tenacious Soviet resistance, and by 27 July its southern units had reached the vicinity of Ukhta, where fighting was particularly hard because of the difficult terrain. In these battles the Finns proved themselves to be masters of forest combat and fought with conspicuous bravery. Some elements of the Finnish Corps also contributed to the capture of the fortifications of Salla.

A few days after the battle began in the XXXVI Corps area, the Russians moved in reserves by the spur rail line from Kandalaksha to Salla. There they launched repeated attacks for nearly a month against German and Finnish forces. Despite Luftwaffe support, the Soviet units

---

*From 22 June to 23 September 1941 the XIX Mountain Corps lost 2,211 men in action, with 7,854 wounded and 425 missing. See Col. (Ret) Kurt Hermann, General Dietl, Muenchen: Muenchner Buchverlag, 1951, p. 231. See also Map No. 11.

†6th SS Mountain Division, an untried, recently formed unit organized for police work in Norway, which was sent to the XXXVI Corps for its first combat assignment.

posed a serious threat to the German ground advance. Only the immediate resumption of the initiative by the Wehrmacht could stave off the danger.

On 27 July the corps again took up its attack in the direction of Kairala, whence the Russians had gone to establish new positions. Although beset with heavy Soviet resistance, the XXXVI Corps was able by 9 August to win the city of Kestenga. Driving toward the east and southeast it formed the left wing of a pincers movement designed to entrap Soviet forces in and around Kairala. Approaching from the south, the Finnish III Corps reached the vicinity of Loukhi, but the German XXXVI Corps was unable to close the ring because of spirited Russian counterattacks. The German unit was thereby forced to halt its offensive for regrouping operations.

The XXXVI Corps resumed its attacks on 20 August, driving toward Kandalaksha. Two days later it had reached a position nine miles southwest of Alakurti, where it was able to hold its ground against furious Russian assaults. On 24 August the Soviet forces began to evacuate their positions and to withdraw toward the area east of Alakurti. Many, however, were already encircled by Finnish and German units. The encirclement battle of Kairala ended on 27 August with the destruction of the Soviet XXXXVI Corps (including the 104th and 122nd Divisions), thus averting for the time any serious Russian threats.[8]

On 3 September 1941, German troops driving eastward from the Salla area crossed the former Russo-Finnish frontier and by the middle of the month reached a line approximately six miles east of Alakurti. This effort, however, demanded much from Wehrmacht units and most of them were completely exhausted as a result. German forces therefore finished mopping up operations and established the Wehrmann Line, which could be held against Soviet counterattacks until winter.

On 22 September Hitler ordered a halt in the attack then in progress in the Finnish III Corps area, and the transfer of troops thereby relieved to the XXXVI Corps, which was to prepare for a resumption of the drive upon Kandalaksha in early October. It was considered essential to sever the Murmansk rail line before winter. The 163rd Division, which had been assigned to the Finnish Command and had performed so well in the battles of the Finnish Army on the Karelian Front, was to be sent via Rovaniemi to Army Command Norway for participation in the operation. The almost stalemated offensive of the XIX Mountain Corps was ordered to cease, with the exception of operations underway on its northern flank, which for reasons of deception and the improvement of defenses had to be continued. Before the onset of winter the mountain troops were to capture the greater part of the Rybachiy Peninsula in order to facilitate naval operations associated with the supply movements passing through the ports of Kirkenes and Petsamo for army forces in Finland.[9]

The directive from the Fuehrer's headquarters arrived just as the first blizzards were raging in the northern sector of the front. A few days later weather conditions were the same along the entire extent of the German-Finnish lines. Under such circumstances it was impossible to carry out the terms of the directive. Instead, troops all along the Lapland front prepared for winter positional warfare, a situation which remained unchanged until the end of 1941.

The Finnish III Corps, parts of which materially assisted the XXXVI Corps in its successful assault on Alakurti, fought skillfully and bravely against Russian forces around Ukhta. It then advanced upon Loukhi, drove to the narrows between Lake Pya and Lake Top by the end of September, and held its ground in an advanced bridgehead, fending off all Soviet counterassaults.*

Under the able leadership of Field Marshal Mannerheim, the Finnish Army in the summer of 1941 reached and crossed the former Russo-Finnish border. Some units reached the Arctic Canal, closing it to traffic in the direction of Murmansk. These objectives were attained in heavy fighting at a considerable cost in life and equipment.†

Luftwaffe Participation

Command and Mission

The tactical staff of the Fifth Air Fleet (with headquarters at Kirkenes) controlled, for tactical purposes only, all of the air units committed against Russia in the Far North. All other command authority over these Luftwaffe units rested with Air Commander North (with headquarters at Stavanger) and with Fighter Command Norway.

---

*See Map No. 11.

†The Finns called even men of advanced years to the colors, and thousands of women and girls were also included among the fighting forces. Like the Germans, the Finns hoped to use all forces possible to effect a speedy end to the campaign. The resulting strain was severe upon the Finnish economy.

The chief of the tactical staff, generally designated as Chief of Air Command Kirkenes (Col. Andreas Nielsen, GSC), had a completely independent mission to perform, a mission which was only roughly defined in the High Command of Wehrmacht directive. More definite commitments were made in conferences between the Chief of Staff of the Fifth Air Fleet and the chiefs of staff of army and naval headquarters in the North. The principal mission was to support all army and naval operations in the Finnish area. This included: (1) the establishment of German air superiority over all combat areas and coastal portions of northern Norway; (2) operations against hostile land and sea forces; (3) operations against Soviet supply routes, especially the Arctic Canal, Murmansk, Arkhangelsk and Kandalaksha; and (4) the protection of German shipping against attacks by the Western Allies.

Because of the scope of German operations, the extent of the war theater, and the paucity of Luftwaffe forces available, these operations could only be performed "as far as possible" under the existing conditions.

Since the Chief of Air Command Kirkenes also had to act as tactical air commander at an army headquarters, close cooperation between Luftwaffe and ground units was assured.

The Air Forces Assigned

In order to accomplish its mission the following forces were assigned to Air Command Kirkenes:

(1) Reconnaissance units consisted of the 1st Strategic Reconnaissance Squadron, 120th Reconnaissance Group; the 1st Tactical Reconnaissance Squadron, 32nd Reconnaissance Group (both at Kirkenes).

(2) Bomber forces consisted of the 5th Squadron, 30th Bomber Wing, stationed at Banak.

(3) Dive bomber units were formed from the 4th Dive Bomber Group, 1st Air Wing, at Kirkenes.

(4) Fighter forces consisted of the 13th Squadron, 77th Fighter Wing at Kirkenes, and 1 swarm* of aircraft from the 76th Twin-Engine Fighter Wing, also at Kirkenes.

---

*Usually 5 or 6 aircraft, not a standard organization or designation of unit strength.

Antiaircraft artillery units were not assigned to Air Command Kirkenes, but were provided by the Luftwaffe Administrative Command Norway, a subordinate unit of the Fifth Air Fleet. Army units in the Far North were furnished with the 1st Battalion, 5th Antiaircraft Artillery Regiment, while 1 mixed antiaircraft artillery battalion was sent to the airfield at Banak, and 1 light and 1 heavy antiaircraft artillery battalions were posted at Kirkenes for the defense of the main air base.*

Ground Service Organization

The only two airfields suitable for operations in the northern Norway area were controlled by the Air Commander Kirkenes, acting under the administrative authority of Air Commander North (Col. Alexander Holle) and Air Administrative Command Norway.

Responsibility for the development of the ground service organization and logistical support for these bases rested with Air Command North. Work had commenced in the autumn of 1940 on the expansion of the two fields, Banak and Kirkenes, although it was not known at the time that they would be decisively important for later operations. This project was accelerated once the plan for a campaign against Soviet Russia became known. Delays kept occurring, however, because of the early winter in those latitudes, and the unfortunate necessity [for the Germans] of transporting everything, down to the last nail, by sea. Preparing the two fields in time for BARBAROSSA was thus a task which required the utmost efforts.

The Finnish airfield at Petsamo was also stockpiled with supplies in case the Luftwaffe had to make use of it in the future. Other Finnish airfields would be available to the Luftwaffe in case of necessity. After the movement of German forces into Finland, the Finnish Air Force offered the central Finnish base of Rovaniemi and the tactical airfield at Kemijarvi for Luftwaffe use. The equipping of these bases was accomplished through the Luftwaffe liaison channels in collaboration with the German general attached to Finnish headquarters and the Supreme Commander of the Luftwaffe, so that German flying units could take over these fields at any time. All of the airfields in the area, however, Norwegian as well as Finnish, were makeshift bases at best. None of them measured up to peacetime standards for European flying fields.

_____

*See Chart No. 6 and Map No. 11.

Because of inadequate runways, supply facilities, billets, and communications, normal safety regulations could scarcely be fulfilled to the letter.

Another factor of importance in this theater was the matter of morale. German airmen, accustomed to much better conditions, often complained bitterly about their situation. Despite apprehensions of German flyers, the necessity to observe greater precautions in landing and taking off at these more primitive fields actually resulted in a lower accident rate than at regular bases in continental Europe. The extreme isolation of the troop units in the Far North, especially the ground personnel who had no momentary escape, as did the flyers, required special welfare measures from German special services organizations. Considerable support was rendered to these units by the Reichs Commissioner for Norway.

Operations

Air Command Kirkenes was under orders to initiate purely tactical operations. Missions of this sort were ordered by special directives, most of which involved support of the army or the naval forces. Its primary function was to eliminate hostile air forces.

This command's first attack began simultaneously with the movement of the main German front across the Soviet border. Since the Russians were unprepared for the assault, they made only a feeble response to these incursions by the numerically weaker Luftwaffe forces. Sixty to seventy Soviet planes were caught on the airfield at Varlamovo and destroyed. The surprise was that the Russians would permit this to happen in view of the devastating losses already suffered in the main combat areas. This probably reflected the serious Soviet problem of inflexibility at command levels, and the terrible disruption of their communications because of the invasion farther to the south.

A second attack delivered on the opening day resulted in massive destruction of communications lines and the central power station at Murmansk. Prisoners later testified to the impact made upon shipbuilding yards, workshops, and factories. Some missions were later flown against Russian airfields with little opposition from Soviet ground or air forces.

A further mission of tactical importance was the severance of the Murmansk railroad line, a route which was interdicted more than

100 times during the first six months of battle. Because this interdiction could not be continuously maintained, the bomber squadron of the 30th Bomber Wing (at Banak) was increased in size to a group. Russians, aware of the need to maintain their traffic over the Murmansk rail line, stockpiled repair materials by the sides of the tracks at various points to facilitate quick repairs. The Luftwaffe succeeded by its steady attacks in preventing a large-scale concentration of power being built up in the Soviet Far North, which had the additional effect of blunting many Russian counterattacks.

In response to requests by the High Command of the German Navy, a number of attacks were made against lock installations in the Arctic Canal during the opening days of the campaign and again late in the summer. Nevertheless, the scanty ship traffic on this canal made it a point of secondary importance to the Luftwaffe. Whenever the locks or other parts of the canal were bombarded, the damage was usually repaired by the Russians in remarkably short time. After 9 September 1941, the day on which Finnish Army units reached the southern part of the water-way (the White Sea Canal) near Petrokrepost, the entire Arctic Canal system ceased to be important as a major shipping route. Thereafter only occasional attacks were made against local traffic in the northern part of the canal.

Other important targets in this area were the installations at Arkhangelsk, the Kandalaksha to Arkhangelsk railroad line, and the hydroelectric plant at Nivskiy, north of Kandalaksha, all of which were successfully attacked by the Luftwaffe.[10]

Support of Army Operations

Effective air support of army operations in the Far North began on 29 June and had favorable as well as unfavorable effects upon the German Wehrmacht. While this assistance permitted ground force units to advance rapidly, it also caused them to become overly dependent upon the protective umbrella of the Luftwaffe. German troops thus reacted in an unusually sensitive manner to aerial attacks when occasional Soviet planes were able to penetrate Luftwaffe defenses.

The IV Dive Bomber Group, 1st Air Wing, supported the operations of the XIX Mountain Corps and performed certain secondary duties as requested, while units of the 30th Bomber Wing attacked targets farther in the Soviet rear area. The dive bombers were especially effective in reducing the batteries on the Rybachiy Peninsula.

From the beginning of the campaign strategic reconnaissance units of the German Air Force carried out their missions over distant Russian terrain, securing valuable photographic material for use by the ground forces and by the air command in conducting counter-air operations. Long-distance reconnaissance flights were often hampered, however, by adverse weather.

During the battle for Salla, which began on 1 July 1941 and lasted for more than a week, the dive bomber group carried out continuous operations against Soviet positions and troop concentrations. From the outset it was obvious that the German ground attack would have failed completely without this air support. About 30 planes participated in each attack, and every Luftwaffe aircrew flew four or five missions daily. The approach leg of these flights was about 112 miles, and upon reaching the target it was necessary for the aircraft to remain over the battle area for at least a half hour in order to hamper Russian movements. Because of these factors, it was not surprising that German aircrews were soon on the verge of complete exhaustion.[11]

As soon as victory was in sight around Salla, the dive bomber group (minus one squadron) was returned to Kirkenes to make preparations to support on 10 July the XIX Mountain Corps along the Litsa River. Especially important targets in Litsa Bay and in Motovski Bay were attacked in an effort to prevent a Russian landing behind the northern flank of the mountain units. Keenly aware of the increased Soviet military activity in this sector, the Commanding General of the Fifth Air Fleet (Generaloberst Stumpff) proceeded to the area himself, and thereupon ordered the transfer of two additional bomber squadrons from Stavanger to Banak, thus enabling the Luftwaffe commander at Kirkenes to form an entire group by the end of July.*

The superiority which Wehrmacht forces in this sector hoped to achieve as a result of operations by a full dive bomber group was completely offset by newly arrived Soviet reinforcements. Spirited Russian counterattacks in the northern sector soon forced the Luftwaffe commander at Kirkenes to commit all of his planes in order to defend the German forward positions. Under such conditions the XIX Mountain Corps could scarcely resume its planned offensive. The Luftwaffe was able to fend off attempted Soviet flanking attacks on the corps' southern perimeter, to silence batteries in the neck of the Rybachiy Peninsula,

---

*See Map No. 11.

and to repel Russian forces which had landed from Motovski Bay on the northern rim of the front in the rear of the mountain troops.

The continuous daylight of the Far North and the exceptionally heavy demands made upon German air units in that theater compelled the Luftwaffe commander to take measures to strengthen his weak organization. On his request the reserve squadron of the IV Dive Bomber Group, 1st Air Wing, was transferred from Christiansand, Norway, and temporarily assigned to the commander at Kirkenes, while the fighter organization in the Far North was increased in size from one squadron to a group by the addition of two squadrons from Norway.

The dive bomber group (Gruppe Blasig),* again minus a squadron, was transferred on 27 July to Rovaniemi, where it was to support the renewed advance of the XXXVI Corps and the Finnish III Corps. In the meantime the Russians had established new advance airfields in the Kandalaksha and Salla areas. Because of this, a squadron of escort fighters was assigned to the bomb group. This air support was a positive contribution to the advance of the XXXVI Corps from Kairala to Alakurti and of the Finnish III Corps in its drive on Loukhi.

During this time the aforementioned Soviet amphibious troops had become a dangerous threat to the northern flank of the XIX Mountain Corps, but Luftwaffe attacks against Soviet naval vessels in Motovski Bay were so successful that the recently landed Russian troops now found themselves virtually isolated and in a most precarious situation. Taking advantage of this fact, the XIX Mountain Corps launched a bold counterattack and on 3 August completely crushed the Russian opposition on their northern flank. Remnants of these Soviet units attempting to escape by sea were continuously attacked by units of the Air Command Kirkenes. From then on German mountain troops (with air support) were able to control the only Soviet land route for the transport of military supplies in the northern sector of the Far North operational area. This compelled the Russians to ship their equipment and supplies by sea from Murmansk, where their transports were highly vulnerable to air attacks.

Unfavorable weather during the month of September prevented good exploitation of Luftwaffe forces in the Far North, especially along the coastal areas. Reconnaissance units were active insofar as conditions permitted. They soon discovered that the Soviet Air Force was

_____

*Named after its commander, Capt. Arnulf Blasig.

195

already receiving considerable amounts of equipment (including aircraft) from the Western Allies. Occasionally fighter planes of Western manufacture were sighted by German flyers.[12]* A number of newer Russian fighters also began to appear, which confirmed German suspicions that the Soviet Union was rapidly modernizing its fighter organizations. However, despite the use of improved aircraft, Russian flyers were still unable to contend successfully with Luftwaffe pilots.

Rocky terrain prevented the establishment of German airfields, which placed Luftwaffe fighter units at a disadvantage when reports came in concerning Soviet attacks upon front line ground units. By the time German fighters were on the scene the Russian attacks had often been completed. Forward warning teams helped to correct this problem, but only the installation of radar in 1942 was really effective in this respect.

Bad weather fronts with considerable fog and rain usually traveled from west to east, allowing Soviet aircraft to take off from their fields while the Luftwaffe remained grounded and unable to intercept them. Conditions were even more unfavorable for German fighters operating in the central sector of the Far North in support of the XXXVI Corps and the Finnish III Corps. Here, the closest Luftwaffe airfield (Kemijarvi) was 60 miles behind the front. Until the Soviet air base at Alakurti was taken, German flyers were at a distinct disadvantage, while Russian airmen could operate from a number of advance bases close to the front lines.

Sometimes the only way to protect front line German troops was by the establishment of fighter patrols over the combat area, a tactic which was quickly recognized by the Russians, who then attacked only when no Luftwaffe fighters were in the air. With the seizure of the base at Alakurti by the XXXVI Corps, two squadrons of Luftwaffe fighters were immediately brought in to this advance base and positive steps were taken to expand its facilities for increased German air traffic. It soon became the main base of the Luftwaffe in central Finland. The acquisition of this field dramatically improved the position of the German Wehrmacht in the North. Soviet efforts to recapture it were easily beaten off by the Luftwaffe.

---

*Because of Lend-lease and other Allied assistance, by the turn of 1942 the Soviet Union had four to five times as many fighters as the Luftwaffe. See Capt. Karl Otto Hoffmann, "Entstehung, Einsatz und Erfolg der Sowjet-Luftmacht," Luftwaffenring, Nr. 8 ("Origin, Operations and Results of the Soviet Air Power," Air Force Ring, No. 8), 8 August 1956. G/VI/2b, Karlsruhe Document Collection.

With an utter lack of understanding of operational possibilities and general conditions in the Arctic, the bomber group was transferred in September to Rovaniemi, where it carried out a few missions against the Murmansk rail line. At the end of the month it was transferred back to Petsamo (where one squadron had remained) for further operations. Before the group could undertake any missions, however, a heavy blizzard blanketed the area. In mid-October, with the airfield snowed in, personnel of the bomber group embarked by sea for Stavanger, where they were then sent to another theater of war. Their aircraft remained behind at Petsamo.

The onset of winter in late September also stopped all operations of the IV Dive Bomber Group, 1st Air Wing, at Kirkenes. This group was concentrated at Rovaniemi in early October, during a period of favorable weather. From this base it was able to operate with success on the Kandalaksha front, striking billets, troop positions, supply columns, and shelters. Attacks were also made against rail lines and facilities, especially those serving the port of Murmansk. The long approach flight from the base at Rovaniemi made it necessary for all dive bombers to carry auxiliary fuel tanks. As soon as the airfield at Alakurti was captured, however, this was no longer necessary. After a period of hard frost, with temperatures dropping at times to 58° below zero Fahrenheit, it was possible to construct an ice airfield on one of the lakes in the Finnish III Corps sector, where one of the dive bomber squadrons, operating in support of the corps, was more or less permanently based.

The closing two months of 1941 were characterized by a marked decrease in both German and Soviet air activity over the northern theater of operations. A withdrawal of German air units to Norway was also rendered impossible by bad weather conditions.

Cooperation with the Navy in Sea Warfare

Air Command Kirkenes had the full responsibility for the defense of northern Norwegian and Finnish coastal waters since the Navy was without combat units in these areas. Only in August were two German destroyers moved in to the Neiden Fjord near Kirkenes. Here they generally remained inactive since the Soviet Navy carried out few operations.

The mission of the German Navy was to protect supply shipments to the Wehrmacht and the Finnish forces via the northern coastal route.

Luftwaffe units of the naval group of Air Command North were responsible for performing reconnaissance tasks for such convoys and their supporting naval escorts. Air Commander Kirkenes was to supply fighters for the defense of naval and sea transport undertakings within the range of the Soviet air forces. Fortunately for the Luftwaffe the Soviet Air Force never made any serious threats against German convoys in this sector. Had it done so, the weak Luftwaffe fighter units from Kirkenes could never have prevailed. As things turned out, fighters based at Petsamo were sufficient to protect convoys passing Vardφ Island bound for Petsamo or Kirkenes.

The greatest danger in this area came from the heavy batteries on the Rybachiy Peninsula, which the Soviets had carefully emplaced and protected. Even dive bombers were subjected to fire from these guns in the course of their attacks, but the Luftwaffe's action successfully prevented any ship sinkings by the concealed batteries.

A further task of Air Commander North was the maintenance of reconnaissance over sea areas east of a line from Spitzbergen to Barents Island to North Cape, and to attack any hostile naval craft observed.

At the end of July a British fleet succeeded in approaching the northern Norwegian coast during a time when the Rybachiy Peninsula was blanketed under a heavy cover of fog. Two British aircraft carriers* were spotted by German observers just as they emerged from a massive fog bank, but this report arrived simultaneously with the news of an attack by carrier aircraft against Kirkenes and Petsamo. Unforeseen circumstances, not the least important of which was the failure of the Russians to launch their diversionary air attack early enough, caused the British venture to fail. The belated Soviet attacks simply alerted German flying units so that they were prepared to meet the enemy attack. By coincidence a German dive bomber unit from Kirkenes was returning to base from a combat mission when it discovered the carriers and auxiliary vessels. Making a snap decision, the squadron leader joined the attack with his planes, strafing the enemy ships with machine guns. Luftwaffe fighters were already engaged in battle against the carrier-borne planes. In the course of the action 28 enemy aircraft were destroyed, 23 by German fighters and 5 more by naval and antiaircraft

---

*These were probably the Victorious and the Furious.

198

guns.   Only one small coastal vessel was sunk by the British force.
Nineteen prisoners were captured by the Wehrmacht.[13]

Although the British prisoners behaved in an exemplary manner
under interrogation, their efforts to maintain military security were
for naught, since one of them had neglected to remove documents concerning the attack and movie tickets for a theater in Reykjavik, Iceland,
from his pockets. From these scraps of paper German intelligence
officers were able to trace the origins of the raid.

Aerial mining of northern coastal waters produced very little
results. Such missions were disliked by Luftwaffe aircrews, who could
see practically no tangible evidence that such mining operations were
effective. Nevertheless, the fact that Russian mine sweepers were
continually and frantically covering the area was proof that the mining
of coastal waters was at least disruptive to the normal course of Soviet
transport activities.[14]

Cooperation with the Finnish Air Force

There was no real operational collaboration between the Luftwaffe
and the Finnish Air Force, since their sectors of responsibility were
hundreds of miles apart and their missions vastly different in character.
Liaison officers were regularly exchanged, however, so that a free flow
of information was assured between Finnish and German leaders in
widely separated combat sectors. There were no causes for friction
between the two powers in 1941, nor were there such later in the war.*

During the winter of 1941-42 the Finnish Air Force voluntarily
placed the airfields at Kemi on the northern tip of the Gulf of Bothnia
and at Pori on the western coast of Finland, north of the Aland Islands,
at the disposal of German air units. Kemi was foreseen as a tactical
bomber base and Pori as the end terminal of the German air supply
route in Finland.

_____

*Editor's Note: It should be remembered that Finns and Germans
fought side by side in 1918 for Finnish independence from Russia, and
that the democracies failed to offer assistance to Finland during the
Russo-Finnish War of 1939-1940. Germans and Finns thus had a
common purpose: to defeat Russia.

Review of Operations in the Far North in 1941

Considering the strength of the Luftwaffe in this area, its operations were highly successful. Great efforts were made by all German personnel to accomplish their missions, despite material and personnel shortages. Yet, in the final analysis, the Luftwaffe failed to attain its objectives in the Far North.

The German High Command should have realized that Russia, as an ally of the Western Powers, would soon be forced to rely on assistance from that quarter, and that such assistance would be forthcoming upon request. It was also not too difficult to see the strategic importance of Arkhangelsk and Murmansk, especially the latter, which remains ice-free all year around.[15] A study conducted by the 8th (Military Science) Branch of the Luftwaffe General Staff showed clearly that more than half of Russia's overseas logistical support came through the ports of the North via the Atlantic route. The events of World War I had already shown the significance of Arkhangelsk and Murmansk to the Russian war economy. If this matter had been soberly examined, it would have been the logical thing to have sent all the forces necessary to close this gap in the North for the duration of the conflict. Had this been done the seizure of the Kola Peninsula and the Karelian area would probably have amounted to a mere mopping-up operation. Far fewer forces could have accomplished the ground objectives if the initial strategic points had been secured at the opening of the campaign.[16]*

The German Armed Forces had its own specific ideas about the allocation of forces and the selection of strategic objectives within the framework of the overall operation against the Soviet Union. Since Finland was treated as a secondary theater of operations from the beginning of the conflict, even the most gifted German and Finnish commanders could not have led their meager forces to a decisive victory. Far greater chances for success might have presented themselves if the Chief of the Joint Command Norway had not divided his forces into three widely separated combat units, but had concentrated upon a single specific strategic objective.

The Luftwaffe's strength was rapidly dissipated over the extensive area of the entire Finnish-Norwegian theater by being required to

---

*See Maps Nos. 1, 2, 3, and 11.

shift quickly from one place to another, extinguishing "fires" at crucial points on the front. In such a situation no decisive results could be expected. The initial phase of operations in Finland will therefore always be considered as a classical example of the narrowly confined continental concepts of the German Supreme Command, and as one of the significant lost opportunities, which, in its total effect, had much to do with bringing about the final failure of German arms.

Chapter 9

THE FOURTH AIR FLEET TO THE CRIMEA
AND ROSTOV-ON-THE-DON

The Battle on the Shore of the Sea of Azov

By late August 1941 Army Group South had completely mopped up the Soviet forces west of the lower Dnepr River, with the exception of units in the strongly fortified naval port of Odessa, which had been invested on the land side by Rumanian forces. Since the Rumanian troops were not strong enough to take the port (German offers of help were at first declined--probably for political reasons), the Rumanian Chief of State, Marshal Ion Antonescu, on 24 September, requested German military assistance.1* Two divisions and very heavy artillery were immediately sent in, which was believed to be sufficient to assure the capture of Odessa.

On 26 September the great battle of encirclement east of Kiev came to an end. While the Sixth Army, the First Panzer Group, and elements of the Seventeenth Army of Army Group South were still engaged in the annihilation of Soviet units trapped to the east of Kiev, other components of the Seventeenth Army had advanced eastward and taken Krasnograd (by Army Group von Schwedler)/ and Poltava (by the LV Corps).

In continuing its push to the east, Army Group South had established bridgeheads across the lower Dnepr at Kherson, Berislav, and Dnepropetrovsk, each providing a favorable jump-off site for future operations. It intended to take the Crimea with the Eleventh Army, to

---

*Editor's Note: Many Rumanians were unenthusiastic about the war with Russia, especially since by this time they had already recovered the territories which were wrested from them on 28 June 1940 by the Soviet Union. Marshal Antonescu, however, recognized that these gains would be short-lived if the Soviet state was able to threaten Rumania anew. He therefore urged all possible Rumanian assistance to Germany's campaign to defeat Russia.

/This group, organized within Army Group Center on 18 July 1941 was disbanded 18 October 1942. It was commanded by General Viktor von Schwedler. See Maps Nos. 7, 8, and 9.

capture the area around Kharkov with the Seventeenth Army, to form the defense of the extended northern flank of the army group by advancing north of Kharkov with the Sixth Army, to destroy the enemy east of Dnepropetrovsk, and then push forward toward the Donets Basin and Rostov-on-the-Don with the First Panzer Group.

The Fourth Air Fleet, directed to cooperate closely with Army Group South, ordered the IV Air Corps to support the Eleventh Army and to attack the Soviet Navy and its bases on the Black Sea, and, as a secondary mission, to support Rumanian forces in taking Odessa. The V Air Corps of the Fourth Air Fleet was ordered to give primary support to the First Panzer Group and, when necessary, to the Sixth and Seventeenth Armies. About mid-September, before the end of the battle of Kiev, the Eleventh Army* and Rumanian units had begun a new offensive toward the east, but just short of Melitopol they encountered stiff enemy resistance and strong counterattacks which compelled them to go over to the defensive.[2]

Strong Eleventh Army forces were turned south to open the way across the Perekop-Ishun isthmus to the Crimean Peninsula.✝ These troops received effective support from the IV Air Corps, whose powerful bomber and dive bomber forces attacked troop concentrations, vehicular columns, tanks, field fortifications, bunkers, and positions on the isthmus of Perekop, destroying 195 trucks and 9 tanks.[3]

On 24 September the First Panzer Group of Army Group South attacked toward the south, opened a small bridgehead at Dnepropetrovsk from the east, and destroyed three Soviet divisions at Novo-Moskovsk. The Italian Expeditionary Corps contributed toward this partial victory by advancing southeast from Kremenchug along the east bank of the Dnepr. After rolling up the Dnepr front as far as Zaporozhye, the First Panzer Group proceeded east and southeast and then turned south to

---

*Because of the death of Generaloberst Eugen Ritter von Schobert on 12 December 1941, the command of the Eleventh Army was entrusted on 17 September to General der Infanterie Erich von Manstein (Field Marshal 1 July 1942).

✝Only two avenues were open to Army Group South for an advance into the Crimea. Since the eastern route, west of Genichesk, was far too narrow for operations, and the Sivash Sea was impassable for infantry, only the isthmus of Perekop could be considered. See Generalfeldmarschall Erich von Manstein, Verlorene Siege (Lost Victories), Bonn: Athenaeum Verlag, 1955, pp. 215-216. See also Maps Nos. 8 and 13.

relieve the Eleventh Army which was fighting in the Melitopol area. The armored group penetrated deeply into the rear of two Soviet armies, while the Eleventh Army renewed its frontal assault.

The High Command of the Luftwaffe reported on 5 October that "the enemy has begun to withdraw from the battle sector Melitopol-Balki in order to evade the threatening encirclement" and that German and Rumanian forces were continuing to pursue him to the Radionovka-Akimovka line, about nine miles west of the Melitopol-Kronsfeld-Balki area.[4] The SS Panzer Division "Adolf Hitler"* broke through Melitopol from the north and advanced to the Berdyansk (now Osipenko) area, where it linked up with armored units of the First Panzer Group which had driven forward to the Sea of Azov. The bulk of the Russian forces withdrawing before the Eleventh Army were thus encircled and destroyed in the "Battle at the Sea of Azov." More than 100,000 prisoners and hundreds of tanks and guns were captured. Soviet troops which had withdrawn in time to escape encirclement were pursued eastward by armored and motorized units of the First Panzer Army.✝ In a rapid forward drive, armored units reached Mariupol (now Zhdanov), which was taken by surprise. The advance continued, proceeding swiftly along the coast by way of Taganrog, which was captured on 2 October, to a position about nine miles west of Rostov-on-the-Don. The bulk of the First Panzer Army, together with the Italian corps, captured Stalino on 20 October and occupied thereby the center of the industrial Donets Basin.

The initial, extremely heavy Soviet pressure against the Eleventh Army was alleviated by attacks of the V Air Corps (overlapping those of the IV Air Corps) upon enemy columns around Melitopol and by V Air Corps support of the swift German armored advance from Zaporozhye toward Berdyansk. At the same time, the threats to the extended eastern flank of the First Panzer Army were removed by air attacks launched against Soviet columns and troop concentrations in the Chaplino-Pavlograd-

---

*1st SS Panzer Division "Leibstandarte Adolph Hitler" was formed from Hitler's bodyguard regiment, the Leibstandarte, and was composed of selected personnel, outfitted with the best equipment available.

✝The four armored groups on the Eastern Front were redesignated as "Panzer Armies" on 5 October 1941, each retaining its original number. From 28 July to 3 August 1941, the Second Panzer Group was known as Panzer Group Guderian. In Combat Zone Center, from 3 July to 15 August 1941, the Fourth Army and Second and Third Panzer Groups made up the Fourth Panzer Army. See Map No. 9.

Postyschevo (apparently Krasnoarmeyskoye) area and against rail movements over the line linking Sinelnikovo, Krasnoarmeyskoye, and Stalino and that which linked Pavlograd, Krasnoarmeyskoye, and Yasinovataya. Air attacks on the railroads leading north from Mariupol, Taganrog, and Rostov-on-the-Don further delayed the transfer of Soviet troops and materiel.

By October autumn rains had become commonplace throughout most of central and southern Russia, turning solid fields into sticky morasses. The effects were soon felt by German divisions all along the front. General von Tippelskirch later recalled that upon advancing to Taganrog the First Panzer Army had encountered a period of bad weather in which muddy terrain "almost completely paralyzed the supply system." Tanks, sinking deeply into the mire, could proceed only at a "snail's pace."[5] Temporary improvements in weather conditions were of little help in accelerating troop movements, for as the High Command of the Air Force reported on 16 October, despite an improvement in weather, "roads and streets are still covered with deep, sticky mud," making movements of motorized units and logistical traffic possible only with great losses from numerous vehicular breakdowns.[6]*

V Air Corps Support of the Sixth and Seventeenth Armies

North of the First Panzer Army, the Seventeenth Army, on 2 October, had advanced toward the Severnyy Donets River south of Kharkov, while the Sixth Army commenced its drive on Kharkov and Kursk. At first, both armies moved ahead well, but Russian resistance increased steadily. Under Marshal Timoshenko, who relieved Marshal Budënny, the Russians defended their positions with bitter tenacity. As a result, the Seventeenth and Sixth Armies, in a struggle lasting for weeks, were able to gain ground only slowly. Moreover, bad weather conditions prevailed in this battle sector. The difficulties caused by the completely saturated ground assumed massive proportions and required the utmost exertion from the already exhausted German troops. Often troops and supplies could be advanced only by the use of the so-called Panje wagons.†

---

*See Figure 34.

†Panje wagons were small, four-wheeled, wooden wagons, with the box of each wagon designed very much like an old-style, wooden coffin. Drawn by two horses or Steppe ponies (Panje horses), they were used in large numbers by the indigenous peasantry of the Soviet Union. See Figure 35.

Figure 34
Wehrmacht vehicle mired down during
the muddy season in Russia, 1941

Figure 35
German workmen building Panje
wagons for transport work

Even the forward detachments had to be served by such vehicles. The noteworthy fact here was that the infantry divisions which were provisionally equipped with Panje wagons advanced more quickly and easily than the motorized troops.

The bomber forces of the V Air Corps continued with excellent results the interdiction of Soviet rail movements around and to the east of Kharkov, which had been started during the encirclement battle of Kiev. Waves of Luftwaffe bombers attacked the enemy rail transport system, which was carrying supplies of all kinds and evacuating industrial goods, machines, and even food from Kharkov and the Donets Basin to the north and east. Severe losses were inflicted upon Soviet locomotives and freight cars around Kharkov. When the weather was suitable for hit-and-run raids, Luftwaffe daylight attacks were carried out deep in the Soviet rear areas as far as the Millerovo-Liski-Voronezh line. Moonlight nights were also utilized for attacks on Russian railroads. These missions were directed against the rail lines connecting Kharkov and Bogodukhov, Kharkov and Krasnyy Liman, Kupyansk and Lisichansk, Lozovaya and Slavyansk, Lisichansk and Valuyki, Millerovo and Liski, Kharkov and Kursk, Kharkov and Kurilovka, Kurilovka and Belgorod, Kursk and Kastornoye, and Kastornoye and Valuyki. The main points of effort were then shifted more and more to the lines connecting Kharkov and Belgorod, Kurilovka and Valuyki, Valuyki and Novyy Oskol, Valuyki and Liski, and Millerovo and Liski. From 23 September to 12 October, 95 trains were destroyed, including 4 ammunition and 4 fuel trains; 288 trains were heavily damaged; 12 locomotives were destroyed and 10 badly damaged. Rail traffic was cut in 64 places.

During this period of rail interdiction far in the rear of Soviet lines, the other tasks of the Luftwaffe were mainly neglected. However, the interdiction program strongly supported the German ground forces, for these successful air attacks considerably delayed, and occasionally prevented, the enemy from carrying out a well regulated logistical movement. The certain and increasing loss of special replacement parts, repair materials, and essential special equipment had a decided impact upon Soviet striking power. The great results achieved by the Luftwaffe lead to the assumption that in many instances the Soviet command was unable to carry out its plans and frequently had to give up its attacks or regroupings, planned on a large scale, after recognition of the effects of German air attacks.

The advance of the Sixth and Seventeenth Armies had been complicated by the fact that the very well equipped and supplied airfields around Kharkov and Bogodukhov--favorably situated near the front--were available to the Soviet air force, permitting increasing attacks which often severely interfered with the maneuverability of German ground forces. German air reconnaissance of these fields showed continuously heavy occupancy. The bases had often before been the targets of German night attacks and daylight nuisance raids. Now, from 25 to 27 September, bomber units of the V Air Corps, under fighter cover, were employed anew in particularly effective attacks against these airfields, destroying at least 43 aircraft on the ground and causing a noticeable reduction in Soviet air activity, especially by the bomber units. German fighter forces protected the air space above the Seventeenth Army and carried out numerous attacks against the airfields at Kharkov in order to system- atically attain air superiority over that city, where, by 28 September, 58 Soviet aircraft had been shot down.

Since the V Air Corps had given up almost all of its fighter units to the Second Air Fleet in the center of the front, only the III Group of the 52nd Fighter Wing was still at the disposal of the corps. Unfortunately, due to maintenance difficulties and the III Group's long, uninterrupted commitment in the East, the daily operational strength of the unit sank to an average of 10 to 15 aircraft, and sometimes even less. With this limited strength, there was no possibility of quickly gaining even local air superiority. In addition, difficulties in building up supply stocks at the German fighter base at Poltava temporarily compelled a further limitation of operations. A certain reserve of fighters also had to be kept back to protect the Poltava airfield from the very numerous Soviet attacks. On 22 October the III Group of the 52nd Fighter Wing was trans- ferred to the IV Air Corps for employment in the Crimea.

Bomber units of the V Air Corps, in support of the Seventeenth Army, attacked Soviet forces lodged in villages, armor concentrations, and columns moving on the roads west of Kharkov, particularly the Kharkov-Valki-Poltava road. Successful attacks on numerous armored trains also brought appreciable relief to German ground forces.

Attacks on the command, traffic, and routing center of Kharkov acquired special significance. In a series of nightly nuisance and hit-and- run attacks, Luftwaffe units effectively bombed the Oshova Station, the southern railroad station, and, in particular, the highways leading into Kharkov from the west. Fires in the western part of the city and in the railroad depot area indicated to German reconnaissance the success of the attacks. Between 2 and 9 October the tank factory at Kramatorsk-- according to reports of intelligence agents (V-Meldungen) the most important of its kind--was repeatedly and successfully attacked, as was the aircraft plant Voronezh IV on 20 October.

About 20 October, although severely hampered by the enemy and the weather, the Seventeenth Army and, north of it, the Sixth Army reached the railroad line extending from Lozovaya through the western outskirts of Kharkov to Belgorod. Prior to the occupation of Kharkov, V Air Corps bomber units repeatedly hit Soviet troops and defense positions in the outskirts of the city and on the east bank of the Lopan River with good effect. At the special request of the Sixth Army, the northeastern part of Kharkov was spared from attack, except for those launched by the ground forces. On 23 October, immediately following a successful heavy bombing attack, advance units of the 57th Infantry Division pressed into the city. On the next day Kharkov was firmly in German hands. While the Sixth Army captured Kursk and continued its advance toward the Don River, the Seventeenth Army pressed south of Kharkov into the industrial Donets Basin. From the beginning of their offensives, both armies had been continually supported by most of the flying units of the V Air Corps, directly by attacks against troop movements and concentrations on the roads and communities close behind the enemy front, and indirectly by attacks against the Soviet rail net in the Severnyy Donets River bend and between the Severnyy Donets and the Don.

Very soon after the end of the fighting around Kiev, air reconnaissance had observed a noticeable increase of heavy rail movements from the Rostov-on-the-Don area to the Caucasus, toward Voronezh and Stalingrad--generally in both directions. In particular, the significance of the line running from Baku to Rostov to Voronezh became increasingly evident. The transportation of troops and war materiel--the lattter apparently from Iran--was definitely confirmed as was the "pipeline" of fuel trains. In clear appreciation of the tremendous importance of these movements, the Luftwaffe attacked this rail line as quickly as the operational and supply situation permitted. It also brought under attack the lines from Tikhoretsk to Stalingrad and from Rostov-on-the-Don to Salsk, as well as (occasionally) that from Novorossiysk to Kropotkin and the approach to Krasnodar.

Inadequate supply of the airfield at Taganrog often prevented its use by bomber forces; its use would have increased the bombers' range into the Caucasus region. The mostly unknown variations in weather characteristics over such great distances and the strong enemy fighter defense along the main route also made operations very difficult. Nevertheless, considerable forces succeeded in flying as far as Mineralnyye Vody, and over a period of several weeks destroyed a large number of trains. The High Command of the Luftwaffe mentioned these attacks in a report of 24 October, stating that in the southern section of the Eastern Front, German fighters, while escorting bombers, flying reconnaissance, and carrying out fighter sweeps, shot 40 Soviet planes out of the sky on 23 October. Most of the Luftwaffe bombers supported the ground forces by attacking "field and artillery positions and communities occupied [by Russian troops] in the area around Ishun" and columns of Soviet trucks withdrawing around Kharkov and Belgorod. Lighter bomber forces attacked various targets on the rail lines connecting Rostov-on-the-Don, Armavir, and Mineralnyye Vody, Krasnodar and Armavir, and Kharkov and Kupyansk, destroying seven trains, one of which was a fuel train, and damaging many others. On the Crimean east coast, off Feodosiya, two bombers sank a medium-sized merchantman.* Lastly, some 25,000 leaflets were dropped over the Ishun area.7

The conveyance of troops and materiel from Caucasia and, especially, Transcaucasia to the areas of Rostov-Stalingrad and Voronezh-Moscow and the evacuation of materiel and industrial equipment from the Donets Basin-Rostov sector were severely interrupted by these railway interdictions. In the course of the attacks, bombers of the V Air Corps (Fourth Air Fleet) alone destroyed 79 trains and damaged 148 others by direct hits.

Conquest of the Crimea

The objective of the Crimean operation was already clearly defined in the OKW directive of 21 August 1941. The Crimea was to be seized to safeguard the vital Rumanian oil region. Mobile forces and other units were to proceed rapidly across the Dnepr to the peninsula before Soviet reinforcements could arrive by land or sea.8/

The Crimean Peninsula was nearly separated from the mainland by the Sivash Sea, a salt marsh or mud flat, which was so shallow that

---

*Editor's Note: These vessels traveled by night whenever possible to avoid German air attacks.

/Editor's Note: It was the Soviet control of the waters of the Black Sea that posed the greatest threat to the Rumanian oil region. As long as this control remained, the Crimea was always a likely place for flanking operations against German units in the South, and served as an air base for attacks against Rumania.

it could not be crossed in assault boats. The narrow isthmus west of Genichesk provided space for only one road and railroad embankment, with numerous bridges. Thus, only the isthmus of Perekop, slightly more than four miles in width, with virtually no cover, heavily mined, traversed by the 50-foot-deep "Tatar Ditch," and with strong field fortifications, could be utilized for the attack. Farther to the southeast, the Ishun defile (which also had strong field defenses), with its salt lakes, then had to be penetrated.* The fighting for the narrow approach to the Crimean Peninsula, the isthmus of Perekop and Ishun, was certain to be exceptionally tough and costly, but there was no other possible way to attack.

Meanwhile, to the west, Rumanian troops, supported by German units, entered Odessa on 16 October and occupied the naval base which the Russians had systematically demolished and evacuated. Evacuation movements of Soviet forces within the harbor of Odessa, as well as at sea (hoping to reach the Crimea or points farther to the east), were attacked by bombers of the IV Air Corps (Fourth Air Fleet) with good results.

Units of the IV Air Corps assisted the southern wing of Army Group South (Eleventh Army), which on 11 October, immediately after the termination of the battle on the shore of the Sea of Azov, turned its full weight against the Crimea. By 19 October Eleventh Army forces had entered the peninsula and had broken through the "stubbornly defended" Soviet positions. The following day the Luftwaffe command commented that "north of Ishun our troops are fighting in the breaches of enemy fortifications which are organized in depth." In defense, the Soviets counterattacked repeatedly at points of German penetration, trying desperately to regain their former positions.[9]

The Russians employed their air forces--actually for the first time in a point of main effort--over the narrow, completely level, steppe-like isthmus. The treeless and bushless terrain offered no cover for the attacking troops of the Eleventh Army against the continuous attacks by very strong Soviet bomber and ground-attack units. General von Manstein, commanding the Eleventh Army, stated later that the Soviet Air Force dominated the sky, and with its bombers and fighters attacked every target sighted. German infantrymen and artillerymen at the front, and even vehicles and horses in the rear, had to be protected by trenches or foxholes.

---

*See footnote f, p. 203.

In order to meet these attacks more effectively, the employment of German fighters was concentrated under the leadership of Col. Werner Moelders (who, for his 100th aerial victory, had been the first officer of the German armed forces to be awarded the Knight's Cross of the Iron Cross with Oak Leaf, Swords, and Diamonds) while bomber units of the IV Air Corps increasingly attacked enemy airfields in the Crimea, in order to strike the enemy at his bases and thus lessen his effectiveness. Concurrently, dive bombers struck the strong ground positions on the isthmus. "Only when Moelders and his fighter wing were brought to the army"* toward the end of the fighting were the Soviet planes swept from the sky by day. But the enemy still continued its attacks at night.[10]

The size and the strength of Soviet air operations on the Eastern Front at this time were greater than at any time since the beginning of the war. During the last half of October, for example, situation reports of the Luftwaffe Intelligence Branch showed that Soviet air strength on the southern front averaged around 130 bombers and 200 fighters. The bulk of these forces was at any given time employed around Ishun.[11] Low-level attacks by Soviet ground-attack planes, and medium-level attacks by Soviet conventional bombers, were carried out around the clock against German infantry which was wearily fighting its way through the numerous, fortified defense lines. At night Soviet air attacks succeeded in penetrating far behind the German front lines.[12] Soviet troops, supported by very heavy artillery fire--60 batteries had been identified by 24 October--carried out without interruption strong counterattacks, partly by hand-to-hand fighting, which were repulsed with very severe losses to both sides.[13] German dive bomber and bomber units hammered incessantly at the enemy. Field positions, concentrations of artillery, bunkers, pockets of resistance, troop concentrations and assembly areas lay under the daily hail of bombs from the IV Air Corps, whose strength on 1 November consisted of 6 bomber, 3 dive bomber, and 4 fighter groups.[14] Despite heavy opposition, bolstered by bad weather and roads and the flooded Chatyrlyk River (south of captured Ishun), the German gains were considerable.

Achieving notable success were the fighters under the direction of Colonel Moelders, which were committed chiefly in fighter sweeps over the battlefield.[15]/ On 27 October, the High Command of the Luftwaffe,

---

*Colonel Moelders became fighter units commander in the Crimea; it appears that his 51st Fighter Wing was never transferred to that area, but remained in the general sector of Army Group Center.

/The 77th Fighter Wing under Maj. Gotthardt Handrick scored its 800th aerial victory on 20 October 1941.

reporting on the assault on the Crimea, stated that on the morning of 26 October German ground forces had renewed their attack on both sides of the Ishun-Simferopol road, penetrating the strongly fortified positions and throwing back the stubborn enemy. The Russians had concentrated most of their strength--eight infantry and four cavalry divisions--against the German center and western flank, but they suffered severe losses when their counterattacks were repulsed. Luftwaffe bomber and dive bomber units, supporting mainly the ground forces, destroyed many guns and vehicles in attacks upon enemy defensive and battery positions, troop concentrations, and moving columns south of the Ishun area.[16]

After ten days of exceptionally hard fighting, the breakthrough down the isthmus was achieved (28 October), opening the way to the Crimea. Units of the IV Air Corps then harried the retreating Russian forces. The Soviet command was no longer able to establish organized resistance to delay the rapidly pursuing troops of the German Eleventh Army. On 1 November Simferopol was taken and on the 16th, Kerch. Except for the fortress of Sevastopol, which was besieged on the land side, the entire peninsula was now under German control and cleared of Russian forces. Thus, the Soviet air base which had been a potential threat to the Rumanian oil region was eliminated.

Following the seizure of the Crimea, continuous air reconnaissance over the Black Sea was particularly important. Considering that in 1941 the Soviets had command of that sea, Russian commando raids or even larger enemy landings from Sevastopol, the eastern coasts of the Black Sea, and the Sea of Azov had to be reckoned with at all times.* However, with the low operational strength of the Luftwaffe reconnaissance forces in the area and with the prevailing adverse weather conditions of rain, fog, and snow, the necessary round-the-clock surveillance was not possible.

Yet during the mopping-up operations, the enemy supply system was attacked not only by the IV Air Corps but by the V Air Corps in over-lapping strikes on the ports of Sevastopol, Kerch, Anapa, Novorossiysk, and others. Shipping in the Sea of Azov and the Black Sea also were continuously attacked. Besides the destruction of supplies, the objective was to delay the embarkation and debarkation of enemy troops, which had been identified in these harbors by aerial reconnaissance, and to destroy the harbor installations. All of these attacks were very successful.

---

*See footnote f, p. 210.

Besides heavy damage to the harbor facilities at Yeysk, Novorossiysk, Primorsko-Akhtarsk, Rostov-on-the-Don, and particularly at Kerch, units of the V Air Corps alone, by concentrated unit attacks and cease-less individual nuisance raids, definitely sank 16 ships totaling about 18,000 gross register tons, and set afire and otherwise damaged 18 other vessels comprising at least 15,000 gross register tons. In December, bombers of the IV Air Corps attacked oil refineries and storage sheds at Tuapse.*

At this point a black day for the Luftwaffe must be mentioned. At the end of the difficult air operations over the Crimean Peninsula, Colonel Moelders flew to Germany to attend the state funeral for Generaloberst Ernst Udet, one of the most famous of German fighter pilots of World War I and a leading figure in the rebirth of the Luftwaffe in the 1920's and 1930's. Coming in in a fog on 22 November 1941, the He-111 aircraft in which Moelders was a passenger lost its second engine and crashed, just short of the airfield at Breslau-Gandau.17 Werner Moelders, the bravest and most successful German fighter pilot in the Spanish Civil War and (at the time of his death) in World War II, was killed. The death of this youthfully fresh, but characteristically mature, Inspector of Fighter Pilots was an irreplaceable loss to the Luftwaffe.╪

On 17 December the Eleventh Army opened its attack on Sevast-opol, supported by a specially organized close support unit of the Fourth Air Fleet. After favorable early progress the Eleventh met stiffening resistance by the fortress garrison so that the enveloping ring could be contracted only very slowly against continuing counterattacks from the fortress area.

Strong Russian forces landed on 26 December on both sides of Kerch, and a few days later at Feodosiya. General Halder noted the effectiveness of these Soviet amphibious operations in his diary entry of 26 December, pointing out that the situation around Kerch was critical within 24 hours after the Russian landings. On 28 December he declared that the Kerch problem was not yet cleared up and that Soviet reinforce-ments were being brought in. Two days later he wrote: "Again a difficult

---

*See Figure 36.
╪General der Flieger Helmuth Wilberg, a World War I flyer, con-sidered at one time to have been the "natural commander" of the Luftwaffe died in an air crash on 20 November 1941. Chief of Special Staff "W," which directed the German expeditionary force in Spain, 1936-1939, and holder of numerous high staff positions, Wilberg was retired 31 March 1938. Thus three of Germany's best known flyers died in the same month and year.

Figure 36
Oil refineries and installations on the Black Sea
Coast burning after German air attacks, 1941

215

day. In the Crimea the enemy landing at Feodosiya has created a
formidable tactical situation. Nevertheless, the army group [South]
has decided to continue the attack on Sevastopol." On New Year's Eve,
Halder reported another day beset with serious problems. At Sevastopol
the attacks of the 22nd German Infantry Division had been unsuccessful
and had to be suspended in order to make forces available for Feodosiya.
"The enemy [has] reinforced himself and expanded." New Year's Day
was likewise unpromising for the German forces in the Crimea. In
Halder's words, the situation was "tense and difficult to clear up without
new forces."

On 1 January 1942 the Luftwaffe temporarily halted the enemy, but
three days later the situation was again critical. The Soviets had sent
small forces ashore at Yevpatoriya and were reinforcing Feodosiya.
These landing operations, supported by strong naval and air units, took
the German defenders completely by surprise, for their naval and reconnaissance had noted neither the preparations for the operation--assembly
of shipping and loading of troops--nor the approach of the Russian forces
by sea from Sevastopol and Novorossiysk. Despite bad weather, all units
of the Fourth Air Fleet were committed against the enemy ashore, in
order to support the weak German ground forces in their resistance and
to destroy the enemy in his bridgehead. While the Soviet force at
Yevpatoriya could soon be destroyed (at least in the beginning Halder
believed this landing to be merely a local tactical operation), the landings
at Kerch and Feodosiya led to the loss of the entire Kerch Peninsula. On
15 January Halder wrote: "On the southern front the attack has begun on
Feodosiya. Good initial success. . . ." On 24 January, however, he
announced that the attack on the Crimea had been suspended.18

From Halder's remarks it is clearly evident that the Soviet
amphibious operations were highly effective. Although at first believed
to be only tactical successes, the landings soon had serious strategic
consequences for the German Army:

(1) The attack upon Sevastopol, which had just commenced, had to
be postponed, but considerable German enveloping forces continued to be
tied down. The capture of Sevastopol was delayed until late in 1942.

(2) Strong elements of the Eleventh Army had to be diverted for
defense against the landed enemy forces at Feodosiya and Kerch.

(3) In difficult and protracted fighting, the Eleventh Army had to
restore the situation in the Crimea and again capture the Kerch Peninsula,
with a corresponding loss of time.

The effect upon Luftwaffe operations was also serious:

(1) The IV Air Corps of the Fourth Air Fleet remained confined to constant direct and indirect support of the Eleventh Army.

(2) The staff and elements of the V Air Corps had been transferred from the Fourth Air Fleet area to Brussels late in November, with the intention of organizing a mine-laying air corps to be used against England. However, half of the staff had to be returned to the combat area of the Fourth Air Fleet as Special Staff Crimea (Sonderstab Krim), under General der Flieger Robert Ritter von Greim, and the intended organization of a mine-laying air corps was discontinued.*

The Setback at Rostov-on-the-Don

The attack of the First Panzer Army on Rostov-on-the-Don had been scheduled for 3 November 1941. With a strong left wing it was to proceed in the general direction of Shakhty, envelop the extended flank of the Soviet front before Rostov and destroy the enemy forces there, take possession of the city, and establish bridgeheads across the Don River. The V Air Corps was to support this operation. The tactical operations staff of the corps was transferred to Mariupol (now Zhdanov) where, in closest collaboration with the operations staff of the First Panzer Army, also at Mariupol, it would carry out the employment of the air units. Delayed by bad ground conditions and fuel shortages, the Panzer attack did not begin until 5 November, but at first it won a good area of ground. Only the left wing of the First Panzer Army (XXXXIX Mountain Corps) was delayed on the Nigishin River⁺ and southwest of Dyakovo by the bitterly fighting Russians. Vigorous action by the close support forces of the V Air Corps at Dyakovo, the key point in the Soviet defense, enabled the 1st Mountain Division to capture the town. Influenced by the air attacks on Dyakovo and by the accompanying waves of attacks on the roads leading east from there, the enemy hastily withdrew, thereby eliminating the

---

*The other half of the V Air Corps staff, under the corps chief of staff, was transferred to Combat Zone Center (Smolensk) in order to prepare for assuming conduct of the fighting in the central sector of the front as the Staff, Luftwaffe Command East (1 April 1942). The VIII Air Corps was released and in May 1942 transferred to Combat Zone South (Crimea). See Map No. 13.

⁺Since no English or Russian version could be determined for this river, the spelling indicated in the German manuscript has been retained.

threat to the flanks of the armored units south of Rovenki, which were then pressing southward.

On 6 November a pouring rain set in which made the roads bottomless and forced the First Panzer Army to temporarily suspend the attack. A few days later a heavy frost further crippled the movements of the motorized units. Vehicles and tanks froze in the mud into which they had sunk and frequently had to be freed with pickaxes. The lack of heating equipment* had disagreeable effects on the flying units although they endeavored by every means possible to carry out flying operations. At 5° Fahreneheit an attempt was even made to preheat the engines with hot-air boxes improvised from the medical service equipment.

Long-range air reconnaissance revealed that Russian traffic on the rail lines north of Rostov-on-the-Don, particularly those leading east from Valuyki, had increased considerably. For the first time, trains consisting entirely of locomotives (40 to 60 in a group) were observed. Bombers of the V Air Corps flew continuous attacks against these trains, so that from 4 to 20 November they destroyed 12 trains and 51 locomotives and damaged 161 trains and 32 locomotives.

German fighters in 578 sorties shot down 65 Russian planes in front of the First Panzer Army. But as a result of the cold, German fighters on alert-readiness (Alarmrotte)/ at the very important advance base at Taganrog were frequently unable to take off during the numerous enemy air attacks. Similarly, antiaircraft artillery guns were often unable to fire because of the lack of nonfreezing grease. On 12 November the 54th Bomber Wing and the 55th Bomber Wing (less one group) were withdrawn from action and transferred to Germany. Thereafter, the bomber forces at the disposal of the V Air Corps consisted of a single group of the 55th Bomber Wing with an average operational strength of 6 to 9 aircraft.

The extremely strained supply situation endangered the overall employment of aircraft in the further course of operations. Derailment

---

*Supplies could not be brought up over the sticky and bottomless roads and paths, nor were the railroads fully operational. Every item of supply for the German Army and Luftwaffe had to be flown to the front. See Figures 37 and 38.

/Alert-readiness (Alarmrotte) units normally consisted of two aircraft and flying personnel ready to take off within a few minutes. In fighter units they were usually already in their planes waiting for an alarm.

Figure 37
German airfield in Russia
during muddy period, 1941

Figure 38
Provisional warming ovens for German
aircraft engines in Russia, 1941

of trains through sabotage considerably delayed the arrival of fuel, and frequent periods of bad weather prevented air supply of units of the Close Support Air Commander. These organizations had only flying personnel and equipment and advance technical personnel at their disposal. Trucks of all kinds, including some from Army service installations, antiaircraft artillery batteries, and Luftwaffe signal units, were borrowed in order to make the most essential vehicles at the airfields available to the Close Support Air Commander, and thus available for operations.

Moreover, winter clothing, rations, motor fuel, and other additional supplies required by units of the Close Support Air Commander had to be brought in by air. The only reason that the fighter and dive bomber units of the Close Support Air Commander were out of action through lack of fuel was because frequent bad weather severely limited operations.

Generalmajor von Waldau, Chief of the Operations Staff of the High Command of the Luftwaffe, remarked in his diary on 21 October, in regard to the supply situation and the influence of weather upon the armies, that at Rostov-on-the-Don "good progress [is] hindered only by fuel and weather conditions."[19] On 15 November he observed that at Rostov there was no progress, sometimes for reasons of supply, sometimes because of weather conditions.[20] That month General Halder commented that both the southern and central sections of the front were "under the influence of wretched weather."[21]

On 17 November the First Panzer Army, with a strong right wing (II Army Corps), renewed the attack on Rostov-on-the-Don. A thrust along the Tuzlov River rolled up the strong Soviet position, and the capture of the Tuzlov bridges enabled the 14th Panzer Division and the 60th Infantry Division (Motorized), which meanwhile had approached the scene, to push toward Rostov. Despite bitter enemy resistance the armored units continued the drive toward the south, and on 19 November stood between three and six miles from Rostov. Strong Soviet forces, comprised of some 10 divisions and 2 armored brigades, attacked the covering party of the First Panzer Army from the northeast, on the road between Nakhichevan and Rovenki and the XXXIX Mountain Corps, in an effort to relieve the troops defending the city. In spite of the extremely stubborn defense by the covering force of the SS "Viking" Division,* the Soviets succeeded in breaking through at several points.

_____

*See p. 56.

In general, however, the Russian attacks were beaten off, and the situation again restored, but only after fairly heavy German losses.

By 20 November the situation on the east flank of the First Panzer Army became so threatening that air support was urgently requested. The Fourth Air Fleet, therefore, assigned at first a group of the 27th Bomber Wing, and shortly thereafter the entire wing, to the V Air Corps for employment against the enemy forces on the east flank.

Because of the weather during the period 17 to 20 November the Close Support Air Commander was unable to intervene successfully, apart from providing scanty fighter cover. During the crisis on the First Panzer Army's eastern flank, however, the Close Support Air Commander--despite a 500-foot ceiling and a light snowfall--responded to the order of the V Air Corps by immediately sending fighters to attack in that area, while Ju-87 units recklessly struck heavily-occupied villages in front of the withdrawing security elements of the SS "Viking" Division. Bombers attacked advancing Russian troops, their billeting centers, rail traffic, and detraining areas deep in the rear of Soviet forces facing the First Panzer Army.

On 20 November von Kleist's First Panzer Army, which had driven past Rostov on the north, forced its way into the city from the east. The next day Rostov-on-the-Don was in German hands. Because of the widespread publicity given to the capture of this important city, Kleist saw the value of holding it for reasons of morale and prestige. In the days that followed, Russian forces, which had probably been brought up in haste from the Caucasus, launched powerful counterattacks. Approximately 14 fresh divisions, with strong armored and air support, ruthlessly and relentlessly attacked the right flank of the First Panzer Army, advancing, in part, over the frozen delta of the Don River. On the 28th the Soviets retook Rostov.[22]

During this period of crisis for Army Group South, a serious conflict arose between Hitler and the commander in chief of the army group, Field Marshal Gerd von Rundstedt. Concerning this affair, Halder wrote on 30 November that the First Panzer Army needed to retire still farther but that Hitler had forbidden its withdrawal to the line running from Taganrog to Mtschus,* along the Mius River, and to the mouth of the Bachmutka River (where it joins the Severnyy Donets). When von Rundstedt replied that Hitler's order was "impracticable" Hitler

_____

*Editor's Note: The spelling indicated in the German manuscript.

relieved him of his command and appointed Field Marshal von Reichenau to carry out his [Hitler's] orders.[23] Thus, von Reichenau became the new Commander in Chief of Army Group South. In his diary entry for 1 December, Halder described the outcome of this change and noted that in a discussion held that day in regard to the situation he [Halder] had asked Jodl (who was present), as Chief of the OKW Operations Staff, to inform Hitler that "to expose troops to a tactical defeat in front of the Mius position is nonsense." By mid-afternoon enemy motorized forces had broken through the SS "Adolf Hitler" Division's intermediate position in front of the Mius River, and von Reichenau requested Hitler's permission to fall back that night to the Mius position. The Fuehrer's permission was granted at once.* Halder commented that they were thus at the point where they could have been the evening before. "Strength and time have been sacrificed and von Rundstedt lost."[24]

North of the First Panzer Army strong Soviet counterattacks compelled the Sixth and Seventeenth Armies to draw back behind the Severnyy Donets. Still near its easternmost point of advance was the extreme left wing of Army Group South (left wing of the Sixth Army), holding positions southeast of Kursk, where it kept contact with the Second Army of Army Group Center.

The withdrawals of the armies, especially of the First Panzer Army, were supported by the V Air Corps, with additional assistance by units of the IV Air Corps. Army Group South concluded that the ceaseless and audacious attacks by units of the Fourth Air Fleet had thwarted the primary Soviet tactical objective, the breakthrough toward Taganrog, and denied them their secondary objective, the isolation of the Rostov salient and the destruction of the southern wing of the First Panzer Army, and that the orderly withdrawal of German ground forces was achieved only by the severe and continuous air attacks against the Soviet offensives. Prisoners and deserters reported that the German air attacks had inflicted tremendous personnel and materiel losses upon the Soviet assailant and that the force of the Russian counterattacks had been considerably diminished, if not broken.

_____

*Editor's Note: Von Rundstedt, an officer of the "old school," took few pains to hide his contempt for Hitler, whom he dubbed "the Bohemian Corporal." Von Reichenau, however, was one of Germany's youngest field marshals, and one who at the time mentioned enjoyed Hitler's confidence.

In concluding the description of this part of the eastern campaign, it can be stated that Army Group South failed to carry out simultaneously its tasks of capturing the Crimea, occupying the Donets Basin, and reaching the Caucasus oil region. The reasons for this failure were, first, that the forces of Army Group South were too weak for such wide-spread objectives, and, secondly, that the weather extraordinarily impaired and hampered the advance, especially of the mobile units. The forwarding of supplies, particularly of fuel and ammunition, came to a standstill; indeed, it even failed completely from time to time. Only uninterrupted air transportation was able to alleviate the temporary, but very critical, supply situation.

In the same way the forces of the Fourth Air Fleet were too weak to support simultaneously the advance of four armies, attack Soviet flying forces and their bases, interdict enemy rail traffic carrying troops and supplies, prevent the movement of oil from the Caucasus, and force the Soviet naval and merchant vessels into their Black Sea ports and there destroy them.

Most of the troops and commands of the Army and the Luftwaffe had been committed directly, without rest, from the heavy fighting at Kiev to the new operations to the south, and they were simply exhausted, the army by the long, wearisome marches and ground combat in the Ukrainian mud and the Luftwaffe from flying unending sorties. Materiel-- tanks, aircraft, and trucks--was likewise worn out and expended in these incessant operations. Recognizing this state of affairs, Halder commented: "The mobile striking power is spent. We must reconcile ourselves to this."[25]

Hoffmann von Waldau, remarking on this extremely critical period, noted on 3 December that 16 Russian divisions had launched an attack which was increasing in intensity. Despite severe losses around Rostov, the Russians pierced the positions of the Leibstandarte (1st SS Panzer Division)* and badly mauled the 60th Infantry Division (Motorized), which had to be withdrawn under violent enemy pressure. (As noted earlier, it was at this time that von Rundstedt, after "a series of misunderstand-ings," had been relieved.) Then, late on 2 December, the Mius River defenses were occupied and expected to hold. Von Waldau noted that at this time there was more need in the Luftwaffe for ground crews and warming devices than for aircraft; moreover, the cold hampered the servicing of the planes, so that there were never enough of them ready for operations.

---

*See footnote *, p. 204.

During the night of 1 December, Hitler flew to Mariupol for a personal conference with the command of the First Panzer Army.* The trip was a success and resulted in adequate clarification of the situation, yet it was clear that the Russian campaign still had not achieved its final objective. Rostov had been lost, together with the bridgeheads east of the Don River, a region which had been foreseen as the starting area for a drive on Maykop.

On the 6th, von Waldau became concerned about Russian troop concentrations around Yeysk, which pointed to a Soviet intention "to attack from the south over the nearly frozen-over Sea of Azov, with a simultaneous envelopment movement in the north." He considered this situation to be most critical since the German forces available, while sufficient to stop a frontal attack, could not halt large-scale flanking movements. With a temperature of almost zero (Fahrenheit) on the 6th, the Sea of Azov continued to freeze. According to von Waldau, the view that an operation across the ice would be too dangerous and costly was not valid where the Russians were concerned because of their disregard for human life; the view also lost validity because of the possible tactical effects and results which might be achieved by such an attack.

On 15 December Army Group South repelled all attacks on the front held by the First Panzer Army, and the Seventeenth Army was holding its positions. The Soviet attacks were further complicated by the condition of the roads. The arrival of reinforcements at the front in this area permitted the Wehrmacht to stabilize its positions for the time being.[26]

When the staff of the V Air Corps and corps troops were transferred from the Fourth Air Fleet to Brussels on 30 November, as mentioned heretofore, it left only the IV Air Corps to carry out the many and varied tasks of the air fleet. The corps supported Army Group South in its new winter positions as best it could in the constant critical defensive battles.[27]

In a critical analysis of the overall situation of Army Group South at the turn of the year 1941-1942 it must be unequivocally stated that, although army group forces had succeeded in occupying the Crimea (with the exception of Sevastopol), and although the army group retained possession of the greater part of the Donets Basin, the German military command nevertheless had, in the Rostov area, suffered its first major reversal in the conduct of its operations in the East.

---

*Commanded by Generaloberst Ewald von Kleist. See footnote /, p. 204.

Chapter 10

WITH THE SECOND AIR FLEET TO MOSCOW

The Double Battle of Bryansk-Vyazma

Since the end of the German advance in the Smolensk area,* the Fourth and Ninth Armies had found themselves in continuous defensive action against incessant Soviet counterattacks east of the Roslavl-Smolensk line. Now, as the encirclement battle of Kiev came to a close, Army Group Center regrouped to continue operations against Moscow.

The initial German successes against Soviet units in the area between the wings of Army Group Center and Army Group South had created a favorable situation for a decisive offensive operation. On 6 September Hitler issued Directive No. 35, which prescribed the measures to be taken against the Soviet forces under Marshal Timoshenko, then in action against Army Group Center. These enemy forces were to be destroyed within the short time remaining before the onset of winter. For this purpose, all Army and Luftwaffe forces which could be spared from the flanks were to be brought together in good time and committed in the operation.

In an integrated operation, Army Group Center's southern wing (Second Army and Second Panzer Group) was to drive toward the southeast and south to meet units of Army Group South (Sixth Army and First Panzer Group) proceeding northeast across the Dnepr, and there to destroy Soviet forces within the triangle formed by Kremenchug, Kiev, and Konotop. Immediately after this operation, elements of the Second and Sixth Armies and the Second Panzer Group were to regroup. Not later than 10 September, motorized infantry divisions of Army Group South (with strong Fourth Air Fleet support) were to attack suddenly from the Seventeenth Army's Kremenchug bridgehead, the attack to proceed northwest via Lubny. And, moving against Poltava, the Seventeenth Army was to seize the Kharkov area. At the same time, the attack on the Crimea, also supported by the Fourth Air Fleet, was to continue from the lower reaches of the Dnepr; the southward drive of the mobile forces to Melitopol were expected to "bring substantial advantages for the mission of the Eleventh Army."

---

*See Chapter 3, p. 44. See also Maps Nos. 4, 5, and 8.

Hitler ordered Army Group Center to prepare for an attack against Timoshenko's army group at the end of September. The object of this action was to destroy the Soviet forces east of Smolensk by a double envelopment, driving in the general direction of Vyazma, with strong armored forces pushing ahead on the wings. Mobile forces were to be concentrated: (1) on the southern wing, probably southeast of Roslavl, to attack northeastward with available units of Army Group Center and the specially assigned 2nd and 5th Panzer Divisions, and (2) in the Ninth Army area, to strike probably through Belyy, with "the strongest possible elements" to be moved from Combat Zone North to support the drive. "Only then, if the bulk of Army Group Timoshenko is defeated in this . . . operation of annihilation," would Army Group Center be sent toward Moscow, its right wing along the Oka River and its left along the upper Volga. The Second Air Fleet, reinforced with units from the northeastern area, was to concentrate its efforts on the flanks of the army group, with most of its dive bomber units (VIII Air Corps) deployed there in support of the mobile ground forces.*

Hitler stipulated that operations in Combat Zone North were to be carried out in conjunction with Finnish forces attacking across the Karelian Isthmus, Leningrad was to be encircled, and Petrokrepost (Schluesselburg) was to be taken not later than 15 September,┼ so that "substantial portions of the mobile troops and the First Air Fleet, especially the VIII Air Corps," would be available for Army Group Center. But first, the Leningrad encirclement ring was to be strengthened, especially on the eastern side, and the Luftwaffe, weather permitting, was to carry out a heavy bombing attack, mainly upon the city water works. Units of Army Group North were to proceed northward across the Neva River as soon as possible to assist the Finnish advance against the former Finno-Russian border fortifications, to effect a substantial reduction in the size of the battle sector, and to eliminate the airfields in that area. To prevent enemy naval forces from escaping into the Baltic, Finno-German forces were to seal off the Bay of Kronshtadt with mines and artillery fire. When forces became available, the Leningrad battlefield was also to be "screened to the east as far as the lower Volkhov," but union with the Finns at the Svir River was not to be attempted until the enemy was defeated around Leningrad.

---

*See Map No. 13.
┼See Maps Nos. 11 and 12.

The Fuehrer directed that the attack by Army Group Center toward Moscow be covered by a flank column from Combat Zone South composed of available mobile forces driving in a northeasterly direction, and on the left flank by Army Group North units, which were to contact the Finns and push ahead "on both sides of Lake Ilmen."*

In a supplemental instruction to Directive No. 35, Hitler required that all motorized divisions of Army Group South be combined with the First Panzer Group for the attack from the Kremenchug bridgehead, because no Fourth Air Fleet units would be "available for the support of an attack from the Dnepropetrovsk bridgehead," a point which was to be held by the 198th Infantry Division and Italian or Hungarian forces.[1]

After the war, Kesselring wrote that, beginning on 15 September, preparations for the attack had been carried out "with burning heart but cool head" and that he had discussed the details of the joint operation with the commanders in chief of the Second, Fourth, and Ninth Armies and the interested armored groups. The tactical mission of the Second Air Fleet units had been preceisely defined: the I and II Antiaircraft Artillery Corps/ were assigned ground tasks at the points of main effort to provide supporting and assault artillery fire, concentrating on the right wing of the army group; the close support units of the Luftwaffe were to clear the way for the ground forces, especially armored units, and attack enemy movements on the battlefield. The heavy bomber forces were to close off the battle area to the rear.[2]

The Second Panzer Group (Second Panzer Army after 5 October 1941) had already launched its attack with strong II Air Corps (Second Air Fleet) support from the Putivl area on 30 September in order to reach Orel as quickly as possible. For this operation the air corps had regrouped and now had its command post at Shatalovo. The 3rd and 53rd Bomber Wings were based at the airfields Shatalovo East and Shatalovo West; to protect these fields, which were repeatedly attacked by Soviet bombers and ground-attack aircraft, a fighter unit was located at an advanced airfield east of the fields. The 28th Bomber Wing was based at Bobruysk, while the 2nd Squadron of the 122nd Long-Range Reconnaissance Group operated from the airfield Smolensk South. The II Close Support Air Commander was assigned two groups of the 1st Dive Bomber Wing, three groups of the 77th Dive Bomber Wing, and two groups

---

*See Map No. 12.
/The II Antiaircraft Artillery Corps had been transferred from Combat Zone South to Combat Zone Center.

of the 210th Ground-Attack Wing, respectively.* The fighter forces of the II Air Corps consisted of four groups of the 51st Fighter Wing and three groups of the 3rd Fighter Wing.

On 1 October the Luftwaffe reported that German armored units had advanced from the Glukhov-Yampol line and that the bulk of the bombers, supporting the ground forces, had successfully attacked Russian troop concentrations and columns of tanks and trucks in the Glukhov-Bryansk-Kursk area.[3]

General Halder remarked in his diary on the following day that the Second, Fourth, and Ninth Armies (of Army Group Center) had begun Operation TAIFUN (Typhoon)/ at 0530 hours "in shining autumn weather" and that the Second Panzer Group, despite a lagging right wing, had gained some ground, although by noon the attack of the other armies and armored groups had won "only 6 to 12 kilometers of enemy territory." In some sectors, even "hurried withdrawal movements" had occurred.[4]

The Second Panzer Group of Army Group Center, continuously supported by II Air Corps units, reached Orel on 3 October; its left wing had turned against the rear of the enemy facing the Second Army at Bryansk. Enemy air activity was very lively, with Soviet bombers and ground-attack aircraft, flying mostly in small formations of three to six planes, continuously attacking the German assault columns and airfields. The II Air Corps laid particular significance upon quickly advancing the close support and fighter units as closely as possible behind the attacking ground forces. Therefore, immediately after the fall of Orel, fighter units were brought forward to the airfield at that point. In the days that followed, this field also became a base for the air transport of supplies, since poor road conditions severely limited the forwarding of supplies and made all such operations on the ground extremely difficult. For example, 132,100 gallons (500 cubic meters) of fuel and other materiel

---

*The 210th Ground-Attack Wing is also frequently designated the 210th Bomber Wing, and was outfitted with Me-110 twin-engine fighters, equipped to carry small (SD-2) fragmentation bombs. See Figure No. 39.

/Cover designation for Army Group Center's operation against the armies of Timoshenko.

Figure 39
Me-110's attacking Soviet ground positions,
Battle of Smolensk, 1941

had to be flown in for the Second Panzer Group.* Furthermore, the II Close Support Air Commander had transferred dive bomber units to this airfield which were deemed to be worthwhile targets by Soviet flyers.

On 4 October Halder observed that Operation TAIFUN was proceeding in a "classic" manner, since the Soviets were cooperating in the development of the encirclement by holding their lines rigidly wherever they had not been attacked.[5] Two days later Halder noted that the pocket would soon be closed.[6] The new large-scale attack had taken the Soviet forces completely by surprise.

Very strong action by the Second Air Fleet--with the II Air Corps reinforced by units of the Fourth Air Fleet and the VIII Air Corps transferred swiftly from the Leningrad area to just north of Smolensk--contributed decisively to all the penetrations and breakthroughs by the ground forces. The II Air Corps supported the advance of the Second and Fourth Armies, and particularly the Second Panzer Group on the right wing of the army group, while the VIII Air Corps deployed its units before the Ninth Army, especially ahead of the Third and Fourth Panzer Groups on the left wing.[7]

The severity of the fighting in Combat Zone Center is shown by the report of the High Command of the Luftwaffe for 4 October, which stated that 48 dive bombers and 32 bombers, supporting ground forces, made successful daylight attacks on rail lines and troop movements in the Sumy-Lgov-Kursk area. Then, 202 dive bombers and 188 bombers, some of them in actions integrated with operations of Panzer units, struck Soviet positions, supply movements, troop concentrations, and rail targets in the Bryansk-Spas-Demensk-Sukhinichi area. Further, some 152 dive bombers and 259 bombers were sent over the Belyy-Sychevka-Vyazma area in support of the army. These attacks destroyed some 22 tanks (including 4 of 52 tons), 450 motor vehicles, 11 horse-drawn limbers, 7 tractors, and 3 fuel depots. In addition, these attacks hit a motor park, destroyed 6 guns and put 7 more out of action, and wrecked a bunker and 3 antiaircraft artillery emplacements. Fires and demolition were

_____

*Meantime, road conditions from Orel to Tula had become so bad that air supply was necessary for the 3rd Panzer Division, which had just arrived at Tula (following Group Eberbach, commanded by Col. Heinrich Eberbach of the 4th Panzer Division). Generaloberst Heinz Guderian, Erinnerungen eines Soldaten (Recollections of a Soldier), appearing in an English version entitled Panzer Leader, Heidelberg: Kurt Vowinckel Verlag, 1951, pp. 208, 222.

inflicted everywhere, particularly at Sukhinichi, Yukhnov, Kaluga, Belyy, and Sudzha. Suffering various degrees of damage were 10 railroad depots, while rail lines were frequently interdicted and 37 trains damaged or destroyed. It was even believed that greater losses than those shown above had been inflicted upon Soviet personnel and materiel, although these additional losses could not be verified.[8] On 7 October the High Command of the Luftwaffe reported that the Soviet front in Combat Zone Center had been pierced at three points and that "some 70 large enemy units" in the vicinity of Bryansk and Vyazma would soon be encircled and destroyed. Soviet resistance there was weakening, and signs of disintegration were becoming apparent. Approximately 800 bombers, comprising most of the bomber strength, supported the ground forces and successfully attacked infantry and tank assembly areas, columns of trucks, and communities occupied by Soviet forces. These attacks took place in the areas of Sukhinichi-Kaluga-Chern and Kholm-Vyazma-Spas-Demensk. In addition to the silencing of four artillery positions, the bombs destroyed several bunkers, 8 machine-gun nests, 40 horse-drawn limbers, 34 artillery pieces, 650 vehicles of various kinds, and 20 tanks.[9]

On 7 October units of the Third and Fourth Panzer Armies met near Vyazma. By 10 October, one pocket of Soviet forces had been formed south and one pocket northeast of Bryansk and one west of Vyazma. Although by 13 October the northern pocket was almost completely annihilated by extremely heavy Luftwaffe attacks, elements of the forces of the two southern pockets (south of Bryansk and the pocket west of Vyazma) succeeded in breaking out to the east by making continuous assaults upon the weak positions in the ring. The escaping forces were then constantly pursued and attacked by units of the II Air Corps. These breakout and breakthrough efforts cost the enemy exceptionally high casualties and materiel losses, because at the normally very narrow gaps in the circle-- frequently bridge crossings over rapid streams, swollen from rain and snow--thousands of men and vehicles were pressed tightly together. Some combat units reported that a bombing miss on such a compact mass of troops and equipment would be simply impossible! The two southern pockets surrendered on 17 and 20 October.*

The extent of these encirclement battles around Bryansk and Vyazma is indicated by the Luftwaffe report of 15 October which announced that the enemy had mopped up in the pocket west of Vyazma; elements of

_____
*See Map No. 9.

some 10 armored and 40 infantry divisions, belonging to four Soviet armies, had been taken prisoner or destroyed. To date, 800 tanks and about 3,000 artillery pieces had been destroyed or captured and over 500,000 prisoners taken. To the south and north of Bryansk entrapped Russians were compressed even more tightly together. The OKL report of 15 October declared that "Their final destruction is imminent." Yet the enemy continued his futile attacks in an effort to escape. German ground forces had pushed on to Pesochyna, north of Kaluga, and to Kliny, northeast of Detchino. Borovsk was taken by armored units, while parts of the Wehrmacht attack force at Vereya battled against superior enemy forces. German infantry troops took Nikolo-Pustyn, north of Gzhatsk, and motorized units pushed forward southeast of Lataschino* to Fedorovskoye. After violent house-to-house fighting Kalinin was in German hands, as "strong enemy counterattacks were repulsed." Similar attacks were halted northwest of Staritsa. Around Rzhev, where military operations were plagued by heavy rains and snow, fighting was still in progress, with German infantry nine miles northwest of that city and five miles west of Sytkovo. Although the snowfall had slowed considerably by 15 October, the "bottomless roads" continued to complicate "large-scale movements and the supply of the troops." In the territory between Vyazma and Kalinin large numbers of Russian stragglers had thrown away their weapons and were trying to reach home.[10]

The antiaircraft artillery of the Luftwaffe had also played a considerable part in the success of the battles of encirclement, as shown by the activity of the II Antiaircraft Artillery Corps, which had been transferred from the area of the Fourth Air Fleet to Combat Zone Center and assigned to the Second Air Fleet for the new operation against Moscow. Thus, on 22 October the High Command of the Luftwaffe reported that in the fighting around Vyazma, this antiaircraft artillery corps had, between 2 and 13 October, shot down 29 Soviet planes; destroyed 17 bunkers, 18 fortified field positions, 14 armored cars, 5 defensive posts, 104 artillery pieces, and 94 machine guns; captured or destroyed 579 vehicles of various types and a freight train; routed 7 columns and a cavalry squadron; and repulsed 23 infantry attacks. The antiaircraft artillery corps also thwarted all enemy attempts to break through the sides of the pocket, mopped up a village housing enemy units, and took 3,842 prisoners.[11] From reports and announcements it is evident that all units of the Second Air Fleet had a large share in the success of the encirclement battles of Bryansk and Vyazma.

Editor's Note: This form is the spelling given in the German manuscript. The English version could not be determined.

After the encirclement of Timoshenko's armies in the Bryansk and Vyazma pockets, German infantry divisions had relieved armored units in the area so that the latter could immediately push on to the east. From 7 October on, the weather, which had at first been good, deteriorated rapidly, and by the end of the month the operations of Army Group Center against Moscow had come to a standstill because of impassable roads. Armored units could no longer move ahead; even the horse-drawn vehicles were immobilized by the mud, which was often three feet deep. In the Kalinin area Army units could only be supplied by air. Toward the end of October, as a result of the completely bogged-down condition of advance airfields, operations of Second Air Fleet units were heavily restricted and, at times, impossible. The heavy snowfall mixed with rain, which began about mid-October, considerably curtailed Second Air Fleet activities and brought every movement of the ground forces to a halt by the end of the month. In his diary entry of 16 October, General von Waldau noted that "the boldest hopes are disappearing under rain and snow. . . . everything remains stuck in bottomless roads," while temperatures fell to as low as 17.6° Fahrenheit, followed by 7 to 8 inches of snow and more rain.[12] Kesselring later wrote that the "unfavorable flying weather complicated air support operations" and that a combination of rain and snow, together with the effects of excessive traffic loads carried by "the heaviest tracked vehicles" and the plowing up of roads by bomb craters, slowed (and after 5 October almost halted) ground movements. Rations had to be air-dropped to some units of the Second Panzer Army, and because of a critical lack of winter clothing troops of this army were subjected to severe physical and mental strain.[13]* As an example of the impact of the weather on flying, the Luftwaffe reported that weather conditions during the night of 20-21 October had been unfavorable for operations along the entire front, with the exception of the southeastern part of the Ukraine. During daylight hours on 21 October, bombing and reconnaissance operations on the front were curtailed because of "low, multi-strata clouds, continuing rainfall, and frequent bad visibility,"[14] but the desire of the Luftwaffe command to fight and the high combat morale of the Second Air Fleet were clearly demonstrated that day when the air fleet, despite the bad weather, committed 168 bombers, 49 fighters, and 2 reconnaissance planes in support of ground operations.

The sustained heavy fighting by the ground forces, the difficulties in command and supply for Army and Luftwaffe, the unprecedented stresses

---

*Editor's Note: Soviet troops were then fully equipped with winter clothing.

on all troops, and the exceptional demands upon men and equipment can be seen from comments by Hoffmann von Waldau and reports of the High Command of the Luftwaffe. [15] Von Waldau wrote on 21 October that local gains had been achieved in the drive on Moscow but that small crises had developed at Kalinin as a result of "desperate attempts by the enemy to hold the most important supply line for the logistical support of his front" in and north of the Valdai Hills, which lay east-southeast of Lake Ilmen. [16] On 23 October the High Command of the Luftwaffe reported that on the preceding day difficult weather and road conditions had made planned movements impossible, and that the determined Soviet defense had permitted "only local successes." German troops reached the Svapa River northeast of Rylsk, while in the sector between Mtsensk and Kaluga infantry forces advanced to the Zusha and Oka Rivers. Wehrmacht forces then won bridgeheads across the Protva River near Vysokinichi and across the Nara south and northwest of Naro-Fominsk. Only at Belev, on the west side of the Oka River, was the enemy able to hang on to a bridgehead. Rear German divisions, often spread out over as much as 25 miles, had great difficulty in closing their ranks. Bad roads made their supply problems especially difficult, sufficient artillery and antitank weapons could rarely be brought forward, and the efforts demanded of the dismounted troops was "unusually high." Soviet defenses were concentrated along the road running from Maloyaroslavets to Moscow, on either side of the highway between Mozhaysk and Moscow, and west of the town of Ruza, with various reinforcements being brought in for support. Futile enemy attacks were also launched against the northern, western, and southeastern parts of Kalinin. [17] On the 22nd the Luftwaffe committed 481 bombers, 123 fighters, and 20 reconnaissance aircraft, mostly in support of the Army, against troop concentrations, tank assembly areas, and communities occupied with Soviet troops, while a smaller number of planes bombed rail lines and some airfields. On the 23rd, sorties were carried out by 458 bombers, 140 fighters, and 17 reconnaissance planes, mainly against armored and infantry concentrations, particularly around Kalinin and the area bounded by Mtsensk, Tula, and the terrain north of Rshev. Then, on 24 October, field positions, artillery emplacements, columns, and communities billeting Soviet forces, especially in the sector around Mtsensk and Tula, were attacked by 441 bombers, 208 fighters, and 13 reconnaissance aircraft, while railroad lines were interdicted by smaller formations. And, as final examples of the extent of the Luftwaffe's daily commitment in the attack against Moscow, on 25 October, 455 bombers, 173 fighters, and 23 reconnaissance planes supported the ground forces by attacks in the areas around Mtsensk, Mozhaysk, Kalinin, and Volokolamsk. Two days later, however, weather conditions permitted only one aircraft to be committed east of the battle area.

By 26 October, bad roads had seriously impaired the advances of the motorized units and infantry in Combat Zone Center, which resulted in a wide separation of those units. Fuel for the armored forces had to be brought up by air transport. Leaving all their heavy vehicles and almost all of their motorized vehicles behind, the infantry forces in the southern sector of Combat Zone Center renewed their attacks.[18]

Besides supporting the ground forces--the principal mission at the point of main effort--the Luftwaffe continually and successfully attacked airfields and railroads. In one of these operations bombers of the II Air Corps destroyed 10 trains loaded with armored vehicles. On another day, direct hits on a rail line destroyed 55 trains and damaged 22 others so badly that they could no longer proceed. One episode from these great battles of annihilation deserves mention because of its distinctive features as a case in which air power alone succeeded in keeping a route open for the ground forces. The enemy, holding a bridge over the Snopot River, was subjected to such a heavy and uninterrupted 1 1/2-hour bombing and strafing attack by close support units of the II Air Corps that his attempts to blow up the bridge were delayed long enough for German armored units to arrive and capture this important crossing.

During the Second Panzer Army's drive to the northeast against Tula, a serious crisis arose in the area around Teploye, some 37 miles south of that city. In the attempt to outflank heavily fortified and bitterly defended Tula, the forward units (right wing) of the LIII Army Corps unexpectedly encountered a strong Soviet combat group consisting of two cavalry and five infantry divisions and one armored brigade.* While the German tanks could move only with difficulty, the Soviet T-34 tanks attacked, unhampered by the mud and mire. When air reconnaissance determined that the enemy was approaching the only firm road in the line of advance of the Second Panzer Army, the Orel to Tula road, along which the army's units were standing in columns, the II Air Corps decided upon an unusual action. Although the weather was so bad that the aircraft ran the danger of colliding with trees on the many small hills of the region, a large number of bombers were employed in very-low-level attacks and actually succeeded in discovering the Soviet tanks which had already arrived close to the Orel-Tula road. Part of them were then destroyed and the remainder forced to retreat. This action, however, was costly to the Luftwaffe, and some of the participating

_____

*Editor's Note: The exposed eastern flank of the Second Panzer Army almost invited an attack by Soviet forces.

bombers even returned home with fragments and splinters from their own bombs in their wings.

The frost which now set in so facilitated the movements of the German armored, motorized, and infantry forces in the next few days that the ground situation was restored by 13 November.[19] It is understandable that the operational strength of the units had sunk unusually low through continuous operations and from the extremely difficult weather and the poor ground conditions. Thus, not only the climate--rain, storms, snow, and cold--but also the constantly diminishing operational strength of the Luftwaffe units reduced the expected destructive effect of German air attacks upon the enemy.

Climate and Time Decide the Issue

After operations had come to a halt early in November, the German command then had to decide whether it would still be possible to achieve the desired objective before winter arrived in earnest. Therefore, in a conference of chiefs of staff held in Orsha on 13 November, the Chief of the Army General Staff, Generaloberst Halder, discussed the overall situation and the intentions of the high command. Some of the primary points of discussion were:[20]

(1) Future conduct of military operations would become increasingly a matter of organization and leadership.

(2) Although the previous operations of the war had proceeded according to plan, it was now time to go beyond the preparation conceived by the Army General Staff.

(3) It was now vital to decide whether the progress of operations against Russia had achieved the objectives desired in 1941, and whether it was still necessary and possible to expand these operations before the end of the year. In consideration of these problems it would be necessary to bear in mind that the continuance of the Russian war, as well as of the entire war, would be generally subject to certain economic restrictions. A shift in emphasis to air and naval operations could also be expected to "play a large role in the future."

(4) The fundamental concept of the Russian campaign in 1941 was "to force a decision that would permit a clear shifting" of the major war

effort from Russia back to England and thereby from ground to naval and air operations.

(5) In respect to the timing of the continuation of operations, General Halder stated that in his opinion the drive on the Caucasus could continue in January, while the Sixth Army and Army Group Center could continue to the end of November, but armored units were to resume the attack only when roads were firm. In these circumstances it was necessary to depart from the principles laid down in the regulations.[21]

In a spirit of excessive optimism caused by a period of mild frost, a renewed assault on Moscow was ordered for 17 November. During the first days of the new attack the weather was actually sunny with only light frosts, and the troops--exhausted as they were by their prolonged, severe battles against a tenaciously resisting foe and by their laborious forward struggle through mud, rain, storms, and heavy snowfall--set out on what they expected would be their last great trial of strength, the capture of the Soviet capital. After a few days, however, the weather changed abruptly. Fog, snow, and temperatures of -22° Fahrenheit and below considerably reduced the operational strength of the Luftwaffe units in Combat Zone Center, which had already been severely weakened by the withdrawal of the staffs of some units of the Second Air Fleet and the II Air Corps for transfer to Italy.*

General von Waldau noted on 15 November that these Second Air Fleet units were being withdrawn slowly from Combat Zone Center "so that the calculated and reported deadlines, transportation, rehabilitation, rearmament, and deployment could be maintained on a large scale." Much detailed work was involved; "trifles, the most exacting observance of which are of decisive importance."[22]

On 13 November, General der Flieger Bruno Loerzer, commanding the II Air Corps, issued an order of the day which proudly enumerated the outstanding performance of all corps units since 22 June. Addressing the men of the corps, Loerzer noted that five months of steady fighting against the Soviets had "essentially destroyed the fighting power of the enemy." The corps had played a decisive role in the battles of Minsk, Bialystok, Gomel, Smolensk, Kiev, and Vyazma-Bryansk. Convincing evidence "of the heroic deeds of the soldiers and commanders of all participating units" were the successes achieved. Between 22 June and 12 November the flying units flew over 40,000 day and night sorties,

_____

*See Maps Nos. 13 and 14.

destroying 3,826 Soviet planes (2,169 in aerial combat and the remainder on the ground), 789 tanks, 614 artillery pieces, and 14,339 vehicles of every type, and probably destroying 281 additional aircraft and damaging 811 more. An additional 240 machine-gun nests, field positions, and artillery emplacements were attacked with "devastating results," while 33 bunkers were put out of action or destroyed. Besides these targets, rail lines were attacked 3,579 times, resulting in the severing of tracks 1,736 times, in the destruction of 159 trains and 304 locomotives, and damage to another 1,584 trains and 103 locomotives. Finally, columns, troop concentrations, and points where trains and vehicles were loaded and unloaded were ceaselessly attacked, inflicting very heavy losses upon the enemy. More than 23,150 tons of bombs had been used in the fighting since 22 June. Antiaircraft artillerymen of the corps well supplemented aerial combat achievements by repulsing 300 attacks by 1,000 planes. The accuracy of German antiaircraft fire was shown by the Soviet loss of 100 aircraft (confirmed) and 23 probables to Luftwaffe Flak units.

Loerzer also praised the work of the Luftwaffe signal service personnel, whose tireless efforts in all kinds of weather had provided the "necessary communications without which a close and satisfactory command of the units of the air corps, would not be conceivable."[23] Despite extremely bad roads and constant threat of enemy attack, the signal men had established and operated some 1,865 miles of wire and transmitted 30,000 teletype and 40,000 radio messages. The aircraft reporting detachments employed in the front lines had created conditions essential for the successful defense against enemy air attacks, while the air traffic control teams had vitally assisted in orienting German air units over the far-reaching expanse of Russian territory. And the liaison parties assigned to front line army units did an exemplary job in relaying "the situation and wishes of the ground forces to the headquarters of the corps," thus making possible successful cooperation, especially with the tank forces. None of this could have been achieved without "the unprecedented and devoted action of the flying crews and the friendly, unflagging readiness of the ground personnel to help." And, Loerzer concluded, "If in such a proud moment of reflection upon our performances we consider also the losses which we have suffered through the death of many a faithful comrade, we know also that the significance of their sacrifice is to point the way to our continued struggle, the battle for victory."[23]

Only the VIII Air Corps remained in Combat Zone Center, where on 1 December it assumed command over the II Close Support Air Commander--formerly under the direction of the II Air Corps. On the ground, army operations were making only slow progress at this juncture and in spite of the best intentions of the air command and its troops, unfavorable weather conditions made it impossible to render to the ground forces the measure of air support they had hitherto received and had become accustomed to expect. Many of the advance airfields now occupied by German units consisted only of a sea of mud which made take-offs and landings impossible.

On the other hand, the Soviets committed their air strength all the more strongly. They could do this because many well-developed airfields were available to them in the Moscow area, fields which could be used in the poorest weather. The nearness of the Germans to the Russian capital also caused the enemy, quite naturally, to strengthen his forces with all available means for the defense of the city. Strong antiaircraft artillery, situated at all of the airfields in the Moscow area, made German counter-air operations exceptionally difficult. Powerful, concentrated attacks against these enemy airfields could not be made because flying forces needed for the attacks were lacking; all units were required for commitment in the immediate situation for the direct and indirect support of the ground forces. The higher army headquarters themselves, despite thorough briefing, showed little or no understanding for the air situation. Yet, in spite of the reduced Luftwaffe support, progress was made along the entire front by Army Group Center.[24]

On 27 November von Waldau noted in his diary that the Russian front showed no "substantial changes" and that although the troops appeared to be "fairly ready" he no longer believed that the offensive could succeed. "Cold, poor condition of equipment and clothing, have limited their striking power." While Istra and Solnechnogorsk, north-west of Moscow, were captured, there was "neither the possibility of effecting a complete encirclement of Moscow nor such a close approach to the capital that the armament works could be eliminated by artillery bombardment."[25] By 3 December von Waldau observed that the attack had generally drawn to a halt with the objective, Moscow's encirclement, unattained. And although "Leningrad can still be reached," Rostov-on-the-Don and its bridgeheads had been lost as starting points for a drive on Maykop. Yet, von Waldau did not see these events as causes for pessimism because a vast territory with highly important manufacturing centers and sources of raw material had been captured, while the Russians had lost about 3,600,000 men as prisoners of war and 1,400,000 dead. Still, he expected the war to become "harder and more prolonged."[26]

The Luftwaffe attacked repeatedly to facilitate the advance of the ground forces, but it could not prevent the German armies in their weary struggle against enemy and weather from being slowly, but surely, exhausted. On 9 December, von Waldau noted that the higher levels of command were finally beginning to appreciate what had been learned about weather conditions, and that this realization was "decisive for the new directive, which essentially determines the winter field position and . . . plans the measures for winter and spring."[27]

On 22 November General Halder commented in his diary that the troops had reached the limit of their endurance, and a week later he recognized the need to issue orders for the transition to winter status. On the 30th, he wrote that Hitler and those closest to him "have no idea of the condition of our troops and move about with their thoughts in a vacuum." Halder lauded the performance of the weakened troops in penetrating organized Soviet positions as a "tremendous" feat, but declared on 1 December that these troops were clearly no longer fit for operations.* Halder wrote on 7 December that neither Hitler nor the High Command of the Wehrmacht (OKW) realized the condition of the German troops and were engaged in "petty faultfinding."[28]

In front of Moscow the Soviets scraped together their last available forces. New, recently formed, in part uneducated, and poorly trained forces were brought up from everywhere for the defense of the city. In continuous counterattacks the enemy attempted to halt the German advance.[29] Generals "Mud" and "Winter" supported the enemy most effectively, and finally with decisive results. The German campaign against the Soviet Union had reached its zenith.

A desperate attempt on 4 December to renew the attack failed. "No command could drive farther ahead these troops, who had given their utmost in the face of incredibly severe conditions." After the many remonstrances of the preceding weeks against overstraining the troops had been ignored, Nature compelled Hitler on 6 December to

_____

*Editor's Note: By this time German ground units had lost scores of men because of frostbite. Expecting to win a short campaign, the High Command had failed to order winter clothing except for the 60 divisions which were to occupy Soviet Russia. Unexpected bad weather and logistical problems, however, prevented even this amount from reaching the front. Many German soldiers were fighting in their regular field blouses in December of 1941.

discontinue the attack, although he ordered the Wehrmacht to hold the territory which it had won.[30]* Thereupon, operations in the center came to a halt, and over the German armies of Army Group Center a terrible crisis now arose which also affected all the other fronts.

The Crisis Before Moscow

On 8 December 1941, Directive No. 39 was issued because the "onset of a surprisingly early and severe winter" with its related supply difficulties had led to the immediate discontinuance of the offensive and a shift to the defensive. The directive required that the defense govern itself according to the following objectives:

(1) Areas vitally important to the Russians for tactical, strategic, or military-economic purposes were to be held.

(2) Forces of the Wehrmacht in the East were to be afforded the greatest possible opportunities for rest and rehabilitation.

(3) Conditions requisite for the renewal of large-scale offensive operations in 1942 were to be created.

In detail, the directive outlined specifically the measures to be taken by the Army with respect to defensive dispositions: winter quarters for front line troops; rehabilitation of all troops, especially those from motorized and armored units; simplification of supply conditions in relation to the location of the front line and the eventual thaw; establishment of defensive positions in the rear areas; and, lastly, special missions, such as the immediate capture of Sevastopol and a winter offensive, when the weather permitted, by Army Group South into the lower Don and Severnyy Donets region to secure a starting point for operations into the Caucasus in the spring.

As the primary task of the Luftwaffe in this period, Directive No. 39 required the German air units to interfere as much as possible with the rehabilitation of Russian armed forces by launching attacks upon the training and armament centers, particularly those at Moscow, Leningrad,

---

*Editor's Note: General Friedrich Fromm, Commander of the Replacement Army, suggested to Brauchitsch, before the futile December offensive against Moscow and while German prestige was high, that peace offers be made to the Soviet Union.

Voronezh, Gorkiy, Shcherbakov, Stalingrad, Rostov, and Krasnodar. Soviet communications "by which the enemy lives and by whose use our own front sectors were threatened" were to be continually interdicted. In addition to counter-air operations, the Luftwaffe was to fully support the ground forces in defense against both Soviet air and ground attacks.

In this directive Hitler approved the organizational boundaries of the army groups and the order of battle and distribution of flying units remaining in Russia, and ordered that, as ground operations ceased, the various units were to be withdrawn, where feasible, for training and rehabilitation. Rest and rehabilitation centers were to be established very close to the front, thereby providing a "ground organization" which would permit "a swift shifting of forces and reinforcements from withdrawn units." This was to provide for defense against possible winter attacks as well as to allow for German winter operation in the Don-Severnyy Donets region.

"Continuous, overlapping, and far-reaching" aerial reconnaissance was particularly important in order to be able to "detect early and to keep under surveillance enemy regroupings." Hitler, moreover, reserved for himself the right to approve any withdrawal of forces from the front before Moscow, which had been earlier foreseen, for operations in the theater of Commander in Chief South.* Air defense would be maintained to protect troop billeting and supply areas and the most important rear area communications. To counter "identified massed concentrations of enemy air attack forces," it was planned to hastily assemble the German fighters into massed fighter forces.

The Navy stood as security for the sea route to Helsinki, which would be less hazardous after the port of Hangö and the island of Osmussaar had been captured, so that these sea lanes could be more fully utilized by merchant shipping and for the supply of German forces in Finland. Small cargo ships, especially designed for use in the Black and Aegean Seas, were to be built in very large numbers in Germany and in the allied and occupied countries.[31]

The envisioned partial withdrawal of Army Group Center began on 13 December. (By that date, in severe fighting, the Germans had

---

*Editor's Note: Field Marshal Kesselring became Commander in Chief South (Oberbefehlshaber Sued) 1 December 1941 in addition to his command of Luftflotte 2 (Second Air Fleet). This assignment covered operations in Italy, Africa, and the Mediterranean areas.

242

pushed to within 12 1/2 miles of Moscow at various points.) Russian forces hit these withdrawal movements with powerful counterattacks, launched by numerically superior, newly arrived, and winter-hardened Soviet forces,* dressed in good winter clothing. These attacks frequently caused very serious crises. The withdrawal battles of the German armies--made especially difficult by the severe cold and the lack of winter equipment among the ground forces--were supported by attack waves of the VIII Air Corps and the II Close Support Air Commander, insofar as weather conditions would permit. In these crucial days--for the first time in the central sector of the Eastern Front--ground personnel of the Luftwaffe and antiaircraft artillery and Luftwaffe signal service units were organized into "Luftwaffe combat units" and committed in ground combat in support of Army units which were fighting under particularly difficult conditions.† Additional help was given by the arrival of an air transport commander (Col. Fritz Morzik) and five Ju-52 groups from Germany for assignment to the VIII Air Corps to carry out urgent air transport duties.††

On 16 December, Hitler issued an order to the ground forces of Army Groups North, Center, and South to hold fast to their positions with "fanatical resistance," without "retreating a step," and to "defend to the last man" the farthest point of advance to the east, in order to maintain the encirclement of Leningrad, prevent the loss of heavy equipment and weapons in the central sector, and, hopefully, to gain time for reinforcements to arrive. Army Group South, meanwhile, was to hasten its capture of Sevastopol so that reserves could be released from the Crimea.

Hitler directed that the VIII Air Corps be reinforced without delay by a full bomber group from the Western Front, three newly activated bomber groups, a twin-engine fighter group withdrawn from the night fighter forces to replenish two similar groups of the VIII Air Corps, four newly activated air transport groups, and one transport

---

*Editor's Note: Many of these new Soviet replacements had been sent in from Siberia, fully equipped with winter camouflage and protective clothing.

†Editor's Note: These Luftwaffe combat units (Luftwaffen-Gefechts-verbaenden) were forerunners of the Luftwaffe Field Divisions (Luftwaffen-Felddivisionen) which were established in the autumn of 1942. Twenty of these divisions were assigned permanently to the German Army 31 October 1943. See various articles on the subject, A/VI/4, Karlsruhe Document Collection.

††See Figure 40.

Figure 40
Panje sleds carrying loads from Ju-52 air
transports, Russia, winter 1941

Figure 41
Iced-up engines of Ju-52 transport plane at a
German airfield in Russia, December 1941

group transferred from the Fourth Air Fleet. The four new air transport groups were to be equipped with the Chief of Training's "last Ju-52's" and all but the most essential courier planes of the various staffs and agencies of the Luftwaffe. These groups were to bring with them elements of the 4th SS Standarte* from Krakow. At the same time the Fourth Air Fleet's air transport group, when transferring to the VIII Air Corps, was to carry a march battalion from Army Group South for a special mission of undisclosed purpose.[32]

The Fuehrer directive concluded with specifications for measures to be taken for the strengthening of the Eastern Front: badly weakened units were to receive replacements; some divisions in the West which were fully equipped for winter were to be moved to Combat Zone Center into places where there were insufficient units, while divisions remaining in the West were subject to possible loss of their winter equipment to units in Russia. In addition, infantry units with little artillery were to be re-equipped first, and all transports were to be "fitted out with ovens and ample food supplies." Army group commands were to establish priorities for bringing up reinforcements and supplies. All German forces in the homeland "which can guard, build, or fight and which are not employed in a vital mission" were to be organized, obtain winter clothing from their present areas, and stand by for transfer to the East.† The availability of all such forces was to be reported directly to Hitler. Finally, besides the four divisions to be provided by the replacement army, the greatest possible number of fighting units, mobile for winter combat, were to be organized in battalion strength and equipped with skis and sleds. Reports on the state of combat readiness and the number of such units were to be made to Hitler.[33]

This Fuehrer directive clearly shows the intervention by the supreme military and political leadership, that is, by Hitler, into details of tactical and strategic operations and into disposition of forces, organization, and training. These Luftwaffe operations also reveal the obligation to use newly activated units, the weakening of the last Luftwaffe forces in the West, the allocation of air transport groups for tactical purposes, and the risky and serious inroads into the training of new crews, especially those of bomber units. By the withdrawal of over 100 Ju-52's, a grievous disruption and curtailment of training activities inevitably had to occur, which sooner or later would lead to a shortage of replacement aircrews at the front.

---

*Editor's Note: A unit corresponding in size to an army regiment.
†Editor's Note: This force included Army guard battalions, Luftwaffe guard battalions, SS units in Berlin, and the Reichs Labor Service from the West and Poland.

In the midst of this crisis, which threatened to expand into a catastrophe, Hitler accepted the resignation of Field Marshal Walther von Brauchitsch and, on 19 December, assumed supreme command of the Army himself.[34]* Von Tippelskirch wrote after the war that at the time Hitler made the decision it was the only one possible which held any promise of success. Hitler alone had led the Army as far as Moscow, he alone had "the suggestive power to give it new impulses," and "he enjoyed the unqualified confidence of the troops." His decision thus had an inspiring influence. Even the higher commanders, despite their frequent critical opposition, clearly understood the "fascinating significance" of Hitler's decision.⧸ After the offensive of 1941 had been halted, Hitler forbade voluntary withdrawal. Application of this "fixed and uncompromising" measure meant that the Army had to dispense with operating in space and led to a series of tactical and strategic crises

---

*Editor's Note: Hitler, angered at the withdrawal of German Army units before Moscow, blamed von Brauchitsch for the situation. Von Brauchitsch, although ostensibly retired for reasons of poor health, was in reality removed by Hitler.

⧸Editor's Note: The Luftwaffe apparently enjoyed a greater measure of Hitler's confidence than did the Army, as may be noted from the remarks of Army leaders. Von Manstein remarked that Hitler "had a certain eye for strategic possibilities as shown by his decision for the plan of Army Group A in the West . . . [but that] he failed in his ability to assess prerequisite conditions and possibilities for accomplishing a strategic thought." He also pointed out Hitler's abject refusal to countenance any arrangement of command except absolute, direct control of operations in the person of the Fuehrer. Erich von Manstein, Verlorene Siege (Lost Victories), Bonn: Athenaeum Verlag, 1955, pp. 303-305, 438. Guderian viewed Hitler as a man "raw in speech and manner," who saw all traditions as obstacles in his revolutionary path. The fall of Brauchitsch, said Guderian, "placed the power of command directly in the hands of Hitler. This was for all practical purposes the end of the old, Prussian-German stamp upon the General Staff." Erinnerungen eines Soldaten (Recollections of a Soldier), Heidelberg: Kurt Vowinckel Verlag, 1951, p. 422. Kesselring has noted that "the most competent leaders, Field Marshals von Rundstedt, von Leeb, List, von Weichs, von Kleist, and von Manstein, as well as Generalobersten Guderian, Hoth, and others, were at some time relieved of their commands [in Russia] by Hitler." Gedanken zum Zweiten Weltkrieg (Thoughts on the Second World War), Bonn: Athenaeum Verlag, 1955, p. 121.

and brought about an extremely serrated front line.[35]*

As was the case in Combat Zones South and North, a crisis now occurred also in the center, where a decision was being sought. This crisis, however, was incomparably greater because the Soviets had naturally assembled their strongest and best units around Moscow and, seeking a decision in their own favor, had gone over to a counteroffensive.[36]

In October 1941 the German supreme command headquarters had been considering the minimum forces which would be required in the East after the cessation of hostilities, with Halder noting in his diary on 8 October that following the eastern campaign it was intended to leave behind under two air fleets the following forces:

(1) Two bomber and three fighter groups, one reconnaissance squadron, and one antiaircraft artillery regiment at Leningrad, and three bomber and four fighter groups, one reconnaissance squadron, and two antiaircraft artillery regiments at Moscow, all units under the command of the First Air Fleet.

(2) Three bomber, three and one-half fighter, and three dive bomber groups, one reconnaissance squadron, and two antiaircraft artillery regiments, all under the Fourth Air Fleet.[37]

But by the end of December the Germans were scraping together all the forces possible to throw against the large-scale Soviet counterattacks which already were beginning, while in contrast to the October plan to leave air units at Leningrad, Moscow, and other key captured places was the teletype message of 24 December 1941 from the OKW, stating that Hitler, confirming his oral decisions, had ordered the High Command of the Luftwaffe to withdraw air units from operations against Britain in order to prepare them for short term operations on the Eastern Front, either in support of Army Group North or Center, as the situation required.[38] The effects of the Soviet counteroffensive on the

---

*Editor's Note: General Plocher believes that no withdrawal was possible on a large scale because of a lack of solid defensive positions to the immediate rear and the probability that German units would have been rolled up in the course of a general retreat. The order by Hitler to defend the front line was, in Plocher's opinion, a wise decision which came at precisely the most favorable time to help bolster the lines.

overall German distribution of forces is clearly evident; the Eastern Front had to be strengthened at the expense of other fronts--in this case, at the expense of operations against England.

In the central sector the Luftwaffe had become what might be called a "fire brigade," which carried on operations and was expected simultaneously to extinguish countless fires. Independent operations by the Luftwaffe could no longer be considered. Because they could be used swiftly and flexibly, flying units were invariably used to give direct support to the harassed armies. Thus in Combat Zone Center the Luftwaffe command had also become completely dependent upon tactical and strategic plans and procedures of the Army. The Luftwaffe had become more and more an effective long-range arm of the artillery and an auxiliary weapon of the ground forces. The Luftwaffe, created originally in the spirit of the Italian General Giulio Douhet* and General-leutnant Walter Wever✝ as an independent strategic force, was now thrown into a battle of annihilation in a downright suicidal manner in support of the Army, thus contradicting all of the wishes and intentions of the founders of the Air Force. ✝✝

A Review of German Air Operations in 1941

In what was then an unparalleled series of victories, the German Wehrmacht, supported on all fronts by the Luftwaffe, in 1941 penetrated deeply into the heart of European Russia, and threatened the very existence of the Soviet Union. During this campaign the Russians suffered terrible losses in both men and materiel, but the magnitude and difficulties of the offensive effort virtually exhausted the capabilities of the German Armed Forces. In these far-flung operations German troops were required to fight in climates to which they were unaccustomed, varying from extreme heat to bitter cold, in dampness, drought, storms, and snow. Because of improper preparations--Hitler firmly believed that the issue could be decided before plans for a long-term war became

---

*Italian general (1869-1930) who was an early advocate of strategic air power.

✝First Chief of the General Staff of the Luftwaffe, a far-sighted, able, and highly respected officer who met his death in an air accident 3 June 1936.

✝✝Editor's Note: One of the principal obstacles to the creation of a strategic air force in Germany was Generaloberst Hans Jeschonnek, Chief of the Luftwaffe General Staff, a man who considered Hitler a genius and who steadfastly opposed the idea of strategic air warfare.

necessary--and the unexpected conditions, the logistical support of the German Army and Air Force was seriously deficient and eventually almost nonexistent. Serious reverses halted the German advance in many parts of the front before 1941 was out, especially in the central sector. Driving rains, endless tracts of deep, sticky mud, and snow storms and freezing cold deadlocked many communication routes and proved to be decisive factors in the first year's operations. By the end of the year it was clear that Germany had failed to reach its desired strategic objectives and that the Soviet Union would not be defeated by Hitler in a "lightning war."

By late 1941 air transport services had become a recognized part, in fact a vital part, of the overall supply program for German forces in the East, but Luftwaffe reserves were insufficient to meet the demands of the time.* Transport aircraft became ever more scarce as the German Air Force attempted to compensate for its losses by withdrawing large numbers of planes from the air training commands. The Luftwaffe, unable to meet its air transport commitments, also used bombers for regular transport and air dropping assignments, with the result that badly needed combat aircraft were lost while performing missions for which they were never intended.

But no demands upon the Luftwaffe were greater than those of the ground forces asking for tactical support. In many cases the only possible means of relieving the perpetual crises in certain areas was to throw all available air forces into action, even aircraft which were barely operational. German Air Force personnel demonstrated a remarkable devotion to duty in their efforts to support the hard-pressed ground forces, but the effects of combat had a much harsher effect upon the Luftwaffe than upon the Army. The air forces, being more complex in character and staffed by technically trained personnel who were difficult to replace, suffered more immediately from the war than did the German Army, with its sounder and more robust organizational structure.

---

*Editor's Note: Once Germany had embarked upon a multi-front war the opportunity for building up a reserve force had passed. Luftwaffe commanders were subsequently forced to support critical places at the front by withdrawing units from other fronts or training centers. War involvement in other areas, therefore, proved to be the "straw that broke the camel's back."

Figure 42
Ju-88-A-15 bomber engines being heated by
warming device at a Luftwaffe base
in Russia, December 1941

Paramount among German failures in 1941 was the stalemate of the Wehrmacht before the gates of Moscow. Luftwaffe leaders generally agreed that the Soviet capital could have been captured that year if: (1) the Balkan campaign had not delayed the opening of the attack upon Russia; (2) troops used for the assault on Moscow had been rested for a shorter time after the end of the battle for Smolensk and thus committed at an earlier date; and (3) climatic factors had been considered, including preparations for winter clothing, cold-resistant lubricants, engine warmers, * wide-tracked vehicles, and other appropriate equipment at the front.

General V. M. Sokolovski of the Soviet Army attributed the German failure to seize Moscow and the successful Russian stabilization of the front to: (1) the strong Soviet will to resist (probably enhanced by imprudent occupation policies of the German government in conquered areas); (2) the increased output of armaments by Soviet factories (a factor which was badly underestimated by German leaders); (3) German weaknesses in rear areas (due in part to poor communications routes as well as to the unwise treatment of the civil populace by German government agencies, which tended to encourage partisan activities); and (4) the loss of faith by German soldiers in the invincibility of their armies. Other Russian leaders could find little reason for the termination of the initially so successful German offensive./ According to Field Marshal Kesselring, one Soviet general called the deadlock before Moscow a "repetition of the incomprehensible miracle of the Marne," which saved "Moscow in 1941 as it had saved Paris in World War I." Some have suggested that the Luftwaffe was surprised by the arrival of winter-trained Siberian troops in Moscow, who helped to turn the tide of battle. Evidence shows, however, that German leaders were aware of the

---

*Editor's Note: Luftwaffe personnel found that engines which were stopped overnight in the sub-zero temperatures could frequently not be started again. Because of this, all sorts of engine warming devices were improvised. See Figures 41 and 42.

/Editor's Note: German forces, elated at the tremendous amount of booty and the number of prisoners captured in western Russia, failed to note that the Soviet field armies had not been defeated, since thousands had withdrawn to the East. German commanders failed to revise their plans accordingly before the arrival of winter, but instead rushed headlong into the interior of the Soviet Union with all available forces. Lacking any reserves, even the slightest reversal of the situation was bound to have disastrous results.

arrival of reinforcements as early as August of 1941 and that the winter arrivals had been sighted by aerial reconnaissance. [39]

The question has been raised whether the Luftwaffe could have done more to support the German Army or to expedite its advance. Greater efforts might have been possible if the forces of the Luftwaffe had not been so thinly spread over such a great area. As the war progressed, attrition destroyed the Luftwaffe's scanty reserves and kept it from fulfilling even the tactical assignments for ground force units. Since the requests of the Army could not be satisfied in all places simultaneously, it should not have been surprising that efforts to gratify all such demands would eventually bleed the Luftwaffe white.

At the beginning of the campaign the German Air Force swept the Soviet Air Force from the skies and destroyed nearly all of its obsolete aircraft. This could have been a decisive victory if the Luftwaffe had been able to stifle the reconstruction of Russian air forces through a destruction of the Soviet aircraft industry and the closing of the ports of Murmansk, Arkhangelsk, and the Black Sea area. This it was not able to do. Strategic objectives in the Soviet Union might have been attained if the Luftwaffe had carried out systematic strategic operations. By the end of October it should have been clear that the "Blitzkrieg" warfare was not going to work. A joint request at that time by the General Staffs of the Army and the Luftwaffe asking for an interruption in operations to prepare for all-out strategic air warfare might have succeeded, but this was not done.* Since all significant operations over Britain ceased about the time of the invasion of Russia, at least two bomber wings should have gone at once to the East for strategic assignments. These units (4th and 28th Bomber Wings) were eventually sent to the East anyway, but by the time they arrived they were desperately needed for tactical purposes and to fill in the gaps caused by the increasing attrition rates among other Luftwaffe combat units.

---

*Editor's Note: Even had the Luftwaffe made the decision to use strategic air power, and even if the High Command of the Wehrmacht had approved this type of action, the question could be fairly raised whether the Luftwaffe had the proper type of aircraft and equipment to carry out such operations. Too, it should be borne in mind that air forces had to be used against the British in the West and in support of German troops still fighting in Cyrenaica.

The principle of concentration of forces was not uniformly observed among Luftwaffe units in the Soviet Union. Real concentrations of air power were observed on only two occasions in 1941, once in the general advance upon Leningrad and again during the offensive against Moscow. At all other places the German Air Force was employed in a piecemeal fashion, usually in accordance with the demands of front line ground units. Unfortunately for the Luftwaffe, German ground forces found themselves in a series of crises at the very time when Air Force reserves were at a critically low ebb and when combat air units were least able to give support. By the winter of 1941-42 the effects of war were beginning to tell heavily upon Luftwaffe organizations in Russia and in other theaters as well. It was the beginning of the death of the German Air Force.

FOOTNOTES

Chapter 1

1. Generalfeldmarschall Albert Kesselring (Ret.), Soldat bis zum letzten Tag (Soldier to the Last Day), Bonn: Athenaeum Verlag, 1953, p. 114. Cited hereafter as Kesselring, Memoirs.

2. General der Infanterie Georg Thomas, "Grundlagen fuer eine Geschichte der deutschen Wehr-und-Ruestungswirtschaft" ("Foundations for a History of the German Armed Forces War Economy"), manuscript of a book written during World War II by General Thomas (National Archives Microcopy No. T-77, Serial 635, Roll 635, Item USA-035, PS-2353). See also Der Prozess gegen die Hauptkriegsverbrecher vor dem Internationalen Militaergerichtshof Nuernberg (The Trial of the Principal War Criminals Before the International Military Tribunal Nuremberg), Vol. XXX, pp. 260-280, F/I/1a, Karlsruhe Document Collection.

3. Ibid.

4. "Fuehrer's Conferences on Naval Affairs," 8 and 9 January 1941, Brassey's Naval Annual 1948, New York: The MacMillan Company, 1948, p. 172.

5. Statement by Col. (GSC) Josef Schmid, at the time Chief of the Intelligence Branch (Ic) of the Luftwaffe General Staff. Cited hereafter as "Statement by Colonel Schmid."

6. Ibid.

7. Generaloberst Franz Halder (Ret.), "Vorbereitungen fuer den Russland und Balkanfeldzug" ("Preparations for the Russian and Balkan Campaigns"). Statements made by Generaloberst Halder for the Allies 1945-46. See also Halder, "Der Russlandfeldzug bis zum Weggang des Generalfeldmarschall von Brauchitsch" ("The Russian Campaign up to the Departure of Field Marshal von Brauchitsch"), G/VI/1, Karlsruhe Document Collection. Cited hereafter as Halder, Russian Campaign.

8. _____, "Erhard Milch," a typescript of unknown author-
    ship prepared by the Studiengruppe (Study Group) at Karlsruhe,
    Germany, p. 12, D/II/1, Karlsruhe Document Collection. Here-
    after cited as "Erhard Milch."

9. Ibid., pp. 13-14.

10. Count Galeazzo Ciano (Hugh Gibson, ed.), The Ciano Diaries 1939-
    1943: The Complete, Unabridged Diaries of Count Galeazzo Ciano,
    Italian Minister for Foreign Affairs 1936-1943, Garden City, New
    York: Doubleday and Company, Inc., 1946, pp. 583-584.

11. Reichsmarschall Hermann Goering, "Rede des Reichsmarschall
    Goering vor den Gauleitern in Muenchen, Fuehrerbau, am 8.11.
    1943, mittags 12 Uhr ueber Fragen des Luftkrieges" ("Address
    of Reichsmarschall Hermann Goering Before the District Party
    Leaders in Munich at the Fuehrer House on 8 November 1943, at
    Noon, Concerning Questions on the Air War"), D/I/2, Karlsruhe
    Document Collection. Cited hereafter as Goering, Air War 1943.

12. Statement by Col. (GSC) Josef Schmid, undated.

13. Statement by Col. (GSC) Torsten Christ, undated, Aide to General-
    major Otto Hoffmann von Waldau.

14. International Military Tribunal, Nazi Conspiracy and Aggression,
    Vol. IX, Nuremberg: International Military Tribunal, pp. 59-60.

15. Ibid., pp. 382-388. See also Prof. Richard Suchenwirth, Historical
    Turning Points in the German Air Force War Effort, USAF
    Historical Studies: No. 189, Maxwell AFB: Historical Division,
    RSI, June 1959, pp. 72-74. Cited hereafter as USAF Study No.
    189.

16. Der Fuehrer und Oberste Befehlshaber der Wehrmacht, Weisung
    Nr. 21, Fall Barbarossa, OKW/WFSt/Abt. L (I), Nr. 33 408/40,
    g.Kdo Chefsache, F.H.Qu., den 18.12.40 (The Fuehrer and
    Supreme Commander of the Armed Forces, Directive No. 21,
    Operation Barbarossa, High Command of the Armed Forces/Armed
    Forces Operations Staff/National Defense Branch (Operations), No.
    33 408/40, Secret Command Matter, Fuehrer's Headquarters in
    the Field, 18 December 1940), G/b, Karlsruhe Document Collection.
    See Appendix I of this study. Cited hereafter as Directive No. 21.

17.   Union of Soviet Socialist Republics, Orientierungsheft, Union
      der Sozialistischen Sowjetrepubliken, unter besonderer Berueck-
      sichtigung der Fliegertruppe und Flakartillerie sowie der Flug-
      ruestungsindustrie im Rahmen der allgemeinen Wehrwirtschafts-
      lage, Stand 1.2.1941, OKL, Fuehrungsstab Ic/IV, Nr. 3500/41,
      geheim (Orientation Manual, Union of Soviet Socialist Republics,
      with Special Consideration of the Air Forces and the Antiaircraft
      Artillery as well as the Air Armament Industry within the Scope
      of the General Military Situation, as of 1 February 1941, High
      Command of the Air Force, Operations Staff, Intelligence Branch,
      Group IV, No. 3500/41, Secret), G/VI/2a, Karlsruhe Document
      Collection.   Cited hereafter as Orientation Manual.

18.   Ibid. See also "Vortrag bei Hitler am 5.12.1940 ueber die
      geplante Ostoperation" (Vortrag Halder) ("Discourse with Hitler
      on 5 December 1940 Regarding the Planned Eastern Operation, "
      a discourse of Generaloberst Franz Halder), G/VI/1, Karlsruhe
      Document Collection.

19.   Generalleutnant Heinrich Aschenbrenner, "Nachrichten ueber die
      russische Ruestungsindustrie, " Nach einem Bericht von General
      Heinrich Aschenbrenner, vor dem Kriege deutscher Luftwaffen-
      attache in Moskau ("Reports on the Russian Armament Industry, "
      from a report by General Heinrich Aschenbrenner, before the
      war German Air Force Attache in Moscow), G/VI/2a, Karlsruhe
      Document Collection.   Cited hereafter as Aschenbrenner Report.
      See also Orientation Manual.

20.   Orientation Manual. See also OKL, Lageberichten Mai u. Juni
      1941 (High Command of the Air Force, Situation Reports from
      May and June of 1941), Karlsruhe Document Collection. See also
      OKL, Generalstab der Luftwaffe, "Russische Luftwaffe 1941, "
      Auszug aus einer Studie der 8 (kriegswissenschaftlichen) Abteilung
      der Luftwaffe (High Command of the Air Force, General Staff of
      the Air Force, "Russian Air Force 1941, " excerpt from a study
      by the 8th (Military Science) Branch of the Air Force), G/VI/2a,
      Karlsruhe Document Collection.

21.   Orientation Manual. See also OKW, Wirtschaft und Ruestungsamt,
      Chefsache Nr. 10/41, den 13.2.1941, "Die wehrwirtschaftlichen
      Auswirkungen einer Operation im Osten" (High Command of the
      Armed Forces, War Economy and Armament Office, "The Military-
      Economic Effects of an Operation in the East"), G/VI/1, Karlsruhe
      Document Collection.

Chapter 2

1. Generalleutnant Hermann Plocher (Ret.), "Luftwaffen - Vorbereitungen fuer Barbarossa" ("The Air Forces - Preparations for
Barbarossa, Russian Campaign"), Karlsruhe Document Collection.
See also Orientation Manual. See also Reichspropaganda Minister-
ium, "Vernehmung des sowjetrussischen Fliegerobersten Wan-
juschkin," den 3.2.1942, Berlin (Reichs Propaganda Ministry,
"Interrogation of Soviet Russian Colonel Vanyushkin," Berlin,
3 February 1942), G/VI/2b, Karlsruhe Document Collection.

2. _____, "Die Lage vor Kriegsbeginn 1941" (The Situation
Before the Beginning of the War, 1941"), an unpublished report of
unknown, but apparently postwar authorship, prepared from
studies of the 8th (Military Science) Branch of the German Air
Force, the Reynaud Documents of 1940, wartime newspapers, and
various other German sources, G/VI/1, Karlsruhe Document
Collection.

Chapter 3

1. Directive No. 21.

2. General Plocher's Commentary: "Each spring all Russian troops
moved from their barracks to tents." See also Orientation
Manual.

3. OKL, Fuehrungsstab Ic, gKdos., Lagebericht Nr. 652, vom
22.6.1941 (High Command of the Luftwaffe, Intelligence Operations
Staff, Secret, Situation Report No. 652 of 22 June 1941), Appendix
70, Karlsruhe Document Collection. Cited hereafter as Situation
Report No. 652 of 22 June 1941.

4. Ibid. See also Situation Reports 653-660, Karlsruhe Document
Collection.

5. Generaloberst Franz Halder, The Private War Journal of Generaloberst Franz Halder, Chief of Staff of the Supreme Command of
the German Army 14 August 1939-24 September 1942, Vol. VI,
(Translated by Arnold Lissance), Washington, D.C.: Office of
the Chief of Military History, 1950, 22 and 24 June 1941. Cited
hereafter as Halder, Diary.

6. Situation Report No. 652 of 22 June 1941. See also Situation Report No. 669 of 9 July 1941, Karlsruhe Document Collection.

7. Generalmajor Otto Hoffmann von Waldau, "Kriegstagebuch" ("War Diary"), Part I, 22 June 1941, p. 49, H/I/1, Karlsruhe Document Collection. Cited hereafter as von Waldau, Diary.

8. Ibid., p. 50.

9. Kesselring, Memoirs, pp. 119-120.

10. Winston S. Churchill, "The Grand Alliance," The Second World War, Vol. III, Boston: Houghton Mifflin Company, 1950, p. 367. Cited hereafter as Churchill, Vol. III.

11. General der Infanterie Kurt von Tippelskirch (Ret.), Geschichte des Zweiten Weltkrieges (History of the Second World War), Bonn: Athenaeum Verlag, 1951, p. 216. Cited hereafter as Tippelskirch.

12. Luftdivision 16, Nur fuer den Dienstgebrauch, "Luftkriegfuehrung," Berlin: Maerz 1940 (Air Division 16, Only for Service Use, "Air War Leadership," Berlin: March 1940), Item 17, F/I/2a, Karls-ruhe Document Collection. Cited hereafter as Air War Leadership.

Chapter 4

1. Tippelskirch, p. 210. See also Directive No. 21.

2. Tippelskirch, pp. 210-211.

3. Ibid., p. 211.

4. Ibid., pp. 210-212.

5. OKL, Fuehrungsstab Ia, V. Flieger Korps, "Das V. Flieger Korps im Osten, 22. Juni bis 30. Nov. 1941," (High Command of the Luft-waffe, Operations Staff, V Air Corps, "The V Air Corps in the East, 22 June to 30 November 1941"), pp. 2-3, G/VI/3c, Karls-ruhe Document Collection. Hereafter cited as V Air Corps Action Report, 1941.

6. Item of unknown origin, taken from the original draft of Generalleutnant Hermann Plocher (Ret.), Karlsruhe Document Collection.

7. V Air Corps Action Report, 1941, p. 3.

8. Situation Report No. 666 of 6 July 1941, p. 28.

9. Halder, Diary, VI, 30 June 1941, G/VI/3a, Karlsruhe Document
   Collection.

10. Situation Report No. 662 of 2 July 1941.

11. Von Waldau, Diary, VI, 6 July 1941, pp. 56-57, H/I/1, Karlsruhe
    Document Collection.

12. Halder, Diary, VI, 6 July 1941, pp. 205-206.

13. Ibid., 11 July 1941, pp. 222-225.

14. Ibid., 12 July 1941, pp. 226-231.

15. Ibid., 13, 15 July 1941.

16. Von Waldau, Diary, Part I, 15 July 1941, pp. 57-58.

17. Situation Report No. 675 of 15 July 1941, p. 20.

18. Halder, Diary, VI, 15 July 1951.

19. Ibid., 10 July 1941.

20. Ibid., 10, 11 July 1941.

21. Ibid., 10, 11, 12 July 1941. See also Kesselring, Memoirs, pp.
    120-122.

22. Situation Report No. 657 of 27 July 1941, p. 12.

23. Ibid., No. 713 of 22 August 1941, p. 35.

24. Ibid., No. 728 of 5 September 1941, p. 26.

25. Halder, Diary, VII, 19 August 1941.

26.   Situation Report No. 710 of 19 August 1941, p. 20.

27.   Halder, Diary, VII, 12 September 1941.

28.   Von Waldau, Diary, Part I, 14 August 1941, pp. 66-67.

29.   Situation Report No. 677 of 17 July 1941, p. 27. See also Situation Report No. 714 of 23 August 1941, p. 36.

30.   Personal accounts of General der Flieger Wilhelm Speidel (Ret.) as told to Generalleutnant Hermann Plocher (Ret.).

31.   Situation Report No. 656 of 26 June 1941, pp. 8-9.

32.   Ibid., No. 674 of 14 July 1941, p. 9.

33.   Ibid., No. 708 of 17 August 1941, p. 11.

34.   Ibid., No. 777 of 26 October 1941, p. 11.

35.   Von Waldau, Diary, Part I, 15 July 1941, pp. 56-57.

36.   OKL, Deutsche Luftwaffenmission Rumaenien, Ia, gKdos., Nr. 17/42 Ia op 3 (LS), vom 7.1.1942 "Kurzbericht ueber den Einsatz der deutschen Luftschutzkraefte in Rumaenien 1941" (High Command of the Luftwaffe, German Air Force Mission in Rumania, Operations, Secret, No. 17/42, 3rd Operations Branch - Air Defense - of 7 January 1942 "Short Report on the Employment of German Air Defense Forces in Rumania 1941"), Appendix 74, Book 2, "Der Feldzug im Osten 1941-1945" ("The Campaign in the East 1941-1945"), Karlsruhe Document Collection.

Chapter 5

1.   Directive No. 21.

2.   Tippelskirch, p. 212.

3.   Ibid., pp. 212-213.

4.   Ibid., p. 214.

5.   Ibid., pp. 214-215.

6. Generaloberst Heinz Guderian (Ret.), _Erinnerungen eines Soldaten_ (Recollections of a Soldier), Heidelberg: Kurt Vowinckel Verlag, 1951, p. 167. Cited hereafter as Guderian, _Recollections_.

7. Directive No. 21.

8. Kesselring, _Memoirs_, p. 119.

9. _Ibid._, p. 117.

10. _Ibid._, p. 120.

11. Halder, _Diary_, VI, 22 June 1941; VII, 18 August, 28 November 1941.

12. Guderian, _Recollections_, p. 140.

13. Interview of General der Flieger Paul Deichmann (Ret.) by General-leutnant Hermann Plocher (Ret.). (Deichmann was then Chief of Staff, II Air Corps.) Cited hereafter as Deichmann Interview.

14. Situation Report No. 655 of 25 June 1941, p. 10.

15. _Ibid._, No. 658 of 28 June 1941, p. 20.

16. Generalfeldmarschall Wolfram Freiherr von Richthofen, "Kriegs-tagebuch des Generalfeldmarschalls Freiherr von Richthofen," ("War Diary of Field Marshal Freiherr von Richthofen"), unpub-lished, in the possession of Frau von Richthofen in Lueneburg, Germany. Cited hereafter as Richthofen, "Diary."

17. Situation Report No. 655 of 25 June 1941, p. 14.

18. Halder, _Diary_, VI, 26 June 1941.

19. Situation Report No. 658 of 28 June 1941, p. 24.

20. Kesselring, _Memoirs_, p. 121.

21. Guderian, _Recollections_, pp. 143-145.

22. _Ibid._, p. 168.

23. Capt. Herbert Pabst, "Kriegstagebuch Stukageschwader 2" ("War Diary of the 2nd Dive Bomber Wing"), H/I/4, Karlsruhe Document Collection. Cited hereafter as Pabst, Diary.

24. Deichmann Interview.

25. Halder, Diary, VI, 11 July 1941.

26. Situation Report No. 660 of 30 June 1941, p. 18.

27. Ibid., No. 661 of 1 July 1941, p. 17.

28. Guderian, Recollections, p. 145.

29. Kesselring, Memoirs, p. 121.

30. Richthofen, "Diary."

31. Guderian, Recollections, p. 156.

32. Ibid., p. 152.

33. Situation Report No. 789 of 29 July 1941, p. 25.

34. Generalkommando VIII Fliegerkorps, Tagesnotiz vom 11.7.1941 (VIII Air Corps Command, Daily Memorandum of 11 July 1941), notations of General der Flieger Wolfram Freiherr von Richthofen, Commanding, Karlsruhe Document Collection.

35. Generalfeldmarschall Albert Kesselring (Ret.), "Kurzbericht des Generalfeldmarschalls a. D. Kesselring ueber den Einsatz der Luftwaffe im Osten" ("Short Report of Field Marshal Kesselring (Ret.) Concerning the Employment of the Luftwaffe in the East"), dated 22 February 1955, Karlsruhe Document Collection. Hereafter cited as Kesselring, "Report."

36. Kesselring, Memoirs, p. 123.

37. Generalkommando VIII Fliegerkorps, Tagesbefehl des Generalfeldmarschalls Kesselring an das VIII Fliegerkorps, 3 August 1941 (VIII Air Corps Command, Order of the Day of Field Marshal Kesselring to the VIII Air Corps, 3 August 1941), Karlsruhe Document Collection.

38.   Situation Report No. 691 of 31 July 1941, p. 21.

39.   Ibid., No. 694 of 3 August 1941, p. 30.

40.   Kesselring, Memoirs, p. 122.

41.   Richthofen, "Diary," 23 July 1941.

42.   Situation Report No. 731 of 9 September 1941, p. 34.

43.   Ibid., No. 723 of 1 September 1941, p. 13.

44.   Von Waldau, Diary, Part I, 27 August 1941.

45.   Halder, Diary, VII, 3 August 1941.

46.   Ibid., 4 August 1941.

47.   Ibid., 14, 15, 21 August and 1, 2, 5 September 1941.

48.   Kesselring, "Report."

49.   Situation Report No. 722 of 31 August 1941, p. 7.

50.   Ibid., No. 723 of 1 September 1941, p. 13.

51.   Ibid., No. 726 of 4 September 1941, pp. 9, 17.

52.   Ibid., No. 729 of 7 September 1941, p. 9.

53.   Tippelskirch, p. 222.

54.   Situation Report No. 663 of 3 July 1941, p. 33.

55.   Ibid., No. 663 of 3 July 1941, p. 33; No. 664 of 4 July 1941, p.
        31; No. 665 of 5 July 1941, p. 33; No. 670 of 10 July 1941, p.
        27; No. 691 of 31 July 1941, p. 30; No. 707 of 16 August 1941,
        p. 40; and No. 708 of 17 August 1941, p. 34.

56.   Ibid., No. 731 of 9 September 1941, p. 34, and No. 735 of 13
        September 1941, p. 33.

Chapter 6

1.   Halder, Diary, VI, 26 July 1941.

2.   Kesselring, Memoirs, p. 126.

3.   Ibid., pp. 133-134.

4.   Tippelskirch, p. 229. See also Halder, Diary, VI, 28 and 29 July 1941; VII, 4 August 1941.

5.   Der Fuehrer und Oberste Befehlshaber der Wehrmacht, OKW/WFSt, Abt. L, Nr. 441412/41, gKdos. Chefs., den 21.8.41, Weisungen an den Oberfehlshaber des Heeres (The Fuehrer and Supreme Commander of the Armed Forces, High Command of the Armed Forces, Armed Forces Operations Staff, National Defense Branch, No. 441412/41, Top Secret Document, 21 August 1941, Instructions to the Commander in Chief of the Army), G/b, G/VI/3a, Karlsruhe Document Collection. See also OKW, WFSt/Abt. L (I Op.), Nr. 441376/41, gKdos., Chefs., den 12.8.41, Ergaenzung der Weisung 34 (High Command of the Armed Forces, Armed Forces Operations Staff, National Defense Branch, Operations Section, No. 441376/41, Top Secret Document, 12 August 1941, Supplement to Directive No. 34), G/b, Karlsruhe Document Collection.

6.   Der Fuehrer und Oberste Befehlshaber der Wehrmacht, "Studie Russlandkrieg 1941, vom 22.8.1941," an OKH und herausgegeben worden (The Fuehrer and Supreme Commander of the Armed Forces, "Study Russian War 1941, of 22 August 1941," issued to the High Command of the Army and the High Command of the Air Force). The original was found in the Historical Branch of the Wehrmacht in "Mappe Barbarossa," and was used in the Nuremberg hearings. G/VI/3a, Karlsruhe Document Collection. Cited here-after as Hitler, "Russian War 1941."

7.   Tippelskirch, p. 233.

8.   Guderian, Recollections, p. 204.

9.   Situation Reports No. 729 of 7 September 1941, No. 730 of 8 September 1941, No. 731 of 9 September 1941, No. 732 of 10 September 1941, No. 733 of 11 September 1941, and No. 734 of 12 September 1941. See also Generalleutnant Herman Plocher (Ret.), "Die Abschnuerung des Schlachtfeldes vor und waehrend der Kesselschlacht von Kiew, 1.9. - 25.9.1941" ("The Interdiction of the Battlefield Before and During the Encirclement Battle of Kiev, 1 September to 25 September 1941"), dated 10 April 1955. Book 2, "Der Feldzug im Osten 1941-1945" ("The Campaign in the East 1941-1945"), Karlsruhe Document Collection. Hereafter cited as Plocher, "Interdiction of Kiev."

10.   Plocher, "Interdiction of Kiev."

11.   Halder, Diary, VII, 18 August 1941. See also 18 September 1941.

12.   Ibid., 18 and 19 September 1941.

13.   Generalleutnant Hermann Plocher (Ret.), "Das V Fliegerkorps im Osten, 22. Juni bis 30. Nov. 1941" ("The V Air Corps in the East, 22 June to 30 November 1941"), p. 74, G/VI/3c, Karlsruhe Document Collection. Cited hereafter as "V Air Corps, 1941."

14.   Plocher, "Interdiction of Kiev."

15.   Guderian, Recollections, p. 185.

16.   Halder, Diary, VII, 10 September 1941.

17.   Situation Report No. 754 of 2 October 1941, pp. 33-34.

18.   Ibid., No. 757 of 5 October 1941, p. 32.

19.   Ibid., No. 734 of 12 September 1941, p. 34.

20.   Generalkommando II Flakkorps, Fuehrungsgruppe Ia, Br. B. Nr. 0753/41 g.Kdos., den 10.9.41, Korpsbefehl Nr. 53, fuer den taktischen Einsatz (Command Headquarters, II Antiaircraft Artillery Corps, Operations Group (Ia), Brigade B. No. 0753/41, Secret, 10 September 1941, Corps Order No. 53, for the Tactical Employment of the Corps), Appendix 77a, Book 2, "Der Feldzug im Osten 1941-1945" ("The Campaign in the East 1941-1945"), Karlsruhe Document Collection.

21.   Guderian, Recollections, p. 199. Based upon a description of the action of the 104th Antiaircraft Artillery Regiment by General der Flakartillerie Walter von Axthelm (Ret.). See also Situation Report No. 751 of 29 September 1941, p. 10.

Chapter 7

1.   Tippelskirch, p. 214.

2.   Directive No. 21.

3.   Tippelskirch, p. 215.

4.   Ibid.

5.   Halder, Diary, VI, 23 June 1941.

6.   Ibid., 4 July 1941.

7.   Directive No. 21.

8.   Halder, Diary, VI, 8 July 1941.

9.   Ibid., 5 September 1941.

10.   Ibid., 5 and 6 September 1941.

11.   Ibid., VII, 2 and 26 December 1941.

12.   Situation Report No. 675 of 15 July 1941, p. 25.

13.   Ibid., No. 657 of 26 June 1941, p. 9, and No. 674 of 14 July 1941.

14.   Ibid., No. 653 of 23 June 1941 and No. 655 of 25 June 1941, p. 8, annex 1, p. 6.

15.   Ibid., No. 665 of 5 July 1941, p. 26.

16.   Ibid., No. 674 of 14 July 1941, p. 25.

17.   Ibid., No. 659 of 29 June 1941, p. 21.

18.   Ibid., No. 666 of 6 July 1941, p. 25.

19.   Ibid., No. 694 of 3 August 1941, p. 24.

20.   Ibid., No. 702 of 11 August 1941, p. 21.

21.   Der Fuehrer und Oberste Befehlshaber der Wehrmacht, OKW/WFSt, Abt. L (I Op) Nr. 441298/41, f. K. Chefs., vom 30.7.41 (The Fuehrer and Supreme Commander of the Armed Forces, High Command of the Armed Forces, National Defense Branch of the Armed Forces Operations Staff, No. 441298/41, Secret Command Matter, of 30 July 1941), G/b, Karlsruhe Document Collection.

22.   Halder, Diary, VI, 29 July 1941.

23.   Ibid., 30 July 1941.

24.   Ibid., 8 August 1941.

25.   Situation Report No. 702 of 11 August 1941, p. 21.

26.   Ibid., No. 721 of 30 August 1941, p. 26.

27.   Ibid., No. 700 of 9 August 1941, p. 8.

28.   Ibid., No. 716 of 25 August 1941, p. 33.

29.   Ibid., No. 714 of 23 August 1941, p. 36.

30.   Ibid., No. 741 of 19 September 1941, p. 27.

31.   Ibid., No. 744 of 22 September 1941; No. 745 of 23 September 1941, pp. 27-28; No. 746 of 24 September 1941, pp. 11, 22, 26; No. 751 of 29 September 1941, p. 29; and No. 760 of 9 October 1941, Appendix 18.

32.   Col. Hans-Ulrich Rudel (Ret.), Trotzdem (Nevertheless), Waiblingen, Wuerttemberg: Verlag Lothar Leberecht, 1950, pp. 32-36, 38-40. Cited hereafter as Rudel, Nevertheless.

33.   Halder, Diary, VII, 12 August and 12 September 1941.

34.   Col. Rudolf Loytved-Hardegg (GSC, Ret.), Interview of Col. Loytved-Hardegg (GSC, Ret.) by Generalleutnant Hermann Plocher (Ret.), undated, Karlsruhe Document Collection. Cited hereafter as Loytved-Hardegg Interview.

35.   Ibid.

36.   Situation Report No. 697 of 6 August 1941, pp. 27, 30.

37.   Halder, Diary, VII, 9 November 1941.

38.   Ibid., 27 September 1941.

39.   Ibid., 4 December 1941.

40.   Loytved-Hardegg Interview.

41.   Excerpt from the Marinedienstvorschrift (M. Dv.) Nr. 601/12
       (German Navy Publication No. 601/12), p. 22, G/IX/2a, Karlsruhe
       Document Collection.

42.   Ibid. See also Appendix 39, unpublished German original manu-
       script "Russlandfeldzug 1941-1945" ("The Campaign in Russia
       1941-1945"), Karlsruhe Document Collection.

43.   Situation Report No. 772 of 21 October 1941, pp. 11-13. See also
       Generalleutnant Hermann Plocher (Ret.), "Der Luftwaffe Einsatz
       bei der Besetzung der Baltischen Inseln Moon-Oesel-Dagoe 1941"
       ("Luftwaffe Participation in the Occupation of the Baltic Islands
       of Muhu, Saaremaa, and Hiiumaa in 1941"), G/VI/3b, Karlsruhe
       Document Collection. Cited hereafter as Plocher, "Baltic
       Operations."

44.   Loytved-Hardegg Interview. See also Plocher, "Baltic Operations."

45.   Oberbefehlshaber der Luftwaffe, Fuehrungsstab Ia, g.Kdos., vom
       7. 4. 1941 (Commander in Chief of the Air Force, Operations Staff,
       Operations Branch, Secret, of 7 April 1941), order establishing
       the missions of Luftwaffe Commander Baltic, G/VI/3b, Karlsruhe
       Document Collection. The fourth task was also accomplished,
       according to oral testimony given by Col. Wolfgang von Wild to
       the author. Cited hereafter as Von Wild Report.

46.   Plotcher, "Baltic Operations." See also Fliegerfuehrer Ostsee,
       KR, Geheim, Abt. Ic, "Abendmeldung des Fliegerfuehrer Ostsee
       vom 18. 9. 41" (Air Commander Baltic, Important War Transmission,
       Secret, Intelligence Branch, "Evening Report of the Air Commander
       Baltic of 18 September 1941"), G/VI/3b, Karlsruhe Document
       Collection.

47. Von Wild Report. See also Loytved-Hardegg Interview and supporting reports by Luftwaffe commanders, G/VI/3b, Karlsruhe Document Collection.

48. Fliegerfuehrer Ostsee, Abt. Ic, Geheim, Lagebericht Nr. 21 vom 2.9.41 (Air Commander Baltic, Intelligence Branch, Secret, Situation Report No. 21 of 2 September 1941), Karlsruhe Document Collection.

49. Excerpts from the Marinedienstvorschrift (M.Dv.) Nr. 601/12 (German Navy Publication No. 601/12), p. 34, Karlsruhe Document Collection.

Chapter 8

1. Directive No. 21.

2. Hermann Hoelter, Armee in der Arktis (Army in the Arctic), Bad Nauheim: Hans-Henning Podzun Verlag, 1953, p. 11.

3. Ibid., pp. 11-12.

4. Situation Report No. 661 of 1 July 1941, p. 9.

5. Ibid., No. 669 of 9 July 1941.

6. Der Fuehrer und Oberste Befehlshaber der Wehrmacht, OKW/WFSt, Abt. L (I Op) Nr. 441230/41, g.K. Chefs. vom 19.7.41, Weisung Nr. 33 (The Fuehrer and Supreme Commander of the Armed Forces, High Command of the Armed Forces, Armed Forces Operations Staff, National Defense Branch [Operations], No. 441230/41, Top Secret Document of 19 July 1941, Directive No. 33), Karlsruhe Document Collection. Cited hereafter as Directive No. 33. See also Der Fuehrer und Oberste Befehlshaber der Wehrmacht, OKW/WFSt, Abt. L (I Op) g.K. Chefs. Nr. 44254/41 vom 23.7.41, Ergaenzung zur Weisung Nr. 33 (The Fuehrer and Supreme Commander of the Armed Forces, High Command of the Armed Forces, Armed Forces Operations Staff, National Defense Branch [Operations], Top Secret Document, No. 44254/41 of 23 July 1941, Supplement to Directive No. 33), Karlsruhe Document Collection. Cited hereafter as Supplement to Directive No. 33.

7. _Ibid._, No. 441898/41, Top Secret Document of 30 July 1941, Directive No. 34. Cited hereafter as Directive No. 34.

8. Situation Report No. 720 of 29 August 1941.

9. Der Fuehrer und Oberste Befehlshaber der Wehrmacht, OKW, WFSt/S (I Op) Nr. 441578/41, g.K. Chefs., F.H.Qu. den 22.9.41, Weisung Nr. 36 (The Fuehrer and Supreme Commander of the Armed Forces, High Command of the Armed Forces, Armed Forces Operations Staff, Lowest Priority, Operations, No. 441578/41, Top Secret Document, Fuehrer's Headquarters, 22 September 1941, Directive No. 36), Karlsruhe Document Collection. Cited hereafter as Directive No. 36.

10. Situation Report No. 658 of 28 June 1941, p. 18, and No. 746 of 24 September 1941, p. 27.

11. Ibid., No. 661 of 1 July 1941; No. 663 of 3 July 1941; No. 664 of 4 July 1941; No. 665 of 5 July 1941; No. 667 of 7 July 1941. See also Halder, _Diary_, V, 1-7 July 1941.

12. Situation Report No. 756 of 4 October 1941, p. 34.

13. _Ibid._, No. 691 of 31 July 1941. See also Maj. Arnulf Blasig (Ret.), "Zusammenarbeit zwischen russische und englische Luftwaffe," Auszug aus einer Arbeit des Majors a.D. Blasig ("Cooperation Between Russian and English Air Forces," excerpt from a work of Major Blasig (Ret.)), G/VI/3c, Karlsruhe Document Collection.

14. Der Reichsminister der Luftfahrt und Oberbefehlshaber der Luft-waffe, Generalluftzeugmeister, GL 6 Nr. 876/41, g.Kdos., Az 74 v. (V), Berlin, den 14. Juli 1941, Kurzbeschreibung der Bomben-Mine "Bm" 1000 (The Reichs Minister of Aviation and Commander in Chief of the Air Force, Chief of Air Force Special Supply and Procurement Services, Document No. 876/41, 6th Branch, Secret, Code No. 74, Administrative, Berlin, 14 July 1941, Brief Description of the Aerial Bomb Mine Bm-1000), Karlsruhe Document Collection.

15. Kaarlo Hilden, "Die Murmanbahn," Suomen Kirja, Helsinki: 1943 ("The Murmansk Rail Line," excerpt from an article by Kaarlo Hilden in Suomen Kirja, Helsinki, 1943), G/VI/3c, Karlsruhe Document Collection. See also "Ueberblick ueber den Einsatz der Luftwaffe gegen die feindliche Versorgungsschiffahrt 1941/42" ("Overview of the Employment of the Air Force Against the Enemy Supply Shipping 1941/42"), Karlsruhe Document Collection.

16. OKL, Generalstab der Luftwaffe, FSt Ic, Wi Nr. 1116/43, g.Kdos., v. 4.4.43 (High Command of the Luftwaffe, General Staff of the Air Force, Intelligence Operations Staff, War Economy No. 1116/43, Secret, of 4 April 1943), Karlsruhe Document Collection.

Chapter 9

1. Halder, Diary, VII, 26 September 1941.

2. Ibid., 21 September 1941.

3. Situation Report No. 749 of 27 September 1941, p. 16.

4. Ibid., No. 757 of 5 October 1941, p. 7.

5. Tippelskirch, p. 235.

6. Situation Report No. 767 of 16 October 1941, p. 5.

7. Ibid., No. 775 of 24 October 1941, p. 8.

8. Der Fuehrer und Oberste Befehlshaber der Wehrmacht, OKW, WFSt/L, Nr. 441412/41, g.Kdos., Chefs., den 21.8.41, Weisungen an den Oberbefehlshaber des Heeres (The Fuehrer and Supreme Commander of the Armed Forces, High Command of the Armed Forces, Armed Forces Operations Staff, National Defense Branch, No. 441412/41, Top Secret Document, Instructions to the Commander in Chief of the Army), G/b and G/VI/3a, Karlsruhe Document Collection.

9. Situation Report No. 770 of 19 October 1941, p. 3, and No. 771 of 20 October 1941.

10. Generalfeldmarschall Erich von Manstein (Ret.), Verlorene Siege (Lost Victories), Bonn: Athenaeum Verlag, 1955, pp. 225-226. Cited hereafter as Manstein.

11. Situation Reports No. 766 of 15 October 1941; No. 769 of 18 October 1941; No. 770 of 19 October 1941; No. 771 of 20 October 1941; No. 772 of 21 October 1941; No. 774 of 23 October 1941; and No. 775 of 24 October 1941.

12. Ibid., No. 773 of 22 October 1941, p. 4.

13. Ibid., No. 776 of 25 October 1941, p. 3.

14. OKL, Gliederung der Luftflotte 2 (fliegende Verbaende), Stand 15. 9.1941, Kesselschlacht von Kiew (High Command of the Air Force, Organization of the Second Air Fleet, Flying Units, as of 15 September 1941, Encirclement Battle of Kiev), Appendix 46, Book 2, "Der Feldzug im Osten 1941-1945" ("The Campaign in the East 1941-1945"), Karlsruhe Document Collection.

15. Situation Report No. 776 of 25 October 1941, p. 13.

16. Ibid., No. 778 of 27 October 1941, pp. 4, 9.

17. Reichsmarschall des Grossdeutschen Reiches und Oberbefehlshaber der Luftwaffe Hermann Goering, Der nachstehende Tagesbefehl des Herrn Reichsmarschalls on der Truppe (Reichsmarschall of the Great German Reich and Commander in Chief of the Air Force, Hermann Goering, The Standing Order of the Day to the Troops [of the Air Force] from the Reichsmarschall), undated. Commemoration of the death of Col. Werner Moelders. Appendix 79, Book 2/d, "Der Feldzug im Osten 1941-1945" ("The Campaign in the East 1941-1945"), Karlsruhe Document Collection.

18. Halder, Diary, VII, 26-28, 30-31 December 1941; 1, 2, 4, 5, 15, 24 January 1942.

19. Von Waldau, Diary, Part I, 21 October 1941, p. 79, H/I/1, Karlsruhe Document Collection.

20. Ibid., 15 November 1941, p. 82.

21. Halder, Diary, VII, 7 November 1941.

22.   Ibid., 28 November 1941.

23.   Ibid., 30 November 1941.

24.   Ibid., 1 December 1941.

25.   Ibid., 29 November 1941.

26.   Von Waldau, Diary, Part I, 3, 6, 15 December 1941, pp. 90-93, 98.

27.   Generalleutnant Hermann Plocher (Ret.), "Zusammenstellung ueber den Gesamteinsatz des V. Fliegerkorps im Ostfeldzug vom 22.6. - 30.11.41" ("Summary of V Air Corps Operations in the Eastern Campaign from 22 June to 30 November 1941"), Appendix 51, Book 2, "Der Feldzug im Osten 1941-1945" ("The Campaign in the East 1941-1945"), Karlsruhe Document Collection.

Chapter 10

1.   Der Fuehrer und Oberste Befehlshaber der Wehrmacht, OKW/WFSt, Abt. L (I Op), g.Kdos. Chefs., Nr. 441492/41, F.H.Qu., den 6.9.41, Weisung Nr. 35 (The Fuehrer and Supreme Commander of the Armed Forces, High Command of the Armed Forces, Armed Forces Operations Staff, National Defense Branch, Operations, Top Secret Document, No. 44192/41, Fuehrer's Headquarters, 6 September 1941, Directive No. 35), G/b, Karlsruhe Document Collection.   Cited hereafter as Directive No. 35.

2.   Kesselring, Memoirs, pp. 128-129.

3.   Situation Report No. 753 of 1 October 1941, pp. 11, 19.

4.   Halder, Diary, VII, 2 October 1941.

5.   Ibid. 4 October 1941.

6.   Ibid., 6 October 1941.

7. Col. Hans Wilhelm Deichmann (Ret.), "Einsatz des VIII Flieger-korps im Kampfraum Mitte 28. 9. 41 - 10. 12. 41" ("Employment of the VIII Air Corps in Combat Zone Center from 28 September to 10 December 1941"). Drawn in part from the diary of Field Marshal Wolfram Freiherr von Richthofen. Appendix 53, Book 2, "Der Feldzug im Osten 1941-1945" ("The Campaign in the East 1941-1945"), Karlsruhe Document Collection. Cited hereafter as "VIII Air Corps, Zone Center. "

8. Situation Report No. 757 of 4 October 1941, p. 18.

9. Ibid., No. 758 of 7 October 1941, pp. 9, 25.

10. Ibid., No. 766 of 15 October 1941, pp. 4-5.

11. Ibid., No. 773 of 22 October 1941, p. 12. See also Appendices 77, 77b, and 77e, Book 2, "Der Feldzug im Osten 1941-1945" ("The Campaign in the East 1941-1945"), several orders from the files of Generaloberst Otto Dessloch (Ret.), Karlsruhe Document Collection.

12. Von Waldau, Diary, Part I, October 1941, p. 77.

13. Kesselring, Memoirs, pp. 129-130.

14. Situation Report No. 773 of 22 October 1941, p. 5.

15. Ibid., pp. 5-6.

16. Von Waldau, Diary, Part I, 21 October 1941, p. 79.

17. Situation Report No. 774 of 23 October 1941, p. 6.

18. Ibid., No. 778 of 27 October 1941, pp. 4-5.

19. Guderian, Recollections, pp. 222-224.

20. Halder, Diary, VII, 13 November 1941.

21. Ibid. See also excerpts from this discussion in G/VI/3b, Karlsruhe Document Collection.

22. Von Waldau, Diary, Part I, 15 November 1941, p. 83.

23. General der Flieger Bruno Loerzer, Generalkommando II. Fliegerkorps, Tagesbefehl vom 13. 11. 41 (General der Flieger Bruno Loerzer, Command Headquarters of the II Air Corps, Order of the Day of 13 November 1941), G/VI/3b, Karlsruhe Document Collection. See also Generalkommando Luftflotte 2, Schematische Leitungsskizze der Fernsprechverbindungen der Luftflotte 2, Nur fuer den Dienstgebrauch, Stand vom 23. 10. 41 (Command Headquarters of the Second Air Fleet, Schematic Circuit Sketch of Telephone Communications of the Second Air Fleet, Restricted, as of 23 October 1941), Karlsruhe Document Collection.

24. Von Waldau, Diary, Part I, 23 November 1941, p. 84.

25. Ibid., 27 November 1941, p. 86.

26. Ibid., 3 December 1941, pp. 91-92.

27. Ibid., 9 December 1941, pp. 93-94.

28. Halder, Diary, VII, 22, 29, and 30 November, 1, 7 December 1941.

29. Generalkommando II Flakkorps, Abt. Ic, "Beurteilung der Lage," Anlage zum Korpsbefehl Nr. 86, g.Kdos., Nr. 0939/41, Korps-Gefechtsstand, den 22. 11. 1941 (Command Headquarters II Anti-aircraft Artillery Corps, Intelligence Branch, "Estimate of the Situation," Appendix to the Corps Order No. 86, Secret, No. 0939/41, Corps Field Headquarters, 22 November 1941), and Generalkommando II Flakkorps, Abt. Ic, "Beurteilung der Lage," Anlage zum Korpsbefehl Nr. 90, g.Kdos., Nr. 0969/41, Korps-gefechtsstand, den 5. 12. 41 (Command Headquarters II Antiaircraft Artillery Corps, Intelligence Branch, "Estimate of the Situation," Appendix to Corps Order No. 90, Secret, No. 0969/41, Corps Field Headquarters, 5 December 1941). See Appendix 77k and 77n, "Der Feldzug im Osten 1941-1945" ("The Campaign in the East 1941-1945"), Karlsruhe Document Collection.

30. Tippelskirch, pp. 241-242.

31. Der Fuehrer und Oberste Befehlshaber der Wehrmacht, OKW/
     WFSt, Abt. L (I Op), Nr. 442090/41, g. Kdos. Chefs., F. H. Qu.,
     Weisung Nr. 39, den 8. 12. 1941 (The Fuehrer and Supreme Com-
     mander of the Armed Forces, High Command of the Armed Forces,
     Armed Forces Operations Staff, National Defense Branch, Oper-
     ations, No. 442090/41, Top Secret Document, Fuehrer's Head-
     quarters, Directive No. 39, 8 December 1941), G/b, Karlsruhe
     Document Collection.

32. "VIII Air Corps in Zone Center."

33. Der Fuehrer und Oberste Befehlshaber der Wehrmacht, OKW/
     WFSt, Abt. L (I Op), Nr. 442182/41, g. Kdos. Chefs., F. H. Qu.,
     den 16. 12. 41 (The Fuehrer and Supreme Commander of the Armed
     Forces, High Command of the Armed Forces, Armed Forces
     Operations Staff, National Defense Branch, Operations, No.
     442182/41, Top Secret Document, Fuehrer's Headquarters, 16
     December 1941), an unnumbered Fuehrer Directive, G/b Karls-
     ruhe Document Collection.

34. Halder, Diary, VII, 19 December 1941.

35. Tippelskirch, p. 244.

36. Generalkommando II Flakkorps, Abt. Ic, "Beurteilung der Lage,"
     Anlage zu Korps-Befehl Nr. 91, g. Kdos., Nr. 0981/41, Korps-
     Gefechtsstand, den 12. 12. 41 (Command Headquarters II Antiair-
     craft Artillery Corps, Intelligence Branch, "Estimate of the
     Situation," Appendix to the Corps Order No. 91, Secret, No.
     0981/41, Corps Field Headquarters, 12 December 1941), and
     Generalkommando II Flakkorps, Abt. Ic, "Beurteilung der Lage,"
     Anlage zu Korps-Befehl Nr. 93, g. Kdos., Nr. 0987/41, Korps-
     Gefechtsstand, den 19. 12. 41 (Command Headquarters II Anti-
     aircraft Artillery Corps, Intelligence Branch, "Estimate of the
     Situation," Appendix to the Corps Order No. 93, Secret, No.
     0987/41, Corps Field Headquarters, 19 December 1941), Karls-
     ruhe Document Collection.

37. Halder, Diary, VII, 8 October 1941.

33.   Auszug aus Fernschreiben OKW/WFSt, Abt. L (I Op.), Nr. 442243/41, g.Kdos. Chefs., 24 December 1941 (Excerpt from Teletype Message of the High Command of the Armed Forces, Armed Forces Operations Staff, National Defense Branch, Operations, No. 442243/41, Top Secret Document), G/VI, Karlsruhe Document Collection.

39.   Halder, Diary, VII, 17 August 1941, p. 46. See also statement by General der Infanterie Guenther Blumentritt, Situation Report No. 757 of 5 October 1941, p. 690.

The Fuehrer and Supreme Commander
      of the Wehrmacht
High Command of the Wehrmacht
Wehrmacht Operations Staff
National Defense Branch (Group I)
No. 33 408/40, Top Secret

Fuehrer Headquarters
18 December 1940

Directive No. 21

OPERATION BARBAROSSA

The German Wehrmacht is to make preparations for the conquest of Soviet Russia in a swift campaign (Operation BARBAROSSA), even before the war against England has ended.

Toward this end, the Army will employ all available forces, with the exception of those required to protect the occupied territories against surprise attacks.

The Air Force will have the important task of making available for the support of the Army in the eastern campaign forces in such strength as to make it possible to count upon a speedy conclusion of the ground operations, and the task of making certain that enemy air attacks will inflict as little damage as possible upon the eastern part of Germany. This concentration of forces in the East will be limited only insofar as it will be necessary to assign sufficient troops to adequately protect the entire combat zone and arms-producing region under our control against enemy air attacks, and to make sure that offensive operations against England, especially her supply shipments, will not come to a halt.

Naval operations will definitely continue to be concentrated against England, even during the entire campaign in the East.

I shall issue the order for the strategic concentration of forces against Soviet Russia, if the occasion arises, eight weeks prior to the contemplated start of operations.

Those preparations which require a longer period to get under way should - as far as this has not been done already - be initiated immediately and be concluded by 15 May 1941.

However, it is of decisive importance to make sure that there is no indication of any plan to attack.

The preparations made by the High Commands are to be based on the following elements:

I.   OVER-ALL OBJECTIVE:

The bulk of the Soviet Army stationed in western Russia is to be annihilated in bold operations and with far-reaching drives of armored spearheads; the withdrawal to the rear of elements [of the enemy] at fighting strength is to be prevented.

Thereupon a line will be reached in rapid pursuit beyond which the Russian Air Force will no longer be able to attack the [German] Zone of Interior. The final objective of the operation is the establishment of a general line extending from the Volga to Arkhangelsk which will constitute a covering line against Asiatic Russia. In this way, the Air Force, if necessary, will be able to destroy the last remaining Russian industrial areas in the Ural.

As a result of these operations, the Russian Baltic Fleet will be quickly deprived of its bases, which will render it unfit for combat. From the very beginning of the operation, we must, by means of powerful blows, prevent the Russian Air Force from taking any effective [counter] measures.

II.   PROSPECTIVE ALLIES AND THEIR MISSIONS:

1. We can count on Rumania's and Finland's active participation in the war against Soviet Russia on the flanks of our operations.

The Wehrmacht High Command (OKW), in accordance with current requirements, will arrange and determine the manner whereby the fighting forces of these two countries will be placed under German command.

2. Rumania's task will consist in pinning down the enemy troops they are facing in joint operation with the German forces stationed there, and on the whole, in rendering assistance in the rear areas.

3.   Finland's mission will be to cover the strategic concentration of the German northern Army Group (parts of the XXI Group) withdrawing from Norway and to carry out joint operations with this group. In addition, Finland will be assigned the task of depriving the enemy of the use of Hangö (Hanko).

4.   We have reason to believe that Swedish railways and roads will be available for the assembly march of the German Army Group North at the latest beginning with the start of operations.

III.   THE CONDUCT OF OPERATIONS:

A.   Army (approval of the plans submitted to me):

In the Zone of Operations, which is divided by the Pripyat Marshes into one southern and one northern part, the emphasis will be placed in the North. Two army groups will be assigned here.

The army group in the southern part - in the center of the over- all front - will be charged with the task of advancing with especially strong armored and motorized units from the area around Warsaw and north there- of and to rout the enemy forces in White Russia. This will perforce make it possible for large portions of the mobile troops to pivot to the north in order to be able to annihilate the enemy forces fighting in the Baltic States, acting in joint operation with Army Group North advancing from East Prussia in the general direction of Leningrad. Only after the success of this most urgent mission has been assured, which should be followed by the occupation of Leningrad and Kronshtadt, should offensive operations for the capture of the important communication and armament center Moscow be continued.

A simultaneous attempt to accomplish both objectives could be justified only by a surprisingly rapid collapse of Russian resistance.

The defense of Norway is still the most important mission of the XXI Group, even during the campaign in the East. Those forces which are available beyond these requirements will be committed in the North (the Mountain Corps), first of all for the defense of the Petsamo region and its ore mines and also of the Arctic Sea Route. Following that, they will push forward, in joint operation with Finnish forces, for an attack against the Murmansk railway and in order to prevent the land shipments of sup- plies destined for the Murmansk area. Whether or not it will be possible to conduct such an operation with larger numbers of German forces (2-3

divisions) advancing from the area of Rovaniemi and south thereof depends
upon Sweden's willingness to place her railways at our disposal for such
a strategic concentration.

The main body of the Finnish Army will be charged with the
mission (in keeping with the progress made by the German northern wing)
of tieing down as many Russian troops as possible by attacking west of or
on both sides of Lake Ladoga, and to take possession of Hangö.

The army group committed south of the Pripyat Marshes will
also attempt a double envelopment. Strong forces concentrated on both
wings are to achieve the complete annihilation of the Russian troops in the
Ukraine west of the Dnepr. The main attack will be directed from the
Lublin area toward Kiev, while the forces concentrated in Rumania will
cross the lower Pruth River and form the other arm of a wide envelopment.
The Rumanian Army will have the mission of tieing down the Russian forces
which are to be caught between the two pincers.

Once the battles south and north of the Pripyat Marshes have
been brought to a successful conclusion, pursuits will be launched with
the following objectives:

In the south the Donets Basin, highly important from a military
point of view, must be seized without delay.

In the north the swift capture of Moscow. The capture of this
city means a decisive victory, politically and economically, and, in
addition, spells the elimination of the Russians' most vital railway hub.

B. Air Force:

The Air Force will be charged with the responsibility to
paralyze insofar as possible the activities of the Russian Air Force and
put it out of commission, and to support the operations of the Army at
its points of main effort, particularly in the Army Group Center area and
along the north wing of Army Group South. According to their significance
for the course of the campaign, the Russian railways will be severed by
air attacks. The most important railroad installations (river crossings!)
will be seized by bold operations by parachute and airborne troops. The
[Soviet] armament industry should not be attacked during the major operations in order to be able to concentrate all Luftwaffe elements against
the enemy air force and for the direct support of the Army. Strategic
attacks, particularly against the Ural region, are advisable only after
the mobile operations have been concluded.

C. Navy:

In this campaign, besides safeguarding our own coast, the Navy will have the mission of preventing the escape of enemy naval forces from the Baltic Sea. After Leningrad has been seized the Russian Baltic Fleet will have been deprived of all its bases. Since its situation will then be completely hopeless, major naval engagements prior to that time must be avoided. After the Russian Fleet has been put out of commission, it will be essential to safeguard the total maritime traffic in the Baltic Sea, including the supply shipments for the northern army (mine sweeping).

IV. All measures which are to be taken by the Commanders in Chief on the basis of this directive should definitely concur in one point: they are to be referred to as precautionary measures in case Russia should change her present attitude toward us. The number of officers who will be assigned to early preliminary duties is to be kept as small as possible, and then only insofar as is necessary for the performance of their individual duties. Otherwise the danger exists that our preparations may become known - the execution date of which has not even been set - and very serious political and military complications will be the result.

V. I await the reports of the Commanders in Chief concerning their future plans which are to be based on this directive.

All services of the Wehrmacht will report to me via the Wehrmacht High Command (OKW) on the measures which they contemplate, including their chronological progress in preparations.

signed: ADOLF HITLER

APPENDIX II

BIOGRAPHICAL SECTION OF IMPORTANT
PERSONALITIES

Generalleutnant Heinrich Aschenbrenner

Served in the infantry in World War I. After the war qualified as a pilot, and from August to September 1931 was attached to the Russian 20th Air Force Brigade during the time when German air units were proscribed. Aschenbrenner served as Air Attaché in Moscow 1939-40 and as Chief of Signals for the German Second Air Fleet 1940-42. With the exception of a tour of duty in Norway in 1943, Aschenbrenner served during the remainder of the war as Chief of Signals of the High Command of the Luftwaffe.

General der Flakartillerie Walter von Axthelm

Von Axthelm served in the field artillery during World War I. Following the war he transferred to the antiaircraft artillery arm. In 1931 he became a General Staff officer in the Reichswehr Ministry in Berlin, and on 1 April 1935 transferred to the Luftwaffe as a member of the Reichs Air Ministry and Inspector of Antiaircraft Artillery. During World War II he became the most prominent antiaircraft artillery officer in the Luftwaffe. His promotion dates of significance were: Colonel, 1 February 1939; Generalmajor, 28 May 1940; Generalleutnant, 1 October 1942; and General der Flakartillerie, 1 April 1944.

Field Marshal Fedor von Bock

A nephew of the famous General von Falkenhayn, who headed Germany's Imperial Army Command 1914-16, Bock was one of Germany's most able commanders. In World War I he won numerous decorations. During the Polish Campaign of 1939 he commanded Army Group North, and in 1940 directed Army Group B in the West. In the invasion of Russia, 22 June 1941, he commanded Army Group Center. On 18 January 1942 he assumed command of Army Group South until he was sent to the Reserve Army 15 July 1942. He was killed with his family on a road in northern Germany by Allied fighters 5 May 1945.

General der Flieger Walter Boenicke

A World War I flyer, Boenicke was an early member of the new Luftwaffe. During 1941 he served as Chief of Staff of the I Air Corps under the command of General Foerster. Promoted on 1 September 1943 to Generalleutnant and on 1 March 1945 to General der Flieger, Boenicke was also active with antiaircraft artillery forces. He died in 1947 while in British captivity.

General der Flieger Rudolf Bogatsch

General Bogatsch served during World War I as an infantry officer of the line and as a General Staff officer. He left the active service to join a unit of "irregulars" organized to combat Polish incursions along the Silesian border in 1921. He served thereafter in infantry and cavalry units in the Reichswehr. On 1 April 1933 he was promoted to Lieutenant Colonel and assigned to the Reichs Air Ministry. Thereafter he held numerous important posts in the new Luftwaffe, including command positions in the antiaircraft artillery forces, and in air administrative and training commands. Holder of the Knight's Cross, he was promoted to General der Flieger 1 July 1941.

General der Infanterie Guenther Blumentritt

Blumentritt was a highly decorated infantry officer in World War I. After the war he served in various capacities in the German General Staff (then called Truppenamt) in the Reichswehr. In December of 1941 he became Oberquartiermeister I (Chief Quartermaster) in the Army High Command, and served in this office until 25 September 1942. From 25 September 1942 to 5 September 1944 Blumentritt was Chief of the General Staff of the German Command in the West, and from 3 February to 20 March 1945 served as head of the German Twenty-Fifth Army. He has rendered invaluable assistance to the German Historical Monograph Project of the U.S. Army under the Office of the Chief of Military History, and has written a number of significant military works.

Field Marshal Walther von Brauchitsch

One of the senior German Army commanders, von Brauchitsch was groomed for General Staff duties even prior to World War I, a war

in which he served with distinction.   Emerging from the war as a Major
in the General Staff Corps, he soon became a leading figure in the new
Reichswehr.   On 4 February 1938 he became Commander in Chief of the
German Army, a post which he held until 19 December 1941.   Retired
ostensibly on grounds of poor health, he was actually forced out by Hitler,
who was angered at Brauchitsch's order to withdraw the German Army
to safer defensive positions in the face of furious Soviet counterattacks
around Moscow.   Hitler then took personal command of the Army, which
thereafter lost its last remnant of Prussian control.

Field Marshal Ernst Busch

An older Army officer who served with honor during World War I,
Busch served in various staff positions in the Reichswehr Ministry during
the 1920's and early 30's.   He commanded the Sixteenth Army in the West
from 15 October 1939 to the end of March 1941, and at the end of May
moved to the East with his unit to prepare for the war against the Soviet
Union.   On 11 October 1943 he relinquished command of the Sixteenth
Army to assume command of Army Group Center, and on 15 April took
command of German Forces in the North (Western Front).   Long suffering
from a heart ailment, he died in 1945 while in British custody.

General-Admiral Rolf Carls

Carls served with distinction in the German Imperial Navy during
World War I.   By 1936 he was Admiral of the German Fleet, and served
during 1936 and 1937 in Spanish waters.   He assumed command 1 November
1938 of the German Naval Station Baltic, and on 21 September 1940
directed German Naval Command North, a post he held until 1 March
1963.   He was promoted to General-Admiral 19 July 1940, and was
killed in an Allied air attack upon Germany in April 1945.

General der Flieger Paul Deichmann

General Deichmann served as an infantry officer, an aerial
observer in the First World War, and later as an officer in the Reichswehr.   In 1934 he transferred to the Reichs Air Ministry as a technical
advisor.   During World War II he served as Chief of Staff of the II Air
Corps in the West and later in Russia.   From 20 August 1942 to 15 June
1943 he was Chief of Staff to the Wehrmacht Command South under Field
Marshal Kesselring.   Deichmann subsequently held other important posts

in the Luftwaffe, including the command of the IV Air Administrative Command (Austria). A recipient of the Knight's Cross, General Deichmann lent invaluable assistance to the USAF Historical Division's German Historical Monograph Project in Karlsruhe as well as to the Fuehrungsakademie of the Bundeswehr.

Generaloberst Otto Dessloch

Dessloch, a senior Wehrmacht officer in World War II, was born in Posen and served during World War I in a Bavarian cavalry regiment and later as a pilot and squadron commander in the West. After the war he served in the Reichswehr. In 1926 he took air training in the Soviet Union, at a time when such activities were forbidden in Germany by the Treaty of Versailles. He became a Generalmajor and Commander of Air Division 6 by 1939, and at the outbreak of war against Russia commanded the I Antiaircraft Artillery Corps. He later commanded the Fourth and Sixth Air Fleets. A Knight's Cross winner, Dessloch survived the war.

Generaloberst Eduard Dietl

Born in Bad Aibling, Bavaria, Dietl served with distinction in the Bavarian Army in World War I. After the war he served in the new Reichswehr. An expert skier and mountaineer, Dietl was active in the formation of the German Mountain Troop organization. In 1941, following a successful campaign around Narvik, he took command of the XIX Mountain Corps in northern Norway and Finland. On 20 January 1942 he assumed command of the German Army Command Lapland, and on 20 June 1942 of the Twentieth Mountain Army. This highly popular and able general (Generaloberst 1 June 1942) was killed in an air accident 25 June 1944.

Generaloberst Nikolaus von Falkenhorst

During World War I von Falkenhorst served with distinction in a Prussian infantry regiment. After the war he remained in service. He commanded the XXI Army Group in the Norwegian Campaign, and on 15 April 1941 assumed command of Army Command Norway in Norway and Finland. On 20 January 1942 he took command of all Wehrmacht forces in Norway, a post he held until 18 December 1944. Sentenced to death by a joint British-Norwegian court after World War II, his sentence was first commuted to life imprisonment, then to ten years, and on 23 July 1953 remitted.

General der Flieger Martin Fiebig

Colonel, 6 January 1938; Generalmajor, 4 January 1941; retired 1955. Fiebig was among those officers who trained in the Soviet Union in the late 1920's. He was a specialist in close support operations and later commanded Air Division 1, VIII Air Corps, II Air Corps, and finally was Commander in Chief of Luftwaffe Command Northeast.

General der Flieger Veit Fischer

Fischer was a veteran of World War I, having served in the Army. He was active in the development of the new Luftwaffe in the early 1930's, and on 20 April 1936 was promoted to Colonel. Prior to the outbreak of World War II he had attained the rank of Generalmajor and on 1 December 1940 was promoted to Generalleutnant. In 1941 and 1942 he commanded Staff for Special Duties in Air Administrative Commands II and I, respectively, and Headquarters of Air Administrative Command Moscow. Promoted on 1 June 1942 to General der Flieger, Fischer later commanded Air Administrative Commands XXVII and VIII.

General der Flieger Helmuth Foerster

A highly decorated veteran of World War I, Foerster served during part of that conflict as a flying officer. He reentered the military service 1 March 1934 as a Lieutenant Colonel in the Luftwaffe. On 1 March 1936 with his promotion to Colonel he assumed command of Bomber Wing "General Wever." He commanded an air division in the Polish Campaign, and by 1 January 1940 had attained the rank of Generalleutnant. He was Chief of Staff of the Fifth Air Fleet in the Norwegian Campaign, a member of the German-French Peace Commission of 22 June 1940, and Wehrmacht Commander in Serbia in 1941. On 22 June 1941 he commanded the I Air Corps (East), and from 1 October 1942 until the war's end served as Chief of Administration, Reichs Air Ministry. He was pensioned (1952) as a Lieutenant Colonel.

Reichsmarschall Hermann W. Goering

Goering, credited with 20 aerial victories in World War I, was the last commander of the famous Fighter Wing No. 1. After the war he promoted aviation ventures in Sweden and Germany, avidly supporting the vociferous Nazi Party, of which he was an early member. Forced to flee to Sweden after Hitler's 1923 "Putsch" in Munich, he returned to the Reich and became a leading political figure. Persuading aging President von Hindenburg to make him an infantry general, the stage was set for his selection 1 March 1935 as Commander in Chief of the Luftwaffe and promotion in 1938 to Field Marshal. On 19 July 1940 he became the only Reichsmarschall in Germany. Congenial, but also ruthless at times, he was fond of sumptuous living, increasingly shirking his command duties, eventually even losing favor with Hitler. Removed from his post 23 April 1945, he only escaped a worse fate by the intervention of his own troops. Tried and sentenced in the main trials at Nuremberg, he took his own life 15 October 1946.

Field Marshal Robert Ritter von Greim

Greim was credited with 28 aerial victories in World War I, in which he earned a hereditary title from the King of Bavaria and numerous distinctions. He helped organize Chiang Kai-shek's Chinese Air Force in the 1920's, and organized the German Commercial Pilot's School in Wuerzburg. He reentered military service 1 April 1934 as a Luftwaffe Major in command of Fighter Wing "Richthofen." In 1939 he commanded Air Division 5, and from 1940-43 commanded the V Air Corps. In July 1943 he assumed command of Luftwaffe Command East (later designated Sixth Air Fleet). Promoted 25 April 1945 to Field Marshal, he was given Goering's post as Commander in Chief of the (then almost nonexistent) Luftwaffe. A Knight's Cross winner, he committed suicide in 1945 shortly after his capture by American forces. Few commanders were more popular among German airmen than Greim.

Generaloberst Heinz Guderian

A World War I soldier who served with distinction, Guderian served in the Truppenamt (Troop Office, a cover for the General Staff after World War I) of the Reichswehr between wars under Col. Freiherr von Fritsch. During the Polish and Western campaigns he commanded an armored group. From May of 1941 to 5 October 1941 Guderian commanded the 2nd Panzer Group in Russia. He was then retired because of differences with Hitler. On 21 February 1943 he was recalled to duty as General Inspector of Armored Forces, a position he held until the end of the war. He was promoted 19 July 1940 to Generaloberst. Guderian wrote a number of books and articles of note after World War II concerning German military history, and died in the 1950's.

Generaloberst Franz Halder

This distinguished staff officer won numerous decorations in World War I, and served as a member of the German General Staff between wars. In early 1938 he became Chief Quartermaster I in the High Command of the German Army, and on 31 August 1938 was appointed Chief of the General Staff of the Army, a post he held until his resignation 24 September 1942. An eminent strategist, Halder often found himself at odds with Hitler, which led to his decision to resign. After World War II he served as the driving force in the U.S. Army's German Historical Monograph Project under the direction of the Office of the Chief of Military History. He also lent assistance to the USAF Historical Division's German Historical Monograph Project.

Generalleutnant Adolf Heusinger

Heusinger served from World War I through World War II, being a distinguished staff officer in each conflict. From 1937 on he was Chief of Operations Branch, Army General Staff, where he became a well known personality. Implicated in the 20 July 1944 plot against Hitler, he was never cleared of charges when the war came to an end. After 18 months imprisonment by the Allies, he was released and later became a highly respected general officer of the West German Bundeswehr. An attempt in December 1961 by Soviet authorities to discredit him by claiming he had been responsible for wartime atrocities was investigated and summarily rejected by U.S. officials.

Generaloberst Hermann Hoth

Generaloberst Hoth was chiefly a combat commander and distinguished himself in both World War I and World War II. He participated in the Polish and Western campaigns, and on 22 June 1941 commanded the 3rd Panzer Group in Russia. On 5 October 1941 he assumed command of the Seventeenth Army, a post which he held until June 1942 when he took charge of the 4th Panzer Army (Eastern Front). In November 1943 he became Commander of German Forces Erzgebirge (Ore Mountains in Bohemia). Hoth, promoted 19 July 1940 to Generaloberst, was tried in the High Command of the Wehrmacht (OKW) trials in Nuremberg 1947-48 and sentenced to 15 years imprisonment at Landsberg.

Generaloberst Hans Jeschonnek

Jeschonnek served ably in World War I and in World War II. Between wars he served in the Reichswehr and promoted various aviation groups. On 1 September 1933 he transferred to the Luftwaffe as a Captain and began his meteoric rise in the Luftwaffe General Staff. By 1 February 1939 he had become Chief of the Luftwaffe General Staff, on 19 July 1940 was promoted to General der Flieger, and on 1 March 1942 to Generaloberst. Although a protege of General Wever, Jeschonnek remained a bitter opponent of strategic air power. He often differed with Goering and occasionally with Hitler, whom he considered a genius. His appointment as Chief of the General Staff of the Luftwaffe represents the first clear break with the older traditions of the Reichswehr. The circumstances surrounding his suicide 19 August 1943 provide an interesting insight into command and policy problems in the Luftwaffe.

Generaloberst Alfred Jodl

Jodl, a Bavarian, served in the field artillery during World War I, winning several significant decorations. After the war he served in a number of staff positions in the "100,000 Man Army." From 1935 to 1939 he headed the Home Defense Branch of the German Army, and on 22 August 1939 became Chief of the German Army Operations Office. From 8 August 1940 until the end of World War II he headed the Wehrmacht Operations Staff. Jodl (Generaloberst 1 February 1944) was tried and convicted in the main trials at Nuremberg, and executed 16 October 1946.

Field Marshal Wilhelm Keitel

This officer entered the military service just after the turn of the century, served ably during World War I, and remained in service after 1918. By 1 September 1939 he had risen to the post of Chief of the High Command of the Armed Forces, an office he held until the end of World War II. Hitler found him useful chiefly because he could rely upon him to be a "Yes man," and one who might help keep the old Reichswehr officers in line; he was, for this very reason, held in somewhat lesser esteem by the professional officer corps. He was often unwilling to contradict Hitler on vital issues. He was tried and convicted in the main trials of the OKW at Nuremberg and later executed 16 October 1946.

Generaloberst Alfred Keller

Keller won the highest decorations during World War I as Commander of Bomber Wing 1, and was an "old eagle," having flown before 1914. He advanced civil aviation enterprises in the 1920's and in 1934 returned to the Army as a Major. On 1 March 1935 he transferred to the Luftwaffe and subsequently served in several administrative commands. On 1 March 1939 he was promoted to General der Flieger and took command of the IV Air Corps. From 22 June 1941 to 28 July 1943 he commanded the First Air Fleet in Russia. A respected Luftwaffe officer, Keller survived the war.

Field Marshal Albert Kesselring

Kesselring, undoubtedly the best known Luftwaffe combat commander to Americans, served with distinction in World War I and later in the Reichswehr. He transferred to the Luftwaffe 1 October 1933 and became a general in 1934. He held several administrative commands until 1938, when he took command of the First Air Fleet. In 1940 he assumed command of the Second Air Fleet and served in the West and in Russia. From 1 December 1941 to 11 June 1943 he commanded the Second Air Fleet and German Forces in the Mediterranean, and from 26 July 1943 to 10 March 1945 commanded Army Group "C" and German Forces in Italy, as well as defense forces in the West and South. Known as "smiling Albert," he was an extremely able and popular commander. After World War II he rendered great assistance to the USAF Historical Division's German Historical Monograph Project in Karlsruhe, where his presence encouraged other German military officers to support the program. Promoted 19 July 1940 to Field Marshal, Kesselring died 16 July 1960.

Field Marshal Ewald von Kleist

Born in a famous Prussian family, 31 of whom had won the coveted Pour le Mérite, Kleist served with distinction in World War I and successfully made the transition from the cavalry forces to armored units after the war. Retired 28 February 1938, he was recalled to duty as Commander of the XXII Army Corps 1 September 1939. He later served in the West and in the Balkans with armored units. On 22 June 1941 he took part in the invasion of Russia at the head of the 1st Panzer Group, and on 22 November 1942 assumed command of Army Group "A" (East), with which he served until 30 March 1944. An eminent field commander, Kleist was delivered to the Tito government in 1946 by the Americans, and in 1948 he was turned over to the Soviet Union, where he is reported to have died in a Russian prison.

Field Marshal Guenther von Kluge

Von Kluge, a Posener, had an outstanding record as a mountain artillery officer in World War I. Between the wars he served in staff, line, and administrative positions in the Reichswehr. He commanded the Fourth Army in Poland, in the West, and along the German-Soviet border. On 22 June 1941 he participated in the Russian campaign with the Fourth Army. On 18 December 1941 he assumed command of Army Group Center, which post he held until his transfer 12 October 1943 to the Fuehrer Reserve. From July 1944 to 17 August 1944 he commanded Army Groups "B" and "D" in the West. An avowed enemy of Hitler, he participated in the plot of 20 July 1944. Summoned to appear in Berlin, obviously for Gestapo interrogation, von Kluge took poison on 19 August 1944. An able and respected officer, he was another of the old Army men who had early become disenchanted with Hitler and his schemes.

Generaloberst Guenther Korten

General Korten served ably in the First World War, in which he won several decorations of note. By 1939 he was one of the leading personalities in the Luftwaffe. From 1 September 1939 to October 1939 he served as Chief of the General Staff of the Fourth Air Fleet in Poland, from early 1940 to July 1940 as Chief of the General Staff of the Third Air Fleet in the West, and in April 1941 assumed the position of Chief of the General Staff of the Fourth Air Fleet in the Balkans, a unit with which he served in Russia as well. From July 1942 he held the commands of the I Air Corps, Air Force Command Don, First Air Fleet, and on 25 August 1943 became Chief of the General Staff, Luftwaffe, a post he held until 22 July 1944. An able staff officer, he was seriously wounded in Count von Stauffenberg's bomb attempt on Hitler's life, and died two days later.

Field Marshal Georg von Kuechler

An outstanding soldier of World War I, von Kuechler later served in the Reichswehr, and held various administrative posts until World War II. He commanded the Third Army in Poland, the Eighteenth Army in the West, and on 22 June 1941 directed the Eighteenth Army in the invasion of the Soviet Union. From 16 January 1942 until 9 January 1944 he was Commander of Army Group North on the Eastern Front. He was promoted to Generaloberst 19 July 1940 and to Field Marshal 30 June 1942. After World War II he was sentenced to 20 years imprisonment as a result of the OKW trials in Nuremberg. In 1951 his sentence was remitted to 12 years and on 18 February 1955 he was freed.

Field Marshal Wilhelm Ritter von Leeb

One of the oldest commanders who served during World War II, von Leeb served with great distinction in the Bavarian Army during World War I. Having retired from active duty 28 February 1938, he was recalled to duty on 3 September 1939 and given the command of Army Group "C." On 1 April 1941 he assumed command of Army Group North, which he commanded until 16 January 1942, when he finally retired from the service. Deeply steeped in the older traditions of the Imperial Army, von Leeb was highly respected by the officer corps, but often differed with Hitler. Promoted 19 July 1940 to Field Marshal, he resigned 16 January 1942.

Generaloberst Alexander Loehr

General Loehr was an Austrian national, born in Croatia, who saw extensive service as a flying officer and as a member of the Austro-Hungarian General Staff during World War I. By 1938 he had become Commander in Chief of the Austrian Air Force, a position he held for a time after the Anschluss of 1938. From 18 March 1939 to 24 June 1942 he commanded the Fourth Air Fleet in Vienna, Poland, the Balkans, and in Russia. Thereafter he commanded German Armed Forces in the Southeast and Army Group "E." His efforts to protect the pro-German Croatians in the closing days of World War II earned him the enmity of Tito's forces. Promoted 9 May 1941 to Generaloberst. Executed after a flimsy trial by the Yugoslavs 16 February 1947.

Generaloberst Bruno Loerzer

A Berliner, Loerzer won numerous distinctions during World War I while serving in Fighter Wing 26. He was credited with 44 aerial victories, making him one of Germany's top "aces." In 1919 he fought in the Baltic, and in 1920 left the service. Between World War I and the early 1930's he promoted various flying ventures. On 1 April 1935 he returned to duty as a Colonel in the Luftwaffe, and by 4 February 1939 had become a general officer and Commander of Air Division 2 (later designated II Air Corps). On 29 May 1940 he was promoted to General der Flieger, and on 16 February 1943 to Generaloberst. Having served on various fronts, he was made Chief of the Personnel Branch, Reichs Air Ministry on 23 February 1943. From 19 June 1944 until the war's end he was Chief of Luftwaffe Personnel, responsible for National Socialist leadership. He survived the war.

Generalmajor Bruno Maass

A World War I flyer, Maass served as Commander of Bomber Wing "General Wever" during 1936-37, as Chief of Staff of the 3rd Luftwaffe Command Headquarters, as Chief of Staff of Luftwaffe Administrative Command VII, and in several positions in connection with the Luftwaffe Mission to Rumania. His final service was performed as a member of the Office of the Commanding General of Aviation, Reichs Air Ministry. Promoted 1 August 1941 to Generalmajor, he was hospitalized in 1944 and saw no further action.

Field Marshal Carl Gustaf Freiherr Mannerheim

A great Finnish statesman and military leader, Mannerheim came from an old military family, and was one of the top cavalry officers in the Imperial Russian Army prior to and during World War I as well as being a member of the Imperial War Council. In December of 1917 he left the Czar's service and took command of the Finnish Army of Liberation. German units were dispatched by the Kaiser to help him drive out the Russians. Mannerheim held the degree of Doctor of Philosophy and made substantial contributions in the field of geography. A great peacetime statesman and officer of the "old school," he again proved his mettle during the Russo-Finnish War of 1939-40 and during World War II, in which he served as Commander in Chief of Finnish Armed Forces.

Field Marshal Erich von Manstein

This famous soldier, the son of General Eduard von Lewinski, was later adopted by General Georg von Manstein. He served in some of the finest units in the German service and distinguished himself in Belgium, East Prussia, Poland, Serbia, France, and Courland during World War I. By 1939 he had become Chief of Staff of Army Group South (von Rundstedt), and on 18 September 1941 assumed command of the Eleventh Army in the East. On 22 November 1942 he took command of Army Group Don, on 14 February 1943 of Army Group South. Many rate him as the finest strategist in the German Army during World War II. A much more reflective and considerate person than Hitler, von Manstein often had differences with his leader. On 30 March 1944, after a final disagreement with Hitler, von Manstein resigned. His work Verlorene Siege (Lost Victories) is one of the best military histories concerning German operations in World War II.

General der Artillerie Erich Marcks

A proven soldier in World War I, Marcks was Chief of the General Staff of the Eighteenth Army by the outbreak of World War II. By 1940 he had become a divisional commander (101st Light Infantry Division). He later became Commander of the LXXXIV Army Corps in the West. Marcks, son of the famous German historian, was promoted 1 October 1942 to General der Artillerie. This officer, whom von Rundstedt called "a superior commander," fell near St. Lô, France, 12 June 1944.

General der Flieger Rudolf Meister

Meister was an aerial observer in several flying units during World War I, and served in Field Flying Detachment 420 of the Freikorps (Free Corps) after World War I. From 1928 to 1930 he received training in the Soviet Union in military aviation. Meister then served with various schools and in General Staff branches of the Luftwaffe. On 19 December 1939 he became Chief of the General Staff, I Air Corps; on 15 October 1940 Chief of Staff of the VIII Air Corps; and on 1 September 1943 he assumed command of the IV Air Corps. Meister became Commander of German Air Forces Denmark on 15 October 1944, and finished his service as Chief of the Luftwaffe Personnel Office.

Field Marshal Erhard Milch

Milch served during World War I as a member of Fighter Group 6. After the war he left the service and entered private aviation business. On 22 February 1933 he was appointed State Secretary of Aviation and given the rank of Colonel in the Luftwaffe. On 20 April 1936 he was promoted to General der Flieger, and on 1 November 1938 to General-oberst. Milch received his Field Marshal's baton 19 July 1940. Although many were at odds with Milch, he was considered to be a competent technical officer, with great talents in this field. He was also the person who blocked the route of subordinates seeking access to Reichsmarschall Goering. He survived the war.

Colonel Werner Moelders

This young officer began his military service in a Reichswehr unit in 1931. By 1935 he had transferred to the Luftwaffe for pilot training. During the Spanish Civil War (1936-39) he became a fighter squadron leader, and was credited with 14 aerial victories. At the outbreak of World War II he commanded a group in the 53rd Fighter Wing. In October 1940 he assumed command of the famous 51st Fighter Wing, and in 1941 took on the additional duties of Inspector of Fighters. This extremely gifted flyer and commander performed exemplary tasks on every front from the opening of the war until his death in an air accident 22 November 1941. At the time of his death he was Germany's top "ace" and had won its highest decorations. His loss was a great blow to the Luftwaffe.

Generalleutnant Andreas Nielsen

Born in Flensburg, Nielsen served during World War I and in the Reichswehr between wars. On 9 November 1923 he participated in the Hitler "Putsch" in Munich, and in 1928 went to Russia for flying training. In 1939 he went to Spain as a Bomb Group Commander in "Legion Condor." He then held a number of important staff assignments. On 19 October 1940 he became Chief of Staff, Fifth Air Fleet (Norway and Finland), a post he held until 24 December 1943 when he became German Luftwaffe Commander Denmark. On 21 May 1944 he became Chief of Staff, Air Fleet Reich, and finally assisted in the demobilization of the Luftwaffe in northern Germany in 1945. After two years of English captivity, he was released and became one of the principal contributors to the USAF Historical Division's German Historical Monograph Project. He died in April 1957.

296

Field Marshal Friedrich Paulus

A World War I and Reichswehr staff officer, Paulus rose to Chief of Staff, Army Group 4 and Quartermaster I of the Army High Command by 1 August 1939. In January 1942 he was promoted to General der Panzertruppe and given the command of the Sixth Army in Russia, which he was forced to surrender 1 February 1943 at Stalingrad. Made a Field Marshal by Hitler 30 January 1943, his marshal's baton was flown in by air just in time for his capture as the first German Field Marshal taken in World War II. His actions during the Stalingrad campaign are still controversial. Later (probably not by choice) he took part in the "Freedom Committee" of captured German officers who sought to "sell" Communism and induce Germany to surrender. Paulus also became an Inspector of the People's Police in East Germany. He is now deceased.

General der Flieger Kurt Pflugbeil

Pflugbeil was a World War I flyer, a member of the Border Police in Upper Silesia in 1919, and back in service by 1920. On 31 March 1928 he went to Russia to receive aerial bombing training. In the early 1930's he served in Germany and in Italy, and in 1935 Pflugbeil transferred to the Luftwaffe. By 1939 he was a Generalmajor, and on 7 August 1939 took command of the VIII Air Corps. From 13 January to 26 August 1940 he directed the Air Administrative Command which served Luftwaffe units in France and Belgium. Thereafter, until 4 September 1943, he commanded the IV Air Corps, much of which time he served in the East. General Pflugbeil, an able commander, completed his service as Commander of the First Air Fleet and survived the war. He died 31 May 1955.

Generalleutnant Hermann Plocher

See "About the Author" in the front part of this study.

Grand Admiral Erich Raeder

This distinguished naval officer was born in Wandsbek in 1876 and had a brilliant record in World War I, in which he saw action in the great "Cruiser Battle" off Dogger Bank in April of 1915, and served as Chief of Staff to Admiral Franz Hipper in the "Battle of Jutland" 31 May 1916. He later commanded the cruiser Cologne, and from 1928 to 31 May 1935 headed the German Naval Command (<u>Marineleitung</u>). From 1 June 1935 to 30 January 1943 he was Commander in Chief of the German Navy, and from that time until the war's end served as Admiral-Inspector of the Navy. Exemplifying the best traditions of the Imperial Navy, he often had serious disagreements with Hitler, resigning his command in early 1943. Tried in the main trials at Nuremberg, he was sentenced to life imprisonment in 1946, freed in 1955, and died in November 1962.

Field Marshal Walter von Reichenau

Von Reichenau served with valor in World War I and remained in service after the war. In the early 1930's he held various significant Army administrative positions. On 1 September 1939 he assumed command of the Tenth Army and served in Poland. In October 1939 he took command of the Sixth Army, a post he held until 30 December 1941 when he was assigned as Commander of Army Group South. Although apparently he enjoyed Hitler's early confidence--he made him a Field Marshal on 19 July 1940--he recognized the Fuehrer's shortcomings. A few weeks prior to his death on 17 January 1942 (heart attack), he had taken over von Rundstedt's command. Questions have been later raised concerning his sudden replacement and unexpected demise.

Generaloberst Hans Reinhardt

Reinhardt served ably in World War I and in the Reichswehr. By 5 October 1941 he had become Commander of the Third Panzer Army, which he directed until 16 August 1944. He then served until 25 January 1945 as Commander of Army Group Center. On 25 January 1945 he assumed command of Army Group North, a post he held just two days. Promoted 1 January 1942 to Generaloberst, he was sentenced in 1948 in the OKW trials at Nuremberg to 15 years imprisonment. On 27 July 1952 he was pardoned and freed.

Field Marshal Dr. Ing. Wolfram Freiherr von Richthofen

A cousin of the famous Baron Manfred, Wolfram also served in Fighter Wing No. 1 during World War I, being credited with 8 aerial victories. He later served in the Reichswehr and during the 1920's earned his doctorate in Engineering at Hanover. In 1936 he went to Spain with "Legion Condor" to assist General Franco. A year later he was Chief of Staff of that unit, and in the last year of war became Commander of "Legion Condor." After experience in the Polish and Western campaigns, he was promoted 19 July 1940 to General der Flieger. On 22 June 1941 he commanded the VIII Air Corps in the East, and on 4 July 1942 assumed command of the Fourth Air Fleet. In 1943 he took command of the Second Air Fleet. Promoted to Field Marshal 16 February 1943. He was once an enemy of dive bombing, but later became a staunch enthusiast of such operations, which he carried out effectively in southern Russia. He died of a lingering illness in Austria on 12 July 1945.

Generalmajor Hans-Detlef Herhudt von Rohden

General von Rohden began his military service before World War I, and later served in that war as an infantry officer. After the war he was given special training for General Staff work. In 1935 he transferred to the Luftwaffe, serving with the Reichs Air Ministry. At the outbreak of war in 1939 he commanded a bomber group in Schwerin, and later became Chief of Staff of the IX Air Corps in the West. For three months in 1941 he was Chief of the General Staff, First Air Fleet in the East, and in 1942 was Chief of the General Staff, Fourth Air Fleet. He served in 1943 as instructor in the Air War Academy, and in 1944-45 as Chief of the 8th (Military Science) Branch of the General Staff of the Luftwaffe. Known afterward for some of his historical contributions to the history of air power, much of his work was unfinished. He died 17 December 1952 in the Taunus Mountains.

Colonel Hans-Ulrich Rudel

Son of a Lutheran pastor in Silesia, Rudel began his service in 1936. Commissioned 20 April 1938, he was immediately assigned to a dive-bomber group. During the Polish campaign he flew as a strategic reconnaissance pilot. He also served in the Western campaign. On 22 June 1941 he was again a dive-bomber pilot, in which capacity he won Germany's highest decorations. Promoted to Colonel 1 January 1945, Rudel flew 2,530 combat missions over the most critical areas of the front, destroyed 519 tanks (enough for an armored corps), numerous fortifications, the 23,500-ton Soviet battleship Marat and many smaller vessels, and remained in the East from 1941 until the war's end. Wounded five times, the last time losing a lower leg, he returned to action and continued his record. Already the recipient of the Knight's Cross with Oak Leaf, Swords, and Diamonds, Hitler devised for him the unique addition of the Golden Oak Leaf. Having survived the war, Rudel went to Argentina, where he works for an aircraft firm.

Field Marshal Gerd von Rundstedt

One of the older officers who served in World War II, Rundstedt represents not only an older age group, but in some respects the better traditions of the old Army. Highly decorated in World War I, he continued to serve in the Reichswehr after the war. Already a general in the 1920's, Rundstedt retired 31 October 1938. With the approach of World War II he was recalled and given the command of Army Group South for the Polish campaign. He then commanded Army Group "A" in the Western conflict. On 22 June 1941 he was in command of Army Group South in the East. Because of differences with the Fuehrer he was retired 3 December 1941. Aloof, aristocratic, and hostile to many of Hitler's ideas and mannerisms (including his coarse language), Rundstedt dubbed him the "Bohemian Corporal." He was again recalled and again retired before being finally placed in command for the Ardennes offensive. Imprisoned in 1945 by British authorities, he was released 5 May 1949 for reasons of illness and advanced age. Von Rundstedt died 24 February 1953.

Generalleutnant Josef "Beppo" Schmid

"Beppo" Schmid, who died 30 August 1956, was a Bavarian who entered the service after World War I, serving with Ritter von Epp's Freikorps (Free Corps). Commissioned in the infantry in the 1920's, Schmid transferred 1 July 1935 to the Luftwaffe, and became a member of its General Staff. On 22 June 1941 this officer was Chief of the 5th Branch (Military Intelligence) of the Luftwaffe General Staff. Schmid held various command positions in the Luftwaffe during World War II, but he is best known as a Luftwaffe intelligence officer in the Luftwaffe General Staff. A colorful and sometimes controversial character, Schmid was a participant in the Hitler "Putsch" of 9 November 1923. After the end of World War II he contributed to the USAF Historical Division's German Historical Monograph Project in Karlsruhe. He died suddenly on 30 August 1956.

Generaloberst Eugen Ritter von Schobert

Ritter von Schobert served with distinction in the German Army during World War I, winning some of the highest awards for valor and a hereditary title from the King of Bavaria. He continued his military service after the war, moving rapidly ahead in the Reichswehr. By 1938 he commanded Army Administrative Area VII (Munich). In June of 1941 he was in command of the Eleventh Army in Rumania and went into battle with his organization. He was killed instantly on 12 September 1941 when his Fieseler "Stork" liaison aircraft landed on a Russian mine.

General der Flieger Hans-Georg von Seidel

A veteran of the First World War, von Seidel was in the General Staff of the Army High Command before the end of the conflict. He left the Army in 1920 as a Captain of Cavalry, and returned to the service 1 April 1934 as a Major in the new Luftwaffe. By 1 September 1939 von Seidel had become a Generalmajor, and on 20 July 1940 was promoted to Generalleutnant. At the opening of the Russo-German war, von Seidel was General der Flieger and Quartermaster of the Luftwaffe. His final assignment was in command of the Tenth Air Fleet. He survived the war.

General der Flieger Hans Seidemann

Seidemann barely missed World War I, having entered the Cadet School before the termination of the conflict. He served later in infantry units in Potsdam and Munich. He transferred 1 July 1935 to the Luftwaffe in the rank of Captain, and rose rapidly in the General Staff. From 1 December 1938 to 30 June 1939 he served as Chief of Staff of "Legion Condor" in Spain. At the outbreak of World War II he was Chief of Staff, VIII Air Corps. On 6 August 1940 he became Chief of Staff, Second Air Fleet, a position he held until 1 August 1942. Seidemann later served (1943-44) as Air Commander Africa, as Commander of Luftwaffe Forces Tunis, and in 1945 commanded the VIII Air Corps. He was promoted 1 March 1945 to General der Flieger.

Generaloberst Adolf Strauss

Adolf Strauss served with great distinction during World War I, winning numerous significant decorations. By 1928 he had risen in the Reichswehr to the rank of Major and belonged to the Staff of the Infantry School in Dresden. He held a number of important posts, including (from November 1938 to the outbreak of World War II) that of Commander of Army Administrative Area II (Stettin). After service in the Polish conflict, he took part in the Western campaign. On 30 May 1940 he assumed command of the Ninth Army, which he later commanded in the invasion of the Soviet Union, until his retirement 15 January 1942. After World War II he was released from British custody 5 May 1949 on grounds of age and ill health.

General der Infanterie Heinrich von Stuelpnagel

This highly gifted commander was an ardent enemy of Hitler. Having served with honor during World War I and in the Reichswehr after the war, he was, by 1938, Chief Quartermaster I in the German Army High Command. In 1940 he presided over the Armistice Commission in France--he was known to speak very good French and to have a sympathetic attitude toward the French people--and later assumed active commands. From 22 June to 5 October 1941 he commanded the Seventeenth Army in the East. He was then retired to the Fuehrer Reserve. From February 1942 to 21 July 1944 he served as German Commander in France. During this time he was active in the plot to kill Hitler, and arrested the SS and SD detachments in Paris to ward off civil war at the time of von Stauffenberg's attempt, 20 July 1944. When the plot failed he set these units free, but he was immediately summoned to Berlin. Near Verdun he attempted suicide, but was rescued by the SS driver. Although blind in one eye, he was tried, convicted, and hung 30 August 1944.

Generaloberst Hans Juergen Stumpff

Generaloberst Stumpff entered military service before World War I, saw much war service during that conflict, and became a General Staff officer in the Reichswehr after the war. In 1933 he transferred to the Luftwaffe as Chief of the Personnel Office, Reichs Air Ministry. From 1 June 1937 to 31 January 1939 he was Chief of the General Staff of the Luftwaffe. During the first part of 1940 he commanded the First Air Fleet. On 11 May 1940, with his promotion to Generaloberst, Stumpff took command of the Fifth Air Fleet (Norway and Finland), a post he held until 5 November 1943. He later commanded defense units of the Reich until the capitulation. He was primarily an administrative officer, and basically an Army man, but received high decorations in both World War I and World War II.

General der Infanterie Georg Thomas

Thomas began his service in 1908, served during World War I, and later in the "100,000 Man Army." By 1 September 1939 he had become Chief of the Economic and War Armaments Office of the High Command of the Wehrmacht. At the end of 1942 he was relieved of those duties pertaining specifically to the War Armaments Office, but continued as Chief of the War Economy Office. On 16 January 1943 he was also appointed General for Special Duties with the Chief of the High Command of the Wehrmacht (Keitel), but on 15 August 1944 he was relieved of all active assignments by Field Marshal Keitel, who thought he painted too pessimistic a picture of Germany's potential and the future course of the war. He remained in the Fuehrer Reserve until the end of the war.

General der Infanterie Kurt von Tippelskirch

This well-known officer won numerous distinctions in World War I, held important offices in the Reichswehr, and was a leading commander in World War II. His most significant commands were the Fourth Army (East) from 5 June 1944 to 18 July 1944, the Fourteenth Army in Italy from December 1944 to 17 February 1945, the Fourth Army (East) from 15 April to 27 April 1945, and finally the dual assignment as Commander of Army Group Vistula (East) and Commander of the Twenty-First Army (East) from late April to the end of the war. Von Tippelskirch has written a number of discourses on military science and a one-volume history of World War II.

Generaloberst Ernst Udet

The internationally famous stunt pilot and aviator Ernst Udet was one of Germany's top aces in World War I. During that conflict he flew in the famous Fighter Wing No. 1 under Baron Manfred von Richthofen, and amassed 62 aerial victories, second only to the famous "Red Knight." After winning Germany's highest decorations, Udet became a commercial and stunt flyer, traveling to Africa, Greenland, the United States, and other countries. In the United States he persuaded the German government to purchase two Curtiss dive bombers, which had made a profound impression upon him. In 1936 he was back in service as Chief of the Technical Office of the Luftwaffe, and a year later was a Generalmajor. Udet held this post until his death, although he found the internal political strife of the German High Command distasteful and depressing. He knew little of the technical aspects of aircraft research and development, and found himself unable to stand fast amid the pressures of rival aircraft firms, all seeking contracts. His suicide on 17 November 1941 was obscured from the public as an "accident which occurred while testing aircraft."

Generalmajor Otto Hoffmann von Waldau

One of Germany's most gifted Luftwaffe General Staff officers, his sudden death in 1943 was a severe blow to the German Air Force. He distinguished himself early in the 1930's as a man with a clear vision for air operations and possible applications of air power. Above the average in his many-sided talents, von Waldau had a more or less running argument with Jeschonnek, an ardent compromiser with Goering and Hitler. He served ably in the early part of World War II as Chief of Operations Branch, General Staff of the Luftwaffe. In early 1942 he was relieved by Goering and soon thereafter posted as a flying commander (Air Commander Africa). In 1943 he became Luftwaffe Commander Southeast (Balkans), where he died in an air accident. His loss was irreplaceable. Before World War II this brilliant General Staff officer had warned of the military potential of the United States and its Allies. Most of his words, however, were unheeded.

General der Artillerie Walter Warlimont

Warlimont served during World War I as a battalion and regimental adjutant and finally as an artillery battery commander. He remained in the Army in the 1920's and 1930's. In 1929 he was a liaison officer with the U.S. Army in the United States. In 1936 he went to Spain at the outbreak of civil war to head up Hitler's assistance program to General Franco, a mission which was handled with great skill and dispatch. In 1937 he held command positions in the artillery, and on 1 November 1938 was appointed Chief of the National Defense Branch, High Command of the Wehrmacht, and Deputy Commissioner for the Chief of the Wehrmacht Operations Office. On 1 January he became Deputy Chief of the Wehrmacht Operations Staff under Jodl, a position he held until released for health reasons on 6 September 1944. Said to have been the mind behind the Wehrmacht Operations Staff and the vehicle through whom Jodl reached the ear of Hitler, he was sentenced to life imprisonment in the OKW trials at Nuremberg. The sentence was later commuted to 18 years, and finally remitted in the 1950's.

Field Marshal Maximilian Freiherr von Weichs auf Glonn

This senior Army officer won numerous laurels as a cavalry officer in the First World War, and remained in service after the fall of the German Monarchy in 1918. Von Weichs served in Poland and commanded the Second Army in the Western campaign and the Balkans, as well as in Russia.   On 7 July 1942 he assumed command of Army Group "B" in Russia, and vainly tried to persuade Hitler to permit the withdrawal of Paulus' Sixth Army from the Stalingrad area.   Von Weichs, who received his marshal's baton 1 February 1943, took over German Forces in the Southeast (Balkans) 22 August 1943.   Tried in the Southeast Trials at Nuremberg, he was released because of poor health 3 November 1948.

Generalleutnant Walter Wever

Wever was in many respects the "Father of the Luftwaffe."   A highly gifted organizer, temperamentally well suited to high command, he demonstrated his talents in World War I and in the Truppenamt (Troop Office, a cover for the German General Staff) of the Reichswehr.   Wever was the first Chief of the General Staff of the Luftwaffe, and held this position until his untimely death in 1936.   He was of a completely different mold than Goering, and saw clearly the future of air power, especially strategic air power.   Wever was keenly aware of the work of Douhet, but he also remembered problems of defense which he considered in relation to future air warfare.   One of Wever's most valuable assets was the ability to inspire confidence, stifle discord, and promote harmony in his organization.   His favorite idea was the creation of a four-engine bomber force capable of flying beyond the Urals and back.   This plane he called the "Ural Bomber."   Some progress was made in this direction, but after his death in an air accident 3 June 1936 his plans were jettisoned.   Had he lived the Luftwaffe might have been a much more formidable organization.

Generalmajor Wolfgang von Wild

Von Wild served as a naval cadet in World War I, was commissioned in the German Navy in 1923, and saw action with irregular units in the Baltic and with Ehrhardt's Naval Brigade in Upper Silesia and Berlin.   In the mid-1920's he transferred to the Luftwaffe, and by 1 September 1939 had risen to the rank of Major.   He participated in the Polish campaign with coastal air units, and on 21 April 1941 was made Air Commander Baltic.   On 30 October 1941 he assumed command of the post Air Commander Atlantic, which he held until 1 November 1942, when he became Air Transport Commander I (Southeast) at Athens.   He held various other important Luftwaffe posts, climaxing his career as Air Attaché to Tokyo. He was promoted 1 March 1945 to Generalmajor.

Generalleutnant Heinz-Hellmuth von Wuehlisch

This highly decorated veteran of World War I was an able officer. As Chief of Staff, First Air Fleet, he was largely responsible for laying the foundation for the initial air thrust into Russia. After 1942 he was Chief of Staff to the Commanding General, Holland, and distinguished himself at Arnhem. At the termination of World War II, von Wuehlisch served as an Air Defense Commander near Hamburg.

APPENDIX III

LIST OF GAF MONOGRAPH PROJECT STUDIES

I.   Published

Study No.	Title
153	The German Air Force versus Russia, 1941
163	German Air Force Operations in Support of the Army
167	German Air Force Airlift Operations
173	The German Air Force General Staff
175	The Russian Air Force in the Eyes of German Commanders
176	Russian Reactions to German Air Power
177	Airpower and Russian Partisan Warfare
189	Historical Turning Points in the German Air Force War Effort

II.   To Be Published

150	The German Air Force in the Spanish War
151	The German Air Force in Poland
152	The German Air Force in France and the Low Countries
154	The German Air Force versus Russia, 1942
155	The German Air Force versus Russia, 1943
156	The Battle of Britain

LIST OF MAPS

1. General Reference Map of the Soviet Union.

2. Metal Processing and Armament Centers in the German-occupied East, 1941.

3. Final Plan for Operation BARBAROSSA, June 1941.

4. Course of German Operations in the East, June and July 1941.

5. Encirclement Battle of Smolensk, early July - 5 August 1941.

6. Air Interdiction of the Kiev Area, 1 September - 25 September 1941.

6a. Breakthrough the Stalin Line--Support by Fourth Air Fleet, September 1941.

7. German Army Operations in the Encirclement Battle of Kiev, 25 August - 25 September 1941.

8. Course of German Operations in the East, August and September 1941.

9. The Seven Great Encirclement Battles of the Eastern Campaign, 1941.

10. Operation BEOWULF for the Conquest of the Baltic Islands, 14 September - 21 October 1941.

11. German-Finnish Theater of Operations (Far North), 1941.

12. The Battle for Leningrad. Encirclement of Russian Forces Around Leningrad and Adjacent Coastal Areas, 16 October - Early December 1941.

13. Course of German Operations in the East, October - End of December 1941.

14. The Battle for Moscow and Results of the Winter Battles of 1941-42.

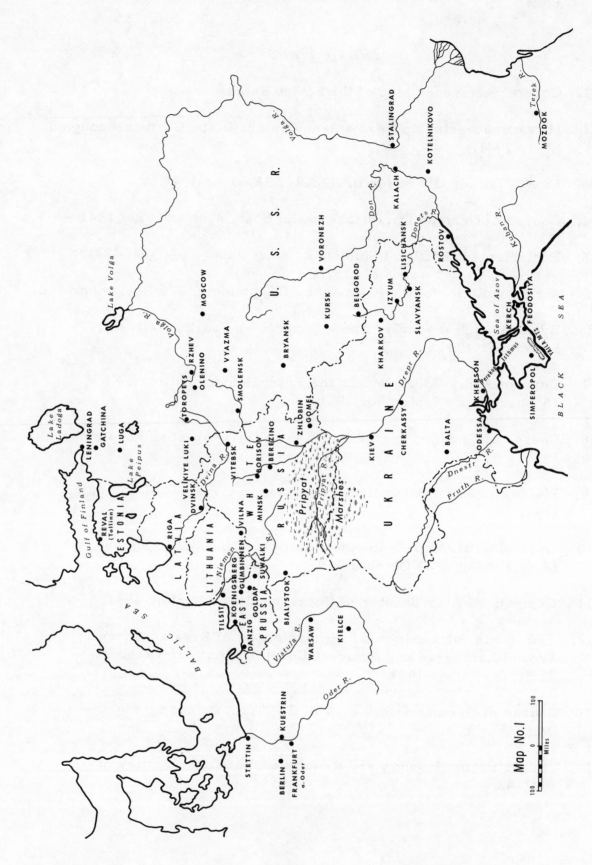

Map No. I

312

Map No. 2
STATUTE MILES
0   100   200   300

Finland
HELSINKI
Gulf of Finland
LENINGRAD
KOHTLA-GOLDFIELD
JEVE
NARVA
REVAL
MARDU
KIVIOLI · SILLANDE
KÜTTJOUD
KOHTLAJARVE

Baltic Sea
Gulf of Riga
Estonia
STARAYA RUSSA
KHOLM
RIGA
LIEPĀJA
Latvia
DAUGAVPILS
DVINA
VITEBSK
VOLGA
RZHEV
VYASMA
MOSCOW
OKA

Lithuania
TILSIT
KAUNAS
WILNO
SMOLENSK
ROSLAVL
SESHINSKAYA
MOGILEV
SCHAZILKI
POLPINO
BRYANSK
OREL
ZNA
KOENIGSBERG
SUWALKI
MINSK

General
BIALYSTOK
BOBRUISK
VYETKA
GOMEL
RECHITSA
DON
BUG
WARSAW
DAVIDGRODEK
PINSK
GORODISHCHE
PETRIKOV
DOMBROVITSA
PRIPYAT

S.

R.

S.

U.

Government
LUBLIN
LVOV
KIEV
DNEPR
DONETS
KRAMATORSKAYA
KONSTANTINOVKA
RYKOVO
MAKYEVKA
STALINO
STRETSUKA
KAMENSKAYA
DNEPROPETROVSK
ZAPOROZHYE
SKOLTAYA REKA
VERKHOVTSEVO
SAKSAGAN
YUGOLETS
CHERNONO-GRIGOROVKA
MARGENETS
KRIVOY ROG
SHOLOKHOVO
MARIUPOL
TARNOPOL
DUNAYEVTSY

NISTROT
NIKOLAYEV
KHERSON
Sea of Azov
ODESSA
YALTA
Black Sea

LEGEND

Iron-Ores		Blast Furnaces	
Steel-Refining Ores	*	Light Metal Works	
Phosphorite	⊛	Armament Works	
Oil Slate		Shipyards	
Blast Furnaces and Steel Mills		Carriage Construction	

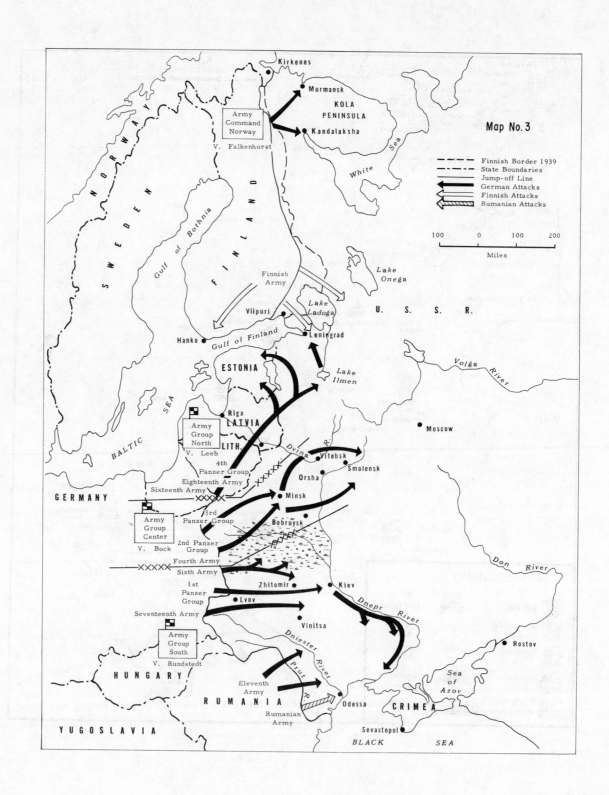

Map No. 3

Finnish Border 1939
State Boundaries
Jump-off Line
German Attacks
Finnish Attacks
Rumanian Attacks

100   0   100   200

Miles

KIRKENES

Murmansk

KOLA
PENINSULA

Army
Command
Norway

V. Falkenhorst

Kandalaksha

White
Sea

N O R W A Y

S W E D E N

Gulf of Bothnia

F I N L A N D

Finnish
Army

Lake
Onega

U. S. S. R.

Viipuri

Lake
Ladoga

Hanko   Gulf of Finland

Leningrad

Volga
River

BALTIC
SEA

ESTONIA

Lake
Ilmen

Riga

LATVIA

Moscow

Army
Group
North

V. Leeb

LITH.

Dvina
R.

Vitebsk

4th
Panzer Group

Orsha

Smolensk

Eighteenth Army

Sixteenth Army

GERMANY

3rd
Panzer Group

Minsk

Army
Group
Center

V. Bock

Bobruysk

2nd Panzer
Group

Fourth Army

Don
River

Sixth Army

1st
Panzer
Group

Zhitomir

Kiev

Lvov

Dnepr
River

Seventeenth Army

Vinitsa

Rostov

Army
Group
South

V. Rundstedt

HUNGARY

Dniester
River

Sea
of
Azov

Eleventh
Army

Prut
R.

Odessa

CRIMEA

RUMANIA

Rumanian
Army

Sevastopol

YUGOSLAVIA

BLACK   SEA

315

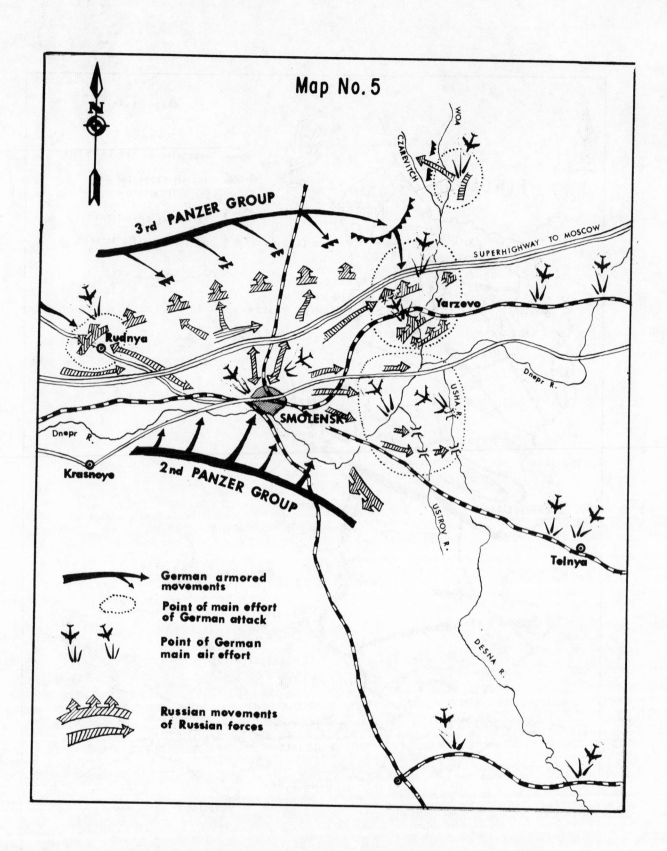

Map No. 5

German armored
movements

Point of main effort
of German attack

Point of German
main air effort

Russian movements
of Russian forces

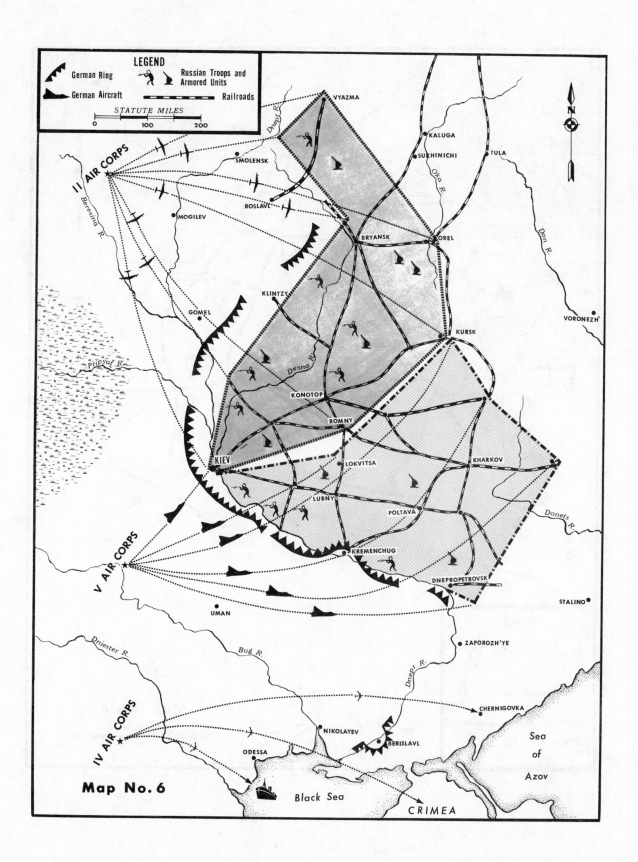

LEGEND

German Ring

German Aircraft

Russian Troops and Armored Units

Railroads

STATUTE MILES

0   100   200

N

II AIR CORPS

V AIR CORPS

IV AIR CORPS

VYAZMA

KALUGA

SUKHINICHI

TULA

SMOLENSK

ROSLAVL

MOGILEV

BRYANSK

OREL

VORONEZH'

KLINTZY

GOMEL

KURSK

KONOTOP

Desna R.

ROMNY

KIEV

LOKVITSA

KHARKOV

LUBNY

POLTAVA

Donets R.

KREMENCHUG

DNEPROPETROVSK

STALINO

UMAN

Pripyat R.

Beresina R.

Dnepr R.

Oka R.

Don R.

Dniester R.

Bug R.

Dnepr R.

ZAPOROZH'YE

CHERNIGOVKA

NIKOLAYEV

BERISLAVL

ODESSA

Sea
of
Azov

Map No. 6

Black Sea

CRIMEA

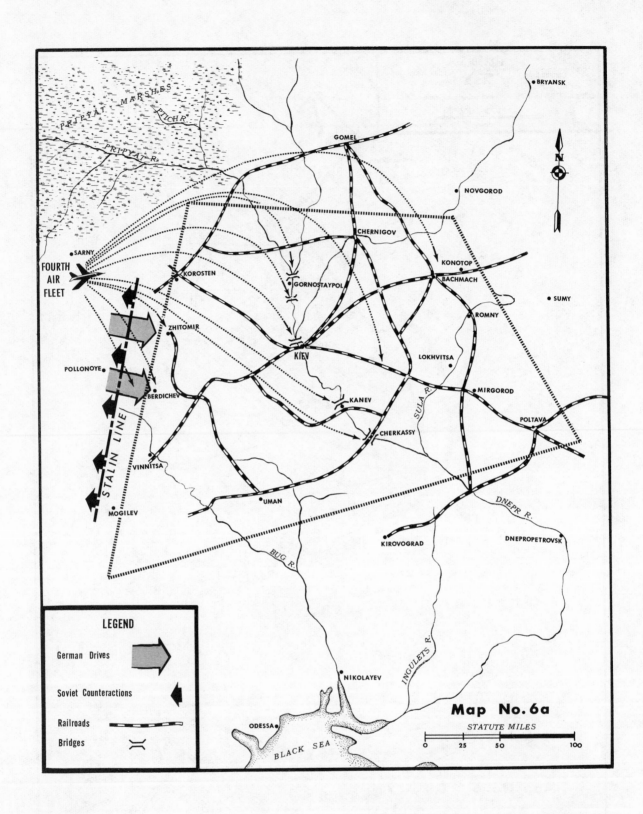

FOURTH
AIR
FLEET

STALIN LINE

PRIPYAT MARSHES

PTICH R.

PRIPYAT R.

SARNY

KOROSTEN

ZHITOMIR

POLLONOYE

BERDICHEV

VINNITSA

MOGILEV

UMAN

BUG R.

NIKOLAYEV

ODESSA

BLACK SEA

GORNOSTAYPOL

KIEV

KANEV

CHERKASSY

KIROVOGRAD

GOMEL

CHERNIGOV

KONOTOP

BACHMACH

ROMNY

LOKHVITSA

MIRGOROD

POLTAVA

SULA R.

DNEPR R.

INGULETS R.

DNEPROPETROVSK

BRYANSK

NOVGOROD

SUMY

LEGEND

German Drives

Soviet Counteractions

Railroads

Bridges

Map No. 6a

STATUTE MILES

0   25   50   100

N

318

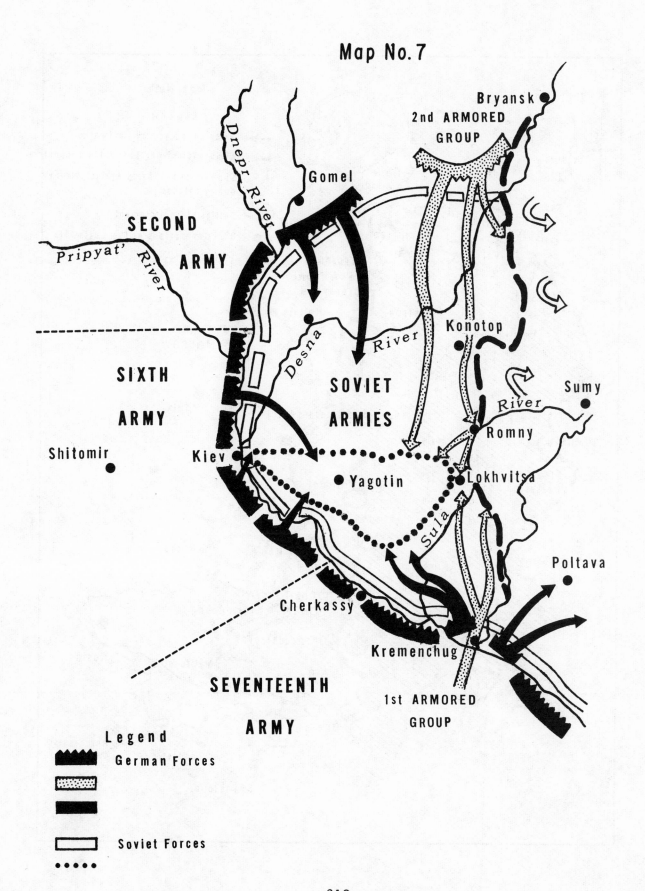

Map No. 7

Bryansk

2nd ARMORED GROUP

Dnepr River

Gomel

SECOND ARMY

Pripyat' River

Desna River

Konotop

SIXTH ARMY

Shitomir

SOVIET ARMIES

Sumy

River

Romny

Kiev

Yagotin

Lokhvitsa

Sula

Poltava

Cherkassy

Kremenchug

1st ARMORED GROUP

SEVENTEENTH ARMY

Legend

German Forces

Soviet Forces

Map No. 8

Legend

→ Army supported by Luftwaffe

➜ Army with strong Luftwaffe support

⌐⌐ Support of the Army against strong enemy attacks

⬭ Battles of Encirclement

✳ Other operations of the Luftwaffe

N

FINLAND

Lake Onega

Lake Ladoga

Baltic Sea *Gulf of Finland*

Leningrad

Reval

Lake Peipus

• Tikhvin

Novgorod

Lake Il'men

Staraya Russa

Gulf of Riga

Ostrov

Kalinin

Riga

MOSCOW

Daugava

Vyazma

• Tula

Kaunas

Orsha

Smolensk

Suwalki

Minsk

Bryansk

Bialystok

Gomel

Voronezh'

Pripyat'

Kursk

Kiev

Romny

Kharkov

Korosten

Donets

Cherkassy

L'vov

Dnepr

Kremenchug

Dniester

Don

Dnepropetrovsk

Rostov

Melitopol'

Sea of Azov

Odessa

Novorossisk

Black Sea

Feodosiya

Sevastopol'

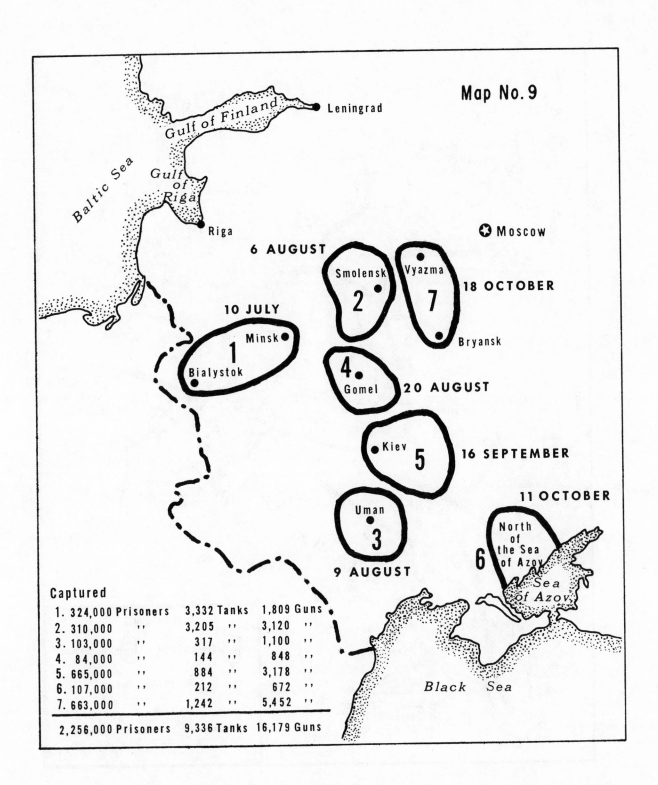

Map No. 9

Leningrad

Gulf of Finland

Baltic Sea

Gulf of Riga

Riga

Moscow

6 AUGUST

Smolensk

2

Vyazma

7

18 OCTOBER

Bryansk

10 JULY

Minsk

1

Bialystok

4

Gomel

20 AUGUST

Kiev

5

16 SEPTEMBER

11 OCTOBER

Uman

3

North
of
the Sea
of Azov

6

Sea
of Azov

9 AUGUST

Black   Sea

Captured

1.	324,000 Prisoners	3,332	Tanks	1,809	Guns
2.	310,000 ,,	3,205	,,	3,120	,,
3.	103,000 ,,	317	,,	1,100	,,
4.	84,000 ,,	144	,,	848	,,
5.	665,000 ,,	884	,,	3,178	,,
6.	107,000 ,,	212	,,	672	,,
7.	663,000 ,,	1,242	,,	5,452	,,
	2,256,000 Prisoners	9,336	Tanks	16,179	Guns

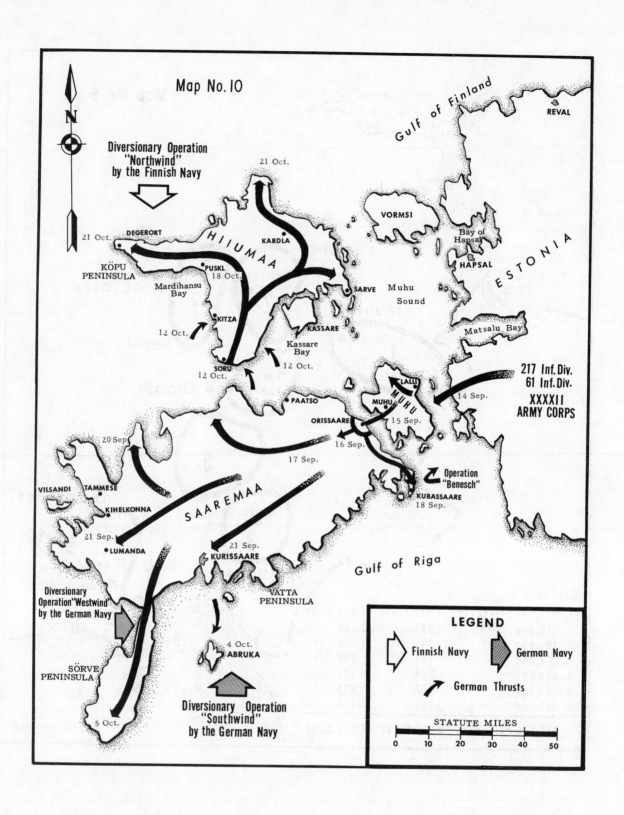

Map No. 10

Diversionary Operation "Northwind" by the Finnish Navy

21 Oct.

Gulf of Finland

REVAL

VORMSI

Bay of Hapsal

HAPSAL

ESTONIA

21 Oct.   DEGERORT

HIIUMAA

KARDLA

KÖPU PENINSULA

PUSKL

18 Oct.

Mardihansu Bay

KITZA

12 Oct.

SORU

12 Oct.

KASSARE

Kassare Bay

12 Oct.

SARVE

Muhu Sound

Matsalu Bay

PAATSO

LALLI

MUHU

217 Inf. Div.
61 Inf. Div.
XXXXII
ARMY CORPS

14 Sep.

ORISSAARE

15 Sep.

16 Sep.

Operation "Benesch"

KUBASSAARE

18 Sep.

20 Sep.

VILSANDI   TAMMESE

KIHELKONNA

SAAREMAA

17 Sep.

21 Sep.

LUMANDA

21 Sep.   KURISSAARE

VATTA PENINSULA

Gulf of Riga

Diversionary Operation "Westwind" by the German Navy

SÖRVE PENINSULA

4 Oct.
ABRUKA

Diversionary Operation "Southwind" by the German Navy

5 Oct.

LEGEND

Finnish Navy   German Navy

German Thrusts

STATUTE MILES

0   10   20   30   40   50

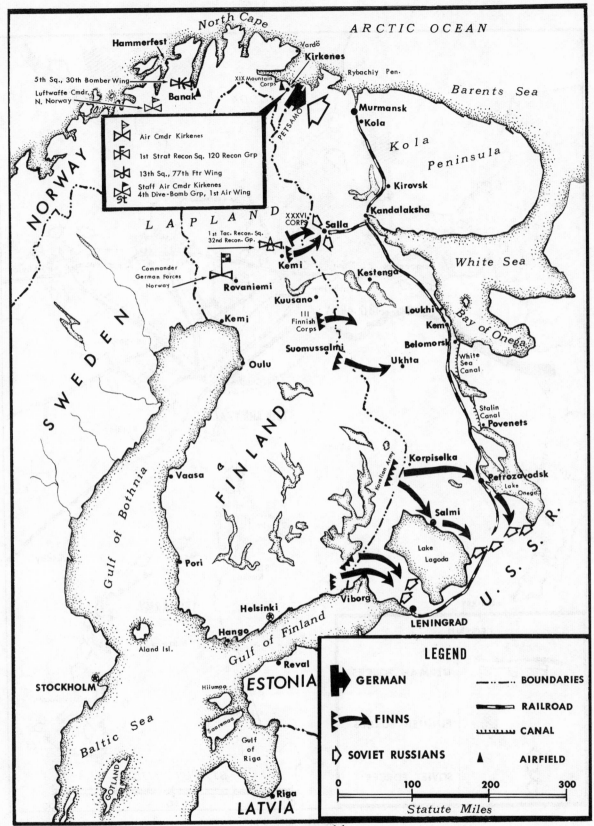

ARCTIC OCEAN

North Cape

Hammerfest

Kirkenes

Vardö

Rybachiy Pen.

Barents Sea

5th Sq., 30th Bomber Wing

Luftwaffe Cmdr.,
N. Norway

Banak

XIX Mountain
Corps

PETSAMO

Murmansk

Kola

Kola

Peninsula

N O R W A Y

Air Cmdr Kirkenes

1st Strat Recon Sq. 120 Recon Grp

13th Sq., 77th Ftr Wing

Staff Air Cmdr Kirkenes
4th Dive-Bomb Grp, 1st Air Wing

Kirovsk

L A P L A N D

XXXVI
CORPS

Salla

Kandalaksha

White Sea

1st Tac. Recon. Sq.
32nd Recon. Gp.

Kemi

Commander
German Forces
Norway

Rovaniemi

Kestenga

Kuusano

Loukhi

Bay of Onega

Kemj

Kemi

III
Finnish
Corps

Belomorsk

White
Sea
Canal

Oulu

Suomussalmi

Ukhta

S W E D E N

F I N L A N D

Stalin
Canal

Povenets

Vaasa

Korpiselka

Petrozavodsk

Lake
Onega

Pori

Karelian Army

Salmi

U. S. S. R.

Lake
Lagoda

Gulf of Bothnia

Helsinki

Hango

Viborg

LENINGRAD

Aland Isl.

Gulf of Finland

Reval

STOCKHOLM

Hiiumaa

ESTONIA

LEGEND

Baltic Sea

Saaremaa

Gulf
of
Riga

GERMAN

FINNS

SOVIET RUSSIANS

BOUNDARIES

RAILROAD

CANAL

AIRFIELD

GOTLAND

Riga

LATVIA

0   100   200   300

Statute Miles

Map No. 11

323

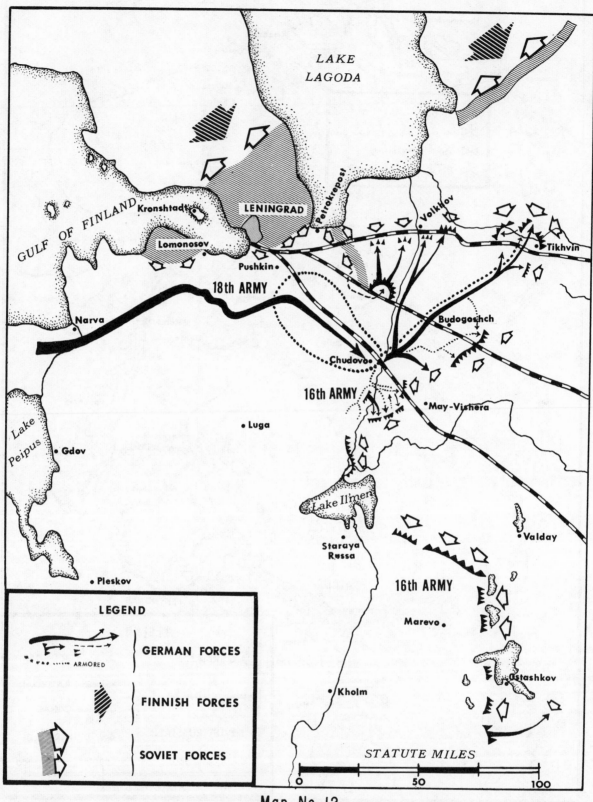

LAKE
LAGODA

GULF OF FINLAND

Kronshtadt

Lomonosov

LENINGRAD

Petrokrepost

Volkhov

Tikhvin

Pushkin

18th ARMY

Budogoshch

Narva

Chudovo

16th ARMY

May-Vishera

Luga

Lake
Peipus

Gdov

Lake Ilmen

Valday

Staraya
Russa

16th ARMY

Pleskov

Marevo

Ostashkov

Kholm

LEGEND

←·····ARMORED	GERMAN FORCES
	FINNISH FORCES
	SOVIET FORCES

STATUTE MILES

0   50   100

Map No. 12

Map No. 13

Legend

⬚ Land conquered by German forces

⬚ Battles of encirclement

→ German offensives

FINLAND

Lake Onega

Lake Ladoga

Baltic Sea

Gulf of Finland

Tikhvin

Leningrad

Reval

Lake Peipus

Novgorod

Lake Il'men

Staraya Russa

Gulf of Riga

Ostrov

Kalinin

Riga

MOSCOW

Daugava

Vyazma

Smolensk

Orsha

Kaunas

Minsk

Bryansk

Suwalki

Gomel'

Bialystok

Kursk

Pripyat'

Kiev

Romny

Kharkov

Korosten

Donets

L'vov

Cherkassy

Dnepr

Kremenchug

Don

Dniester

Dnepropetrovsk

Rostov

Sea of Azov

Odessa

Black Sea

Sevastopol'

325

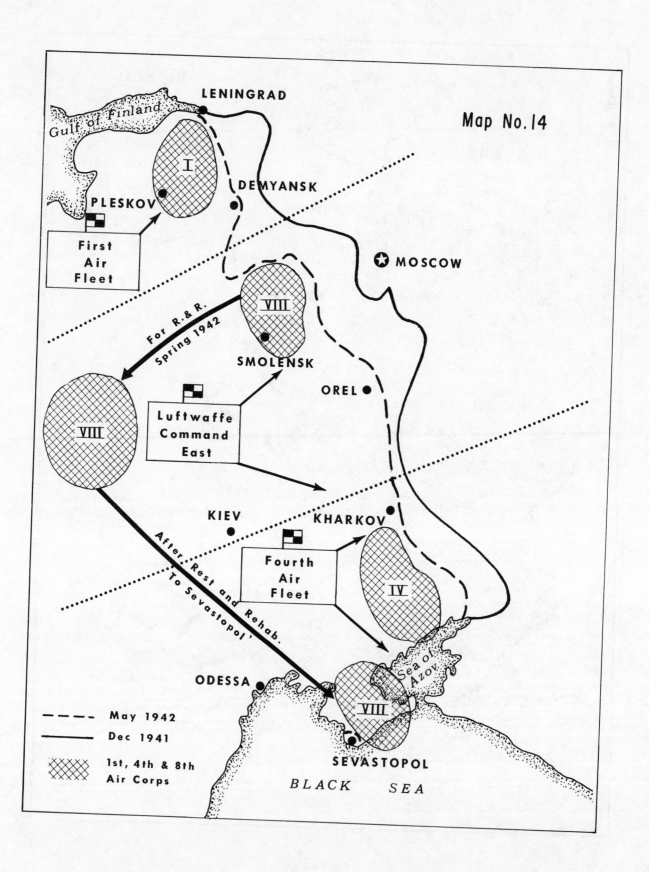

Map No. 14

LENINGRAD

Gulf of Finland

I

PLESKOV

DEMYANSK

First
Air
Fleet

MOSCOW

For R. & R.
Spring 1942

VIII

SMOLENSK

OREL

VIII

Luftwaffe
Command
East

KIEV

KHARKOV

Fourth
Air
Fleet

IV

After Rest and Rehab.
"To Sevastopol"

Sea of
Azov

ODESSA

VIII

SEVASTOPOL

BLACK   SEA

– – – –   May 1942

─────   Dec 1941

1st, 4th & 8th
Air Corps

LIST OF CHARTS

ORGANIZATION OF THE HIGHER COMMANDS OF THE

LUFTWAFFE
22 June 1941

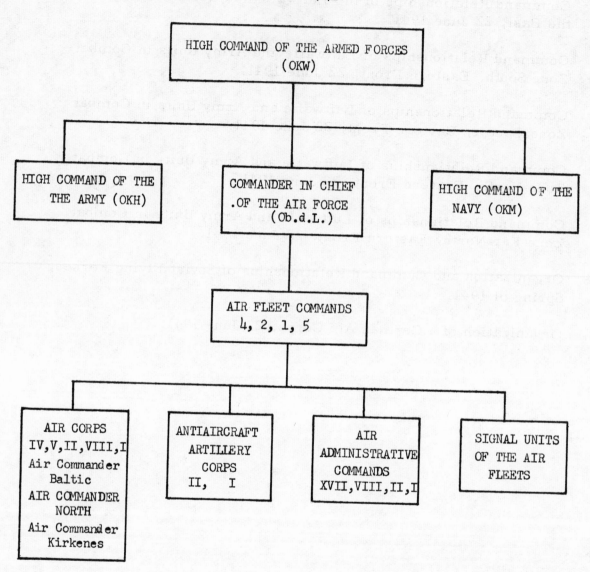

Chart No. 1

COMMAND RELATIONSHIPS IN THE EAST 22 JUNE 1941

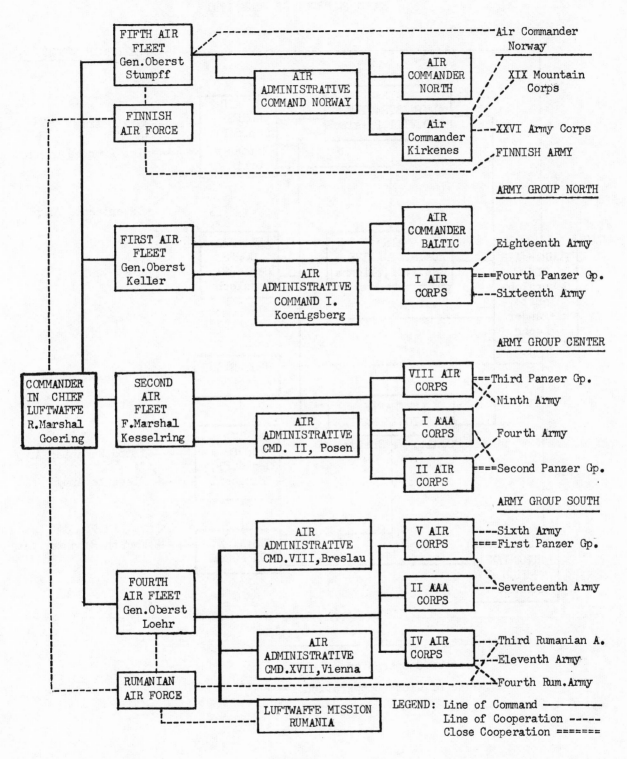

Chart No. 2

COMMAND RELATIONSHIPS IN COMBAT ZONE SOUTH

EASTERN FRONT 22 JUNE 1941

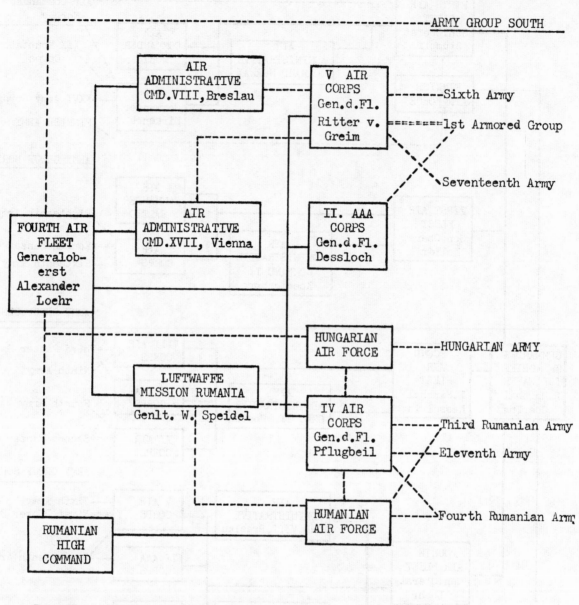

Legend: Line of Command _____

           Line of Cooperation -------

           Line of Close Cooperation =====

Chart No. 3

COMMAND RELATIONSHIPS IN COMBAT ZONE CENTER

EASTERN FRONT 22 JUNE 1941

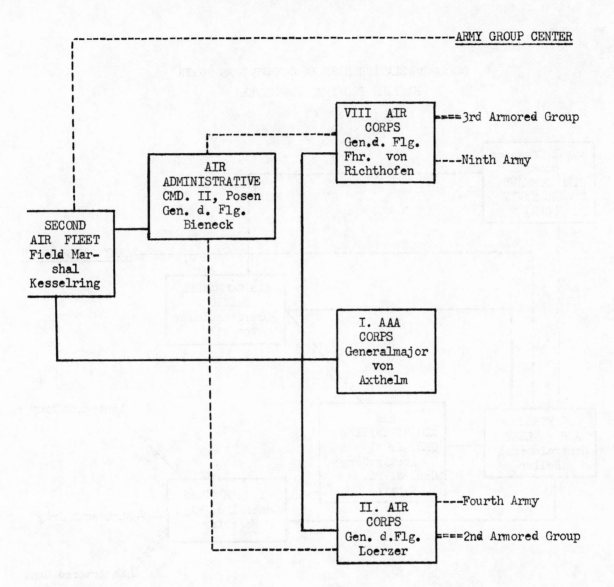

Legend: Line of Command _____
        Line of Cooperation --------
        Close Cooperation==========

Chart No. 4

COMMAND RELATIONSHIPS IN COMBAT ZONE NORTH
EASTERN FRONT 22 JUNE 1941

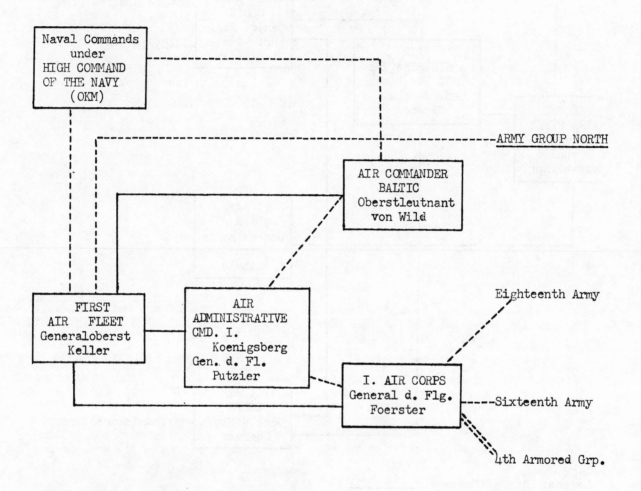

Legend: Line of Command ─────────
        Line of Cooperation ───────
        Close Cooperation ═════════

Chart No. 5

COMMAND RELATIONSHIPS IN COMBAT ZONE FAR NORTH

EASTERN FRONT 22 JUNE 1941
(Finnish Area)

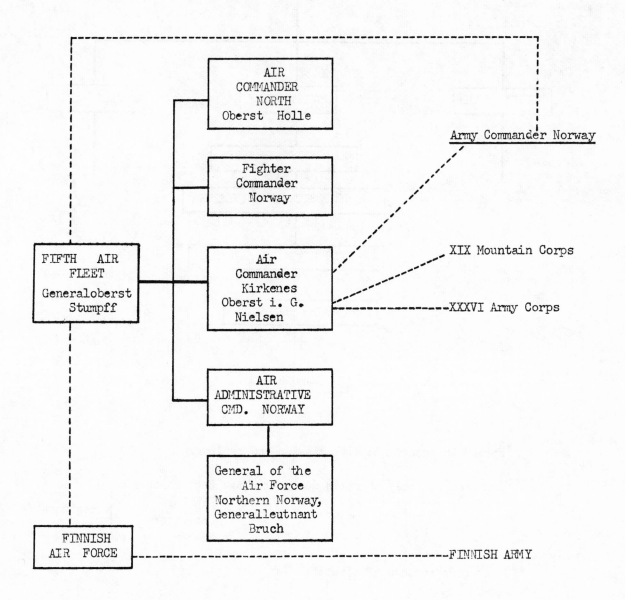

Chart No. 6

ORGANIZATION AND COMMAND RELATIONSHIPS OF

SOVIET AIR FORCES, SPRING 1941

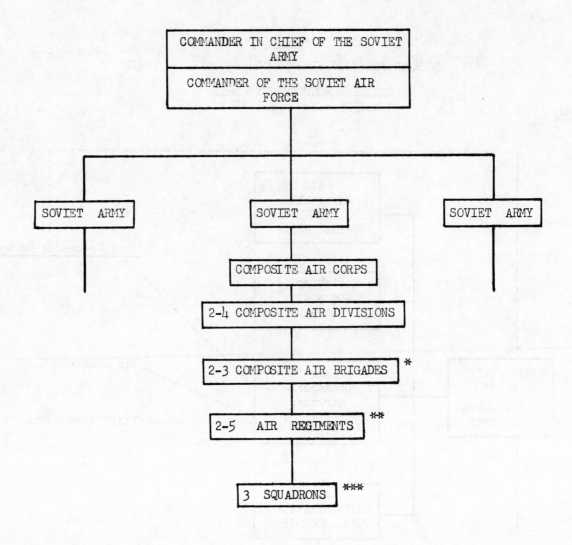

```
┌─────────────────────────────────┐
│ COMMANDER IN CHIEF OF THE SOVIET │
│              ARMY                │
├─────────────────────────────────┤
│ COMMANDER OF THE SOVIET AIR      │
│              FORCE               │
└─────────────────────────────────┘
```

SOVIET ARMY   SOVIET ARMY   SOVIET ARMY

COMPOSITE AIR CORPS

2-4 COMPOSITE AIR DIVISIONS

2-3 COMPOSITE AIR BRIGADES *

2-5   AIR   REGIMENTS **

3   SQUADRONS ***

*Formed in accordance with mission and employment

**Composed entirely of units designated as: Reconnaissance
Fighter
Destroyer
Bomber } Regiment

***Each squadron has 27 aircraft

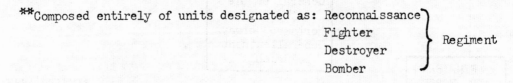

Chart No. 7

ORGANIZATION OF A GERMAN AIR CORPS

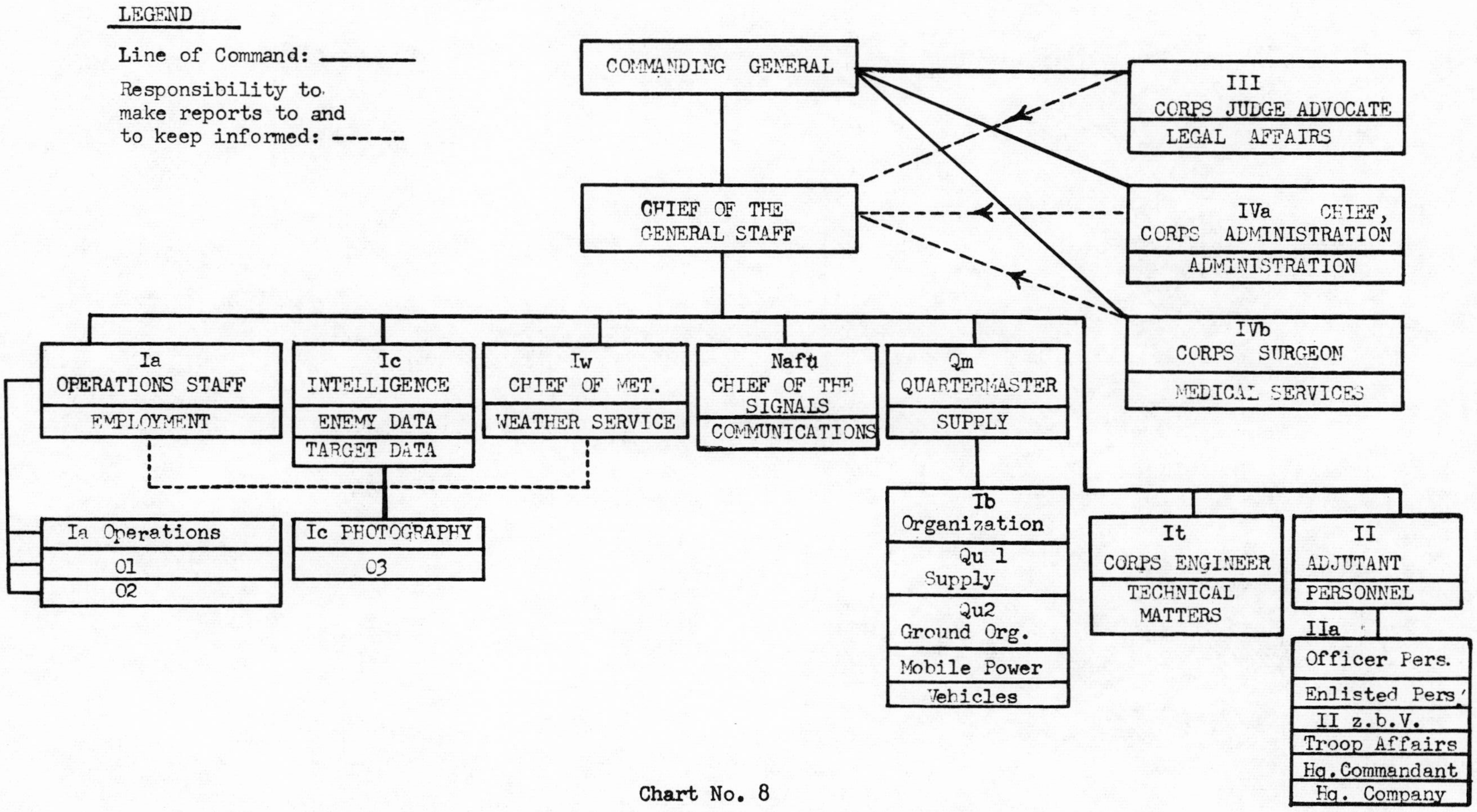

LEGEND

Line of Command: ───────

Responsibility to.
make reports to and
to keep informed: ───────

Chart

III — CORPS JUDGE ADVOCATE — LEGAL AFFAIRS

IVa — CHIEF, CORPS ADMINISTRATION — ADMINISTRATION

IVb — CORPS SURGEON — MEDICAL SERVICES

COMMANDING GENERAL

CHIEF OF THE GENERAL STAFF

Ia — OPERATIONS STAFF — EMPLOYMENT

Ia Operations — O1 — O2

Ic — INTELLIGENCE — ENEMY DATA — TARGET DATA

Ic PHOTOGRAPHY — O3

Iw — CHIEF OF MET. — WEATHER SERVICE

Naft — CHIEF OF THE SIGNALS — COMMUNICATIONS

Qm — QUARTERMASTER — SUPPLY

Ib — Organization — Qu 1 Supply — Qu2 Ground Org. — Mobile Power — Vehicles

It — CORPS ENGINEER — TECHNICAL MATTERS

II — ADJUTANT — PERSONNEL

IIa — Officer Pers. — Enlisted Pers' — II z.b.V. — Troop Affairs — Hq.Commandant — Hq. Company

Chart No. 8

335